Tenth Edition

Infants, Toddlers, and Caregivers

A Curriculum of Respectful, Responsive, Relationship-Based Care and Education

Janet Gonzalez-Mena

Napa Valley College

Dianne Widmeyer Eyer

Cañada College

Mc
Graw
Hill
Education

INFANTS, TODDLERS, AND CAREGIVERS: A CURRICULUM OF RESPECTFUL, RESPONSIVE, RELATIONSHIP-BASED CARE AND EDUCATION, TENTH EDITION

Published by McGraw-Hill Education, 2 Penn Plaza, New York, NY 10121. Copyright © 2015 by McGraw-Hill Education. All rights reserved. Printed in the United States of America. Previous editions © 2012, 2009, and 2007. No part of this publication may be reproduced or distributed in any form or by any means, or stored in a database or retrieval system, without the prior written consent of McGraw-Hill Education, including, but not limited to, in any network or other electronic storage or transmission, or broadcast for distance learning.

Some ancillaries, including electronic and print components, may not be available to customers outside the United States.

This book is printed on acid-free paper.

1 2 3 4 5 6 7 8 9 0 DOC/DOC 1 0 9 8 7 6 5 4

ISBN 978-0-07-811034-4
MHID 0-07-811034-3

Senior Vice President, Products & Markets: *Kurt L. Strand*
Vice President, General Manager, Products & Markets: *Michael Ryan*
Vice President, Content Production & Technology Services: *Kimberly Meriwether David*
Managing Director: *Bill Glass*
Executive Director of Development: *Lisa Pinto*
Brand Manager & Managing Editor: *Penina Braffman*
Brand Coordinator: *Adina Lonn*
Associate Marketing Manager: *Alexandra Schultz*
Director, Content Production: *Terri Schiesl*
Content Project Manager: *Jolynn Kilburg*
Buyer: *Jennifer Pickel*
Cover Designer: *Studio Montage, St. Louis, MO*
Cover Image: *©Ariel Skelley/Blend Images LLC*
Compositor: Cenveo® Publisher Services
Typeface: *10/12 Janson Text LT Std*
Printer: *R. R. Donnelley*

All credits appearing on page or at the end of the book are considered to be an extension of the copyright page.

Library of Congress Cataloging-in-Publication Data

Gonzalez-Mena, Janet.
    Infants, toddlers, and caregivers : a curriculum of respectful, responsive, relationship-based care and education / Janet Gonzalez-Mena, Dianne Widmeyer Eyer.—Tenth edition.
        pages cm
    ISBN 978-0-07-811034-4 (alk. paper)
    1. Child care—United States.   2. Child development—United States.   3. Education, Preschool—Activity programs—United States.   I. Eyer, Dianne Widmeyer.   II. Title.
HQ778.63.G663   2015
362.7—dc23   2014009804

The Internet addresses listed in the text were accurate at the time of publication. The inclusion of a website does not indicate an endorsement by the authors or McGraw-Hill Education, and McGraw-Hill Education does not guarantee the accuracy of the information presented at these sites.

To Magda Gerber, Emmi Pikler, and Anna Tardos

About the Authors

Way back in the 1970s Janet Gonzalez-Mena and Dianne Widmeyer Eyer met when they were both teaching early childhood education in a community college. The program focused on preschool even though infants and toddlers were starting to come into child care programs.

The two authors decided to do something about that problem. Janet became an intern in a program called the Demonstration Infant Program, where Magda Gerber taught her unique philosophy of respect and responsiveness for infant-toddler care on which this book is based. Janet's internship helped her earn a master's degree in human development. In the 1980s Gerber and others created a new program called Resources for Infant Educarers (RIE), through which Janet was made a RIE Associate, the highest certification. Dianne completed a second master's degree in special education, and together the two worked to expand the field of early childhood education to include infants and toddlers, special education, and family child care providers. Writing this book together was one of the things they did.

A few years later both authors became more involved with family child care. As director of Child Care Services for the Family Service Agency of San Mateo County, California, Janet supervised a network of family child care homes that served infants and toddlers as well as preschoolers. Under her direction, the agency opened a new infant center and also created a pilot program of therapeutic child care for abused and neglected infants and toddlers. Dianne worked with the Child Care Coordinating Council of San Mateo County to develop a training program for family child care providers at Cañada College. This curriculum also models the Gerber philosophy of respect and responsiveness for infant-toddler care.

Janet went on to teach at Napa Valley College, retiring in 1998. Today she continues to educate infant-toddler caregivers in different settings. She trains trainers in WestEd's Program for Infant/Toddler Care (PITC) and speaks at conferences in the United States and abroad. As a longtime (43 years) member of the National Association for the Education of Young Children (NAEYC), Janet served two terms on the Consulting Editors Panel. She worked on a Head Start project to create a user's guide for their Multicultural Principles. Janet is becoming an internationally recognized author as some of her books are translated into German, Chinese, Japanese, and Hebrew. Janet belongs to the California Community College Early Childhood Educators, BANDTEC, a diversity trainers' network, and serves on the board of Pikler/Lóczy Fund USA.

Dianne continued teaching at Cañada College, where she developed several curriculum specializations in early childhood education and child development, including children with special needs, family support, "Safe Start" violence intervention and prevention in the early years, and home-based child care. She has been a member of NAEYC since 1970. Dianne retired from Cañada College in 2005 after 36 years of teaching and 27 years as the ECE/CD Department Chair. She continues to coordinate a grant, which she wrote in 2000, with First 5 San Mateo County to support the early childhood education (ECE) workforce by recruiting and retaining teachers in the early care and education field.

The current interests and passions of both authors still relate to education. Dianne's interests involve supporting literacy skills for adult second language learners and providing specific supports related to career development for the diverse population in the ECE workforce. She was able in 2010 to extend the First 5 grant; "Bridges to Success" creates a curriculum specialization in "school readiness." There is also expanded outreach to support "ready schools" in the community. In her downtime, Dianne enjoys hiking, gardening, and music. Janet's up-close and personal interests lie in her grandchildren including her young granddaughter Nika, "a RIE baby," who is now 7, her 23 month old grandson, Cole, and his baby brother, Paul. She also speaks around the country and sometimes abroad about Pikler, Gerber, and RIE. Her grander pursuits involve working with early educators and others around diversity and issues of equity and social justice.

Brief Contents

Contents

chapter 4

Play and Exploration as Curriculum 71

chapter 7

Motor Skills 131

part 3   Focus on the Program 255

Preface

The Philosophy of Infants, Toddlers, and Caregivers

The first edition of this book came out in 1980 and was called *Infancy and Caregiving*. It was 141 pages, nine chapters, pen and ink graphics (no photography except on the cover), and had few pedagogical features. Magda Gerber wrote the Foreword. She called it "a book that so sensitively represents my life's work." She went on to write, "This approach stresses the importance of respectful responsive and reciprocal adult-infant interactions. . . . If we could improve the care of infants, we could improve the world. . . . We'll find a way. We will at least make a *dent* in the world." She pointed out that the original book was that dent. If she were alive today, she'd say that the nine editions that followed are continuing to make that dent.

The Tenth Edition of *Infants, Toddlers, and Caregivers* is a hallmark. In the 34 years since its first publication, an entire generation has grown up. Each revision has examined and expanded issues in the early care and education field. Reviewers have donated thoughtful detail, and readers have used this information to change the way they interact with very young children. But with each edition the cornerstone of the text has been the same—the philosophy of Magda Gerber and the theory of Emmi Pikler.

Magda Gerber was an infant-toddler expert who originally came from Hungary and settled in Los Angeles, California. She credited the roots of her work to Emmi Pikler, a pediatrician, researcher, and theorist who founded a residential nursery in Budapest in 1946 after World War II. The focus of this nursery was to care for infants and toddlers whose families could not and to provide them with a strong start in life. This first nursery became a model for other residential nurseries once it was learned that the children who spent their first three years in this very particular kind of residential care grew up to be stable, productive adults. Their ability to establish long-term relationships was a great accomplishment for institutional care. Emmi Pikler died in 1984, but the Pikler Institute, incorporating research and training, continues in operation today. It no longer provides residential care but focuses on day care for infants and toddlers, as well as parent education.

Janet Gonzalez-Mena, coauthor of this text, was a student of Magda Gerber's in the 1970s and continued to be a close friend until Gerber's death in 2007. Gonzalez-Mena has been able to observe and study at the Pikler Institute, as well as assist in trainings in the United States conducted by Anna Tardos, present director of the Institute and daughter of Emmi Pikler. Gonzalez-Mena's experience with these three amazing women confirmed for her how much the Pikler research and the Gerber philosophy can help infant-toddler centers in the United States and around the world.

Magda Gerber's work has been known in the United States for a number of years, and its reputation continues under the auspices of the organization Gerber founded, Resources for Infant Educarers (RIE). Emmi Pikler's work was little known in the United States until a few years ago because for much of her career Hungary was behind the Iron Curtain. Magda Gerber was one of the first to publish some of Pikler's research in English. A new edition of what's called the RIE Manual is now available and updated with further work in English, some of which has been written by Gerber's followers. You can find the RIE Manual at www.rie.org. Pikler's works in English can be accessed at www.Pikler.org and at the European website for Pikler, which is www.aipl.org.

The approaches to infant-toddler care created by these two women *has* made a "dent" in the early care and education world. The authors of this text are proud and humble to support these approaches.

The Ten Principles: A Philosophy of Respect

A keystone of both Magda Gerber and Emmi Pikler's work is *respect*. Until Gerber introduced its use to the United States, the word *respect* was not part of the vocabulary of most American infant-toddler caregivers. Respect is one of the major themes that runs throughout *Infants, Toddlers, and Caregivers*, and respect is an important component of the curriculum the book advocates. This curriculum is all-inclusive and centers on connections and relationships. Briefly, the term *curriculum* is about educating, but in the infant-toddler world, *care* and *education* are one and the same. In this book, curriculum has to do with respecting and responding to each child's needs in warm, respectful, and sensitive ways that promote attachment and allow children to explore and play on their own. Curriculum embraces everything that happens during the day—whether the child is alone or with other children or having sensitive interactions with an adult. Those adult-child interactions may be part of caregiving activities, both planned and unplanned, but they go way beyond. Even the down times during the day, when caregivers just hang out with the little ones, can include the kinds of interactions that make up curriculum.

Perhaps the most important feature of this book is the consistency with which it outlines well-established practices designed to promote infants' and toddlers' total well-being. The book also looks at the importance of sensitive care and good program planning, and the impact they have on the identity formation of infants and toddlers.

The Ten Principles found on pages 10–16 are the underlying framework for this book. Respect is an attitude that shows up in behavior. Respectful behaviors on the part of caregivers are the basis of the Ten Principles, which show how respect applies to treating babies as people when caregiving, communicating with them, and facilitating their growth, development, and learning. The book refers to the Ten Principles in every chapter. In addition, a Principles in Action feature in each chapter uses a scenario to further explain the individual principles.

A Focus on Application and Practice

Knowing *about* is different from knowing *how to*. Knowing *about* means learning theory. Knowing *how to* puts theory into action. We purposely organized this book to emphasize action because we know that even people with considerable understanding of infants and toddlers have trouble acting on that understanding unless they have also learned to *apply* theory. Knowledge does not necessarily build skill.

Caregivers who have knowledge but lack confidence in their ability to use it may suffer from "analysis paralysis," which prevents them from making quick decisions, stating their feelings clearly, and taking needed action. A common pattern when analysis paralysis strikes is inaction, indecision, then overemotional or otherwise inappropriate reaction, followed by more inaction. When adults have analysis paralysis and either cannot react or react inconsistently, infants cannot learn to predict what will happen as a result of their own actions. This learning to predict what effect they have on the world is a primary accomplishment of infants in early life.

Terminology

In this book, the youngest children—those from newborn to walking—are called infants. Children who are walking (from about a year old to two years) are called young toddlers. Children from two to three are called older toddlers. Children from three to five are called preschoolers. Please note that these labels and descriptions apply to children who are typically developing. When development is atypical, the labels and descriptions don't fit as well. For example, a child who has reached the stage when other children walk may have many other characteristics of that age group even though she doesn't walk; not all toddlers toddle, but that doesn't mean they should be thought of as infants.

If you visit many infant-toddler programs, you will find that the adults in the teacher/caregiver role go by different titles. *Educarer, teacher, caregiver*, and *infant care teacher* are four different terms used. In this book we have mainly used the word *caregiver* to emphasize the importance of "caring" in programs for the youngest children. The caregiver role incorporates that of teacher and educator.

Organization of the Text

By starting with the *interactive aspect of caregiving*, we highlight this philosophy from the beginning pages. Thus the book is organized in a unique way. Part 1 (Chapters 1–4) is about caregiving. It focuses on the caregivers' actions and relationships with the children and how these actions and relationships make up the curriculum. Part 2 (Chapters 5–11) presents child development information, along with the curriculum implications of that information. It also includes topics related to early childhood special education. Part 3 (Chapters 12–14) takes a programmatic point of view (looking at both center and family child care programs) and includes environments as well as adult-adult relationships. Appendix A gives a checklist for determining quality in infant-toddler programs. Appendix B includes a popular and well-used environmental chart that combines the information from all three parts of the book into one concise but comprehensive chart designed for practical use in program planning and implementation. The glossary at the end of the book consists of the key terms from all the chapters.

A Focus on Diversity and Inclusion

Honoring diversity and including children with special needs in infant-toddler programs is a strong point of this text. Topics related to early childhood special education appear throughout the text, but also have their own place at the end of each chapter in Part 2. We have focused more on cultural differences and inclusion with each edition. Though we present a cohesive philosophy, we urge readers to recognize that there are multiple views on every aspect of infant-toddler care. Strive to honor differences and work respectfully with families who represent them. It is important to respect and respond to linguistic differences in positive ways, supporting the child's home language, whatever it might be.

Our emphasis on self-reflection helps caregivers who might feel uncomfortable in the face of differences. Only when caregivers understand themselves can they understand infants, toddlers, and their families. Sensitivity is an important qualification for anyone who works with very young children. For that reason, the reader is asked to focus on personal experience throughout this book.

New to the Tenth Edition

We made five additions to this edition.

First: Even Greater Focus on Play

Play has become a huge interest for early childhood professionals as academics and school readiness issues creep down into the nursery! In light of that development, the play chapter in this book has been expanded. Eva Kallo's overview of play is now included and gives more structure to what Magda Gerber and Emmi Pikler taught for many years. As infants and toddlers play, they run into problems. Immobile babies struggle with how to get the toy just beyond their reach, and toddlers struggle with how to make something large fit into something smaller. It is so easy for adults to help out and make both children happy by showing the toddler how the pieces fit together or by putting the toy within reach of the baby. Both Gerber and Pikler cautioned against the goal of just making children happy, and taught adults not to rescue children who were working on solving a problem. Sticking to something and not giving up, even when frustrated, is the kind of trait that benefits adult personalities and makes them successful people, even more than being born with a high IQ. Traits like persistence are the subject of researchers such as Angela Duckworth, who labels the subject of her research "*grit*." Gerber would be surprised at the term *grit*, but that's just what she supported! It is clear from the work of Pikler that grit starts in infancy and is influenced by the adult's willingness to allow and even encourage problem solving.

Second: The Issue of "Screens" for Infants and Toddlers

New to this edition is the subject of "screens" for infants and toddlers. The American Academy of Pediatrics and other researchers have focused a good deal of attention on the effect of electronic devices with screens in the first two or three years of a child's life. What do very young children learn from them? Certainly not language as the videos designed to make babies "smart" like the genius they were named for used to advertise. Does it hurt young children's development if the focus on digital images takes them away from time spent in the real world with people and objects? Most likely. Does it matter if the screens are interactive such as Skype on computers or FaceTime on smart phones? Maybe. The research is just now being conducted by the American Academy of Pediatrics. Stay tuned.

Third: Focus on Self-Regulation

Self-regulation is also getting a good deal of attention these days. Children who start school need to be able to regulate their behavior and the feelings behind their behavior to succeed in classrooms. If you look back to the beginning, self-regulation is a lot more than just a school readiness issue. Self-regulation is a whole system that starts at birth and continues to develop throughout life. It is not just about "being good" but involves body processes, feelings, and cognition. Though we have added aspects of self-regulation in most of the chapters in this edition, we have put it in the spotlight in the play chapter. Self-regulation is about moving from an automatic response to a more considered one. It's about making choices that serve the individual. During play, aspects of self-regulation show up as a physical skill, as emotional development, and also in intellectual achievement as infants and toddlers figure out how to make things happen that they want to happen. Through play babies begin to develop the ability to move from an automatic or habitual response to making a choice that promotes a playful intention. They work on gaining self-control rather than going on automatic. As babies grow into toddlers, they begin to make believe. That kind of play is directly connected to self-regulation as they gain experience by playing out various scenarios. By toddlerhood self-regulation helps them improve focus, and they practice acting appropriately in ways that keep the play moving. A toddler talking to herself shows how self-regulation is developing, and this increased focus enables her to play with another toddler.

Fourth: Language Development Research

Babies are born with the ability to hear the sounds in all languages, even though few grownups have that ability. Patricia Kuhl, a neuroscientist, has studied babies' neural networks and provides expanded knowledge on how infants manage to move away from hearing the sounds of multiple languages to focusing on their mother tongue. Between 8 and 10 months, increases in brain activity enable infants to become excellent native speakers, as the ability to hear sounds in other languages decreases. The good news is that training can increase the capacity for native speakers to differentiate sounds in nonnative languages. We continue to learn more about language development as the brain research continues.

Fifth: Website Resources

The quality and quantity of websites has grown a great deal in the last few years. Many websites have been added to the Tenth Edition to provide the reader with immediate access to in-depth information. These resources are embedded in the chapters where the specific topic is being discussed and encourage critical thinking. They also encourage the reader to explore more content across the curriculum in other areas related to early care and education. The websites are updated frequently, and many represent professional organizations that have been serving the needs of very young children and their families for many years.

Retained Features

A What Do You See? feature starts each chapter by showing a child or children in a situation related to the material to follow and immediately engages the student in the chapter's subject matter. Students are encouraged to think back on these scenes later in the chapter. In some of these scenes the age of the children is mentioned, but not all. We left out age labels in the spirit of Magda Gerber, who used to say, "Why does it matter how old the child is?" She was an advocate for appreciating what a child was able to do, whether he was the "right age" or not.

The Video Observation is a popular feature in each chapter that introduces and encourages students to think about the issues and concepts presented in online video clips related to the chapter material. At the book's Online Learning Center, students can watch these live-action examples of what they are reading about and can respond to questions analyzing what they observe in each video clip.

The Principles in Action feature is a case study scenario followed by questions to help students apply the content they have learned to a "real-life" situation. The Principles in Action connects to the Appropriate Practice feature through boxes called Appropriate Practice in Action. The Appropriate Practice feature summarizes points of the National Association for the Education of Young Children (NAEYC) guidelines for developmentally appropriate practice related to the chapter topics. Each Appropriate Practice feature has four sections:

1. Overview of Development
2. Developmentally Appropriate Practice
3. Individually Appropriate Practice
4. Culturally Appropriate Practice

Sections 2 through 4 list points to keep in mind and practical suggestions for interacting with infants and toddlers based on the NAEYC guidelines.

A Developmental Pathways feature is included in each of the chapters in Part 2. Each feature begins with generalizations about stages of development by showing a chart of behaviors related to the chapter topic (for example, attachment, perception, or motor skills), and then uses examples of two different children to show diverse developmental pathways. The details of each example are explored as to what you see, what you might think, what you might not know, and what you might do.

The For Further Reading and References lists for each chapter have been expanded and updated. In order to keep the book compact and affordable to students, this edition has the References in the book's Online Learning Center at www.mhhe.com/itc10e. There instructors and students will also find a variety of resources to help them teach from and learn from the text.

Pedagogy

Each chapter contains a pedagogical system designed to provide learning support for students and to encourage students to reflect on and apply what they learn. Pedagogical features include:

- **Focus Questions** that prepare students for the content to follow
- **Boldfaced in-text key terms** that highlight key terminology and define it in context of the paragraph in which it appears
- **The Principles in Action** boxes that allow students to apply the principles to scenarios
- **Appropriate Practice** boxes that provide practical suggestions related to the NAEYC guidelines for developmentally appropriate practice and refer to the Principles in Action boxes, showing how appropriate practice can be applied to the scenarios

- **Developmental Pathways** boxes that list typical development and variations
- **Online Resources** sections that list study resources available to the student at the Online Learning Center
- **Chapter Summaries** that contain key ideas of the chapters
- **Key Terms** sections that list all key terms from the chapter, with page references, and that are collated in an end-of-book glossary
- **Thought/Activity Questions** that encourage students to review, reflect, and apply what they are learning
- **For Further Reading** lists that suggest additional readings
- **Video Observation** features in each chapter with pedagogy to help readers think about the video clips they view at the Online Learning Center
- **NAEYC Program Standards** listed in the margins next to related material
- **Reflection** questions designed to help readers consider their own feelings and experiences that relate to what they are reading

Student and Instructor Resources and Supplements

For the Student

- The **Online Learning Center** at www.mhhe.com/itc10e includes related Web links, practice quizzes, video observations, flashcards and other interactive exercises, chapter references, a glossary, and Spanish language resources.
- **English-Spanish Early Childhood Glossary:** The Online Learning Center offers an English-Spanish glossary of Early Childhood terms taken from the text. Ofelia Garcia of Cabrillo College developed this glossary to support Spanish-speaking students and students who anticipate working in communities where English is not the first language.
- *The Caregiver's Companion: Readings and Professional Resources:* Available separately, *The Caregiver's Companion* includes practical articles to extend student understanding of important topics, observation guidelines, and a wealth of forms to use when becoming a professional caregiver.

For the Instructor

- The instructor's side of the Online Learning Center contains an instructor's manual, PowerPoint slides, and a test bank.

- *Observing Infants, Toddlers, and Caregivers:* This video, free to adopters of this text, includes real-life scenes of infants, toddlers, and caregivers. Use this video with students to practice observation techniques and to show the real worlds of young children and their caregivers. In addition, you can have students watch video clips online, as each chapter contains a Video Observation feature with discussion questions.
- More instructor resources are available at the **Online Learning Center** at www.mhhe.com/itc10e.

Acknowledgments

We would like to acknowledge and thank the reviewers who provided feedback that helped us prepare this Tenth Edition of *Infants, Toddlers, and Caregivers.* These instructors include:

Helen M. David, EdD, *University of California, Los Angeles*
Denise Da Ros-Voseles, *Northeastern State University, Broken Arrow, Oklahoma*
Linda A. Dove, *Western Michigan University*
Cynthia P. Galloway, *Horry-Georgetown Technical College*
Sharon Hirschy, *Collin College*
Marsha Peralta, *Folsom Lake College, Los Rios Community College*
Norma Simpson, *Heartland Community College*
Ruslan Slutsky, *The University of Toledo*

Resources for Caregivers

Available separately is *The Caregiver's Companion: Readings and Professional Resources.* *The Caregiver's Companion* includes twenty-one readings regarding the Ten Principles; curriculum; keeping toddlers safe and healthy; culture, identity, and families; and including infants and toddlers with special needs. Readings include:

"Caring for Infants with Respect: The RIE Approach" by Magda Gerber

"Curriculum and Lesson Planning: A Responsive Approach" by J. Ronald Lally

"Respectful, Individual, and Responsive Caregiving for Infants" by Beverly Kovach and Denise Da Ros

"Facilitating the Play of Children at Loczy" by Anna Tardos

"A Primary Caregiving System for Infants and Toddlers" by Jennifer L. Bernhardt

Excerpt from "Our Moving Bodies Tell Stories, Which Speak of Our Experiences" by Suzi Tortora

"The Development of Movement" by Emmi Pikler

"How Infants and Toddlers Use Symbols" by Karen Miller

"Preparing for Literacy: Communication Comes First" by Ruth Anne Hammond

"Helping a Baby Adjust to Center Care" by Enid Elliot

"Toddlers: What to Expect" by Janet Gonzalez-Mena

"Creating a Landscape for Learning" by Louis Torelli and Charles Durrett

"The Impact of Child Care Policies and Practices on Infant/Toddler Identity Formation" by J. Ronald Lally

"Cross-Cultural Conferences" by Janet Gonzalez-Mena

"Sudden Infant Death Syndrome" by Susan S. Aronson

"Supporting the Development of Infants and Toddlers with Special Health Needs" by Cynthia Huffman

"Breastfeeding Promotion in Child Care" by Laura Dutil Aird

"Cultural Dimensions of Feeding Relationships" by Carol Brunson Phillips and Renatta Cooper

"Cultural Differences in Sleeping Practices" by Janet Gonzalez-Mena and Navaz Peshotan Bhavnagri

"Talking with Parents When Concerns Arise" by Linda Brault and Janet Gonzalez-Mena

"Strategies for Supporting Infants and Toddlers with Disabilities in Inclusive Child Care" by Donna Sullivan and Janet Gonzalez-Mena

The Caregiver's Companion also provides eighteen forms for tracking and relaying information:

Registration Form
Tell Us About Your Child
Identification and Emergency Form
Infant Feeding Plan
Daily Information Sheet
Sign-In Sheet
Diapering Log
Feeding Log
Allergy Notice
Sample Exposure Notice
Medication Schedule

Individual Child's Record of Medications Given
Incident Log
Incident Report
Documentation of Concern for a Child
How Are We Doing? Family Feedback Form
Developmental Health History
Physician's Report Form—Day Care Centers

Additionally, *The Caregiver's Companion* includes observation guidelines, observation forms for use with the video observations on the text's Online Learning Center, and an outline of a parent handbook.

part one

Focus on the Caregiver

Principles, Practice, and Curriculum

Focus Questions

After reading this chapter you should be able to answer the following questions:

1 What kinds of interactions grow into the relationships that are so important in infant-toddler care and education?

2 What is an example of an adult behavior that shows respect to an infant or toddler?

3 What are some key words or phrases for at least 5 of the 10 principles of infant-toddler care and education?

4 Can you define the word *curriculum* as it applies to infant and toddler care and education?

5 What are the roles of adults in infant-toddler curriculum?

6 What are the three knowledge bases of developmentally appropriate practice as defined by the National Association for the Education of Young Children (NAEYC)?

What Do You See?

A five-month-old is lying on the floor with several play materials scattered within reach. She is contentedly surveying the five other infants and toddlers who are in the room with her. Reaching now and then, she caresses a toy first with her eyes, then with her hands. As we look more closely, we can see that some moisture has crept onto the infant's outer clothes in the area of her bottom. The infant hears a step, and her eyes travel in the direction of the sound. Then we see a pair of legs and feet traveling along in the direction of the infant. A voice says, "Caitlin, I'm wondering how you are getting along."

The legs move over close to the blanket, and Caitlin looks up at the knees. Her eyes brighten as the rest of the person appears in her visual range. A kind face comes close. Caitlin smiles and makes a cooing noise. The caregiver responds, then notices the dampness of the clothing. "Oh, Caitlin, you need a change," the caregiver says. Caitlin responds by smiling and cooing.

Reaching out her hands, the caregiver says, "I'm going to pick you up now." Caitlin responds to the gesture and the words with an ever-so-slight body movement. She continues to smile and coo. The caregiver picks her up and walks toward the diapering area.

Did you notice that there was a lot more going on here than just a diaper change? This scene illustrates several of the basic principles of this book. Think back on it as you read. Do you know what it means to respect a baby as a person? We'll answer that question when we return to this scene later.

This book is based on a philosophy of infant-toddler care and education that is summarized in a curriculum or framework of 10 principles for practice. The philosophy comes from the work of two pioneers in infant-toddler care and education: Emmi Pikler and Magda Gerber. Pikler was a Hungarian pediatrician and researcher who got started in group care in 1946 after World War II by creating an orphanage for children under age three. Called the Pikler Institute today, the program is still running under the direction of Dr. Pikler's daughter, Anna Tardos. Magda Gerber, friend and colleague of Pikler, brought what she knew to the United States in 1956 and eventually started a program called Resources for Infant Educarers (RIE). Her followers across the United States and elsewhere have been training caregivers and parents since 1976. Although Pikler's approach and Gerber's philosophy are not identical, they are in tune with each other.

Relationships, Interactions, and the Three Rs

Relationship is a key term in infant-toddler care and education. In the opening scene you saw an example of how interactions like the one between Caitlin and the adult caregiver can lead to a close relationship built on respect. Relationships between caregivers[1] and very young children don't just happen. They grow from a number of interactions. So **interaction**—the effect that one person has on another—is another key term. But relationships don't grow from just any kind of interactions; they grow from those that are *respectful*, *responsive*, and *reciprocal*. You can think of them as the three Rs of infant-toddler care and education, or **three-R interactions**. The caregiver's interaction with Caitlin was obviously responsive—the caregiver responded to the child and the child to the caregiver. The responses were linked in a reciprocal way, that is, a give-and-take kind of way, forming a chain of interaction, with each response triggered by the previous one and leading into the next response by the other person. The difference between responsive and reciprocal may be hard to understand. When a caregiver is responsive, it means he or she pays attention to what the infant initiates and replies to it. Reciprocal is a whole chain of responses going back and forth between the caregiver and the baby. Each response is dependent on the one that came before it. What was respectful about them?

Behaviors indicating respect may not be as obvious as those indicating responsiveness and reciprocation. Did you notice that the caregiver walked up to Caitlin in a way that enabled the child to see her coming? The caregiver consciously slowed her pace and made contact before checking to see if Caitlin needed a diaper change. It's not uncommon to observe caregivers rush over and swoop up a baby unexpectedly and start feeling the diaper without a word of acknowledgment to the person inside the diaper. Imagine how you would feel if you were the baby. That's disrespectful. Instead, Caitlin's caregiver initiated a

Reflect

When were you involved in a respectful, responsive, and reciprocal interaction? Describe what that was like. Then contrast that description with an experience you've had with a disrespectful, unresponsive, nonreciprocal interaction. What are the implications of your experiences for working with infants and toddlers?

conversation by talking to Caitlin. She kept it going by responding to Caitlin's smiles and coos. She also talked to Caitlin about what she was going to do before she did it. This scene illustrates a responsive interaction chain that is the basis of effective caregiving. A number of interactions such as this kind of diaper changing build a partnership. This feeling of being part of a team instead of an object to be manipulated is vital to wholesome development. Reciprocal interactions like these promote attachment between caregiver and child. Another benefit from a series of such interactions is that the baby develops a cooperative spirit. Newcomers who observe at the Pikler Institute are surprised to see babies in their first weeks of life demonstrate cooperation. And that spirit of cooperation doesn't go away—it becomes a lasting habit!

Caregiving Routines as Opportunities for Three-R Interactions

It is no coincidence that the first example in this book is of an interaction involving diapering. There's a message here. Relationships develop through all kinds of interactions, but especially during ones that happen while adults are carrying out those essential activities of daily living sometimes called caregiving routines. Think about how diapering is a time when caregivers and children are in a one-on-one situation. If you count all the diaperings in a child's life, the total probably comes to somewhere between 4,000 and 5,000. Imagine the opportunities that will be lost if adults focus only on the activity, regard it as a chore, and don't bother to interact with the child. And that happens a lot because a common diapering practice is to distract the child somehow—often with a toy or something interesting to look at. Then the caregiver focuses on the chore, manipulating the child's body, and hurrying to get finished. This is the opposite of what we advocate.

It may seem that anyone who is warm and friendly can care for infants and that anyone with patience and nurturing qualities can work with toddlers. Certainly those are valuable characteristics in caregivers, but caring for children under three involves more than just going by instinct or by what seems to work. Going back to that opening scene, perhaps you can see that the caregiver was doing more than just what felt right. She had training in a particular way of caregiving. In fact, what you saw was a caregiver whose training was influenced by RIE, the program Magda Gerber created. You saw a caregiver who could have been trained either at RIE, or at the Pikler Institute in Budapest.

Ten Principles Based on a Philosophy of Respect

Now let's look at the 10 principles that underlie this book, principles that come from the work of Magda Gerber who began formulating them in the 1970s:

1. Involve infants and toddlers in things that concern them. Don't work around them or distract them to get the job done faster.

2. Invest in quality time, when you are totally available to individual infants and toddlers. Don't settle for supervising groups without focusing (more than just briefly) on individual children.

3. Learn each child's unique ways of communicating (cries, words, movements, gestures, facial expressions, body positions) and teach yours. Don't underestimate children's ability to communicate even though their verbal language skills may be nonexistent or minimal.

4. Invest time and energy to build a total person (concentrate on the "whole child"). Don't focus on cognitive development alone or look at it as separate from total development.

5. Respect infants and toddlers as worthy people. Don't treat them as objects or cute little empty-headed people to be manipulated.

6. Be honest about your feelings around infants and toddlers. Don't pretend to feel something that you don't or not to feel something that you do.

7. Model the behavior you want to teach. Don't preach.

8. Recognize problems as learning opportunities, and let infants and toddlers try to solve their own. Don't rescue them, constantly make life easy for them, or try to protect them from all problems.

9. Build security by teaching trust. Don't teach distrust by being undependable or often inconsistent.

10. Be concerned about the quality of development in each stage. Don't rush infants and toddlers to reach developmental milestones.

Let's look further into each of the principles.

Principle 1: Involve Infants and Toddlers in Things That Concern Them

Caitlin isn't just the recipient of her caregiver's actions; she's a participant in what happens to her. She and her caregiver do things together. If the caregiver had given Caitlin a toy to play with to keep her occupied while she changed her diaper, the whole tone of the scene would have been different. The partnership would have vanished, and in its place would have been a distracted child and a caregiver dealing with a damp bottom and a wet diaper instead of a whole child. Or if she had distracted Caitlin with other sorts of entertainment, the caregiver still would have had Caitlin's attention, but the focus would have been on fun and games rather than on the task at hand.

The caregiver's primary goal in this scene was to keep Caitlin involved in the interaction as well as focused on her own body and on what was happening to it. Diapering then became an "educational experience," through which Caitlin increased attention span, body awareness, and cooperation. A number of experiences like these give Caitlin an education in human relations from which she can build her whole outlook toward life and people.

There is a rumor that infants and toddlers have short attention spans. Some people say they can't pay attention to anything for very long. You can test that rumor for yourself. Watch an infant or toddler who is actually involved in something that concerns and interests him. Clock the amount of time spent on the task or event. You may be surprised at what a long attention span infants and toddlers have when they are interested, because they are involved.

Principle 2: Invest in Quality Time

The scene between Caitlin and her caregiver is a good example of one kind of quality time. The caregiver was fully present. That is, she was attending to what was going on; her thoughts were not somewhere else.

Two Types of Quality Time Magda Gerber called the kind of quality time illustrated by the diapering scene **wants-something quality time**. The adult and child are involved in a task the caregiver has set up. Diapering, feeding, bathing, and dressing fit into this category of quality time. If the caregiver pays attention to the child and asks in return that the child pay attention, the amount of wants-something quality time mounts up. In child care programs this can provide the one-to-one interactions that may be difficult to attain in a group setting. Wants-something quality time is educational. Examples of this kind of quality time occur throughout the book.

Another kind of equally important quality time is what Magda Gerber called **wants-nothing quality time**. This happens when caregivers make themselves available without directing the action—for instance, just sitting near babies, fully available and responsive but not in charge. Just being with toddlers while they play, responding rather than initiating, describes this type of quality time.

Floor time is a variation of wants-nothing quality time that the Child-Family Study Center at the University of California at Davis uses in their toddler program. Floor time is a concept they credit to Stanley Greenspan's work. When a toddler is exhibiting difficult behavior, instead of putting her in time-out and trying to ignore her, the caregivers do the opposite. They don't withdraw attention; they give more. The child is given a half hour of one-to-one time with an adult whose sole goal is to be *responsive* to that child and that child alone. The adult sits on the floor, available to the child. The environment is conducive to play, as there are interesting toys within reach. The adult has no plan or expectation but just waits to see what the child will do and then responds. This is the opposite of the common approach in programs where teachers and caregivers become even more directive rather than less in the face of difficult behavior.

The adults at the Child-Family Study Center are directive only when they remove the child from the classroom. They explain where they are going, but use no shame and no punishing overtones. Floor time may seem like being sent to the principal's office, but it's more like play therapy. However, the staff members aren't therapists, and floor time isn't therapy. It's merely wants-nothing quality time. For a half hour the child is given total attention.

Does the child become "spoiled" with such lavish attention? No. According to reports, this approach works miracles. Its effectiveness seems to lie in the fact that it meets the child's needs.

Reflect

Think about the benefits of quality time for an infant. Can you remember a time when someone was fully available to you without being directive? What was that like for you? Can you understand from your own experience how that might benefit an infant?

Many psychotherapists attest to the benefits of being fully present to another person without being directive; yet most of us seldom get this kind of attention from the people in our lives. Think for a moment of the delight of having someone's whole attention at your command for more than a moment or so.

This kind of quality time is easy to give, but often not understood or valued. Caregivers just sitting on the floor where babies and toddlers are playing sometimes feel as though they are not doing their job. They want to play the role of teachers, which they interpret as "teaching something." It is very hard for most adults to be around small children and not be directive. Being receptive and responsive is a skill most adults need to learn; it doesn't seem to come naturally.

Another kind of quality time—perhaps the most commonly understood kind—is shared activity. The initiating mode moves back and forth between adult and child during playtimes as the two enjoy each other's company. These times are often rewarding for the caregiver in ways that the other two kinds of quality time are not.

The Right Amount of Quality Time An interesting aspect of quality time is that a little goes a long way. No one wants (or can stand) intense interaction all the time. An important skill to develop is reading a baby's cues that say, "I've had enough! Please leave me alone." Some younger babies say it by turning away—or even going to sleep. Children (and adults) need to be private sometimes. Although privacy is not an issue with all families, for some it is a strong cultural value. In infant-toddler programs and in family child care, time alone is hard to attain. Some children manage to be alone only by sleeping. Others can focus inwardly and ignore what's going on around them. The adult can help young children gain private time by providing small spaces.

When people never have time alone, they get it by drifting off, by not paying attention, by being elsewhere mentally if not physically. This attitude becomes a habit, so that when this person spends time with others, he or she is "only half there." "Half-there" time, even lots of it, never equals "all-there" time.

Being able to "turn off" is an issue for both caregivers and infants and toddlers. No adult can be expected to be completely present and responsive to others all day, every day. Both adults' and babies' needs must be provided for in programs if the adults are to be effective caregivers.

Of course, every person's life is filled with time that is neither quality time nor private time. Children have to learn to live in a busy world of people. They are bound to be ignored or worked around sometimes. The point is that there is a difference between quality time and other kinds of time and that all children deserve and need some quality time in their lives.

Quality time is built into the daily routine when diapering, dressing, and feeding become occasions for close one-to-one interactions. In group care, when a caregiver is responsible for several babies or a small group of toddlers, paying attention to just one child may be difficult unless caregivers free each other up by taking turns supervising the rest of the children. It is up to the director to ensure that each caregiver be freed at times from responsibility for children other than the one she is changing or feeding. That means that it must be permissible, and even encouraged, for a caregiver to focus on just one child.

In family child care where there is no other adult, the caregiver has no one else to turn to when she feeds or diapers a baby. But caregivers can still focus on just one child by setting up a safe environment and encouraging the rest of the children to play on their own. Of course, the caregiver must still keep a watchful eye on the group—a skill that can be developed with practice. It's amazing to watch an experienced caregiver give full attention to one child but still manage to catch a dangerous or forbidden action going on in another part of the room.

Principle 3: Learn Each Child's Unique Ways of Communicating and Teach Yours

Notice how the communication between Caitlin and her caregiver worked. The caregiver talked directly to Caitlin about what she was going to do, using body movements that matched her words. Caitlin used her body, facial expressions, and voice to communicate her responses. The caregiver responded to her responses by interpreting, answering, and discussing. The caregiver did not carry on endless chatter. She said little, but what she said carried a lot of meaning, backed up by action. She is teaching Caitlin to listen, not tune out. She is teaching that talking is communication, not distraction. She is teaching words and language in context, by talking naturally, not repeating words over and over or using baby talk. She also communicated with her body and with sounds other than words, and she responded to Caitlin's communication (sounds, facial expressions, and body movements). The communication between Caitlin and her caregiver went way beyond words.

No one knows a baby's or toddler's system as well as those people to whom he or she is attached. For that reason (and others), programs for infants and toddlers should encourage attachment between the children and the caregivers.

It's also important to note here that each of us uses a system of body language that is particular to our culture and, within the culture, that is specific to gender and perhaps social class as well. Just one example is in the difference in how men and women in white, European-derived North American culture cross their legs. Another example is the contrasting walk between the African American man and the African American woman. These are unconscious positions and movements, but members of the culture know them well. Children learn the rudiments of culturally based nonverbal communication from adults in their lives, as well as creating their own specific body language.

Eventually babies come to depend more on words to express themselves in addition to other means of communication. They learn to express needs, wants, ideas, and feelings more and more clearly. They also learn to enjoy language for itself—to play with words, phrases, and sounds. Adult reactions and encouragement to use language facilitate their development. By late toddlerhood most children can express themselves in words, though, of course, they continue to use nonverbal communication throughout their lives.

Reflect

Think about someone you know very well. Can you picture some ways that person communicates with you without using words?

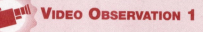

VIDEO OBSERVATION 1

Baby Crying

See Video Observation 1: Baby Crying for an illustration of some of the principles in Chapter 1. You'll see a baby on a blanket crying. This is not a unique way of communicating, but it is communication. The caregiver comes around to pick the baby up. Notice how she comes from the front rather than approaching from the side or rear. That's a sign of respect, so she won't surprise the baby.

Questions

- How does the baby communicate that she needs something?
- How does the caregiver prepare the baby to be picked up?
- Notice that the baby is lying on her back. Do you know why? If not, you'll find out as you read further in the book.

To view this clip, go to **www.mhhe.com/itc10e**. Click on Student Edition, select Chapter 1, and click on Video Observations.

It is important to recognize that some cultures value and depend on verbal exchanges more than others. European Americans tend to use direct communication. Because babies can't talk (in fact, the origin of the word *infant* can be traced back through Middle English to Old French, where it is a combination of *in* ["not"] and *fans* ["speaking"]), researchers at the University of California at Davis discovered that they could introduce direct communication to babies by teaching a gesturing system called baby signs.[2] Caregivers from highly verbal cultures need to be extra sensitive to children who use a good deal of nonverbal communication instead of words.[3]

Young children should see adults using words that match their nonverbal communication. If the face and body movements say one thing and the words say something else, children are receiving double messages, which get in the way of true communication. They not only have problems deciding which to believe, but they model after the adult and thus learn to give double messages themselves. Clear communication is important.

Principle 4: Invest Time and Energy to Build a Total Person

Recent brain research supports the goal of building a total person instead of concentrating on cognitive development alone. Because of all the talk about school-readiness, some parents realize that the early years are important ones in intellectual growth. Whether or not they have heard about the brain research, they may expect to see some evidence that caregivers are providing "cognitive activities." Their concept of cognitive activities may be based on what they know about preschool. They may expect caregivers to teach such concepts as colors, shapes, and even numbers and letters through an activity approach.

On the other side, caregivers, also concerned with intellectual development, may think that the way to promote it is through specialized equipment, exercises, or activities. Books and programs are readily available to, as they say, "stimulate cognitive development." Catalogs and stores are full of toys, equipment, and gadgets advertised as making babies smarter. Of course, providing a rich environment with interesting things to do is desirable. And, yes, it can promote cognitive development. But be careful about falling into the trap of thinking that you can stimulate cognitive development without working on physical, social, and emotional development at the same time. It isn't the clever little toys that you provide or the so-called learning activities you do with the children that make a difference. It's the day-to-day living, the relationships, the experiences, the diaperings, the feedings, the toilet training, and the free play and exploration that contribute to intellectual development. And those same experiences help the child grow physically, socially, and emotionally as well.

Think of how rich the experience of diapering will be for Caitlin. She will be immersed in **sensory input**—visual, auditory, tactile, olfactory. How often are caregivers and parents told to hang a mobile over the changing table so that the diapering can be an "educational experience." How limited an experience a mobile provides compared with what Caitlin will enjoy with her respectful, responsive, reciprocal caregiver without something overhead to distract her.

Principle 5: Respect Infants and Toddlers as Worthy People

Respect was not a word usually used with very young children until Magda Gerber introduced this concept. Usually worries about respect go the other way, as adults demand (or wish for) children to respect them. There is no better way to gain respect for yourself than to model it for children.

What does it mean to respect a child? The diapering scene provides an example. Before the caregiver did anything to Caitlin, she explained what would happen. Just as a respectful nurse warns you before putting a cold instrument on your skin, so Caitlin's caregiver prepared her for what was to come. Until you realize the difference, the natural tendency is to pick up a child without saying anything. Babies are often carried around like objects, even when they are old enough to walk and talk. Adults often pick a child up and put him or her in a chair or stroller without a word. That kind of action is not respectful.

To clarify the concept of respecting an infant, try imagining how a nurse would move a fairly helpless patient from a bed to a wheelchair. Then just change the players and imagine one is a caregiver and one is an infant. Except for the size and weight involved, if the adult is treating the infant with respect, the scene should look much the same.

To better understand the concept of respecting a toddler, imagine you have just seen a man fall off a ladder. Think how you would respond. Even if you are strong enough, you would probably not rush over and set him back on his feet. You'd start talking first, asking if he was hurt or needed help. You'd probably extend a hand if he indicated he was all right and started getting up. You'd comfort him if that was called for. Most people have no trouble responding respectfully to an adult.

Why then do adults rush over and pick up a fallen toddler without a moment's pause? Why not see first what it is the toddler needs? Maybe all that is required is some reassurance—not physical help. Perhaps the child is angry or embarrassed and needs an adult who can accept those feelings and allow expression of them. Perhaps the toddler needs nothing and without adult interference will get up and go about his business on his own. More aspects of respect come out in the next scene.

Twelve-month-old Brian is sitting at a low table with several other children eating a piece of banana. He is obviously enjoying the experience in more ways than one. He has squashed the banana in his hand and crammed it in his mouth, and it is now oozing out between his teeth. He is relishing it. He reaches for his mouth with the very last piece and, plop, it falls on the ground. He stretches out a hand for it, but the caregiver is quicker. "I'm sorry, Brian, but the banana is dirty now. I can't let you eat it." Brian's eyes open wide, his mouth drops open, and a sorrowful wail comes forth. "That's all the banana we have," the caregiver adds as Brian reaches out to her for more. She sits back down at the table after having disposed of the dropped piece. She offers him a cracker, saying, "We're out of bananas, but you can have a cracker instead." Brian rejects the offered cracker. Aware now that he will get no more, he begins to scream.

"I see how unhappy you are," says the caregiver calmly but with genuine compassion. "I wish I had more banana to give you," she adds. Brian's screams become more piercing, and he begins to kick his feet. The caregiver remains silent, looking at him as if she really cares about his feelings.

The other children at the table are having various reactions to this scene. The caregiver turns to them and explains, "Brian lost his banana, and he didn't like it." She turns back to Brian. He continues to cry. The caregiver waits. Sobbing, he gets off his chair, toddles over to her, and buries his head in lap. She touches him on the back, stroking him soothingly. When he has quieted down, she says, "You need to wash your hands now." He doesn't move. She waits. Then gently she repeats, "You need to wash your hands, Brian. I'll come with you," she adds. Turning the table over to another caregiver, she gets up and walks slowly across the floor with Brian. Brian is licking globs of banana from his fingers. A last sob escapes from his lips as he reaches the sink.

The caregiver respected Brian's right to have feelings and to express them.[4] She offered support without gushing sympathy. Because she did not distract him with great amounts of warmth or entertainment, he was able to pay attention to what was going on inside himself. He was learning that it was all right to respond honestly to the situation.

Sometimes adult attention is so rewarding that children associate anger, frustration, or sorrow with attention. They use their feelings to manipulate. We would all be better off to ask directly for what we need than to use emotional displays to get hugs and touching. That's why the caregiver remained available but let Brian indicate what he needed. She did not pick him up but let him come to her. When he was ready for comfort, she was there to give it to him, but it didn't come so early that he was not able to express himself.

Following are some examples of less respectful ways to respond to Brian.

"Stop that screaming—that's nothing to get so upset about—you were almost finished anyway."

"Poor little Brian, let's go play with the doggie that you like so much—look, Brian—see him bark—bow-wow!"

Principle 6: Be Honest about Your Feelings

In the last scene the child was encouraged to recognize his feelings. He was angry, and he was not asked to pretend to be something else. What about adults? Is it all right for caregivers to express their anger to young children? Yes. Children in child care need to be around real people, not warm, empty role-players. Part of being a real person is getting angry, scared, upset, and nervous now and then. Here is a scene showing a caregiver expressing anger:

A caregiver has just separated two children who were coming to blows over a toy. "I can't let you hurt Amber," she says to Shawn, who is 18 months old. She has him firmly but gently by the arm when he turns to her and spits in her face. Her expression changes from calm to anger, and she takes his other arm as well. Looking him right in the eyes, she says clearly, but with emotion in her voice, "I don't like that, Shawn. I don't want you to spit at me." She lets go, stands up, turns her back, and walks away. When she is a few steps away, she gives a quick glance back to see what he is doing. He hasn't moved, so she walks to the sink and washes her face. She keeps an eye out to make sure he doesn't return to hitting Amber. By the time she comes back, she is calm. Shawn is climbing up the slide, and things have returned to normal.

This caregiver was saying honestly what effect Shawn's action had on her. Notice how she expressed her feelings. She didn't put on such a show that it encouraged him to do it again for his own entertainment—a problem that can occur when displays of adult anger are dramatic and lengthy. She didn't blame, accuse, judge, or belittle Shawn. She merely verbalized her feelings and connected them clearly to the situation. She let Shawn know what made her angry and stopped him from continuing the action. Having expressed herself, she left the scene. In short, she neither masked her feelings nor blew up.

Expressing her feelings seemed to have been enough to let Shawn know that this behavior was unacceptable. She didn't have to do anything further about it—this time, at least. If it occurs again, she may have to do something more than just tell Shawn how she feels.

Compare the reaction of this caregiver with the times you've seen people angry with a child, yet smiling and talking in a honeyed voice. Imagine the difficulty a child has in reconciling the two sets of messages at the same time.

Principle 7: Model the Behavior You Want to Teach

All the caregivers in the previous scenes have been modeling behavior that is acceptable for children as well as adults. You've seen examples of cooperation, respect, honest feelings, and communication. Take a look at how this principle works in a more difficult situation—when aggression is involved.

Shawn and Amber are struggling over a rag doll again. A caregiver starts to move near them. Before he reaches the pair, Shawn reaches out and gives Amber a slap on the arm. She lets out a wail. The caregiver kneels on the floor before the two children. His face is calm; his movements are slow and careful. He reaches out and touches Shawn, rubbing his arm on the same spot where he hit Amber. "Gently, Shawn, gently." At the same time he strokes Amber. Shawn remains silent. Amber continues to wail. The caregiver touches her again. "You got hit, didn't you, Amber? It hurt!" Amber stops crying and looks at him. All three are silent for a moment. The caregiver waits. Shawn clutches the doll and starts to walk away with it. Amber grabs it. The caregiver remains silent until Shawn raises his arm to hit again. "I can't let you hurt Amber," he says, catching the arm midair. He touches him softly. "Gently, gently." Amber suddenly jerks the doll and Shawn lets go unexpectedly. Taking the doll in triumph, she starts across the room. Shawn looks sad, but remains in the same spot. The caregiver stays near. "She has the doll," he observes. Amber sees a ball at her feet, drops the doll, and picks up the ball. She throws it and runs after it giggling. Shawn moves quickly over to the doll, picks it up, holds it tenderly, and coos to it. The scene ends with both children playing contentedly, and the caregiver is no longer needed.

Notice how this caregiver modeled gentleness—the behavior he wished to teach. A more common approach when an adult arrives on the scene of a dispute is to treat the children with even more aggression than they have been displaying themselves. "I'll teach you to play rough," growls the adult, jerking the child by the arm and squeezing it. This approach models the very behavior the adult is trying to eliminate. Luckily he didn't shake the child because he knew that was dangerous and could cause harm.

The caregiver in the Shawn-versus-Amber scene knew that both children needed assurance that control would be provided when needed. It is frightening to both aggressor and victim when there is no protecting adult around to stop the violent action. The aggressor needs to be dealt with gently and nonjudgmentally. The victim needs to be dealt with empathetically but not sympathetically (that is, acknowledging her distress without feeling sorry for her). Sympathy and a good deal of attention may reward victims. In that way they learn that being victimized pays off in adult love and attention. How sad that some children actually learn to become victims.

Principle 8: Recognize Problems as Learning Opportunities, and Let Infants and Toddlers Try to Solve Their Own

The same scene also illustrates this principle: Let children, even babies, handle their own problems to the extent that they can. The caregiver could have stepped in and taken care of this tugging situation by creating a solution for the conflict. He didn't, however. He let the toddlers make a decision themselves. (Though he did, of course, keep them from hurting each other further.) Very young children can solve more problems than many people give them credit for. The caregiver's role is to give them time and freedom to work on the problems. That means not responding to every frustration immediately. Sometimes a bit of facilitating will move a child forward when he or she gets stuck on a problem, but the facilitating should be the least help necessary, leaving the child free to work toward his own solution.

In a DVD called *On Their Own with Our Help*, Magda Gerber illustrated this principle.[5] A baby crawls under a low table, then tries to sit up. When he discovers he can't, he starts crying. He doesn't know how to crawl out again, and he looks very fearful. Instead of rescuing him (it would have been easy to just lift the table up), Magda guides him out—reassuring and directing him with both her words and her hands.

Magda is using an approach called **scaffolding**. This term comes from Jerome Bruner and fits with the theory of Lev Vygotsky. To scaffold, adults keep a constant eye out for a child who is in a situation in which there is a potential for learning. The adult sensitively structures that situation so that problem solving is encouraged and supported. Sometimes scaffolding requires a little assist; sometimes the adult presence is all the scaffold an infant or toddler needs.

Problems can be valuable learning opportunities. Another of Gerber's DVDs, *See How They Move*, illustrates this principle. The viewer is treated to scene after scene of children doing **gross motor** problem solving all by themselves. The adults stay back and let the children work without interference. The only scaffold provided is the adult presence, which is enough to allow the children to freely experience their own ways of moving and exploring.[6]

Principle 9: Build Security by Teaching Trust

For infants to learn to trust, they need dependable adults. They need to know that they will get their needs met in a reasonable amount of time. If it's food they need, food arrives in a timely manner. If it's comfort, a caregiver is there to provide it in the way that works best for the particular child. If it's rest, the caregiver is there to help her settle down in a place that's safe, peaceful, and quiet. If it's movement that is needed, the adult situates the baby so movement

Reflect

Have you ever been rescued from a problem in a way that frustrated you? Have you ever seen an infant in the same situation? How did you feel? How do you think the infant felt?

is possible. When infants discover that they can express a need and it will be satisfied, they develop trust in the adults who care for them. In this environment they learn that the world is a secure place for them.

The examples have shown dependable adults who met needs as well as offered strength and support. They didn't trick the children. One of the times adults are most tempted to deceive children is during good-bye times. When everyone knows that a child is going to suffer loudly with protests and wails when the parent leaves, some are willing to trick the child to avoid a scene. However, it is much better when the parent leaves a child by saying good-bye outright, and the caregiver accepts protests and wails. While providing security, support, and empathy, he or she can express acceptance of the baby's right to be unhappy. The baby learns that he can predict when his mother will go, rather than worrying constantly that she has sneaked away when he was occupied. He knows that as long as she hasn't said good-bye, she is still around. He comes to depend on his knowledge that the adults around him don't lie to him or trick him. Learning to predict what will happen is an important part of building trust. Always being happy isn't.

Principle 10: Be Concerned about the Quality of Development in Each Stage

We live in the period of the hurried child (a term coined by David Elkind in his book by the same title). The pressure starts at birth, as many parents anxiously await the time their child reaches each milestone, comparing his or her progress with that of other children or with developmental charts. The message is everywhere—"Fast is better." Books advertise "Teach your baby to read." Institutes promise miracles. When adults have this hurry-up attitude, babies are propped up before they can sit on their own, walked around by the hand before they can even stand by themselves, taught to ride a tricycle when they can barely walk.

Caregivers feel the pressure from every side—from parents, sometimes even from directors, as they are urged to speed up development. Yet development cannot be hurried. Each child has a built-in timetable that dictates just when he or she will crawl, sit up, and start to walk. The way caregivers can help development is to encourage each baby to do thoroughly whatever it is that he or she is doing. The important learnings come when the baby is ready, not when the adults decide it's time.

Take crawling as an example. Instead of standing the child up and continually encouraging him or her to walk, it is better to celebrate the crawling. The only time in his life that he'll ever be so conveniently close to things on the floor is the same time in his life when he is so very curious about everything that is within reach and just beyond it. Caregivers can provide experiences and opportunities for him to develop not only his crawling but also his curiosity.

If you are to help counteract the pushy approach, you need to sell parents on the idea that perfecting skills children are working on now is more important than pushing children to develop new ones. The new ones will come when the child has thoroughly practiced the old ones. The age at which a child first walks in no way correlates with whether or not he or she will become an Olympic runner.

The 10 principles for respectful adult-infant interactions carry with them regard for the individual. That means that differences are honored. Children are not all alike, and we want to emphasize that. Certainly the research done on ages and stages resulting in charts of milestones might lead us to believe the goal is for all children to be "normal." However, in this book we are anxious to set aside those ideas and regard each child as being on a unique path of development. Every child has strengths and challenges; we want to focus more on strengths than weaknesses and to support the child in meeting the challenges. We also want to point out that the young child comes embedded in a cultural and family context. We can't ignore that there are different ideas about what children need and how they grow. If a particular practice advocated in this book doesn't fit what a family believes is good for their children, their value system, or their goals, you can't ignore the difference. You and the family need to talk. One of our goals for caregivers is to honor diversity even when it doesn't fit what the caregiver believes or is in conflict with the program policies. Another of our goals is to help those who work with or will work with infants and toddlers to see the importance of partnering with parents.

Curriculum and Developmentally Appropriate Practice   A word that is being used now more frequently in connection with infant-toddler care is **curriculum**. The term literally means "course"—as in a course of study. You can think of infant-toddler curriculum as the word *course* applies to a river. Like a course of study, it is a path from one point to another. But with a river there's a meandering flow. Using the principles on which this book is based means that the child not only gives input but is actually in charge of his or her own curriculum—in partnership with caregivers (who are partners with the family). So moving from point A to point B is not something that adults control except by the way they set up and adapt the environment according to each child's interests and changing needs. Besides being environmental planners, caregivers acting as curriculum designers also have roles as facilitators of learning, supporters of development, and assessors of both.

NAEYC Program Standard 2
Curriculum

NAEYC Program Standard 4
Assessment

Developmentally appropriate practice has three knowledge bases from which to determine appropriate practice. The guidelines for making decisions about developmentally appropriate practice tell early childhood professionals to consider the following:

1. *Practice based on research and child development principles that relate to typical development.* Developmentally appropriate practice (DAP) is both a general term and a specific term relating to this particular knowledge base.
2. *Practice that fits what is known about individual differences.* We're calling this knowledge base individually appropriate practice (IAP), and it relates to all kinds of differences, including variation from the norms guiding DAP and differences that may or may not be specifically related to disabilities or other kinds of mental, physical, or emotional challenges.
3. *Culturally appropriate practice.* Culturally appropriate practice (CAP) includes practices that come from differences in perceptions, values, beliefs, priorities, and traditions outside the mainstream American culture.

It's important to realize that a practice may fit research and child development principles but may not fit some children and their families. In that case we can't call that practice appropriate in the larger sense. That's why we can't just go by research and child development principles. A practice can't be considered appropriate if it is culturally inappropriate. Bridging cultures is a concept that is carried throughout this book, and caregivers are continually challenged to look for ways to create culturally consistent environments and practices for infants, toddlers, and their families without giving up what they believe are best practices. Instead of educating parents out of their culture, the goal is to create bridges across gaps that may lie between culturally diverse families and the culture of the program or the early childhood culture in general.

Curriculum and Developmentally Appropriate Practice

The 10 principles of respectful care correspond to the NAEYC document called *Developmentally Appropriate Practice*. In each chapter we will show you how the two sets of ideas parallel each other. We will also show you some dilemmas like the following one.

The Principles in Action

Principle 5 Respect infants and toddlers as worthy people. Don't treat them as objects or cute little empty-headed people to be manipulated.

The caregiver understands how important it is to respect even the youngest infant. She always talks to the babies to prepare them for what will happen; in fact, she never does anything to them without telling them first. She always thinks of them as people. That's why she talks to them all the time. In her culture, words are considered the ultimate way to communicate. A parent in the caregiver's class who is of a different culture never tells her baby what she's doing or why. In addition, she "wears" her baby in the baby carrier of her culture and never puts the child down until she has to change her or when she leaves. The caregiver has explained principle 5 to the mother. The mother explained to the caregiver that in her culture, they think babies should have very close contact at all times. It makes them feel secure, she says. In her culture, adults don't talk to babies. Why should they? With all the body contact, communication is going on all the time. The ultimate is to communicate without words. That means you're very close to someone when you can do that. She admits that the caregiver has a different idea about what babies need. The caregiver wants to be culturally responsive, but she thinks she needs to understand more about what the term *respect* means to this mother.

1. Should the caregiver try to educate the parent about this child development principle? Why or why not?

2. Does one perspective make more sense to you than the other? If yes, which one and why?
3. Do you feel yourself taking sides in this situation?
4. What are the issues in this situation as you see them?
5. What does the idea of respecting babies mean to you?

Appropriate Practice

Overview of Development

Quality care is about relationships. Relationships are part of every aspect of early development. Babies learn trust through daily interactions with dependable adults. They build a sense of security when they find they can communicate their needs and are rewarded with a sensitive response. They grow confident when they discover they can manage the challenges they meet. All this depends on relationships that grow through continuity of care and are developmentally, individually, and culturally appropriate.

Developmentally Appropriate Practice

The following are samples of developmentally appropriate practices:

- Adults are especially attentive to infants during caregiving routines, such as diaper changing, feeding, and changing clothes. The caregiver explains what will happen, what is happening, and what will happen next, asking and waiting for the infant's cooperation and participation.
- Adults ensure that every infant receives nurturing, responsive care.
- Diaper changing, feeding, and other routines are viewed as vital learning experiences for both babies and caregivers.
- Adults express healthy, accepting attitudes about children's bodies and their functions.
- Caregivers ask parents what sounds and words their toddler uses so that the caregiver will understand what the child is saying when she uses beginning speech or a home language that the caregiver does not understand.
- Adults respond quickly to toddlers' cries or other signs of distress, recognizing that toddlers have limited language with which to communicate their needs.
- Adults recognize that routine tasks of living such as eating, toileting, and dressing are important opportunities to help children learn about their world, acquire skills, and regulate their own behavior. Meals and snacks include finger food or utensils that are easier for toddlers to use, such as bowls, spoons, and graduated versions of drinking containers from bottles to cups. Adults support and positively encourage children's attempts to dress themselves and put on shoes.

Source: Carol Copple and Sue Bredekamp, eds., *Developmentally Appropriate Practice in Early Childhood Programs*, 3rd ed. (Washington, DC: National Association for the Education of Young Children, 2009.)

Individually Appropriate Practice

The field of infant-toddler care is moving toward including more children of differing abilities and challenges in child care programs that have traditionally served only typically developing children. The need, then, is for caregivers to create inclusive environments, making sure that spatial organization, materials, and activities enable all children to

Appropriate Practice *(continued)*

participate actively. If every child is to receive nurturing responsive care, it must be individualized. The amount of adult intervention needed varies by individual child. Some need less and some need more. For many children it's enough to create a rich environment and let them experience it in an open-ended way. Adults can spend more time responding to what those children initiate than the reverse. Other children profit from selective and sensitive interventions. You will see examples throughout the book of diverse paths of development and adult responses to them.

Culturally Appropriate Practice

Caregivers honor cultural and family differences by listening to what parents want for their children and responding in culturally sensitive ways. Taking a partnership approach, caregivers discuss all decisions about how to best support children's development.

The principles explained in this chapter may not fit for everybody. Some families may find the caregiving practices shown in this chapter and elsewhere to be too standoffish. It may be uncomfortable for families in which the focus is more on teaching the child that he or she is a member of a group instead of an individual. Child-rearing practices reflect this focus, and some adults

may downplay individuality. Instead of encouraging independence, families may instead focus on interdependence. The two are not mutually exclusive. Indeed, all families want their children to have relationships *and* grow up to be individuals who can stand on their own two feet. The perspective about what children need most to learn is what differs. We can't ignore the difference because the independence-interdependence dimension influences outcomes. We can't condone practices that are in opposition to what families want for their children. It may feel like a serious dilemma, but through building relationships of trust and understanding, caregivers and parents can figure out together what's best for this child in this family in this society.

Appropriate Practice in Action

Think about what you just read here and then go back and look at the Principles in Action on page 18. You will encounter dilemmas such as these throughout the book but will continually be asked to honor differences. It takes an open mind to do that. Would you be willing to try to understand *how* exactly to honor this parent's practice? You won't find the answer in this book. Each case is different; the outcome of the dilemma comes from interaction and communication between the people involved.

Summary

This chapter is about principles, practices, and curriculum and is based on 10 principles related to a philosophy of respect, which come from Magda Gerber and connect to the approach of Dr. Emmi Pikler. An explanation of each of the 10 principles takes up most of the chapter.

Relationships, Interactions, and the Three Rs

- Relationships are a cornerstone of infant-toddler care and education. They come from interactions, especially three-R interactions—that is, respectful, responsive, and reciprocal interactions.
- Caregiving routines are opportunities for three-R interactions as shown in the opening diapering scenario.

Ten Principles Based on a Philosophy of Respect

- Key words or phrases for the principles are: (1) involvement, (2) quality time, (3) communication, (4) total person, (5) respect, (6) honest feelings, (7) modeling behavior, (8) problems as opportunities, (9) security and trust, and (10) quality of development.

Curriculum and Developmentally Appropriate Practice

- The word *curriculum*, as it applies to infants and toddlers, can be defined as a course of study, a framework for practice, or a plan for learning that is all-inclusive and centers on connections and relationships.
- Curriculum in this book relates to NAEYC's developmentally appropriate practice, which is based on three bases of knowledge: child development principles, individual differences, and cultural differences.
- The 10 principles of respectful care fit developmentally appropriate practice and can also be looked at in light of cultural differences.

Key Terms

curriculum 17	relationship 4	wants-nothing quality time 7
floor time 7	scaffolding 15	wants-something quality time 7
gross motor 15	sensory input 11	
interactions 4	three-R interactions 4	

Thought/Activity Questions

1. Explain two of the principles in the chapter.
2. What are some common themes that seem to run through all the principles?
3. Observe in an infant-toddler program and see if you can find evidence that it is using any of the 10 principles.
4. Visit an infant-toddler program and ask to see any written materials they have, such as a brochure, a parent booklet, registration materials. Compare and contrast what you read about the program with the information in this chapter.

For Further Reading

Magda Gerber, ed., *The RIE Manual for Parents and Professionals*, expanded edition, ed. Deborah Greenwald with Joan Weaver (Los Angeles, CA: Resources for Infant Educarers, RIE, 2013).

Ruth Anne Hammond, *Respecting Babies: A New Look at Magda Gerber's RIE Approach* (Washington DC: Zero to Three 2009).

Beverly A. Kovach and Susan Patrick, *Being with Infants and Toddlers: A Curriculum that Works for Caregivers* (Tulsa Oklahoma: LKB Publishing, 2012).

Deborah Carlisle Solomon, *Baby Knows Best: Raising a Confident and Resourceful Child, the RIE Way* (New York: Little Brown, 2013).

chapter 2

Infant-Toddler Education

Focus Questions

After reading this chapter you should be able to answer the following questions:

1 If you were describing the educational approach of this book to someone, what three words would you *not* include in the definition of infant-toddler education? Explain why those three words are not appropriate for infants and toddlers.

2 How can you describe what infant-toddler education is?

3 What does the word *curriculum* mean in relation to infant-toddler education?

4 What does it mean to take a problem-solving approach to infant-toddler education?

5 Can you name and explain four roles adults take to support problem solving in infants and toddlers?

What Do You See?

Emily is sitting on a soft rug when she sees a big, bright ball. She scoots on her bottom over to it, pushing with one leg and hand. She reaches out and touches the ball; it rolls away from her. She looks excited as she throws herself from sitting onto all fours and crawls quickly after the ball. She reaches it and tries to hold it, but it slips out of her arms and rolls away again. She follows it to where it has stopped by a small bed with a doll on it. She reaches for the doll with one hand while balancing on the other and her two knees. She picks up the doll by one foot and drops it. She takes the blankets off the bed one by one, holding each to her cheek and comparing their textures. She picks up the last blanket by a corner of the binding and rubs it gently across her lips. Then she's off again, crawling over the doll. As she does, she looks up and sees a picture on the wall at her eye level. It's a photo of the doll's face. She sits back on her bottom, staring at the picture. She then looks at the doll lying under her one leg. "Yes, they are the same," says the adult nearby, who has been sitting on the floor watching her. Emily turns, gives him a smile, and then she's off again to see what else she can discover.

You just saw an example of infant education. If it didn't look like much to you, please read on. As you do, think back to this example. We will return to it later in the chapter.

Child care programs for infants and toddlers are necessarily educational, whether or not that is their primary purpose. There is no way to keep children for a number of hours every day without educating them. You can leave your car in a parking garage in the morning and expect to find it in the same condition that night when you pick it up again. But children aren't cars. Children are changed as the result of their child care experiences. How they are changed and what they learn can come without thought or planning, or the changes can be planned for in a systematic way. This chapter looks at a **philosophy of education** that is appropriate for infants and toddlers in child care. A philosophy of education means the set of theories or concepts related to development and the learning of knowledge and skills.

What Infant-Toddler Education Is *Not*

Infant Stimulation

The word *stimulation* is synonymous with the word *education* in the minds of many when talking about infants. In this book the word *education* means that which takes place in a developmentally appropriate environment and involves relationships. If you are concerned primarily with merely stimulating—with doing something to the baby—you ignore a vital requirement for learning and development: babies need to discover that they can influence the people and things around them. Yes, they need stimulation, which they get from objects and, more important, from people. But they need to perceive their own involvement in these stimulating experiences. Their involvement comes when they are able to have some effect on—that is, interact with—the people and things that are part of the experiences. When stimulation is provided without regard to the baby's initiative or response, the baby is being treated as an object.

The attention on infant stimulation came partly in response to some crib-bound, institutionalized babies who failed to thrive. Being left alone, without much sensory input, but more important without attachment, they naturally failed to thrive. But adding mobiles, music boxes, or dangling objects to the crib isn't the answer. Getting somebody to meet the baby's needs is what is called for—not merely providing stimulation.

In group care for infants, the problem is usually overstimulation rather than the opposite, as sights and sounds bombard the infants. So, in order to meet individual needs, infant education for some may involve cutting down the stimulation—the sensory input—rather than adding to what's already present in the environment.

Babysitting

The opposite view of infant stimulation as infant education is that all you have to do with babies is watch out for them and keep them safe; they'll develop fine on their own. In this view, babies are rosebuds that just need water, air, good soil, plant food, and sunshine to open up to their full potential. The idea of professionally trained caregivers seems superfluous. For someone who is an instinctively good caregiver and is caring for an easy baby, that may all seem true. It's when caregivers are faced with a baby whose needs are hard to determine—one who doesn't respond positively to attempts to get close, or one who lacks the kinds of behaviors that attract adults—that it becomes obvious that this view needs to be reexamined. Then put those caregivers into a situation where each has a number of babies to manage, and some of the babies are quite demanding. Without training, instincts alone may not work so well, and caregivers will have their hands full. Further, the easy-to-get-along-with babies in this situation may well be ignored, which means their development may be compromised. Infant education is a lot more than just babysitting.

Preschool

Education for infants and toddlers in child care is often built on the model of part-time preschools, where the children come in for a few hours in the morning and engage in a variety of activities set up especially for their learning. Circle time, when children are gathered as a group with a teacher in charge, isn't nearly as useful for infants and toddlers. Teachers spend more time herding than involving the infants and toddlers in activities. Infants and toddlers don't do well with preschool-type activities, but instead explore the equipment, toys, and materials in ways that no one ever intended. They bang puzzle pieces, draw on themselves instead of on the paper, and put beans in their mouths instead of gluing them down into the puddles they've produced with glue bottles on paper. They look incompetent because they don't conform to the expectations of adults regarding either process or product.

Rather than find a more appropriate approach, some programs dedicated to this model seem to just wait for the toddlers to grow up and try to tolerate them in the meantime. But while they're waiting, they spend a lot of time restricting the children and teaching them to use the materials in certain ways rather than letting them explore, which is what both infants toddlers are designed to do! Inhibiting infants' and toddlers' exploratory urges is detrimental to their education.

What Infant-Toddler Education Is: The Components

Notice in the vignette at the beginning how Emily was exploring her environment and learning from her explorations. She was stimulating her senses on her own. Nobody was doing that to her. There was an adult nearby to appreciate what she was doing without interfering. He added a few words to support Emily's experience when she was comparing the picture to the doll. Without providing particular activities or setting predetermined outcomes, this scene was a perfect example of infant education. What we didn't see here, but will in chapters to come, was how the care component fits into the total picture. When infant-toddler education comes in a package with play, exploration, and caregiving, everything that happens in the program can become educational. For education to occur, the teachers must understand how infants and toddlers develop and learn. They must also be able to adapt teaching strategies and care routines to meet the individual needs of all infants and toddlers in their care, including those with special needs.

NAEYC Program Standard 1
Relationships

Staff in programs that regard infants and toddlers as immature preschoolers and use an activity approach get frustrated with all the "noneducational" time spent in caregiving and transition times. In contrast, the Pikler Institute in Budapest, the residential nursery started by Emmi Pikler, sees care and education as a package and feels that learning goes on every minute of the day.[1] Resources for Infant Educarers (RIE), Magda Gerber's program that started in Los Angeles, also refuses to separate care and education.[2] Both Pikler and Gerber and their respective programs are in tune with Nel Nodding's work at Stanford University on the ethics of care. Nodding, though not focused on the earliest years, nevertheless makes a strong case for care being a vital ingredient of education at all levels![3] All three of these theorists feel the primary focus of the first three years should be to establish a close and continuous relationship, which also fits with what brain research indicates.[4] Education then grows out of the relationship that results from caregiving.

Curriculum as the Foundation of Infant-Toddler Education

NAEYC Program Standard 2
Curriculum

For a care program to be educational, there must be a curriculum. The appropriate curriculum should be a plan for learning and development that is all-inclusive and centers on connections and relationships with each individual infant or toddler in a center- or home-based early care and education program. Trained caregivers who respond to and respect each child's individual needs in warm and sensitive ways that promote attachment focus on both education and care. Respectful and responsive curriculum is based on relationships that occur within planned and unplanned activities, experiences, and happenings.

A curriculum is not just a book of lesson plans or activities for a day, a month, or a year. It's not a package of posters, books, toys, and materials that go along with themes of the month. It's not a set of forms with blanks to fill in about what to do each day or season. A curriculum is much more complex than any of these things. It can be defined simply as a plan for learning, but to understand what that means in terms of infant-toddler programs takes a whole book. That's what this book is about.

NAEYC Program Standard 1
Relationships

Think of the curriculum centering on relationships. In fact, the WestEd Program for Infant-Toddler Care—the largest training effort in the United States that is related to the first three years—calls what it teaches a "responsive,

VIDEO OBSERVATION 2

Toddler Playing with a Tube and a Ball

See Video Observation 2: Toddler Playing with a Tube and a Ball for an example of problem solving. This is another simple example of the kinds of educational experiences children choose for themselves. This boy is older than Emily, who appears in the scene at the beginning of the chapter. He is exploring and experimenting, too, but is focused on just one problem.

Questions

- What problem is this boy trying to solve?
- What do you think about his persistence? Are you surprised that he has such a long attention span?
- What do you think made the boy pick this particular problem to solve?

To view this clip, go to **www.mhhe.com/itc10e.** Click on Student Edition, select Chapter 2, and click on Video Observations.

relationship-based curriculum." This curriculum is explained in many volumes of guides, manuals, videotapes, and what are called video magazines. The training in this curriculum is extensive, and it focuses on the individual needs and interests of each child and also the child's family.

Although a curriculum does not have to be written out, labeled, or even talked about as such, somewhere there is a framework for decision making based on a philosophy that guides action. The framework and philosophy may only be in the heads of the founders of the program, but it must somehow be conveyed to everyone who works with the infants and toddlers in the program. It helps if that framework or curriculum is in writing, but the most effective way to teach the framework to the people working with the children is through training.

**NAEYC Program
Standard 6**
Teachers

Implementing the Curriculum

To implement the curriculum, infant care teachers, caregivers, educarers, and family child care providers need the skills to understand typical development, atypical development, and diversity. In addition, they must have observation skills so they can be appropriately responsive minute by minute and over time. Here's where more writing comes in. In order to plan for each child and for the group, detailed record keeping is a must. Only then are caregivers able to effectively reflect on what they see, assess what each child needs, and plan environments and experiences for individuals and for the group that are a good fit. They also must be able to adapt the environments and experiences that work for typically developing children so they work for *all* children, no matter what kinds of physical, mental, or emotional challenges individuals bring to the program.

To carry out a curriculum, a caregiver must have goals or desired results, which are often unwritten and even unspoken, but which most often are holistic and relate to the image of whole, healthy children who are able to reach their full, unique potential as individuals and as group members. When expressed or written, the goals (sometimes called outcomes) are usually related to three developmental domains—which we can think of as mind, body, and feelings. Feelings include the ability to relate to others. To use more sophisticated language, goals or outcomes are usually organized by the cognitive, physical, and social-emotional domains. Some programs also have separate spiritual and/or creative goals. Curricula at higher levels of education can focus on the mind alone, but that doesn't work for infants and toddlers. There is no way to separate intellectual needs and interests from other needs and interests at this beginning level.

Assessing the Effectiveness of the Curriculum: Observing and Recording

Any curriculum depends on caregivers determining what children need and are interested in, both as individuals and as a group, which is an assessment process. Two parts of the assessment process are discussed here: observing and recording children's behavior. See Figure 2.1 for a summary of ways to record observations in writing.

Observation as an assessment process can't be overemphasized. Caregivers should develop and practice observation every day. Informal observation should become a daily habit, indeed a mode of being.

Recording Observations   Observations can be recorded in a number of ways, written, taped, or video recorded, and may include anecdotal records, formal written observations, or daily logs. **Anecdotal records** are descriptions of anything that captures your attention and are recorded or written as notes on the spot, or, if written later, as notes on whatever sticks in your mind. By keeping anecdotal records, you may notice that some children don't capture your attention very often

Figure 2.1 Ways of Recording Observations

Anecdotal records	A description of something written on the spot or afterwards, that records something brief that seems to have some meaning.
Running records	A formal written observation taken first as notes and later written up in sentences and paragraphs.
Daily logs	Can be used to record times and details about diapering, feeding, sleeping.
Individual journals	Can be kept on each child and written in by staff members.
Two-way journals	Can be in something that goes home for parents to write in and comes back each day with the child. A variation of the hard copy two-way journal is the two-way e-mail journal.

or in the same way as others. You need to observe those children more carefully and keep records of what you observe.

Formal written observations are called **running records** and involve carefully and objectively noting everything that happens as it happens. They can be recorded and transcribed later or written as notes and then rewritten later. See Figure 2.1 for a summary of ways to record observations. Or video can be used, with the observer commenting on what's being observed in objective, nonjudgmental terms. Still photographs, video without commentary, audio recordings of babies' vocalizations and toddlers' conversations are also record-keeping devices, sometimes called **documentation**, that provide visual and auditory representations of learning and development. Carefully kept records and documentation of all sorts can provide important information that shows patterns used to assess individual developmental pathways.

Ongoing assessment tells how the child is doing; where the leading edge of learning, growth, and development lies; and what might be needed next. Russian researcher Lev Vygotsky called this leading edge the **zone of proximal development**. The environmental chart in Appendix B can be used as a guide to the expected sequence of development and the kinds of behaviors that indicate progress.

Developmental Profiles When you keep good records, a developmental profile emerges that provides a picture of each child's development so caregivers can plan an individualized program. This picture should include the range of general and specific interests and needs for each child and the developmental tasks he or she is working on. It also should include the family's goals and expectations. Using developmental profiles, the caregiver can individualize the curriculum so that it meets each child's specific and special needs. This developmental picture also can help the caregiver notice any particular issues or concerns that may need to be discussed with the family and perhaps even with specialists. Some concerns call for professional observations, testing, and other kinds of evaluation. Certain kinds of interventions may be called for depending on what the assessment shows.

Special training is needed to do these more sophisticated assessments, but caregivers do informal assessments on a daily basis as they work with children and learn what they know and can do. Magda Gerber used to say that caregivers should let the child be the teacher, and, indeed, a good part of assessment is learning the child and what he or she has to teach you about his or her interests, skills, knowledge, capabilities, and needs. Of course, caregivers also learn from the family, not *just* from the child.

Daily Logs and Two-Way Journals   Staff must also be able to relate to parents and other family members in ways that provide a good exchange of information so that what goes on outside the home matches, complements, or harmonizes with what goes on inside the home. One kind of record that has been mentioned only briefly so far is a daily log kept by the primary caregiver. The daily log has multiple uses. It can be a way for parents to receive a comprehensive and detailed report when they arrive to pick up their children. Some records have to do with the various caregiving activities and contain specific information that links to home. Diaper changes, elimination patterns, food offered and consumed, length of naptime, and any outstanding events are all interesting information that will help parents know what their babies might need or want after they take them home. This information is especially important in preverbal infants who can't make their needs or interests known. Some programs have a two-way journaling system where parents bring in a journal in which they've recorded what the caregiver might need to know about how the night and morning went. The caregiver uses that same journal to record the events and details of the day, and then the journal goes home again with the parent and child.

Because it is so hard to pin down curriculum or say exactly what infant-toddler education is (as stated earlier, this whole book is about infant-toddler education), the rest of this chapter will focus on one topic—infants and toddlers learning to solve problems and how adults can help them learn.

Education as Facilitating Problem Solving

One way to describe a focus of an infant-toddler curriculum is to pay attention to the development of problem-solving skills in children. That way of thinking about curriculum differs from both the stimulation and activity-centered points of view. A major aspect of the education in this book is based on a *problem-solving approach* in which babies and toddlers learn how to make things happen in their world. Sensory input comes about mostly as a result of the children's actions. The children are in charge. The adults are facilitators rather than *stimulators*.

What kinds of problems do infants and toddlers face? Watch an infant or toddler for just one hour, and you will go a long way toward answering that question. You will note that infants and toddlers deal with a variety of kinds of problems, including physical ones, such as hunger or discomfort; manipulative ones, such as how to get a toy from one hand to the other or how to get one

The Principles in Action

Principle 8 Recognize problems as learning opportunities, and let infants and toddlers try to solve their own. Don't rescue them, constantly make life easy for them, or try to protect them from all problems.

Jasmine rides down the path in the play yard on a tot-sized tricycle, pushing with her feet on the ground instead of using the pedals. She runs off the edge of the concrete walk, and the bike tips over, spilling her into the sand. She lets out a lusty yell and lies on her back with the bike on its side next to her. A caregiver arrives in a hurry and crouches down next to Jasmine but doesn't touch her. She looks into her face and asks, "Are you OK?" Jasmine cries louder. The caregiver says, "You fell down." Jasmine stops crying and looks at her and nods. "You went right off the edge." Jasmine nods again. She starts to roll over on her side. Her caregiver offers a hand to help her. She refuses it and gets up, brushing herself off. The caregiver looks her over carefully and sees no scrapes or red marks, but says again, "Are you OK?" "OK," Jasmine responds. She reaches for the bike handle. The caregiver gets out of her way. She struggles a little but persists until she rights the bike. The caregiver doesn't help. The caregiver says, "You did that all by yourself." Jasmine grins and pulls the bike back to the cement. She has a broad smile on her face as she rides off.

1. Do you see this as an example of infant education? Explain your view.
2. What if the parent had watched this and become uncomfortable that the caregiver was so standoffish? What might you have said to the parent if you had been the caregiver?
3. Why might the parent have been uncomfortable?
4. Do you have a different idea about how the caregiver should have handled this situation?
5. What would you have done and why?
6. Is this a problem you would try to prevent if you were the caregiver? If yes, how? If no, why not?

block to balance on top of another; and social and emotional problems, such as coping with separation from a parent or caregiver or trying to interact with a peer who is not interested in interacting. Some problems are specific to particular levels of development and will eventually be solved. Others are specific to the situation and may or may not be solved. Still others are ones the child will be dealing with, in one form or another, throughout his or her lifetime. Education for children under three lies in learning to deal with this enormous variety of problems, learning various ways to approach them, and learning when the problems can be solved and when to give up. As babies continually experience the problems that come from everyday living, the problems they encounter in play as well as in being fed, changed, dressed, bathed, and put to sleep, they eventually become toddlers who come to see themselves as problem solvers. If they come to see themselves as good problem solvers, and indeed they are, then they will have been, by the definition of this book, well educated.

The Adult Role in Facilitating Problem Solving

NAEYC Program Standard 3
Teaching

The primary function of the adult in infant-toddler education is to facilitate learning rather than to teach or train. Start by appreciating the problems the babies encounter. Allow them to work on solving those problems themselves. Also, as caregiver, you will present problems to the babies while you provide for their needs and set up the environment for their play and exploration. You facilitate infant education by the way you direct and respond to the problem-solving baby during wants-something and wants-nothing quality time.

The two kinds of quality time relate to two ways of being with an infant or a toddler in an educational way, which we'll call **caregiver presence**. To get an idea of these two ways of being, try this exercise. Find someone who is willing to be your mirror. Stand facing that person, and ask the person to copy each of your movements. Then, using your body, facial expressions, and hands, do something for the "mirror" to copy. You may want to move around. After you have experienced being the doer, try being the mirror. When you finish, discuss the experience with your partner. What role did you prefer—doing or mirroring (leading or following)? What was hard about each one? What are the advantages and disadvantages of each?

This mirroring exercise shows the kind of reciprocal interactions that constitute the responsive relationship first discussed in Chapter 1. It also illustrates the two kinds of caregiver presence—active and receptive. Perhaps you prefer the active mode—being a leader and directing what is going on. Or perhaps you prefer the receptive mode—following the child's lead and being responsive. To be a good infant-toddler educator, you need to develop both modes, no matter what your preference. Knowing which you prefer can help you concentrate on improving the other.

Notice in the following scene how the adult's being receptive or active works when the child has a problem to solve.

Jason, 14 months, toddles in crying loudly and holds his fingers out in front of him.

"Oh, Jason, something happened to you," says the caregiver.

Jason continues to cry and holds his fingers up for inspection. The caregiver touches his fingers gently. "It looks like you hurt your fingers," he says in a calm but understanding voice.

Jason pulls his fingers away and tugs at the caregiver's pants, indicating he wants to show him something.

"You want me to come." He verbalizes Jason's desire and follows him to an area behind a partition, where another adult and several children are on the floor. Jason, sobbing, leads him directly to a cupboard with the door standing ajar. His cries change slightly as he nears the scene of the accident.

"You pinched your fingers in the door?" guesses the caregiver.

Jason, angry now, picks up a wooden block and gets ready to throw it at the cupboard door.

"I see you're mad, but I won't let you throw the block. You might hurt something," says the caregiver firmly, holding Jason's arm.

Jason seems to reconsider. He puts down the block and goes to the cupboard. Still crying, he closes the door and opens it again. He is very careful in his actions.

"Yes, you can do it now without pinching." The caregiver puts Jason's actions into words.

Jason ignores the words and continues to open and close the door. The angry cries subside and pained whimpering takes their place. He sits down by the cupboard and remains there crying.

"Let's go put some cold water on your fingers," says the caregiver, bending over to him with his arms out.

This scene shows both active and receptive presence, with an emphasis on receptive. Only twice did the caregiver take the lead. Notice that the caregiver was calm and not overemotional, though he was able to empathize with Jason (to feel his hurt). Because he did not get drawn into the situation and could provide support to Jason in his pain, he facilitated Jason's problem-solving abilities. The scene might have been very different if the caregiver had given Jason advice or "taught him a lesson." The scene might also have been very different if the caregiver had offered sympathy. Imagine if he had picked up Jason and murmured phrases like "Oh, poor Jason, you got hurt, poor, poor little boy." But the caregiver gave neither advice nor sympathy. Instead, he gave his full, calm attention, both receptive and active, thereby giving Jason the support, strength, and acceptance he needed to pursue the problem he had encountered. This scene shows infant-toddler education at work.

The adult role of directing and responding to infant-toddler problem solving is made up of four skills. The adult must be able to ascertain the optimum level of stress for the child faced with a problem, provide appropriately for the child's need for attention, give feedback, and model desired behavior. These roles are summarized in Figure 2.2.

Figure 2.2 The Four Roles of the Adult in Infant-Toddler Education

1. **Determining optimum stress levels:** observing and deciding how much stress is too much, too little, and just right.

2. **Providing attention:** meeting children's needs for attention without manipulative motives.

3. **Providing feedback:** giving clear feedback so that infants and toddlers learn the consequences of their actions.

4. **Modeling:** setting a good example for infants and toddlers.

Determining Optimum Stress Levels   One way the adult facilitates learning is by being sensitive to the stress levels of babies and toddlers. This sensitivity is important in scaffolding learning. When a young child faced with a problem is going beyond a tolerable frustration level, a little nudge from the adult can reduce the frustration enough so that the child can continue to work to solve the problem.

When a sensitive adult scaffolds as part of infant-toddler education, he or she provides the smallest bit of help possible, not to get rid of frustration but to keep the child working on the problem. This type of help improves attention span and teaches children that they are capable problem solvers.

Most adults want to shield their charges from uncomfortable feelings. They don't realize that stress and frustration are an important part of infant-toddler education and come naturally with problem solving. In order to develop physically, emotionally, and intellectually, children occasionally need something to fight against, to pit their will and strength against. In this way they can discover that they are competent problem solvers. With no stress, no frustrations, and no problems, children have no way to try themselves against the world. Consequently, their education is severely limited. A young parent, thinking about stress as a part of infant education, wrote the following:

> *I was watering my garden the other day and I found out more about stress and development. I'd been watering every day for some time and found that some of my seedlings weren't growing deep roots. As I thought about it—if a plant doesn't have some stress factors so that it has to look for food and water, its roots won't grow as deep, and therefore it won't be as stable in the world. Its foundation will be too shallow.*[5]

Optimum stress is the right amount of stress—not too much and not too little. The right amount of stress means that it is enough to energize and motivate the child toward activity, including problem solving, but not so much that it hampers or inhibits the child's ability to act or solve a problem. Believe it or not, stress can promote learning and development, but it has to be the right amount. It's the caregiver's job to decide what is optimum stress for each child and then try to allow for it. Opportunities will arise naturally in daily life.

How can you decide what is enough stress? You can decide the optimum level of stress by watching the child's actions. Children under too much stress are not able to solve problems effectively; they may become greatly emotional, or they may withdraw.

You can also decide what is enough stress by being empathetic (imagining what a child is actually feeling) and by remaining calm and not being swayed by either the child's emotions or your own. Being calm gives a perspective that facilitates good decision making.

What should you do if children are either overstressed or understressed? Take a look at the problems each child faces. Perhaps there are too many of them, in which case some changes need to be made to cut down on the number. They may be too hard to solve, in which case the child may need more help.

If children are underst_stressed, they may not be encountering enough problems in their lives—perhaps not enough is happening, the environment is lacking in variety or interest, or someone else is solving the children's problems.

Providing Attention   The way an adult responds to a child's actions is an important part of infant-toddler education. The adult response has a lot of power because infants and toddlers essentially live on attention from others, especially the others who are important to them. For each individual there is an optimum amount of attention—optimum again, not maximum. If the person gets enough attention, satisfaction results. An individual who doesn't get enough will seek it in a variety of ways.

Some typical ways to get attention that people learn early in life are:

- By being attractive to look at
- By being kind and sweet
- By being smart, skilled, capable, competent, or talented
- By misbehaving
- By being loud
- By talking a lot
- By talking little
- By being outgoing
- By being shy
- By being sick
- By being helpless

Are you aware that girls are more likely to be noticed for their looks than for their capabilities? How long do you think it takes for children to fall into patterns where they tend to get attention by taking on confining sex roles?

If babies find that smiling, cooing, and being peaceful are not enough, or toddlers find that playing and keeping a low profile does not bring them attention, they will try other behaviors. Children seriously in need of attention will find out how to "push the buttons" of the important people around them. Adults must recognize when children are trying to get attention by upsetting them and when children are directly communicating their real needs. It is not always easy to tell the difference. Take a look at the following scene:

A caregiver is sitting in a comfortable chair feeding a 6-month-old a bottle. A 17-month-old, Mike, at her feet, keeps tugging at her arm and trying to reach the bottle. Another adult removes Mike and tries to engage him in play while explaining that his caregiver is busy right now. When she turns her back to settle a dispute in another part of the room, Mike walks over to another child and grabs the toy he is playing with. Both caregivers admonish Mike, who glows with the attention. As soon as they turn back to their various occupations, Mike goes to the doorway separating the playroom from the kitchen. He hangs on the gate across the opening and fusses.

"You just ate!" responds his caregiver from her chair. "It's hard to believe that you're still hungry, but I'll get you a snack when I finish feeding Sierra," she tells him,

Reflect

Think of a time in your own life when stress was good for you. Can you relate your experience to that of an infant or toddler in group care? How good are you at telling the difference between optimum stress and too much stress in your own life? Does this ability relate to how you can tell when a child is having too much or too little stress?

Reflect

Think about how you satisfy your own needs for attention. How aware are you of the ways you get people to pay attention to you? List some ways you get attention from other people. Are you satisfied with the ways you get attention? Would you want infants and toddlers to get attention in the same ways?

then settles her gaze back on the baby she is feeding. Mike walks over immediately and pulls all the toys off the shelf and stomps on them. Both caregivers admonish him. Again he glows with the attention. But when both withdraw it, he starts throwing toys over the gate across the open kitchen door. Again he has two adults' full attention. The free adult helps him retrieve the toys and put them back on the shelf while his caregiver in the chair watches and comments from time to time. When order is restored, she puts her attention back to the feeding while the other caregiver starts to change a diaper. The scene ends as Mike walks over and slaps a child who has been playing quietly in the corner all this time.

In this scene Mike continually gets attention for undesirable behavior. It's easy to see that he knows how to get attention when he needs it, even when both caregivers are busy. There is no easy answer to this problem. However, if both caregivers are aware that he needs attention, they can concentrate on giving it to him when he is not misbehaving. Perhaps he'll have less need for adult attention when it's difficult to give it to him. The adults can also put into words what it is that he needs by saying things like "I know you need my attention right now, Mike."

If you are generous with your attention during caregiving times, most children can go on about their business during playtimes when you can't respond to them in playful ways. They won't hunger for adult attention. But if a child has learned that misbehavior is satisfying in terms of the reward it brings, you must change your approach.

Start by ignoring undesirable behavior that is designed to attract your attention (without disregarding needs or safety, of course). At the same time, pay lots of attention to behavior that is desirable. Be specific when you talk about the behavior—don't just throw out nonspecific global judgments like "good boy." Instead, say things like "I really like the way you're playing with that toy, Mike. You put the toy back when you're finished. Good for you, Mike. You're letting me feed Sierra without interrupting. You're doing a good job of waiting. You're being gentle with Jacob."

When behavior needs to change, **positive reinforcement** can be quite effective. Positive reinforcement is defined as a response to a behavior that strengthens the likelihood of its being repeated—in other words, a reward. Rewards work, especially when you are changing learned behaviors—that is, those that have been inadvertently rewarded in the past, such as Mike's bids for attention.

But don't go overboard in using positive reinforcement. Attention and praise work and are powerful motivators. However, they can be addictive. Many activities are rewarding for their own sake. They lose that reward when adults add external rewards to the intrinsic ones. So, when a toddler is playing and an adult constantly interrupts to praise her, the message is that the activity itself is not that great, so the child needs motivation. Eventually the child gets the message and that comes to be the case. It's easy to spot a child who is used to a lot of praise while playing. She is the one who constantly looks to the adult after each little accomplishment while playing. She seems to constantly need someone to say

"Wonderful! You stacked that block on the other one." The accomplishment itself is empty without the adult praise.

When children are overpraised, they may lose touch with their own feelings and motives. They look around after every act to see if they did it right. They seek approval for everything they do. Activities and accomplishments are pleasing only for the external rewards they bring. In short, these children cease to get pleasure and satisfaction from the activities themselves.

In *Toward a Psychology of Being*, Abraham Maslow states that when a child is faced with a conflict between inner delight at his own accomplishment and the rewards offered by others, he "must generally choose approval from others, and then handle his delight by repression or letting it die, or not noticing it or controlling it by will power. In general, along with this will develop a disapproval of the delight experience, or shame and embarrassment and secretiveness about it, with finally, the inability even to experience it."[6]

Providing Feedback   Closely related to the subject of praise and attention is feedback. Part of infant-toddler education depends on the child getting clear feedback, or responses. Feedback comes both from the environment and from people. Children need to learn what effect their actions have on the world and on others. If they drop a glass of milk, it spills. That's feedback about the qualities of liquids. The child needs no further feedback about milk. Now what's needed is a response about how to remedy the situation. "The milk spilled. You need a cloth to sop it up" is a good response.

Some things children do result in caregivers expressing pain or anger. That expression is also feedback. For example, a child who scratches a caregiver can be told, "It hurts when you scratch me. I don't like it." The message should be clear if the feedback is to be useful to the child. If the caregiver responds to a scratch in a honeyed voice, smiling all the while but holding the child tightly as if angry, the child gets a mixed message rather than clear feedback.

Adults also can help provide feedback about the environment and verbalize the reaction they see in the child. In this way children learn to give themselves clear feedback. Here is an example of that principle:

Jamal is playing with several other toddlers when his caregiver comes in the door. As Jamal rushes over, he slams his elbow into a table. He approaches his caregiver crying.

His caregiver says, "Oh, Jamal, I saw that. You bumped your elbow on the table." Jamal confirms his caregiver's statement by holding his elbow up.

"Me!" he exclaims.

"Yes," replies his caregiver. "Right here is where you bumped it." He touches the spot gently.

Jamal goes back to the table that he bumped. "Table!" he explains.

"Yes," confirms his caregiver. "Right there—you bumped your elbow right there on the table." He knocks on the table. "It's hard."

Jamal touches the table. "It hurt when you hit your elbow on it," continues his caregiver.

"Hard," repeats Jamal. He cries less now. He concentrates on his elbow, then the table, then his elbow again.

Reflect

Think of a time in your own life when feedback was useful to you in a problem-solving situation. Can you apply your own experience to that of an infant or a toddler?

Jamal's caregiver helped him focus on what just happened, and Jamal learned something about cause and effect. Jamal was shown what hurt him and gained some understanding of the relationship of the pain to the source. His caregiver helped Jamal understand the full experience rather than letting him get lost in the pain, yet he didn't deny Jamal's pain or distract him from it.

Sometimes helping a child get feedback is just a matter of standing back and seeing if the child realizes what just happened and can figure out how to deal with it. Other times it helps to put words to the situation. The properties of objects are something infants and toddlers study intensely in their first three years. They want to know all about most every object they encounter. They learn through experience as they manipulate everything they can get their hands on. That's why it's important that they be in an environment set up for them with a variety of objects for them to explore. They gain feedback through their explorations.

Talk to children about what they may be experiencing. "It's heavy, isn't it?" "You like the smooth feeling of that ball." In the first vignette in this chapter, the adult put words to the connection the child seemed to be making between the doll and the picture. Language gives them labels for their perceptions; helps them analyze, sort, and compare; and provides a means to store their perceptions of an object away for future reference. Putting language into children's experiences from the very beginning of life pays off later when they reach school age. Hart and Risley's classic research shows how a larger vocabulary predicts greater school success. Be careful not to interrupt a child's concentration, though. Use language sensitively so that it adds to the experience rather than disturbs it. Use language to help out in problem solving if the child isn't reading the physical feedback. Saying, "That puzzle piece won't go in if you put it that way" will be more meaningful if the child is sitting there banging the piece in frustration rather than twisting and turning it to find a way to make it fit. Wait, though, until there are signs that the child is about to give up trying. That's the time to do some scaffolding. Give a little hint about what to do. For example, say, "Try turning it over." Adult feedback isn't useful just for helping children understand how objects work. It's also good for helping children understand the behavior of other children. "He didn't like it when you grabbed the book from him." Or "He ran away because you shouted at him." As you read through the many examples in this book, notice the number of times that adults give children feedback about their effects on others.

NAEYC Program Standard 3
Teaching

Modeling   Practice, don't preach! **Model** the behavior you want from the child.[7] To model means to set an example by performing behaviors, actions, and interactive styles that the children observe and imitate. What you do speaks louder than what you say. For instance, if you want to teach the child to share, you need to *be* a sharing person yourself. You need to share your own possessions with others if that's what you expect a child to do. You can teach children to perform the actions of sharing by using rewards and punishments, or you can *make* them share by using your size and power. But neither of these approaches will make children become sharing people. They will become sharing people (with lots of modeling) only after they gain the concept of possession. Toddlers need to learn this concept (hence all the "Me!" and "Mine!" statements you hear when you work with children in this age group).

Children model after other qualities of their caregivers as well—qualities such as gentleness. Children who are treated gently are more likely to treat other children gently. Respect is another example. Children who are treated with respect are more likely to be respectful to others than children who are not.

Another example of modeling behavior is expression of anger. If you work all day, every day in an infant-toddler center, your own anger is bound to be an emotion you'll deal with at least occasionally. The children pick up on how you cope. If you smile and sing and deny that you're feeling furious, they learn to hide their feelings too. (And they learn to give the same mixed messages you are giving.) But if you use the energy to confront the source and problem solve, they learn that way of dealing with conflicts. Or, if confrontation is not appropriate, they can learn your coping mechanisms, such as working out the feelings through talking about them, through redirection into physical exercise or expression, or through soothing activities. (For some adults, washing dishes is as soothing as water play is to children.)

In short, modeling behavior is more effective than teaching it. Just think of the habits, mannerisms, attitudes, gestures, and expressions you use that came straight from your parent(s). We pick up behaviors and mannerisms without even being aware of doing so and without being taught. As a caregiver, you must be conscious of the behavior you model so that what you do and what you say are in accordance with each other.

Obviously, no one can be a model all the time. Everyone acts in ways they would rather not have children imitate. If you expect to be a perfect model, you set yourself up for disappointment. However, as you respond to your own weaknesses, your own imperfections, and your humanness, you are modeling. For example, when you make a mistake, you can show the children that mistakes can be forgiven by forgiving yourself. When you're feeling needy, you can tune in to your needs, modeling for the children that responding to needs is important. When you bring modeling to the conscious level of awareness, you can make decisions about it. Modeling is a powerful tool and can work either for you or against you. Because caregiving is already a difficult task, you may as well have all your tools working for you.

Modeling works with children—and it also works with adults. As parents watch you working with their children, they may see approaches they never thought about before. There's a saying that applies here: actions speak louder than words. And it's not just *your* actions—the same goes for the parents and

Appropriate Practice

Overview of Development

According to the National Association for the Education of Young Children (NAEYC), quality care combines care and education. Some of the components of quality care include recognizing that ages birth to three cover a large span of developmental differences and must be broken down into three stages: young infants (ages birth to 9 months), mobile infants (ages 8 to 18 months), and toddlers (ages 16 to 36 months). Each age group needs particular environmental adaptations and sets of responses from caregivers. For a program to be educational, the caregiver must create a safe, interesting, developmentally appropriate, and orderly world. To do this requires individualized care in small groups with primary caregivers. Continuity of care is important, too, so that infants and toddlers are with the same caregiver for (ideally) three years. Care is educational when it's developmentally and culturally appropriate and when caregivers exhibit responsive interactions.

Developmentally Appropriate Practice

The following are samples of developmentally appropriate practices that relate to infant-toddler education:

- There is sufficient continuity of care to ensure that every infant (and family) is able to form a relationship with a primary caregiver. As the caregiver comes to know a few infants very well, she is able to respond to the temperament, needs, and cues of each baby and to develop a mutually satisfying pattern of communication with each child and family.
- Adults engage in many one-to-one, face-to-face interactions with infants. Adults talk in a pleasant, calm voice, using simple language and frequent eye contact, while being responsive to the child's cues.

- Warm, responsive interactions with infants occur throughout the day. Observing the infant's cues, the adult is able to judge when the baby would like to be held, carried to a new place, or shifted to a new position. Adults often talk to babies, especially older infants, about what is going on.
- Children are acknowledged for their accomplishments and helped to feel increasingly competent and in control of themselves.

Source: Carol Copple, and Sue Bredekamp, eds., *Developmentally Appropriate Practice in Early Childhood Programs*, 3rd ed. (Washington, DC: National Association for the Education of Young Children, 2009).

Individually Appropriate Practice

Caregiving routines must be individualized so that they meet each child's specific needs. One infant may need special positioning on the diapering table to keep from becoming stiff, while another may need to be held on a pillow because skin-to-skin contact bothers her. Still another may need extra support to sit up so that he can feed himself finger food.

Culturally Appropriate Practice

One difference in view between caregivers and parents may be about children feeding themselves. In families where the tradition is to spoon-feed children for the first few years, the idea that they are left to feed themselves in the first two years may be upsetting. As one mother said, "I love to feed my baby. I don't want to stop just because he can feed himself. Feeding is a way I show him I love him." Remember that appropriate practice means that caregivers and parents confer in making decisions about how best to support children's development or to handle problems or differences of opinion as they arise.

Appropriate Practice in Action

Look back on the Principles in Action scene on page 31 and reconsider your answers. After reading this chapter would you answer any of the questions differently? Now analyze that scene in terms of the information in the last bullet in the "Developmentally Appropriate Practice" section of this Appropriate Practice box.

- Did the caregiver acknowledge Jasmine's accomplishment? Do you think the caregiver helped Jasmine feel increasingly competent and in control of herself?

Now look at the "Culturally Appropriate Practice" section of the Appropriate Practice box.

- How might this scene have been different if Jasmine's culture saw the adult role as solving the problem for her instead of letting her solve the problem?
- What could you do if the caregiver's approach and the family's approach were different?

other family members. Step back and watch how they interact with their children. Learn how they diaper, feed, and hold their babies. We can all learn from each other.

If you think of yourself in partnership with the families, you'll be right in tune with a growing movement called "family-centered care and education." There are several reasons for this movement, one of which is a reaction to what traditionally has been called child-centered programs. A number of early childhood leaders perceive that the path to high-quality programs leads in the direction of focusing on families instead of just on their children.[8] See Figure 2.3 for why it's important for early care and education professionals to partner with parents. Also check out www.parentservices.org, an ongoing project to bring programs and parents together to benefit families and the educational entities that serve them.

Figure 2.3 The Benefits of Partnering with Parents

1. Children always come embedded in the context of a family and a community.[9]
2. When a program focuses on families, children's learning and development are optimized.
3. Professionals and families have different funds of knowledge and skills—when they share what they know in two-way exchanges, everybody benefits.
4. The goal of child rearing is to produce adults that fit in with their family and culture[10]—though bicultural goals may be important to the family too.
5. Though professionals may have sets of outcomes to strive for, so does the family, and these outcomes may differ.
6. Preserving diversity is a survival issue for all of us.[11]

Infant-Toddler Education and School Readiness

We can't talk about education in the first three years without mentioning the connection between getting children off to a good start and what happens when they get into school later on. It's important to note that although infant-toddler education as explained in this chapter and throughout the book may not look like a "school-readiness" approach, it can indeed give children the foundation they need for success in school.

Early care and education is a societal economic investment.[12] Some policy makers examine the brain research and regard early childhood education as an investment that can make an important difference in later outcomes, especially for children in low-income families. When families don't have what they need to give their children a healthy, secure, caring beginning, their children are at risk for falling behind when they get to school. Indeed, many of them enter kindergarten already behind. That's where society can help. Although early childhood programs can certainly benefit all children, those from middle-class families tend to do well in school even if they never use outside services.[13]

Two programs demand special attention for addressing the particular issues facing low-income families with infants and toddlers. One such program was started by Geoffrey Canada in New York and is called the Harlem Children's Zone or HCZ for short.[14] The goal of the HCZ is to prepare every child from birth on to go to college and graduate. The program is a comprehensive one involving the whole community—not just focusing on children. Parents enroll in parenting classes when pregnant and they continue to attend when their babies are born. Parents learn parenting skills, how to access community resources, and enjoy many incentives to continue to learn and support their children's development and learning.

Canada discovered that he couldn't just focus on parents, but also had to focus on the programs that served them, including child care programs, which he worked on improving. As the children graduate from infant-toddler programs they go on to preschool programs that are carefully monitored for quality. It took Canada and his workers years to make sure that every educational experience involving the children was a quality one—right up through school. The first class of parents graduated in 2000 from what Canada calls Baby College. Their children have been followed and the success rate is notable! In May 2009 test results showed that 100 percent of third graders scored on or above grade level in math and 94 percent in reading.[15] HZC and Baby College work![16]

It is interesting to note that, though Canada's primary goal is to raise test scores once the children are in school, what parents learn about infants and toddlers in Baby College is good solid child development information related to caregiving and other parenting practices. The curriculum for the parents is, in fact, quite compatible with the information in this chapter and the rest of this book.

Another program for infants, toddlers, and their families worthy of mention has been going since the 1990s. That program is a federally funded nationwide program targeting low-income families and is called Early Head Start. This infant-toddler version of the larger Head Start program (started back in the mid-sixties) expanded greatly under the Obama administration. Like Harlem Children's Zone, Early Head Start has comprehensive services and focuses on families as much as on infants and toddlers. The programs vary in structure and delivery systems, but again, what is emphasized is based on sound child development research about how infants and toddlers learn. What parents learn in Early Head Start is also quite compatible with what is in this book.[17] Infant-toddler education doesn't look like school, but it does get babies off to a good start, which boosts their chances of later success.

Summary

Infant-toddler education means that respectful, consistent, caring adults meet children's needs by adapting to their individual abilities and interests while supporting their exploration, discovery, relationship building, and problem solving.

What Infant-Toddler Education Is **Not**

- Infant stimulation, or doing things to babies with the aim of stimulating their senses, is not a focus of this book's approach to educating infants and toddlers.
- Babysitting, or just watching out for very young children to keep them safe, ignores the need for trained infant care teachers who understand how care and education go together.
- A preschool model, especially one in which the educational focus of the day occurs only during circle time and when specific activities are available for the children.

Components of Infant-Toddler Education

- Curriculum is the foundation of infant-toddler education. Curriculum can be thought of as a plan for learning.
- The ways in which trained adults focus on and appreciate the problems that infants encounter in daily living in a rich and responsive environment.
- Assessing the curriculum is an important component of infant-toddler education and is an ongoing process using adult observation, plus recording and analyzing what is observed.

- Problem solving as a component of infant-toddler education involves trained adults planning for, supporting, and occasionally facilitating problem solving when the infant shows he or she really needs the facilitation.
- The means by which trained adults plan for, support, and occasionally facilitate problem solving, but only when infants show they need help.
- The roles that trained adults take to support problem solving in infants by determining optimum stress levels, providing appropriate attention, providing appropriate feedback, and modeling behaviors they wish to see in the children.

Infant-Toddler Education and School Readiness

- School readiness depends on parents or parent substitutes giving babies a healthy, secure, caring start in life.
- When families can't give babies a good beginning, those children are at risk for falling behind when they get to school.
- Two programs address the particular issues facing low-income families with infants and toddlers. One is Geoffrey Canada's Harlem Children's Zone. The other is Early Head Start. Both programs offer comprehensive services, including parent education and support.

Key Terms

anecdotal records 28	model 38	positive reinforcement 36
caregiver presence 32	optimum stress 34	running records 29
documentation 29	philosophy of education 24	zone of proximal development 29

Thought/Activity Questions

1. What makes an infant-stimulation program different from one that focuses on infant education?
2. What are four roles adults can play in infant-toddler education?
3. How would you define the term *curriculum* as it relates to an infant-toddler center-based program? Would the definition be different in a family child care home?
4. Think of an answer to give a parent when he or she asks, "Do children learn anything in your program, or do they just play?" How can you explain that your program is educational, not "just babysitting"?

For Further Reading

Mary Benson McMullen and Peggy Apple, "Babies (and Their Families) on Board! Directors Juggle the Key Elements of Infant/Toddler Care and Education," *Young Children* 67(4), September 2012, pp. 42–48.

Deb Curtis, Kasondra L. Brown, Lorrie Baird, and Anne Marie Coughlin, "Planning Environments and Materials that Respond to Young Children's Lively Minds," *Young Children* 68(4), September, 2013, pp. 26–31.

Linda Gillespie and Sandra Petersen, "Rituals and Routines: Supporting Infants and Toddlers and Their Families," *Young Children* 67(4), September 2012, pp. 76–77.

Paul Tough, *How Children Succeed: Grit, Curiosity, and the Hidden Power of Character* (Boston: Houghton Mifflin Harcourt, 2012).

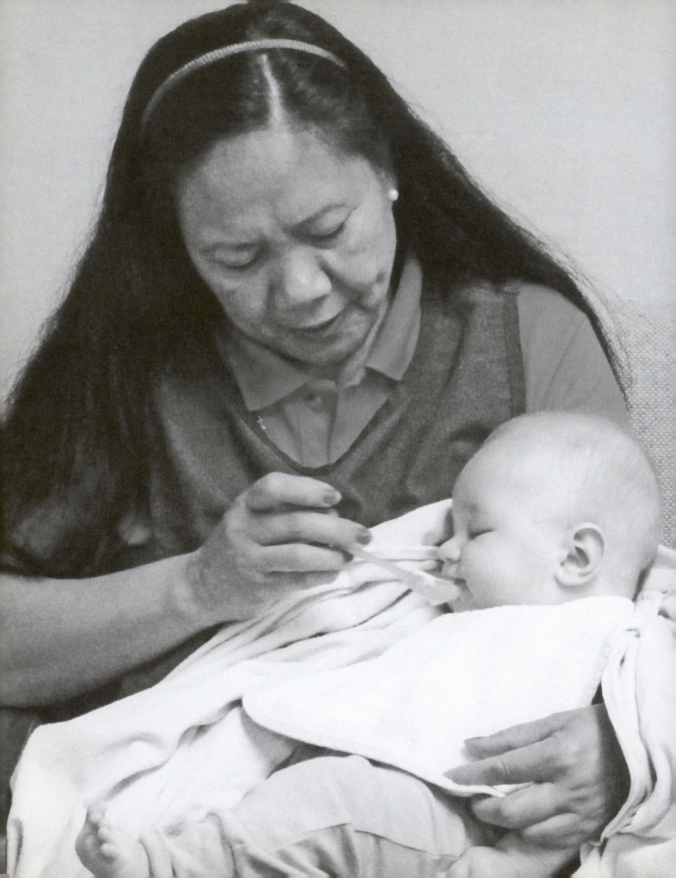

chapter 3

Caregiving as Curriculum

Focus Questions

After reading this chapter you should be able to answer the following questions:

1 How does caregiving build the relationships on which curriculum depends?

2 Curriculum involves planning for learning, and learning is connected to attachment, so what are some ways that programs can plan for attachment?

3 How can caregivers assess the long-term and immediate needs and development of infants and toddlers?

4 What are caregiving routines? Name six of them.

What Do You See?

Four toddlers ranging in age from 14 to 16 months are seated at a low table intently watching a caregiver who has several plastic cups in his hand. He turns to the child on his right and holds out two cups. "Do you want the green one or the blue one, Aiesha?" he asks, holding out first one and then the other. Aiesha reaches for the blue one. The caregiver puts the other cup on a table behind him and brings a pitcher around in front of him.

"Now everyone has a cup," he says, looking at the expectant children. "Here's the juice—it's apple," he says, pouring a small amount of juice in a tiny pitcher. He hands it to Xian, who grabs the pitcher and pours with great excitement, missing his cup. The caregiver hands him a cloth. "Here's a cloth for the spill," he says calmly. Xian quickly swipes at the spill, then looks carefully at the juice left in the pitcher. With precise movement, he pours the small amount into his cup. He abandons the pitcher and concentrates then on the cup, with a satisfied look on his face.

"Your turn, Nicole," says the caregiver, refilling the pitcher and passing it to her. She takes the pitcher, pours some juice, then shoves the pitcher toward the next child, who receives it gratefully. The child next to her bangs his cup, yelling, "Me!"

"You want your juice, Yei Hoon," says the caregiver.

"No!" says Yei Hoon, emphatically, pointing to a banana.

"Oh, you want a piece of banana," says the caregiver.

Keep this scene in mind as you read this chapter and begin to think about caregiving as curriculum. Later we will revisit this scene.

Thinking Again About Infant-Toddler Curriculum

NAEYC Program Standard 2

Curriculum

As stated earlier, curriculum at higher levels of education can focus on the mind alone, but that doesn't work for infants and toddlers. There is no way to separate intellectual needs from other needs at this beginning level. Meeting basic needs through caregiving activities provides multiple opportunities for infants to learn to solve all kinds of problems. Learning to solve problems is an important part of any curriculum for infants and very young children. Infants become good problem solvers when they have a trusting relationship. This chapter focuses on how that kind of relationship starts and grows from the interactions between adults and infants or toddlers that occur during caregiving routines such as diapering and feeding.

Like other curriculum approaches, we are presenting an activity-based approach; however, the activities we see as most important are *not* the ones adults set up specifically for children's learning but instead are those that occur throughout the day, *every day*—the essential activities of daily living, or caregiving routines. So unlike most other books, when the word *activity* occurs here, it usually refers to caregiving routines. We also want to make it clear that the word *curriculum* doesn't apply to just any old approach to diapering, dressing, grooming, washing, or feeding, but rather to a consciously considered approach. That's what this chapter is about—how to take the approaches that turn everyday routines into curriculum. We are basing this approach to curriculum on Emmi Pikler's work in Hungary and what Magda Gerber's Resources for Infant Educarers (RIE) Associates teach.[1]

Let's look at the aspects of caregiving activities that promote learning and development. The quality of the interactions matters. Learning and development as well as deepening relationships occur when the interactions are respectful, responsive, and reciprocal. To make the interactions effective, caregivers need observation and assessment skills. Using these skills helps the caregiver to know each child so that the interactions are individually effective and promote a close, warm, sensitive relationship between the child and the adult.

Planning for Attachment

NAEYC Program Standard 1

Relationships

One important component of the curriculum as it occurs during caregiving activities is **attachment**—a tie to a special person. Through sensitive caregiving interactions, attachment grows, especially when there is consistency and, over time, children come to know the person who provides the care. Development, learning, and attachment are vitally related. From attachment come feelings of trust and security. Lifelong learning and attitudes can be initiated on the diapering counter while babies are being washed, dressed, and groomed, and during feeding times. These essential activities of daily living provide multiple sensory experiences, much pleasure and satisfaction, and an opportunity to learn social and physical skills—all of which form the foundation of the intellect. Interactions with consistent caregivers build structures in the brain that have long-lasting cognitive effects, supporting our position that caregiving is curriculum.

Young children need attachment to someone who, in turn, gives them a feeling that they are important—that they matter. Although most infants and toddlers in child care are attached to their parent(s) or other family member(s), if they are to spend long hours away from them, attachment to caregivers is additionally beneficial. Both caregivers and children benefit from attachment because communication is enhanced and needs are understood. The caregiver is rewarded by the child's feeling for him or her, and the child gains a feeling of importance. Through attachment, the child knows that he or she is being cared *about* as well as *for*.

Policies That Support Curriculum as Caregiving

Three policies need to be in place to make a caregiving curriculum:[2]

- A primary-caregiver system
- Consistency
- Continuity of care

Let's examine each of these policies more closely. Attachment is promoted by assigning each caregiver to a small number of infants or young toddlers in what is called a **primary-caregiver system**. The idea behind this system is that if caregivers see three or four children as their own special charges, they can promote a stronger attachment than might happen if attachment were left to chance or if all the caregivers related to the whole group without differentiation. It's also important to create a system of teams so that there is always a familiar adult present if the primary caregiver is absent. In a smoothly working primary-caregiver system, caregivers interact with children other than their special charges.

Consistency is important to aim for. When change is carefully thought out and minimized, infants and toddlers learn that they can predict what will happen. Their feelings of powerlessness are minimized, and a sense of security grows. Magda Gerber was clear that things should be done in the same way that the child is used to so the child isn't always thrown off balance by trying to adjust to something new all the time. In the United States, where novelty is highly valued, adults may have problems going along with the idea of consistency.

The Pikler Institute has firm policies about predictability.[3] Babies are picked up in the same way by every caregiver. Their routines are carried out the same way every day. Young babies are fed in the same order so they come to know when it is their turn. Observers at the Pikler Institute are impressed at the degree of predictability they see. Having the same person there to relate to in ways that are predictable is a part of consistency. Predictabilty plus the caregiver teaching the child, from newborns on, to be cooperative has amazing results. Observers at the institute were impressed by the spirit of cooperation shown even by toddlers, who are often known to be uncooperative! Learning cooperation is part of an infant-toddler curriculum.

Continuity of care—that is, staying with one caregiver for several years—is lacking in programs where children are "moved up" whenever they reach another developmental level, leaving behind their old room and teacher and sometimes even their companions, depending on the policy. Some programs that enroll babies in the first three months move them a number of times before their first birthday. Other programs follow a school model, moving the children every year to a new classroom and teacher. A program that values continuity of care finds ways to keep the group together with the same adults and either adapt the environment or move into a new room when they outgrow the old one. With older children, this system is called looping.

Assessment

NAEYC Program Standard 4
Assessment

Any curriculum depends on caregivers determining what children need, both as individuals and as a group. Assessment is a means of determining what a child needs at any given time, which is the first step in performing caregiving tasks. Infants and toddlers can't always let you know what they need, so you have to learn to read signs. Attachment helps here, because you get to know children well enough to understand their unique ways of communicating, as stated in principle 3.

When you do pick up signs that a child or the group has a need, put what you perceive into words. If you aren't sure what the signs mean, ask out loud—in words—even to very young infants. Look, listen, and feel for the answer. If you are beginning to learn the child's system of communication, you may get your answer directly from the child. By taking this approach, you're beginning to set up a two-way communication pattern that will serve the child well for the rest of his or her life. Children (even the youngest) who are encouraged to express their needs and interests can become quite skilled at doing just that. But also be aware that expressing needs directly is not appropriate in all cultures, so be sensitive to what the parents want for their child.[4]

Determining the Child's Real Needs Adults sometimes develop a singular approach to responding to signs that a child needs something. "Oh, he's tired; he needs a nap," may be one caregiver's standard response. Another caregiver may wish to feed all cranky children. Or a caregiver may tune in to his or her own needs. The caregiver who thinks the heat is down too low may say, "He's cold," in spite of the fact that the child is plenty warm to the touch. Children who are given food when they aren't hungry or are bundled up when they aren't cold may lose the ability to determine what they need, or they may learn to substitute one need for another. Certainly, comforting with a bottle often works even if the child doesn't need food. That's how the bottle can become a substitute for cuddling or attention. How many adults reach automatically for food when they

Reflect

How do you determine your own needs and get them met? Can you remember a time when you needed something that you could not get by yourself? How did you communicate this need? Were you direct about it? Was your message received? Did you get the results you wanted?

have some other kind of need? This behavior can be learned in the early years. With childhood obesity a growing problem, it's worth paying attention to infants and toddlers who look at food as a comfort device. The question is, What are they really needing that they aren't getting? When we know the answer, we can focus on meeting the real need instead of substituting food. One need that is often unmet is the need for fresh air and outdoor exercise. At the Pikler Institute, where the children are remarkably healthy, they not only play outdoors every day year-round, but they eat and sleep there too. Even newborns sleep in an open-air screened porch. While the older children are outdoors, the rooms are aired so when the children come in, they aren't greeted by hot, stale air. Breathing fresh air is a simple good-health measure and meets a need all of us have.

When Needs Conflict   In infant-toddler care it sometimes happens that an adult's or the group's needs or interests conflict with an individual child's needs or interests. A child must be awakened from a nap because it is time to go home, or a child must be fed early for some reason or must wait to be fed. At the Pikler Institute the infants are fed in a particular sequence that the children come to know well. Although they may protest when they have to wait, the children know they will be fed. They learn to trust that their turn will come, and they learn to predict. If things change all the time, children are confused. When consistency is present, they know what will happen and they feel more empowered than when they can neither predict nor control.

A word about crying: crying is communication. When adults regard it in that way, they feel different about it than when they perceive it as an annoyance that they just want to go away. The hungry baby who is crying needs to be acknowledged, even if you can't meet her needs right away. She is communicating.

Children can cope with their individual needs being put on hold. They are **resilient**—that is, they can adapt to hardship or recover from it. However, it can do permanent harm if very young children continually have to wait and have no way to predict when their turn will come. When program or adult needs and interests always take precedence over infant and toddler needs and interests, or when meeting needs is done on a haphazard basis, children may experience negative long-term effects.

Caregiving Routines

The principles on which this book is based are an integrating theme in this section. For caregiving routines to become curriculum, they can't be done mechanically. Each time a caregiver interacts in ways that focus fully on the individual child while performing one of those essential activities of daily living, the time spent furthers connections. When caregivers manipulate the child's body and put their attention elsewhere, they lose the opportunity to let the child experience an intimate human interaction. It's the accumulation of intimacy during these numerous interactions that turns ordinary tasks into a relationship-based curriculum.

Feeding is a time when attachments are formed.

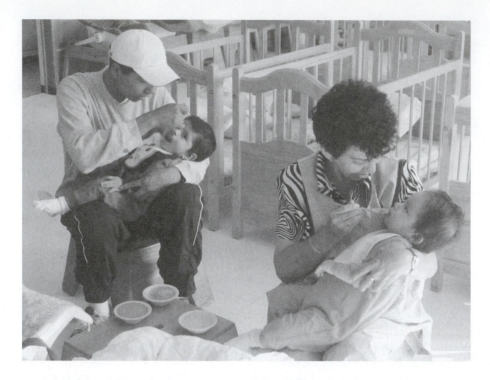

Feeding

Programs for infants and toddlers, in both centers and family child care, should make every provision possible for nursing mothers. Both mothers and infants benefit, even though it may be less convenient for caregivers. Help the mother feel welcome and provide a place for her and her infant to be quiet and comfortable. Breastfeeding has advantages over bottle feeding that shouldn't be ignored. It boosts the baby's immune system and lowers the risk of allergies. Breast milk is made by humans for humans and naturally contains just the right balance of fat and protein. The supply responds to the demand, and the content of the milk changes as the baby's needs change.[5] An added bonus is that cultural food preferences show up in breast milk, giving babies a taste of their own culture away from home. Anything a caregiver or family child care provider can do to encourage mothers to breast-feed, and to make breastfeeding easier for them, should be done.

Promoting Breastfeeding   The trend now is to encourage breastfeeding. It's one approach to heading off childhood obesity, an issue of nationwide concern. The American Academy of Pediatrics (AAP) is promoting breastfeeding and in a newsletter called *Breastfeeding: Best for Baby and Mother* reports several projects in progress. One is a breastfeeding program developed for providers of pediatric and obstetric care serving families of racially and ethnically diverse backgrounds.[6] Pediatricians and obstetricians are in a position to provide information and support to pregnant women and new mothers in ways that can encourage them to breast-feed instead of using formula. In providing educational materials and other resources, and also sensitizing health care professionals to cultural differences in breastfeeding, the program has the potential to make a significant difference in increasing breastfeeding rates among culturally diverse populations.

Another breastfeeding project reported in the AAP newsletter is a program instituted by the U.S. military to support breastfeeding mothers who may be separated from their nursing infants for days or weeks at a time during field-training exercises.[7] The project works with military mothers to make it possible for them to pump, store, and transport breast milk back to headquarters while out in the field. The purpose of the project (besides infant nutrition) is to retain trained soldiers. If the military can figure out how to get breast pumps out to the field, give soldiers a time and place of privacy to pump and store the breast milk sanitarily, plus deliver it in a timely manner to infant caregivers, it's time for the rest of the industrial and business world to do the same. It's also time for child care providers to team up with nursing mothers to provide the very best nutrition for their babies.

Release Time for Feeding   Bottle-fed infants deserve the same kind of one-to-one attention and physical closeness that breast-fed infants receive. A well-organized center will find ways to release a caregiver to sit and feed an infant while holding him or her, without requiring that the caregiver jump up and down to take care of the needs of other children. In family child care this **release time**, when a caregiver can pay attention to just one child while someone else watches the rest, is harder to come by, but caregivers who make it a priority to hold each baby while feeding can find ways to work it out.

Imagine yourself as an infant with a bib covering your chest.

Hear a familiar voice say to you, "Here's some applesauce for you." Look around and see a spoon, a hand, and beyond it a small dish of applesauce. Take time to really perceive all this. Feel the coziness as well as the anticipation. Hear the same voice say, "Are you ready?" See the spoon come up to your face. There is plenty of time for you to open your mouth for the bite. You feel the applesauce in your mouth. You taste it. You notice the texture and the temperature. You thoroughly explore this bite before you swallow. Some goes down your throat; some runs down your chin. You look up to find the familiar face. Seeing the face adds to your pleasure. You open your mouth again. You feel a gentle scraping on your chin and the next bite comes into your mouth. You explore it. When you swallow, you get an excited feeling in anticipation of the next bite. You look at the face again. You reach out, and your fingers touch something soft and smooth. All these feelings are present as you open your mouth for the next bite. Anne Morrow Lindbergh[8] described a good relationship by comparing it to a dance where partners are fully alive in the present and are able to create a pattern by moving to the same rhythm. Could you see the previous feeding scene as something like a dance? The key to effective caregiving is a good relationship.

Compare that first feeding to this one:

You feel yourself plopped into a high chair without a word. A strap is put around your middle, and you are left alone with an empty tray. You pound on the tray. It's cold and hard, as is the back of the chair. You feel impatient. It seems like forever that you are sitting there. You squirm and twist. Suddenly there is a spoon in between your lips forcing them open. You look toward the source of the spoon, at the same time tasting applesauce. You wiggle your tongue around, swallowing down the bite. The spoon again comes between your lips, and your teeth are forced open. You take another mouthful while looking into an expressionless face of a person who seems to have her mind somewhere else. You enjoy the taste and feeling of the applesauce as you push it around in your mouth and out between your teeth and down your chin. You feel metal scraping your chin harshly. More applesauce comes into your mouth. You take a second mouthful into the first, which you haven't swallowed yet. You work on swallowing while you feel scrape, scrape on your chin as the spoon gathers up what is running down. You swallow a little of the big load, and you get ready to swallow more. Before you can, the spoon finds its way in between your teeth again. You sense a bit of urgency to get this down before the next load. More applesauce squishes out and runs down your chin. You feel the spoon—scrape, scrape, scrape—Hold on to that feeling now and stop imagining.

Feeding time should be quality time. One reason is that during feeding, attachments are formed between caregivers and the children they feed. For this reason, the same caregiver should feed the same babies daily, if possible.

NAEYC Program Standard 1
Relationships

When infants begin to feed themselves, the mess level rises dramatically. Most caregivers are willing to put up with the mess because they value independence. They want children in their care to learn **self-help skills**. Accepted practice in the United States is to let or even encourage children to take over their own feeding as soon as they are able. Usually when a baby grabs the spoon, he or she is given one and allowed to try getting it to the mouth.

Figure 3.1 gives some ideas on how to help children become self-feeders.

Eating is an emotional process. The adults bring to a feeding situation feelings, ideas, and traditions that have nothing to do with the immediate experience but rather come from their own personal history and culture. People have strong feelings about what should or should not go on at the table. The way they eat seems to

Figure 3.1 Hints on Promoting Self-Help Skills at Meals

1. Use child-size utensils.

2. Provide finger food such as banana chunks (unless a family strongly disapproves).

3. Give only small amounts of food. It's better to let children ask for more than to discourage them with too large a portion. Also, it's easier to clean up a small amount.

4. Allow children to explore and experiment with the food (unless a family strongly disapproves), but be aware of your own limits. End the meal before you become uncomfortable. A tension-free setting promotes good digestion.

VIDEO OBSERVATION 3

Children Feeding Themselves

See the Video Observation for Chapter 3 to view a mealtime and the interaction between an adult and a child.

Questions

- What about this scene makes eating "curriculum"?
- What is this child gaining from this experience besides food?
- What can you tell about the philosophy of this program from watching this scene?

To view this clip, go to **www.mhhe.com/itc10e**. Click on Student Edition, select Chapter 3, and click on Video Observations.

define who they are. The point is that eating is connected with strong feelings, and these feelings affect the way an adult approaches or reacts to children eating.

It is also important to recognize that not all cultures view early independence, self-feeding, and big messes in the same way. Although you may not wish to do it yourself, you should respect the fact that a parent may continue spoon-feeding a child long past the age you approve of.[9]

Understanding each child's signals, giving some choices, defining limits clearly, reacting honestly, and interacting responsively are all keys to pleasant feeding experiences. Ending a meal for children when their hunger has been satisfied is important. Children cannot be expected to refrain from playing with their food if they are full and it is still in front of them.

Review the scene at the beginning of this chapter and reflect on how it illustrates the principles on which this book is based and the themes of this chapter. The caregiver was respectful, responsive, and reciprocal. The effect was a pleasant atmosphere at the table. The caregiver worked to understand each child's signals and responded by giving words to their wishes. He gave them some choices without setting out a whole smorgasbord. He set some limits.

NAEYC Program Standard 3
Teaching

Perhaps you have not seen toddlers eating at a low table instead of in high chairs. Seating them together provides a more social experience than seating them high up, side by side, in rows. They have more choice about leaving when finished. They don't have to wait for an adult to take them down. If independence is a value, this simple technique goes a long way toward promoting it.

Although the scene at the beginning was not from the Pikler Institute in Budapest, there are some similarities, because there toddlers eat together at low tables. What this scene did not show is what happens when a child isn't able to eat at the table within the limits at the Pikler Institute. There, they say the child simply isn't ready, so they take the child back to an earlier stage and spoon-feed him ahead of the others. It's not a punishment, but merely recognition that the child needs more adult help. At the Pikler Institute they never push or urge a child forward. Readiness is not a worry, but a fact. The caregiver is there to meet the child's need for dependence during caregiving routines for as long as it lasts. You might think that with this policy, children would remain helpless for a long time; however, children have strong urges for independence. That fact shows at the Pikler Institute as children learn to feed and dress themselves surprisingly well at a younger age than many children in the United States, where early independence is often emphasized.

**NAEYC Program
Standard 5**
Health

Of course, there is more to feeding infants and toddlers than just making sure the food gets into their mouths. Care and attention need to go into ensuring that sanitation is part of the picture. Food preparation, feeding, food storage, and cleanup should all be in accordance with local and national health standards. The procedures should be posted and monitored. Feeding and diapering should be kept entirely separate, and different sinks should be used for each. Some dangerous mistakes to avoid include:

- Heating bottles or jars of baby food in microwave ovens, because they can have hot spots that burn the baby's mouth.
- Keeping partially used bottles of breast milk or formula and serving them later, because they can be contaminated and unhealthy.
- Feeding commercial baby food out of the jar and putting the jar back in the refrigerator, because, again, contamination can be a problem.

What about starting solid foods? Parents should be the guide about when to start solid foods and what foods to start with. Although for many years and in many cultures, some parents started solid food before four months, the standard recommendation now is to start solids no sooner than four to six months. Traditional starter foods are rice or barley cereals that are made especially for babies and mixed with formula or breast milk. Foods should be introduced one at a time, with only a taste to begin with; the amount should be increased gradually. Foods to avoid in the first six months because they may produce allergic reactions are wheat cereals, white flour (including bread), eggs, and citrus fruits. Nuts and peanut butter should be avoided for much longer, not only because of allergies, but because they can be a choking hazard. Other foods to avoid up through the toddler years are hotdog rounds, marshmallows, popcorn, whole grapes, and anything else that might lodge in the throat.

Nutrition as it relates to obesity has become a problem as the numbers of obese children increase. According to the *Journal of the American Dietetic Association*, the rate of obese Americans has doubled since the mid-1980s.[10] The problem starts in infancy, and you'll know why when you see what else the research, called "Feeding Infants and Toddlers Study," reported in this journal says. Children between one and two years old take in 30 percent more calories than they need, and many of these calories come from french fries, pizza, candy, and soda. Up to one-third of the children ate no fruit or vegetables, and of those who did eat a vegetable, it often was french fries. In fact, 9 percent of the children studied who were between 9 and 11 months old ate french fries at least once a day, and 20 percent of those 19 months to 2 years old ate fries daily.

Diapering

Look at the following diapering scene. Notice how the adult is in perfect tune with the baby.

The adult leans over the baby on the diapering counter. The two are face-to-face, and the adult has the baby's full attention as she talks to him about changing his diaper. The baby isn't lying sideways so he has to turn his head to see the adult's face; the counter is built so that he lies with his feet at her belly. The adult waits now for the tension to leave his muscles before she begins. She is gently directive as well as responsive. She tells him to do something and waits for a facial or body response before continuing. She talks to him each step of the way, always keeping him focused on the task itself and their interaction around it. The way she is doing the diapering is building the relationship between them. When she's finished, she holds out her arms and says, "I'm going to pick you up now." The baby responds with a slight forward thrusting of his head and body in anticipation and comes willingly into her arms with a little smile on his face.[11]

This diapering scene was based on an observation by one of the authors at the Pikler Institute in Budapest. Although this diapering went smoothly, they don't always, even at the Pikler Institute. Children go through periods of being uncooperative. It is important that they do so, even though it is hard on the caregivers. Resisting is a sign of growth; by resisting, children assert their individuality and independence. Even so, the principles are still the same—try to engage the baby and get him to cooperate. Don't give up trying to involve him in the task. Acknowledge his feelings and verbalize them for him. This is the time when many caregivers go for the distraction technique—they find something entertaining to keep the baby's mind off what is happening to him. Though it may be tempting, we advise not going that route. One of the great dangers of the early years is teaching babies that they need to be entertained. Entertainment is addictive, and once babies get into this habit, breaking it is difficult. Equally important is the warning that when diapering is done without the baby's full awareness and participation, it no longer is an intimate human experience that furthers relationships. It leaves the realm of curriculum.

Sanitation procedures are also important for diapering to prevent the spread of disease. These procedures should be in accordance with local regulations and health requirements, which should be posted in the diapering area for all to see. The diapering area must be away from food preparation and must be used specifically for diapering, not for other things as well. The following diapering procedure has been borrowed from WestEd's *Program for Infant-Toddler Caregivers Guide to Routines* (2nd edition):

1. Check to be sure the diapering area has been sanitized since the last diapering. If not, discard used paper, spray with a bleach solution, and put clean paper down.
2. Remove the used diaper and dispose of it in a covered container.
3. Wipe the child with a clean, moist cloth or baby wipe. Wipe girls from front to back to prevent urinary and vaginal infections. Dispose of the used cloth or wipe in the container provided. If gloves are used, remove and discard them. To prevent the spread of germs, remove gloves after completing the soiled part of the diapering and before starting the clean part.
4. Put a clean diaper and clean clothes on the child.
5. Wash the child's hands under running water. Babies often touch their bottoms at the diaper-changing station, which are loaded with germs. Washing their hands after diapering helps prevent the spread of germs from the diapering procedure, and it begins to teach them the lifelong hygiene habit of washing their hands after going to the bathroom. Return the child to the play area.
6. Clean and sanitize the diapering area by discarding used paper in the container provided, spraying the area with a bleach solution, wiping lightly with a paper towel to spread the bleach solution around, and discarding the paper towel. Put down a clean paper when the bleach disinfectant has air-dried.
7. Wash your hands thoroughly.

Although program policy or local regulations may require gloves, they are not necessary for every diapering. If the child has diarrhea or blood in the stool or if caregivers have open sores on their hands, then gloves are required.

Toilet Training and Toilet Learning

What used to be called **toilet training** is now called **toilet learning** by those who use a readiness approach and involve the child in the process. At the Pikler Institute it is called sphincter control—that is, control of the muscles specifically related to elimination. The ideas at the Pikler Institute relate more to toilet learning than to toilet training because they see it as a developmental process rather than a type of training. In any case, this way of looking at moving from diapers to toilet is regarded as a natural progress of the partnership involved in diapering. When children are around others in child care situations, they often start to use the toilet when they are old enough to want to imitate the other children they see who are out of diapers.

Here are some hints for making toilet learning easier:

1. Help children feel physically secure by providing potties (if licensing allows) or very low toilets, if possible. The easier it is for children to get on and off the toilet by themselves, the more independence is promoted.
2. If appropriate, ask parents to dress children in loose, simple clothing they can remove themselves (elastic waistbands rather than overalls, for example).
3. Be gentle and understanding about accidents.
4. Avoid power struggles. You can't win them, and children can be left with long-lasting effects if toilet learning has been a highly emotional affair.

Most programs try to cooperate with the family when it comes to toileting. In many programs the policy is not to initiate toileting until the parent suggests it; then the staff is assured that the child will find consistency at home and in the program. Consistency may be more difficult if the parent is from a culture that believes in toilet training and sees it as a first-year task. Although staff may not be willing to try to "catch" children and put them on the potty at a young age, it is important to respect a different view. Those educated as caregivers in the United States and other Western countries may be concerned that toilet training is a harmful approach, especially when undertaken before the third year. It's important to understand that this is not a worldwide view. Around the world, and also in the United States, some families use the toilet training approach and their children do not show harmful effects. Toilet training is quite different from the toilet learning or sphincter control approach. We won't explain it here, but we want to acknowledge that differences exist.[12] We urge caregivers to respect diversity in perceptions, timing, and styles of toileting.

Washing, Bathing, and Grooming

Most programs leave bathing up to parents except under very special circumstances. Some parents become insulted if their children are sent home cleaner than they arrived. Cleanliness can be a great point of conflict between parents and caregivers if they have different standards. Parents may be angry if a child with hard-to-wash hair comes home with a head full of sand. Cultural issues can give people different perspectives on the subject of cleanliness, so respect ideas that differ from your own.

Hand washing before meals is not as touchy an issue as bathing. Hand washing is popular with most children and can even be the highlight of the day for some toddlers. Short attention spans lengthen appreciably when toddlers are sent off to wash. Hand washing can be the most pleasant self-help skill to learn if low sinks are available and toddlers are allowed to use them at their leisure. In fact, hand washing can become a major activity because toddlers greatly enjoy the sensory properties of soap and water.

Grooming can be another touchy subject. How groomed children should look during the day and when the families arrive to pick them up is a matter of opinion. One family arrives to pick up their toddler whose hair is uncombed and whose clothes provide a record of everything she got into that day. The family is

NAEYC Program Standard 5
Health

delighted to see that she had a busy day. Another family may be unhappy that their baby isn't clean and combed. They regard the baby in a different light. Another family whose daughter is in the same condition as the first toddler is horrified that she's not properly groomed. They are less upset about their son, whose clothes are even more filled with spots, spills, fingerpaint, and dirt than the daughter's. Hair can be a big issue, as mentioned previously. Most caregivers don't have the extensive knowledge needed to understand the care of all kinds of hair. Some caregivers don't care about hairdos, and some children care even less. Some of those caregivers are critical of parents who spend a good deal of time creating elaborate hairdos on their toddlers. When thinking about honoring diversity, include differing hair views in your thinking!

Differing Needs and Perspectives

Children who come to the program with medical issues, disabilities, or other physical challenges must be accommodated during caregiving routines. Their needs may differ from those of the other children. Specialized instructions from parents or outside experts may be necessary. For example, asthma treatments may be required. Or the child may have a feeding tube that needs specialized care. Parents or specialists may have information about how to put children into positions that allow them the most freedom of movement. It's important that caregivers have that information. By experimenting, caregivers may discover what works best on their own, but that should be in addition to what the parents and specialists already know. For example, some infants are hypersensitive to touch and cry when picked up. That crying may be reduced if the baby is placed on a pillow and picked up that way. But don't ever put babies down by themselves on a pillow, because it puts them at risk for suffocating.

It is beyond the scope of this book (or any book) to tell you everything you need to know about every child who might come into infant-toddler care with medical issues or disabilities. What you do need to know is that there are resources for finding out. The first resource is the child's family. They may well be connected to specialists who also can help you understand the condition and what is needed. And, certainly, as with all children, you can look to the individual child to teach you about himself or herself. Careful observation will help you understand the messages the child gives. Look for signs of discomfort and notice what distresses the child. Find ways to make the child more comfortable and ease the distress. *Remember principle 3: Learn each child's unique ways of communicating (cries, words, movements, gestures, facial expressions, body positions), and teach yours.* Even children with no words at all have ways to let you know what they need. You just have to learn to read their signals. Don't underestimate children's ability to communicate even though their verbal language skills may be nonexistent or minimal.

Paying close attention to the baby sometimes takes so much energy that caregivers don't notice the signals they receive from families. It's possible that the family's ideas about what should be happening with their child are different from

NAEYC Program Standard 4
Assessment

the caregiver's or the program policies. Cultural practices related to caregiving routines may not be the same as what the caregivers are seeing. Take feeding, for example. What to feed and how are cultural matters. When to start solid foods may seem cut and dried, based on the latest research, but cultural and family traditions may not go by the research. Besides, research changes over time. Take sleeping, for example. Generation after generation of parents in this country were told by their pediatricians to put their babies to sleep on their stomachs. Since the 1990s, however, pediatricians have been giving the opposite advice—that babies should sleep on their backs. The reason is to reduce the risk of sudden infant death syndrome (SIDS), or crib death. Times change.[13] See Figure 3.2 for a summary of risk factors for sudden infant death syndrome.

One of the strong messages in this book is to encourage self-help skills. The reason for this message is the sometimes unspoken goal of creating an independent individual. Not all parents are as interested in their children becoming independent individuals as they are for them to feel strong, lasting family ties. Caregivers must respect what families want for their children and honor diversity. You'll see that as a continuing theme throughout this book. We can't tell you what to do when you run into a cultural bump except to talk it over. When caregivers and families are in close communication, they can work out their differences in ways that are good for children, families, and caregivers. Each situation has a unique solution, so we can't just list them here for you. Human relations are complex matters, and human relations are what we are talking about.

Dressing

Caregivers can promote autonomy by setting up tasks in such a way that the child makes maximum contributions.[14] You can easily see examples of this principle in dressing activities. For instance, when taking off the socks or booties of even a very young baby, you can pull them half off and ask the child to finish the job. It takes little coordination when the task is set up like this. Even young babies get real pleasure and satisfaction from helping out. The idea is to simplify the task just the right amount so that the child gets practice in the dressing and undressing process. At first it takes longer to work cooperatively, but as child and

Reflect

What do you know about cultural differences in caregiving routines? How does what you know differ from what's shown in this chapter? What would you do if you were told to "follow the book" and you didn't believe in it? What would you do if a parent's beliefs about carrying out a particular routine differed from yours?

Figure 3.2 Reducing the Risk of Sudden Infant Death Syndrome (SIDS)

1. Always place babies on their backs to sleep, even for naps.

2. Place the baby on a firm mattress, such as in a safety-approved crib.

3. Remove soft, fluffy bedding and stuffed toys from the baby's sleep area.

4. Make sure the baby's head and face remain uncovered during sleep.

5. Do not allow smoking around the baby.

6. Do not let the baby get too warm during sleep.

Source: Adapted from The Back to Sleep Campaign, www.nichd.nih.gov/publications/pubs/safe_sleep_gen.cfm.

Even toddlers need a little
help sometimes.

caregiver come to see themselves as a team, the earlier patience pays off. By toddlerhood, children who were encouraged to help dress and undress themselves have become proficient and need very little help except with such things as buttons and starting zippers.

Notice in the Principles in Action scene how the caregiver tried to involve the baby but had a hard time because, although the baby might have been trying to cooperate, he couldn't control his muscles. Sometimes a caregiver needs more knowledge than he or she has. This scene is an example of that situation.

Here is a scene that shows how it would be if the caregiver did not aim for teamwork:

Imagine yourself a young toddler. You are about to be taken outside for a walk. Without anything being said to you, you feel your arm being grabbed. You're thrown off balance. Then you find yourself being hauled over to a coatrack. Your arm is held tight and then thrust into a sleeve. Your thumb gets stuck and stretches back as the sleeve comes up your arm. Then you feel yourself being swung around. You feel annoyed. When the other sleeve comes up your other arm, you stick your thumb out on purpose. Then you become all floppy. Finally a face comes down near yours, but the eyes look only at the zipper, which is resisting getting on the track. You feel the hands struggle with the piece of metal; then suddenly the zipper moves upward. It stops only when it touches your neck and feels cold, uncomfortable, and tight. The face disappears, and you're left standing alone while the child next to you is readied in the same impersonal way.

Not a very enjoyable experience, was it? This child was being treated more like an object than a person.

Napping

It is important that infants be allowed to rest according to their individual needs rather than according to someone else's schedule. Infants' sleep patterns change—sometimes from day to day as well as over a period of time. No one napping schedule will fit all babies in a program, and each baby's personal schedule changes from time to time.

Not all babies express their need for rest in the same way. Experienced, sensitive caregivers learn to read each child's signals, which may range from slowing down and yawning to increased activity and a low frustration threshold.

Parents are the best source of information about their baby's sleep patterns and needs. Experienced caregivers are aware how useful it is to know that the baby woke up extra early that morning or got less sleep than usual over the weekend. They understand fussy behavior in a different light if they know the reason for it.

Reflect

Can you remember a time in your own life when you were treated as an object? If you can, then you know why it is important not to treat a child (of any age) that way.

The Principles in Action

Principle 1 Involve infants and toddlers in things that concern them. Don't work around them or distract them to get the job done faster.

The caregiver is trying to dress Nicky, who has cerebral palsy. Since this baby is new to this caregiver, the caregiver still has to learn not only about cerebral palsy, but also about Nicky as an individual. The caregiver always tries to involve Nicky in the dressing, but it's hard because muscle control is a challenge for him. Furthermore, the caregiver is trying to put a one-piece stretch-pajama outfit on him and it's a little tight. She starts with a foot and the toes curl. It's hard to fit them into the foot of the pajamas. She wants to get Nicky to relax but doesn't know how to help him. When she finally gets one foot in, she picks up one leg; the other one comes, too, in a scissoring motion. And then his ankle goes into a spasm. She talks to Nicky but is getting more and more frustrated. She finally gives up and goes and gets a loose-fitting two-piece outfit that goes on much more easily. She's happy that she was able to adapt to this situation and vows to talk to the mother about what she can do to make it easier on her and Nicky.

1. What would you have done if you were the caregiver?
2. Are there some other devices that would make dressing this baby easier?
3. Could the caregiver learn about some strategies to use in dressing this baby?
4. Did principle 1 work here, or is this a case in which it didn't work?

Babies should be put down to nap in a way familiar to them.

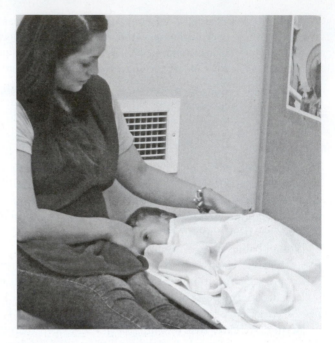

Babies should be put down for a nap in the way most familiar to them. However, it's also important that every caregiver know the results of recent research regarding the relationship between sleeping position and SIDS. SIDS is the label given to unexplained deaths, usually, but not always, occurring when a baby is sleeping. SIDS is not the same as smothering, choking, or dying from a disease. Infant deaths are labeled SIDS only when no cause can be found. For years, North American pediatricians have told parents and caregivers to put babies to sleep on their stomachs. Research now shows that *back sleeping* is associated with lower risk of SIDS. The evidence is compelling.[15] Figure 3.2 shows some concrete steps you can take to reduce the risk of babies dying of SIDS.

Each baby should have a personal crib that is located in the same spot every day. That kind of consistency and security may help the baby feel at home faster. Decisions about when to put a baby in the crib and how long to leave him or her there depend on the adult's perception of the particular child's needs. Some children need to be confined for some time before they can fall asleep, even when they are very tired. They may play or cry before sleeping. Other children fall asleep immediately. The waking-up period also takes some adult judgment. Does the child wake up energetic, active, and ready to play, or is there a long transition period between sleeping and waking during which the child may need to remain in the crib or on the cot? Reading a young child's signals about rest needs is not always easy. Again, the parent is a good source of information. Find out what kind of self-calming behaviors a child has and encourage them. Some children stroke a blanket; others twist their hair. The most common self-calming behavior is thumb sucking. Ask how the child naps at home. Can you use some of the same devices or rituals the parent uses? Perhaps a favorite toy or blanket provides comfort.

Once again, cultural factors may enter into attitudes about sleeping. Some cultures see being alone in a dark room as the way to promote independence. Others feel that babies should not sleep alone. You may not agree with an attitude that is different from your own, but be sure to respect it. If you can't do what the parent wants, talk about it with him or her. Negotiate, discuss, and exchange viewpoints. Don't just ignore a parent's wishes and do what you think is best.

As children move through toddlerhood and nap only once a day, they can learn to rest according to a group schedule. However, individual needs are still important, and provision should be made for the toddler who needs a quiet time earlier in the day, if not an actual nap.

Toddlers who feel nervous, scared, or distrustful may have sleep problems that consistency would help alleviate. A favorite toy or blanket may also provide needed security. Sometimes a caregiver can do nothing at the moment to promote security but must acknowledge the child's insecure feelings and wait until he or she eventually learns that it's a safe place. In some programs, the children who need it have a back rub to help them go to sleep. Here are some further hints about how to help toddlers get to sleep.

1. Provide visual privacy for those children who need it. Some toddlers are too stimulated by being near another child to go to sleep.
2. Provide a quiet, peaceful atmosphere. Some programs use soft music to help. Start winding down before nap time.
3. Make sure all children get plenty of fresh air and exercise. Being tired is the best motivator for napping.
4. Don't let children get overtired. Some children have a hard time settling down to sleep when they are exhausted.

Caregiver Lynne creates a ritual around naptime. The toddlers she cares for are old enough to have an established group naptime. So after lunch she starts transforming the room so that it suggests sleeping instead of play. The toys are hidden away, lights are turned down, windows shaded, and there's a quiet story time for children who settle down that way. As stimulation is lowered and the environment gives the message about what's expected, the children's activity level goes down and rest comes easier.

If adults regard caregiving tasks as vital learning experiences, they are more likely to approach them with patience and attention. In group care, even when the adult-child ratio is good, an infant's main opportunity to enjoy a long period of one-to-one interaction is during caregiving times like feeding, diapering, and dressing. If those times are used well, babies require far less adult attention during the other periods of their day. Babies can go about their play (interacting with the environment and with the other babies) with no more than general supervision from an adult who may be watching a number of babies.

As toddlers develop self-help skills, this built-in one-to-one time diminishes. Therefore caregivers must provide it in some other way, even to the oldest toddlers. The fact that required ratios of adults to children may change when the children are about two adds to the difficulty of giving the kind of individual attention each child needs. Some get it by being charming and appealing to adults.

Others get it by exhibiting unacceptable behaviors. Some don't get it at all. One way to ensure that all children are getting individual attention, once the caregiving tasks are no longer such a focus during the child care day, is to keep brief anecdotal records. If during naptime you write a single sentence about each child in your care that day, you'll soon see the patterns. You'll see that some children stand out because of their behaviors. Some children are practically invisible, and it's hard to think of anything to write about these youngsters. Once you see these patterns, you can make better conscious decisions about how to make sure that all children get individual attention each day.

When infants and toddlers are treated with respect and caregiving is done with a teamwork approach, relationships grow—relationships that help children learn about themselves and the world. They come to anticipate what will happen to them and realize the world has some predictability. They learn they have some power to influence the world and the people in it. They begin to make sense out of life. When used to their fullest, these times can become focuses in children's days—something they look forward to—their chance to "dance" with their partner!

Appropriate Practice

Overview of Development

According to the National Association for the Education of Young Children, the uniqueness of each young baby demands that caregivers learn babies' rhythms, when they eat, how they want to be held for feeding or comforting, and when they sleep. Caregivers' abilities to read babies' signals about needs and to respond appropriately help young babies develop a feeling of security. This same sensitivity is needed as young babies grow into mobile ones and become explorers. The exploration doesn't stop during caregiving routines, so it is up to caregivers to make the best of the child who is trying to touch everything while struggling to get off the diapering counter. Toddlers are concerned about who they are and who is in charge and continually test to find out. Independence and control are primary issues, and these can emerge during caregiving routines.

Developmentally Appropriate Practice

The above overview is a summary of how caregiving relates to curriculum, giving examples of how meeting needs through caregiving routines changes as the baby progresses through developmental stages. Following is a sampling of specific developmentally appropriate caregiving practices:

- Adults adjust to infants' individual feeding and sleeping schedules. Infants' food preferences and eating styles are respected.
- The infant sleeping area is separate from active play and eating areas. Babies have their own cribs and sheets brought from home. Family members bring special comforting objects to personalize their baby's crib. Infants' names are used to label every personal item.
- Infants have their own diapering supplies and extra clothes within reach of the changing table.
- Adults respect children's schedules with regard to eating and sleeping. Toddlers are provided snacks more frequently and in smaller portions than older children are. Liquids are provided frequently.
- Adults work cooperatively with families in encouraging children to learn to use the toilet. When toddlers reach an age when they feel confident and unafraid to sit on a toilet seat, caregivers invite them to use the toilet, help them as needed,

provide manageable clothing, and positively rein-force them. The toilet is child sized, in a well-lit, inviting, relatively private space. Children are taken to the toilet frequently and regularly in response to their own biological needs.

- Caregivers plan a transition into naptime with a predictable sequence of events. They choose a quiet activity, such as reading a story. Toddlers get their own stuffed toys or blankets and go to their cots; soft music or a story tape may be played for toddlers who are still awake.

- Teachers work in partnership with parents, communicating daily to build mutual understanding and trust and to ensure the welfare and optimal development of the child. Caregivers listen carefully to what parents say about their children, seek to understand parents' goals and preferences, and are respectful of cultural and family differences.

Source: Carol Copple and Sue Bredekamp, eds., *Developmentally Appropriate Practice in Early Childhood Programs*, 3rd ed. (Washington, DC: National Association for the Education of Young Children, 2009).

Individually Appropriate Practice

- Toilet training may vary greatly depending on children's physical and mental capabilities. Whenever it starts and however long it lasts, harshness should be avoided.

- Some children need more attention to feeding than others. Careful positioning for children old enough to feed themselves can make a big differ-ence if those children are to use their hands capably. If they tend to slip in the chair, using nonskid cloth on the seat can help. Food texture can be an issue for some children with neurological involvement. Such procedures as massaging the throat to help swallowing or using a cloth or toothbrush to "wake up the mouth" can facilitate muscle control.

Culturally Appropriate Practice

Not all families value independence and individuality in the same way, and many have a different set of pri-orities for their children. Families whose goal is to downplay independence in order to help children see themselves first and foremost as members of the family or of the group in general may have a differ-ent approach to caregiving routines. Spoon-feeding children beyond toddlerhood is common practice among some cultures. Toilet training, on the other hand, may start in the first year of life. Both practices stress interdependence over independence. These practices may startle caregivers who have grown up in families where such things are frowned on. Remember that developmentally appropriate prac-tice mandates that professionals work in partnership with parents to build mutual understanding and trust. The goal is to ensure the welfare and optimal development of the child. Chapter 13 looks at issues of identity development, which ties in to this issue of different ideas about caregiving practices.

Appropriate Practice in Action

Look back on the Principles in Action scene on page 63 and reconsider your answers. After reading this chapter, would you answer any of the questions differently? Now analyze that scene in terms of the information in the last bullet in the "Developmentally Appropriate Practice" section of the Appropriate Practice box.

- What do you think was this caregiver's attitude about a partnership with the parents? Do you think she plans to learn something from them?
- What do you know about positioning a child with cerebral palsy so he has more control over his muscles? How could you learn more?

Now look at the "Culturally Appropriate Practice" section of the Appropriate Practice box.

- Was the caregiver stressing self-help skills?

Appropriate Practice *(continued)*

- If this caregiver's major goal is to encourage self-help skills in Nicky, what if the mother has a different idea about what he needs? How would the caregiver find out? If the two have different goals, what should they do?

- What are your ideas and feelings about downplaying independence in children with the challenges Nicky has, even if encouraging independence is culturally inappropriate?

Summary

Those essential activities of daily living called caregiving routines are part of the curriculum when they offer young children the opportunity for deepening relationships and for frequent personalized experiences related to cooperation and learning.

Thinking Again about Infant-Toddler Curriculum

- Infant-toddler curriculum means planning for learning, which includes providing for growing attachment during caregiving routines.
- To make caregiving routines (those essential activities of daily living) into curriculum means three policies must be in place—a primary caregiver system, consistency, and continuity of care.
- Assessment is part of meeting each child's needs during caregiving routines. Assessment in this chapter means determining each child's needs at any given time.

Caregiving Routines

- Feeding includes providing for breastfeeding mothers, bottle feeding, spoon feeding, and eventually self-feeding. Developmental appropriateness is important and at the same time, cultural differences should be discussed and honored.
- Diapering should be done in such a way that the baby is a partner in the process and learns to cooperate with the caregiving instead of being distracted with a toy or by other means.
- Toilet training and toilet learning are two different approaches. Toilet learning is developmentally appropriate and happens when the child is ready. Toilet training is often culturally appropriate and can occur much earlier than toilet learning.
- Washing, bathing, and grooming includes varying practices and expectations. What satisfies families may not be the same as what satisfies caregivers. Honoring diversity is important.
- Children's differing needs and disabilities must be taken into account and accommodated when carrying out caregiving routines.

- Dressing, like the other routines, should be carried out so the child is encouraged to cooperate and eventually learn self-help skills.
- Napping varies by age and by individual. Caregivers must know about and eliminate risk factors for Sudden Infant Death Syndrome (SIDS).

Key Terms

attachment 48
continuity of care 50
primary-caregiver system 49

release time 53
resilient 51
self-help skills 54

toilet learning 58
toilet training 58

Thought/Activity Questions

1. What does attachment have to do with caregiving as curriculum?
2. What are some ways that programs promote attachment?
3. Does attachment usually happen more easily in family child care homes? Why or why not?
4. What caregiving routines does a caregiver perform throughout the day, and what is an example of how to make them into curriculum?
5. What do you know about cultural differences in caregiving routines? How does what you know differ from what's shown in this chapter? What would you do if you were told to "follow the book" and you didn't believe in it? What would you do if a parent's beliefs about carrying out a particular routine differed from yours?

For Further Reading

Carol Copple, Sue Bredekamp, and Janet Gonzalez-Mena, *Basics of Developmentally Appropriate Practice* (Washington DC: National Association for the Education of Young Children, 2011).

Judit Falk, "When We Touch the Infant's Body," *The RIE Manual: Expanded Edition*, ed. Deborah Greenwald (Los Angeles: Resources for Infant Educarers, 2013), pp. 162–167.

Linda Gillespie and Sandra Petersen, "Rituals and Routines: Supporting Infants and Toddlers and Their Families," *Young Children* 67(4), September 2012, pp. 76–77.

Janet Gonzalez-Mena, "Cultural Sensitivity in Caregiving Routines: The Essential Activities of Daily Living," in *Infant/Toddler Caregiving: A Guide to Culturally Sensitive Care*, 2nd ed., ed. Elita Amini Virmani and Peter L. Mangione (Sausalito, CA: WestEd and Sacramento, CA: California Department of Education, 2013), pp. 56–65.

Maria Vincze, "The Meaning of Cooperation During Care," in *Bringing up and Providing Care for Infants and Toddlers in an Institution*, ed. Anna Tardos (Budapest: Association Pikler-Lóczy for Young Children, 2007), pp. 39–55.

Maria Vincze, "Feedings as One of the Main Scenes of the Adult-Child Relationship," in *Bringing up and Providing Care for Infants and Toddlers in an Institution*, ed. Anna Tardos (Budapest: Association Pikler-Lóczy for Young Children, 2007) pp. 93–104.

Maria Vincze, "From Bottle Feeding to Independent Eating," in *Bringing up and Providing Care for Infants and Toddlers in an Institution*, ed. Anna Tardos (Budapest: Association Pikler-Lóczy for Young Children, 2007) pp. 105–126.

chapter 4

Play and Exploration as Curriculum

Focus Questions

After reading this chapter you should be able to answer the following questions:

1 What are the four adult roles this chapter discusses as important for facilitating the play of infants and toddlers?

2 What is a primary consideration when setting up an environment for play and why is it important?

3 Why should you step back and observe after encouraging interactions?

4 What are five environmental factors that influence play in an infant-toddler care and education program?

5 How is a *happening* different from an *activity*?

What Do You See?

Tyler is on the floor with a simple wooden puzzle on one side of him and plastic nesting cups on the other. Next to him is Kevin, who reaches over and removes two of the puzzle pieces. Tyler picks up the puzzle board and drops it. The pieces clatter together when they hit the rug, which makes Tyler smile. Kevin looks at the puzzle and then at Tyler. Tyler takes the puzzle piece Kevin has in his hand. Kevin looks surprised. Then Tyler picks up another piece off the floor and bangs the two pieces together. He drops both pieces and Kevin picks them up. Tyler picks up the plastic nesting cups and walks over to a low platform, which he steps up on. He raises his arms in the air, then he quickly sits down and begins taking the nesting cups out. First he takes out the small one; he taps it on the wooden floor of the platform and cocks his head to listen to the noise. His fingers are working on the second one—feeling the shape, grasping the edge—and now it's out. He taps this one on the floor, too, before laying it down next to the first one. One by one he takes out the cups and taps each. When he gets to the last one, he lays it at the end of the row and looks satisfied. Then he puts them back together again as slowly and carefully as he took them out.

What you saw in the opening scene may not have looked like much to you. The way infants and toddlers play isn't the same as the way older children play. It takes an understanding of who toddlers are and what they are interested in to appreciate a scene like this one. It also takes good observation skills to notice the details. We'll go back to this scene later to discuss it.

NAEYC Program Standard 2
Curriculum

A main ingredient of any infant or toddler program should be play and exploration. Infants' and young toddlers' play is more exploration than the kind of play children three years and older exhibit. We want to be sure that readers recognize what is happening in that opening scene. They are playing, though it may not seem so to everybody. Early childhood educators and researchers have long recognized play as vital to growth and learning. It is natural to young children and should be regarded as an *important* use of their time, not as something secondary or optional.[1]

A little book called *The Origins of Free Play* by Kallo and Balog gives a clear overview of play at the Pikler Institute in Budapest starting with play objects for infants under a year old. Descriptions and photos show how they develop manipulation skills. The authors go on to show how children beyond a year old use their perceptive skills to collect objects, stack them, and build with them. The benefits of play are enormous and go far beyond the kinds of things we talk about so easily, like developing skills and learning concepts. Play can be an avenue to early literacy skills, for one thing. According to one study, play is where many paths to literacy come together and "emerging understandings are integrated, practiced, and tested in a safe environment."[2] In fact, if you look carefully at play, you can find all aspects of the kinds of skills children need for the foundations of reading and writing.

One benefit of play is the way it facilitates the development of self-regulation. Through play babies begin to develop the ability to move from an automatic response to one involving choice that promotes the baby's intention. A toddler talking to herself shows how self-regulation is developing and as such gives increased focus that allows her to play with another toddler. Playing together depends to some extent on self-control. The development of self-regulation increases intentionality and includes both emotional control and cognitive awareness. Play offers children opportunities that come from nowhere else. Through play, children get involved in open-ended exploration. They are not confined by rules, procedures, or outcomes. Children at play have self-direction. They have power. Through total absorption during play, they make discoveries they might otherwise never make, they work on problems, they make choices, and they find out what interests them.

Reflect
What are the models from your own childhood that you carry in your head today? Can you relate your own experience to Papert's "gears"?

In the foreword to *Mindstorms*, Seymour Papert writes about how, as a child, he fell in love with gears.[3] He spent hours playing with circular objects, turning them as if they were gears. Much later, this led to him turning gears in his head and making chains of cause and effect, and he used gears as his model for learning mathematics.

The way we respond to infants and toddlers at play by giving them freedom, by helping them pursue their special interests, and by providing resources may result in children gaining lifelong models such as Papert's gears (see Figure 4.1).

Giving infants and toddlers freedom to move is a concept we wish to emphasize. Play in infants involves movement; if they cannot move freely, they can't fully engage in play. Unfortunately, families and caregivers tend to restrict babies' activity, rather than encourage it. This is something not usually considered

Figure 4.1 Three Ways Caregivers Create Curriculum out of Play

Caregivers create curriculum out of play in these three ways:
1. By giving children freedom
2. By helping them pursue their special interests
3. By providing resources

before the baby can get around, yet movement, from the first months of life, is important for brain development. It's also important for cognitive development. Magda Gerber made this point to those who studied with her long before scientists understood the brain as they do now. Magda was way ahead of her time! In school, physical education focuses mainly on the body. In infancy and toddlerhood, physical movement is about learning—not just to use the body, but to use the brain as well.[4] Elena Bodrova and Deborah Leong discuss how play influences development in their book *Tools of the Mind: The Vygotskian Approach to Early Childhood Education*.[5] They explain that Vygotsky had an integrated view of play when he wrote about its contribution to cognitive, emotional, and social development. He saw play as a tool of the mind with its roots in the manipulation and exploration of infancy and toddlerhood.

Free play and **exploration** is a theme of this chapter. By free play and exploration we mean undirected but monitored active play when children have choices to pursue their special interests without continual adult control or expected outcomes. Figure 4.2 shows seven supporting factors from Magda Gerber that serve as a foundation for play and exploration in babies. The list is adapted from Carol Garhart Mooney's book. Letting free play and exploration remain free is difficult for some adults once they recognize how important activity is for infants and toddlers. They want to set up specific adult-created activities with objectives and plan for and control outcomes. This is especially true for programs with children from low-income families because of the urgency to prepare them for later schooling. We urge those adults who want to create

Figure 4.2 Seven Factors that Support Play and Exploration in Babies

1. Being an **active participant** in their routines
2. Adults' **sensitive observations** and understanding what the baby needs
3. **Consistency**, including clearly defined limits
4. **Basic trust** in the baby as an initiator, explorer, and self-learner
5. Safe, cognitively challenging, and emotionally nurturing **environments**
6. **Uninterrupted play** when babies can play on their own at their own pace
7. **Freedom** to explore and interact with objects and other babies

activities and objectives—lessons—to appreciate what children gain from free play by observing them. You'll see that given a safe, developmentally appropriate, and rich environment, they create their own objectives and lessons, which are far more effective than those you set up.

Some visitors to an infant-toddler program arrived in the morning to see the children playing freely with a variety of toys. They were impressed with how involved and interested the children were. But then the director arrived breathless, apologized that things were late in starting that morning, and proceeded to organize groups, get out "activities," and herd toddlers into chairs around tables. Here they were drilled on names of objects in pictures, told to match shapes, and shown how to make circles and squares out of play dough. The teachers who had earlier been playing a background role, except when there was a call to be responsive, suddenly took charge of everything. The focus became very objective oriented. When the visitors later had a look at individual education plans, they discovered that cognitive objectives were defined very narrowly (for example, "shown pictures of a dog, a horse, and a cat, child will identify two out of three").

No wonder "playtime" was so objective oriented. But instead of setting objectives for the way a child is to interact with materials, the adult should observe what the child is actually doing and appreciate what the child is getting out of it, even if it isn't immediately obvious. For example, if someone had watched Papert twirling round objects, he or she might well have missed that Papert was creating a model of gears in his head. How different his outcome might have been if he had been redirected continually to do some kind of activity with a particular objective that an adult had in mind.

One reason adults sometimes want to control toddler play is that they don't understand it as exploration. Go back and review that scene at the beginning of the chapter. Did you note that Tyler was exploring with his senses? He wasn't working the puzzle, he was enjoying the feel and the sound of it and of the nesting cups. He has no interest in using the materials "the right way." Tyler is figuring out his own way of discovering the properties of each material. Simple as this scene is, it is a good example of a young toddler playing. Preschool play is easier to understand because it can look involved and productive, and it fits into categories such as "dramatic play" or "art" or "block building." Toddler play may not look like much; toddlers seem to dabble at things. Sometimes they seem to just be wandering around, often carrying objects with them. But if you watch carefully, you see that they are neither uninvolved nor in transition. They are walking and carrying. They are making choices. In addition, perhaps they are enjoying the sensory changes as they move about. Sometimes they are keeping contact with the person they are most attached to (touching home base) when they explore the environment.

Toddlers are easy to satisfy as long as they have room to move and things to examine and manipulate. They may seem to have short attention spans because of their gross motor focus and the need to change location. However, they can also get very involved, especially in problem solving or a self-chosen sensory activity. Toddlers at a sink with soap, water, and paper towels can spend up to half an hour if they are allowed to, messing around. (That's not a short attention span.)

Reflect

Recall an early play experience of your own. Relive it, if you can. Think about what you got out of this experience. How can you use your own experience to understand the importance of free play for infants and toddlers?

Adult Roles in Play

The caregiver takes many roles in supporting infants and toddlers in their play. Although we separate them for discussion, in reality they are all related to each other—with safety as one overarching theme and learning through interaction as another. Both of these roles are mentioned in Figure 4.2.

Setting Up Environments for Play

Safety is of primary importance and involves setting up a healthful environment free from hazards, then carefully monitoring what goes on in it. Without safety, there is no free play. Although some children are bigger risk-takers than others, most children are comfortable only when they feel secure and know no one will let them get hurt. Thought must be put into the age and individual developmental level of each child and of the group as a whole. Health and safety hazards can be an individual as well as a group issue. Careful attention must be given to safety issues for children who may have physical or other challenges. Safety is the key to exploration for all children. By exploration we mean the act of discovering and

Children gain eye-hand coordination from manipulating toys.

examining what's around the child—the people and objects, as well as the properties of those objects—through touching, mouthing, smelling, seeing, and hearing. Only in a safe, developmentally appropriate, and interesting environment can children have opportunities to make the kinds of discoveries that further their development and learning. When thinking about exploration, look again at the age and developmental level of each child. Also take children with challenges into consideration so that they have equal opportunity to safely interact with as much of the environment as possible. For example, consider how children gain eye-hand coordination from manipulating play objects; then think about the child who is severely visually impaired. Make sure that child feels safe enough to get to the toy shelf, knows that toys are there, and is able to discover that those toys have features (such as making a noise) that could give the child experiences with ear-hand coordination.

When you are thinking about play environments, don't consider just the indoor environment. Infants and toddlers need to be outdoors as well, every day if at all possible. They need not only fresh air, but also some experiences in a more natural environment than indoor spaces provide. Exercise in fresh air is good for both the body and the mind. Too many children now grow up on cement and asphalt, rather than in a variety of natural textures that aren't only smooth and hard—textures like grass, sand, and even dirt. Too many children see nothing but bright plastic toys. If the next generation grows up with no experience with nature, who will be out there trying to preserve natural habitats, the rain forest, and open spaces?

Encouraging Interactions and Then Stepping Back

Children learn from other children. By interacting with their peers, infants and toddlers learn much about the world, their power in it, and their effect on others. Through the kinds of problem-solving situations that present themselves in child-child interactions, youngsters come to learn such valuable skills as how to resolve conflicts. The adult's role in these child-child interactions is to encourage them and then step back until needed. Sensitive caregivers know when to intervene. Timing is crucial. If you step in too soon, valuable learning is lost. But if you step in too late, children can hurt each other. Timing and **selective intervention** are important skills for caregivers to acquire in order to facilitate infant-toddler social play. What do we mean by selective intervention? Intervention means interfering or interrupting, and it is selective when it is limited to those times when the effect will be positive. Selective intervention should be used to protect (as in an unsafe situation) or to help facilitate learning when needed. Figuring out when to sensitively intervene appropriately is an adult skill that is important in facilitating play. But remember that encouraging children to solve their own problems is an important part of their education, so stepping back and not intervening is another adult skill that is equally important to practice. Adults should remain available while infants and toddlers are playing, giving wants-nothing quality time. They should refrain from

VIDEO OBSERVATION 4

Toddlers Playing Outside

See Video Observation 4: Toddlers Playing Outside for an illustration of toddlers playing pretend.

Questions

- How could you explain this scene to someone who says to you, "They aren't doing anything important—just messing around"?
- How is the play of these children the same as and different from the play of the two boys in the opening scene of this chapter?
- What makes this scene "curriculum"? What are the children gaining from it? Consider the developmental domains of mind, body, and feelings.

To view this clip, go to **www.mhhe.com/itc10e**. Click on Student Edition, select Chapter 4, and click on Video Observations.

interrupting the child who is really absorbed in play. Absorption is a quality we should value.

Adults can be part of the play, but they must remain in a playful mode, open to what happens, without setting goals or playing for particular results. Otherwise the play ceases to be play and becomes an adult-directed "activity." You'll see examples throughout this book of adults in a wants-nothing mode, being with children.

Be careful about becoming a child's entertainment device. Some children get hooked on adults playing with them and are unable to play with other children or on their own when the adult steps back. In some programs, such as at the Pikler Institute, caregivers are trained to allow children to play uninterrupted. They don't play with them. As a result, the quality of the play there is exceptional. Children need no adult entertainment and little intervention. This is the result of the emphasis put on adult-child interaction and cooperation during caregiving

Reflect

Have you ever experienced a time when play was not playful? What happened? What was that like?

times, so that children have a close trusting relationship and feel secure enough to explore and play on their own and with each other.[6]

Supporting Problem Solving

NAEYC Program Standard 3
Teaching

Adults support problem solving. The caregiver must have sensitivity to recognize the intellectual value of the many problems that arise during free play. Maria can't get the ring on the stick; Blake's block stack keeps falling over; Jamal can't reach the toy just beyond his grasp. The frustrations from these kinds of problems seem to interrupt free play, and it's tempting just to solve the problem for the child. But rescuing a child takes away a potentially valuable learning experience.

Adults provide scaffolding for children's problem solving. It takes skill to know when to help. Often adults do too much and interfere with the child's ability to solve the problem. They deprive the child of discovering his or her own approach. The key to scaffolding effectively is to determine the point at which the child is about to give up. A small assist at just the right time will keep the child working on the problem. If it's too early or too late, the child loses interest. It's not that caregivers have to "motivate" children. Rather, the assist is the type of support that helps children stay with something long enough to finally gain a sense of satisfaction. Satisfaction is the kind of reward that lingers and is remembered the next time a problem arises. Figure 4.3 provides a quick look at eight adult roles in infant-toddler play. Magda Gerber gave some advice about scaffolding:

> *Allow children to learn on their own, without interference. . . . We are child-loving people—too eager, so we think, "Oh, poor baby would like to get that toy but can't reach it," so we push it nearer.*[7]

Angela Duckworth, a researcher who is also interested in problem solving, has studied perseverance and passion as commendable traits in people. She uses the term "grit" and points out the advantages of having it. Magda didn't use that

Figure 4.3 Adult Roles in Infant-Toddler Play

1. Encouraging interactions and then stepping back
2. Practicing selective intervention
3. Providing time, space, and materials
4. Remaining available but not interrupting
5. Providing safety
6. Supporting problem solving
7. Providing scaffolding
8. Observing

term, but she was all for helping very young children follow their passions and work on the problems they encountered along the way. She helped her many students see how their inclination to rescue got in the way of the development of what Duckworth now calls grit.

Observing

The adults in a child care program that stresses free play sometimes look as though they aren't doing anything. Some people think that adults in a wants-nothing mode—available but not directive—look too passive. They may look passive, but they are busy observing. Observation is a key role if a caregiver is to understand what's going on and figure out how to promote learning. Keen observation skills are vital for all caregivers. Sitting still, focusing attention, and just taking in what's happening comes easily to some adults, but for those who don't naturally come by them, these skills must be learned. When adults are in an observer role, the pace of the children tends to slow down because the adult energy influences what's going on around them. A slow pace gives infants and toddlers a chance to focus their attention. *Remember principle 7: Model the behavior you want to teach*. While observing, you are modeling that mode of being, which benefits the children in more ways than one.

Read the following scene, which shows adults facilitating free play, and decide for yourself if the adults are too passive.

NAEYC Program Standard 4
Assessment

The play area is set up for older toddlers, who are busily exploring what has been put out for them. Two adults are sitting on the floor on opposite ends of the play area. In one end of the room four children are carrying around large plastic blocks. One seems to have a plan in mind; one is just carrying a block seemingly without regard to where she is going. A third child has built a four-block enclosure and is sitting in the middle of it. Another child is walking across the blocks that are lying flat on the rug. The first child lays down another block and joins the child who is walking on top of the blocks. The child who was wandering around comes over and takes the block that the child has just set down and a tussle starts. The teacher, who has been observing from a distance, comes to sit by the two children ready to intervene, but one child lets go and leaves and the other abandons the block he was fighting for, so the teacher goes back to her original position. At the other end of the room, a group of children is playing around a table set with plastic dishes. A child brings a "cup of coffee" from the table over to the adult on the floor. He pretends to drink it. The child takes the empty cup and goes over to the play sink to wash it, while another child who has just given a doll a bath gets the empty cup from the first child and gives the "baby" a drink out of it.

Contrast that scene to this one:

A group of toddlers sits on a rug with an adult directing a "circle time." She is singing a song that has a finger play to go with it. Some of the toddlers are trying to make their fingers perform, and others are just sitting watching her. None of them are singing. She finishes that song and starts another. Two children begin to squirm, but most are watching and listening. One child gets up and wanders off and a second one follows. Another adult captures the two escapees and herds them back to the group saying, "Circle time isn't over yet." By the third song all but one of the children are squirming and making attempts to escape. The herding adult is having trouble keeping them all together. The other adult gets out a flannel board and begins to tell a story. She briefly captures most of the group's attention, but then one child comes up and tries to take the figures off the flannel board. The others can't see, so they get squirmy again and two start wrestling. As we leave this scene the two adults are getting chairs and firmly planting each child in one. It is clear that they *will* learn to sit still at circle time.

The adults in the second scene are *doing something*. It is more obvious what they are doing in this scene than in the first scene. They are being teachers. They are playing the role that most people expect them to play.

Which scene appealed most to you?

Did you notice that the toddlers in both scenes are making choices, as is appropriate in the play mode, but in the second scene choices weren't part of the plan? Did you notice how heavily taxed the adults were by being in charge?

Adults who are uninitiated to early childhood principles and practices can understand a program where children are engaged in adult-directed "learning activities" but may be critical of one where the adults just sit on the floor and respond. Parents may prefer that caregivers *teach* and look like they are in control of what is happening. They may not understand the role of facilitating learning through self-directed free play. Further, the caregivers themselves may feel like babysitters when in the wants-nothing mode during free play time. They may resist this role. All these factors work against a curriculum in which free play is a main ingredient. Caregivers need to find ways to articulate what they are doing so they can counteract the pressure that comes from all sides to *teach* infants and toddlers rather than let them play. What the adult does do that is more important than teaching is to structure the environment so that it is conducive to play and respond to children when appropriate.

Environmental Factors That Influence Play

NAEYC Program Standard 9
Physical Environment

You can't just put infants and toddlers into a room and expect great things to happen. Careful consideration needs to be given to the size of the space and how it fits the size of the group and the age span of the children in it. Then the adult needs to think about what is in the room and how appropriate it is for infants and toddlers. There are basic built-in features of the space and the furniture and equipment, plus what the adults bring as movable equipment, toys, and materials. What is to happen in the space is a factor in deciding how to set it up and what it needs. How much choice is to be encouraged is a consideration when setting up the environment. The degree of choice given to the children depends on the philosophy of the program and the age of the children; culture can have an influence too.

The Principles in Action

Principle 2 Invest in quality time, when you are totally available to individual infants and toddlers. Don't settle for supervising groups without focusing (more than just briefly) on individual children.

Mike has been working as a caregiver in a small infant-toddler center for some time. Fiona is a new caregiver in the center. Today the two caregivers are working together with a group of six infants. Except for one baby who is asleep, the others are on a soft rug surrounded by toy shelves. One baby who is not yet crawling is snuggled close to Mike and has several toys in reach. The others are crawling around between the toy shelves; they touch base with Mike and Fiona. Fiona gets up and goes into the kitchen area and begins cleaning out a drawer. Then she goes into the laundry area and folds sheets. Mike in the meantime holds out his arms to a boy who has crawled over to him with a book. He takes the book and reads it to the boy and to a girl who has crawled over to him. The baby on the floor reaches for the book and Mike hands her a plastic one, which she puts in her mouth. Mike notices that Fiona is still in the laundry area. "What are you doing, Fiona?" "Well," she responds, "I see that you can handle the kids, so I thought I should look busy in case the director comes in. We don't want him to find both of us just sitting around playing with the children!" Mike sees that Fiona still has some things to learn about how this program operates and the value of wants-nothing quality time. The director knows that what Mike is doing is an important part of the curriculum of this center. He'll expect Fiona to be doing the same.

1. Do you agree with what Mike is doing and thinking?
2. Would all directors be like Mike and Fiona's?
3. What if Fiona is the kind of person who can't stand to just sit around responding to children but enjoys keeping busy all the time?
4. If a parent came in and complained that the children weren't learning anything, what would you say about what Mike is doing?

Group Size and Age Span

An important environmental factor is group size. Larger groups tend to be over-stimulating, and quieter children get ignored. It's much harder for children to truly get absorbed in play in a large group than in a small one, even when the adult-to-child ratio is good.

Mixture of ages is another environmental factor. Adult preferences in age mixtures in groups vary. Some programs work well with a variety of ages; others work equally well with most of the children about the same age.

If you do mix ages, be aware of protecting the youngest children. In the case of infants mixed with toddlers, you must protect those who can't move around from those who can. One way to do this, if they are in the same room, is to fence off a portion of the room for the immobile children. Don't just keep them in playpens and cribs. They need floor space and room to stretch and move, as well as interactions that come from several infants and adults sharing floor space.

Setting Up the Environment to Support Play

NAEYC Program Standard 9
Physical Environment

Caregivers aren't providing structure by directing the play itself, but they structure the play environment. You can do away with most rules by setting up the environment so that a good deal of undesirable behavior is eliminated. For example, if the children aren't allowed to play in the kitchen, put a gate across the access. For a summary of what's involved in setting up the environment to support play, see Figure 4.4.

Make sure that everything in the environment is touchable and even **mouthable**. Mouthable, of course, means that an object is clean and safe for infants to put into their mouths. You can expect older children not to put things in their mouths, but infants and toddlers learn through mouthing. Sanitize toys periodically rather than restricting children from their natural inclinations.

Provide for **gross motor activity** inside as well as outside. Gross motor activity is an activity using the large muscles of the arms, legs, and trunk, such as climbing, rolling, sliding, and running. Toddlers run, climb, roll, and jump all the time—not just when invited to. You should think of your toddler play area as a gym more than a classroom and set it up for active play.

Provide plenty of softness, both for the active play and for the quiet times. Cushions, pads, mattresses, and foam rubber blocks on the floor invite children to bounce, roll, and flop down, as well as cuddle and snuggle with books or stuffed animals.

Reflect

Where was your favorite place to play as a child? How can you use your own experience to design a play environment for infants and toddlers?

Provide hard surfaces as well. A vinyl floor provides a contrast to carpeting and is interesting to crawlers as well as beginning walkers. Hard surfaces also make cleanup easier when you set up such activities as cooking or perhaps water play. (A thick bath mat under a plastic dishpan gives toddlers a chance to play in water without making too big a mess.)

Make available toys that can be used in many ways rather than toys meant to be used in only one way. Large foam blocks are an example. They can be hauled

Figure 4.4 Setting Up the Environment to Support Play

1. Keep play space separate from caregiving areas.
2. Make sure everything in the play space is touchable.
3. Provide for both fine and gross motor activity.
4. Provide both soft and hard materials and play surfaces.
5. Let children find unique ways to combine toys and materials.
6. Put out the right number of toys.
7. Provide the right number of choices.

around, stacked, put together to make a structure, or sat upon. There is much more to do with large foam blocks than, say, a battery-operated or wind-up toy that puts the child in the role of a spectator.

Let children combine toys and materials as much as possible. If they want to haul stuffed animals into a block structure they have built, let them. If they take pots and pans out of the play stove to put the play dough in, let them.

Of course you can't let everything be combined. Play dough in the water play table makes a mess nobody wants to have to clean up and wrecks the play dough besides. If you don't want something combined, make a clear **environmental limit**. An environmental limit is a physical barrier that keeps a child or material out of or inside of a given space and is often accompanied by a verbal limit. Fencing off stairs provides an environmental limit. Keeping the play dough inside when the water table is set up outside is another form of an environmental limit. Another example is leaving the play dough in the cupboard when water play is available inside. Without an environmental limit or in addition to one, verbal limits become important. "Water stays in the water table" is a clear and positive statement of a limitation.

Determine the right amount of toys to make available. Don't put out more than you can stand to pick up. Watch out for **overstimulation** or too much sensory input. Excited toddlers who have too many choices are more apt to make themselves and everyone else unhappy than those who have just enough to do. On the other hand, bored toddlers in a nearly empty room create as many behavior problems as those in a room overstuffed with toys and people. Be aware of the optimum number of things to do. You can judge the right number by the children's behavior. The optimum number changes with the day, the group, and even the time of year.

Happenings

We avoid the term *activities* when we focus on play because we want to move away from a preschool model for infants and toddlers. Instead, we use the term **happenings**, which broadens the idea of what infants and toddlers engage in and learn from. The use of the term *happenings* is intended to encompass the simplest event as well as more prolonged and complicated experiences. We borrowed the term from James Hymes, a pioneer in early childhood care and education and a longtime leader in our field. We've been asked over the years to include ideas for activities in this book, and we have resisted. Instead, we offer numerous examples throughout the book in the various scenarios. We do not point out that they are happenings. We leave it up to the reader to notice. We also avoid creating learning goals and objectives for happenings, because once an adult has a specific outcome in mind, the happening leaves the realm of free play and becomes something else. That doesn't mean that happenings are accidental. Lots of intention goes into planning for play for infants and toddlers. Intention is an important part of NAEYC's developmentally appropriate practice, a cornerstone of this book.

Happenings put the focus on the child's experience and they can be very simple and still be deeply satisfying. Again, when we use the word *happenings*, we don't mean they always occur by happenstance. Some things do come up by chance, and when they arise, it's the adult's job to take advantage of them. The first fall day after a big wind, a happening can be raking leaves in the play yard.

Other happenings are planned for by bringing them into the environment purposely. A favorite at one center is an ongoing collage. A large piece of contact paper put up on the wall (sticky side out) invites the children to stick various items on it. The continual rearrangement of the elements of this collage shows clearly how much more important the process is than the product at this age. We often think of infants' and toddlers' attention span as quite short, but the nature of this happening and the caregivers' ability to support and encourage the children showed otherwise. When older children's interest in a particular theme or subject lasts for a long period, it is often called a project. The sticky collage wasn't exactly a project. We like to think of it as an extended happening.

Some happenings that toddlers enjoy are modified versions of preschool activities. For example, easel painting can be done with plain water on chalk boards or thick soapsuds (colored with food coloring) on plexiglass easels. Sponge painting can become squeezing sponges in trays with a little water covering the bottom.

Even a passing rainstorm sets the environment up for a happening like this one.

One clever caregiver who knew how much infants and toddlers enjoy pulling tissues out of their box made a toy consisting of a tissue box filled with scarves tied together. Another simple happening the very young enjoy is crumpling tissue paper. (Use white so that if it gets wet, you don't have dye all over everything.)

Simple food preparation tasks (mashing bananas or peeling hard-boiled eggs) can delight toddlers. Even snapping spaghetti can be involving and satisfying for toddlers.

Free Choice

The environment should be set up to provide choices. Free choice is an important ingredient of play. Here is a scene that shows a playroom set up to encourage free play with numerous choices.

One end of the room is fenced off. In it three infants are lying on their backs, waving their arms, and looking around. An adult sits near them, rearranging brightly colored scarves to be within the reach of each child. A floppy beach ball is also available. One of the infants grabs it, waves it in the air, and lets it go. It lands near another of the infants, who regards it briefly, then turns back to gaze at the red scarf standing puffed up near his face.

Beyond the small fenced-in area is a larger space where nine young toddlers are playing. Two are busily engaged in crawling in and out of the rungs of the ladder that is lying flat on the floor. One leaves to sit in an empty laundry basket nearby. He climbs out, turns it over, then crawls under it. He lifts it up to look out at two children who are trying on hats from a collection they have found in a box near a shelf of toys. One of these children puts three hats on his head, then picks up two in his hands and runs over to the fence and throws the hats, one by one, into the area where the infants are lying. He giggles delightedly at the reaction he gets from the surprised infants. The other hat player in the meantime has loaded several into the back of a small toddler trike and is riding around the room. He stops at a low table where several children are squeezing plastic zip-top bags full of different substances. He looks at the caregiver sitting there when she says to one of the squeezers, "You really like the soft one, don't you?" He briefly pokes one of the bags. Finding it interesting, he abandons the hats and the trike and sits down at the table to explore the other bags.

In another area of the room, a girl is hauling large plastic-covered foam blocks from one corner and piling them on the couch, which is pulled out a few feet from the wall. Then she climbs up on the couch and proceeds to throw the cushions over the back until she has nearly filled the space. She gets down, walks around, and jumps on the pile she has made.

In another part of the room, a child is sitting with an adult on a large mattress (which actually is two sheets sewed together and filled with foam rubber scraps). The two are "reading" a book together. They are joined by one of the bag squeezers, who plops down on the adult's lap and takes the book away. It is quickly replaced by the other child, who has a stack of books next to her on the mattress.

In this scene the children have a number of choices. Free choice is an important ingredient of play as well as an important prerequisite to learning.

The Problem of the Match

J. McVicker Hunt talked about the relationship of learning to choice in terms of what he calls the "problem of the match." He said that learning occurs when the environment provides experiences just familiar enough that children can understand them with the mental ability they have already attained, but just new enough to offer interesting challenges.[8]

Learning occurs when there is optimum incongruity between what is already known and a new situation. If the situation is too new and different, children withdraw, become frightened, ignore it, or react in some way other than learning. If it is not novel enough, children ignore it. They won't pay attention to what has already become so much a part of them that it no longer registers.

McVicker Hunt relates to Jean Piaget's theory on assimilation and accommodation. Thinking evolves through adaptation as children seek to make sense of the environment by modifying it to fit personal needs as well as modifying the way they think in response to something new in the environment. Piaget saw adaptation as a two-part process—he called one part assimilation and the other accommodation. Assimilation means that new elements of experience are incorporated into existing structures of thought, which creates a tension when they don't fit. That's where accommodation comes in—new mental patterns are created or old ones are transformed in order to include the new information and make it fit.[9] This is another way of explaining McVicker Hunt's problem of the match.

The question is, how can you set up an environment so that it has elements of optimum incongruity? How does anyone know exactly what a match is for each child in his or her care? The first answer is to have some knowledge of ages and stages (see the environmental chart in Appendix B).

The other answer is by *observation*. When you watch the children, you have a good idea what kinds of things to put into the environment for your particular group. By providing a number of choices of appropriate toys, objects, and occurrences and letting the children play, you give them the opportunity to move to novel situations and novel uses of materials. No one is more creative than infants and toddlers when it comes to inventive uses of materials and objects. They have a need to learn, a desire to understand. Caregivers can capitalize on this need by letting them determine their own use of the environment (within reason of course). By directing children with either praise or pressure, we distract them from the inner delights mentioned by Abraham Maslow in Chapter 2. Children get these inner delights from struggling with a problem that matches their learning level.

Sooner or later children in an interesting, challenging environment are bound to find a problem that they want to solve but can't. They "get stuck." If they can't figure out the next move, the adult can intervene by providing a tiny bit of help.

Sometimes it's hard for adults to wait when they can solve a problem so easily. But if they wait, they provide children with the best learning opportunities. Don't rescue children from problems; help them problem solve.

And don't push children. Here's another view of "getting stuck." Sometimes children get stuck by becoming satiated with something. They have had enough of some activity. *Adults* decide that children are bored, and they want to do something about it—quickly! Many adults have a great fear of boredom for infants as well as for themselves. This fear has perhaps been heightened by the trend for infant stimulation and pressures for academics before kindergarten. Yet boredom is educational and can be considered part of the curriculum or learning plan of any program. Maslow was clear that there is no need to push children forward in their development. They will push themselves when they are ready.[10]

Children cannot push themselves on until they have done very thoroughly what it is they need to do. Until they have reached the state of boredom, they are still motivated by unfinished business and can't move on. Boredom, when they finally attain it, provides the push to move on—but the push comes from within, not from without. They can then leave behind the old level, the old needs, and deal with the new ones, giving them their full attention. When the push to move on comes from without—from the adult or the environment—children never quite satisfy themselves. They may move on to the next stage, task, or activity with leftover feelings from the previous one, perhaps unable to give full attention to the new one.

Magda Gerber used to say, "In time, not on time," meaning that each child has his or her own timetable and adults should respect that individuality. Emmi Pikler also had strong feelings about not pushing children to reach milestones and new stages. Both encouraged infants and toddlers to do thoroughly whatever it was they were doing, rather than urging them forward. That's a different way of looking at development that doesn't necessarily reflect common practice in the United States today; however, one of the authors has seen the results of the Gerber philosophy and the Pikler approach with her own eyes, and they are impressive!

A final word about pushing babies to learn more using technology. This chapter has described how play brings about the developmental unfolding of intelligence, but play as we know it is slowly being eroded at all age levels by screens—those interesting, colorful, moving/changing, shiny things that adults and older children spend so much time looking at. Of course, toddlers want them too—even infants, when they see them. Danger lies in the way very young children are distracted away from the real objects they can touch and manipulate and from the human face, voice, and touch that are so important to peer relationships as well as to attachment to family members. Screens for babies were originally advertised to make them smarter. Who could resist! Now we know from research that babies can become addicted to screens but don't show the same vocabulary advancement as babies without screens who had people who talked to them face to face.[11]

Appropriate Practice

Overview of Development

According to the National Association for the Education of Young Children, infants and toddlers love challenges and are interested in everything. When they are free to explore because warm adults encourage and take pleasure in their interests and skills, they grow, develop, and learn. Young infants play when they feel secure in a relationship. They play with people and objects using all their senses. They enjoy practicing a new skill and exploring objects and people by grasping, kicking, reaching, and pulling. A responsive and stimulating environment with plenty of time to fully experience the people and things in it provides young infants with the simple joys of relating. Mobile infants with their increased skills expand their playfulness by exploring space as well as objects and people. They develop their muscles through these explorations. They also develop cognitively as they experience and learn about what's around them. A sense of security allows infants and toddlers to make use of their capabilities to continually make discoveries and learn through playing.

Developmentally Appropriate Practice

The following are sample practices that link play as curriculum to the statement above:

- Playful interactions with babies are done in ways that are sensitive to the child's interests and level of tolerance for physical movement, loud sounds, or other changes.
- Adults show their respect for an infant's play by observing the child's activity, commenting on it verbally, and providing a safe environment. The quietly supportive adult encourages the child's active engagement.
- Adults frequently observe the infant at play. Appropriate games, such as peek-a-boo, are played with interested infants, the adult being careful not to intrude on how the infant wants to play.

- Adults engage in reciprocal play with toddlers, modeling for children how to play imaginatively—for example, playing "tea party." Caregivers also support toddlers' play so that children stay interested in an object or activity for longer periods of time and their play becomes more complex, moving from simple awareness and exploration of objects to more complicated play like pretending.
- Children have daily opportunities for exploratory activity, such as water and sand play, painting, and clay or play dough manipulatives.

Source: Carol Copple and Sue Bredekamp, eds., *Developmentally Appropriate Practice in Early Childhood Programs,* 3rd ed. (Washington, DC: National Association for the Education of Young Children, 2009).

Individually Appropriate Practice

Older infants and toddlers who are not mobile on their own need a more hands-on approach from caregivers than the typically developing mobile infant and toddlers. They can use what exploratory skills they have when caregivers move them around, find ways for them to move themselves, and make environmental adaptations that make it easier for these children to participate and play.

Culturally Appropriate Practice

Some families may not value play in the way others do. Some may not have an environment at home that allows for safe play and exploration. Others may not have a tradition of free play for children. It is important for caregivers to honor differences and seek to understand them.

Appropriate Practice in Action

Look again at the Principles in Action feature on page 81.

- Can you see the connection between the quality time in principle 2 that Mike is giving the children in his care and the points made in the "Developmentally Appropriate Practice" section of this Appropriate Practice box?

- Consider culturally appropriate practice. What might Mike or Fiona do if the families in the program did not have a safe environment for play at home and/or did not have a cultural tradition of free play for children?

Summary

Play and exploration are vital parts of the curriculum and important ways that infants and toddlers develop and learn. For infants and toddlers play involves movement that is greatly facilitated when they have the freedom to move to the extent they are able, rather than being restricted. Giving babies and toddlers free choice in a rich, developmentally appropriate, and interesting environment facilitates learning best. One of the things they develop during play is self-regulation.

Adult Roles in Play

- Setting up environments for play and making safety the primary consideration so that children are free to explore and discover
- Encouraging interactions and then stepping back so infants and toddlers aren't interrupted
- Supporting problem solving so that infants and toddlers learn persistence and come to see themselves as capable
- Observing as a way of understanding each child in each situation to promote learning

Environmental Factors That Influence Play

- Group size and age span influence the amount of attention children receive. Appropriate group size and a reasonable age span enable children to become absorbed in play.
- Setting up the environment to support play is an important factor in encouraging productive play. Truly productive play does not involve sitting infants and toddlers in front of screens, such as television or other handheld digital devices.
- The kind of happenings that occur are factors that facilitate rich play, exploration, and learning. Happenings include both planned and unplanned occurrences and include intentionality on the part of the caregivers.
- The amount of free choice available is a vital factor as infants and toddlers know what they need and can pursue what interests them.
- The problem of the match is a factor that enables children to choose happenings that match their interest and level of learning.

Key Terms

environmental limit 83
exploration 73
free play 73

gross motor activity 82
happenings 83
mouthable 82

overstimulation 83
selective intervention 76

Thought/Activity Questions

1. How is the term *model* used in this chapter?
2. If play is so important, should adults let children play freely? Why or why not?
3. Most books on infant-toddler care and education use the term *activity*. Why don't we?
4. What is scaffolding and what does it have to do with play?
5. What is the problem of the match, and how is it related to Piaget's theory on assimilation and accommodation?
6. What are some advantages of the caregiver being in an observation mode?

For Further Reading

Laura Berk, "Make-Believe Play: Wellspring for Development of Self-Regulation" in *Play-Learning: How Play Motivates and Enhances Children's Cognitive and Social-Emotional Growth*, ed. Dorothy G. Singer (New York: Oxford University Press, 2006).

Deb Curtis, Kasondra L. Brown, Lorrie Baird, and Anne Marie Coughlin, "Planning Environments and Materials that Respond to Young Children's Lively Minds," *Young Children* 68(4), September, 2013, pp. 26–31.

Alison Gopnik, "Let the Children Play, It's Good for Them!" *Smithsonian Magazine*, July-August, 2012.

Enid Elliot and Janet Gonzalez-Mena, "Self-regulation: Taking a Broader Perspective," *Young Children*, (67)5, January 2011, pp. 28–33.

Éva Kálló and Györgyi Balog, *The Origins of Free Play*, trans. Maureen Holm (Budapest: Association PiklerLóczy for Young Children, 2005).

Rae Pica, "Babies on the Move," *Young Children*, 65(4), July 2010, pp. 48–49.

Deborah Carlisle Solomon, *Baby Knows Best: Raising a Confident and Resourceful Child, the RIE Way* (New York: Little Brown, 2013).

Zero to Three, 30(1), September 2009. The whole journal is dedicated to the subject of the importance of play.

part two

Focus on the Child

chapter 5

Attachment

Focus Questions

After reading this chapter you should be able to answer the following questions:

1 Define *attachment*. What factors influence its development?

2 How is brain development influenced by attachment?

3 Why is it important to know about *attachment milestones*?

4 What are some circumstances in which Ainsworth's patterns might be questionable when it comes to understanding and labeling the degree or kind of attachment?

5 What can adults do to foster attachment in young children? Include any unique issues related to children with special needs.

What Do You See?

A small baby, lying on the floor on a blanket in the family room of the home where he is being cared for, is crying. A reassuring voice comes from the other room. "I know you are hungry! I'm coming!" The cries cease at the sound of the voice, but then begin again when no one immediately appears. The family child care provider hustles into the room carrying a warm bottle. "I'm sorry you had to wait." The crying continues. "I know, I know. I'm going to pick you up now so that you can eat." She bends over with her arms outstretched and gently lifts the baby. The crying slows down; the caregiver walks across the room to sit down in a soft chair.

As he is picked up, the baby's whole body shows his anticipation of what is to come. He stiffens and his arms wave in excitement. He looks intensely into his caregiver's face. Once settled into the chair, he begins to squirm frantically, his mouth searching for the nipple. As it comes into his mouth, he closes his eyes, clenches his fists, and sucks furiously. "There you are. That's better, isn't it?" coos the caregiver. He begins to relax after a few minutes, and both adult and child settle back, moving around until comfortable. "You were really hungry, weren't you?" The baby continues to suck without stopping; after a few moments, he begins to ease up a little. His fists unclench, and one hand reaches out, groping. The caregiver touches his hand with her finger; he wraps his fingers around her finger and holds on tight. The caregiver snuggles him a little closer and kisses the top of his head. He opens his eyes and looks up at her. She looks back, a warm smile on her face. He stops sucking and lets go of the nipple. With his gaze fixed on his caregiver's face, his mouth breaks into a big grin. Then he snuggles in even closer and continues to suck contentedly, his little fist wrapped around her finger, his eyes looking into hers.

This is what **attachment** looks like! It is a complex, ongoing process. Its definitions may vary, but in essence it involves a *closeness* and a *responsiveness* to an infant. This chapter discusses this important and special two-way relationship between an infant and an adult, and describes how brain development is influenced by early quality-care experiences. It examines behavioral milestones related to attachment, the measurement of secure and insecure attachment patterns, and related contemporary issues. It also discusses the importance of early intervention for a child with special needs to avoid a disruptive attachment. Continuity of care and the importance of responsive relationships are discussed throughout the chapter as key to the development of early healthy attachments. Very young children are both competent and vulnerable, and they rely on consistent and positive experiences with one or more special adults to become secure and self-reliant.

Brain Research

We have learned more about the human brain in the last 10 years than in the previous 100! See Table 5.1 for a summary of how our understanding of brain development has changed. Today technologies in neuroscience that are noninvasive (they don't interfere with natural brain function) are making detailed exploration of the brain possible. Amazing tools exist for mapping the brain and for understanding brain chemistry, as well as for appreciating the effects of environmental factors. This information has taught us many valuable lessons about how infants learn and why early experience is so vital to development. Looking at a brief overview of how the brain functions may help to foster an appreciation of just why particularly responsive, positive experiences are so important to an infant's early development.

Table 5.1 Rethinking the Brain	
Old Thinking	**New Thinking**
How a brain develops depends on the *genes* you are born with.	How a brain develops hinges on a complex *interplay* between the *genes* you're born with and the *experiences* you have.
The *experiences* you have before age three have a *limited impact* on later development and learning.	*Early experiences* help to shape the architecture of the brain, which can affect both development and learning.
A *secure relationship* with a primary caregiver creates a favorable *context* for early development and learning.	*Early interactions* don't just create a context; they *directly affect* the way the brain develops.
Brain development is *linear;* the brain's capacity to learn and change grows steadily as an infant progress toward adulthood.	Brain development is *nonlinear;* there are prime times for acquiring different kinds of knowledge and skills throughout life.

Source: Rima Shore, *Rethinking the Brain: New Insights into Early Development.* Copyright 1997. Revised 2003. Families and Work Institute, 267 Fifth Avenue, New York, NY 10016. 212-465-2044. www.familiesandwork.org.

Brain Building Blocks and Brain Circuitry

The basic building blocks of the brain are specialized nerve cells called **neurons**. Each neuron has an **axon**, or output fiber, that sends energy, or impulses, to other neurons. Neurons also have many **dendrites**, which are input fibers that receive the impulses from other neurons. The dendrites grow and branch out forming "dendrite trees" that receive signals from other neurons. These connections, or **synapses**, are formed as an infant experiences the world. The connections used regularly in everyday life become reinforced, or protected, and become part of the brain's permanent "circuitry." The human brain at birth is still very immature, so these early experiences can have a dramatic effect over time on an infant's growth and learning.[1]

In the early years, young brains produce almost twice as many synapses as they will need. The dendrite trees grow and become very dense. By age two, the number of synapses a toddler has is similar to that of an adult. By three the child has twice as many synapses as an adult. This large number is stable throughout the first 10 years, but by adolescence about half of these synapses have been discarded or "pruned." The brain *prunes*, or selectively eliminates, unnecessary synapses.

The key question is, how does the brain *know* which synapses, or connections, to keep and which ones to prune, or discard? Early experience seems to be much more critical than first realized. Experiences activate neural pathways, and information in the form of chemical signals gets stored along the pathways. Repeated experiences strengthen specific pathways. A particular pathway takes on a "protected" status; it is not pruned because it has been repeatedly used. This is a normal, lifelong process of brain neural development. Pruning, however, is not a "use it or lose it" scenario, as earlier brain research sometimes described it. Unused synapses are pruned, but neurons remain intact for later learning.[2] This helps to explain the brain's amazing plasticity, or flexibility, if it experiences damage or trauma.

Quality Experiences and Stable Neural Pathways

This text emphasizes the importance of quality experiences and responsive care for very young children. Now brain development research indicates that these early experiences, if repeated, actually form stable neural pathways. The way we think and learn has everything to do with the extent and nature of these pathways. When a very young child experiences something new, or a problem, brain activity increases and neural pathways grow. If neural pathways are strong, signals travel quickly and the child can solve problems easily.

Pause for a moment and think about a 10-month-old child whose mom is taking him to his child care provider as she goes off to work. He may experience a certain amount of stress (this is called "stranger anxiety" and will be discussed in more detail later in the chapter). However, when his caregiver is familiar with and can be responsive to his stress signals, he comes to *know* that he will be OK (the caregiver is a familiar friend and today his blanket is of particular comfort to cuddle and smell). His mother will return. In his brain, connections have been formed that allow him to separate with relatively little effort. Through his experiences he has

NAEYC Program Standard 1
Relationships

Invest in quality time. Be available and responsive.

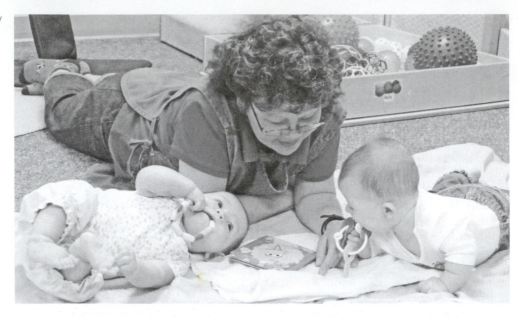

already developed efficient neural pathways. Responsive, positive experiences stabilize connections in his brain. These very early connections in the brain are related to attachment experiences. *Remember principle 2: Invest in quality time, when you are totally available to individual infants and toddlers.* Don't settle for supervising groups without focusing (more than just briefly) on individual children.

Through attachment, two individuals come together and stay together. John Kennell defines attachment as "an affectionate bond between two individuals that endures through space and time and serves to join them emotionally."[3] The mother is usually the first and primary attachment the baby makes, but babies are becoming more and more strongly attached to their fathers, especially as working mothers spend more time out of the home. When infants experience child care at a young age, these secondary attachments (people other than their parents) become very important.

Attachment to caregivers differs from that to parents in many ways. One obvious way is in duration. The long-term, even lifetime attachment a parent has is a much shorter period for caregivers. From day one, caregivers know that the children will leave their charge long before they grow up. The departure may come without warning because parents' lives and need for child care sometimes change suddenly. There is a big difference in this expectation of permanence of the adult-child relationship between parents and caregivers.

Parental attachment, this feeling of closeness, starts right at birth for some. In the ideal situation, where parents and an alert newborn are allowed time together to get acquainted, what is called "bonding" may occur as they fall in love in a very short time. It might even be called "love at first sight." This love at first sight can occur between caregivers and children, too, as an adult and a child are drawn to each other at first meeting. More commonly, attachment grows slowly over time as individuals get to know each other and learn each other's special ways of communicating. These special ways grow and change as children reach developmental milestones. The brain research now available to parents and caregivers validates that warm, positive interactions stabilize connections in the brain. High-quality, responsive care must be provided for this critical process called *attachment* to thrive.

Mirror Neurons: Actions and Observations

Brain research may give us additional insight into the attachment process and how infants seem to promote their own attachments. **Mirror neurons**, and their implication for human brain evolution, may be one of the most important discoveries related to brain development in the last decade. A mirror neuron is a neuron that fires both when an animal (and, it is now believed, a human) acts and when the animal observes the same action performed by another animal. The mirror neuron system was initially found by neuroscientists studying monkey brains and tasks involving intentional movements. Mirror neurons, located in the front of the brain, were active when monkeys performed certain motor tasks; they were also active when the monkeys *observed* another monkey perform the same tasks. Interestingly, the monkeys did not imitate the activities when robots performed them—only when another monkey did. Mirror neurons distinguish between biological and nonbiological actors and seem to have some awareness of intention or goal (most of the activities involved getting food!).[4]

Evidence suggests that a similar observation action matching system exists in humans. We have all no doubt observed young infants imitating the mouth movements of their caregiver or parent during feeding or playtimes. This mouthing is one of the early "attachment behaviors" infants may use to extend the experience of getting food or social interaction. Imitation seems to foster a *link*— mimicry binds and brings people together. Neuroscientists and child development professionals are currently looking at the role of mirror neurons and social (attachment) understanding. A neural system that allows a brain to observe and then imitate the observed movement would be an ideal learning and social system—and that's what mirror neurons do.[5]

Current brain research continues to support the following significant findings:

- Nature (genes) and nurture (environment) interact on a continuous basis.
- Early responsive care and warm, stable relationships foster attachment and lead to healthy brain growth.
- By the age of three, the brains of young children are two-and-a-half times more active than the brains of adults.
- Very young children participate in their own brain development by signalling their needs.
- Strong neural pathways are created by experiences, especially responsive relationships.

EXPLORE the following websites for more information and resource material.

Zero to Three provides numerous resources that support the healthy development of infants, toddlers, and their families; material is updated regularly.

www.zerotothree.org/brainwonders

Better Brains for Babies provides families and child care professionals with current research-based information on early brain development.

www.fcs.uga.edu/ext/bbb

The Principles in Action

Principle 9 Build security by teaching trust. Don't teach distrust by being undependable or often inconsistent.

"Look at this dolly, Cameron," says her mother as she tries to get 12-month-old Cameron involved in the dress-up area. The two have just arrived, and this is the mother's first day to leave her daughter. The caregiver approaches, says hello, and then gets down at Cameron's level. The baby looks at her. Cameron has visited the center several times and recognizes the caregiver, but she's never stayed without her mother. She smiles happily and holds out a doll to show the caregiver. When the caregiver stands up to talk to the mother, she discovers the mother is gone. She had said earlier that she can't stand to see her daughter cry, so apparently she just decided to sneak out. Cameron continues holding the doll, but then she looks around and can't find her mother. She looks puzzled, and then she begins to cry. She ends up wracked in sobs, and the caregiver has a hard time comforting her. The caregiver decides to speak to the mother at the end of the day and tell her about the importance of saying good-bye so that her daughter can predict when she is going to leave. In her experience, children who have no good-bye ritual can't relax because they never know when people come and go in their lives. She knows that trust is an important issue for Cameron, and she knows it will take time. The first step is to get the mother to say good-bye. Imagine that you are this caregiver.

1. How do you feel about the mother's behavior?
2. How do you feel about Cameron?
3. How do you feel about the situation?
4. Do you agree that the caregiver should talk to the mother? Why or why not?
5. Could the mother's behavior come from a cultural difference?
6. What else might you do to help Cameron establish trust?

Milestones of Attachment

Important milestones of attachment influence mental, social, and emotional development. A baby's crying, pulling away from strangers, and trying to follow a departing parent indicate how attachment changes. Looking at these behaviors in more detail clarifies how competent an infant is.

Attachment Behaviors: Birth to Six Months

Babies are designed to promote their own attachment. Think for a moment about the variety of behaviors that attract adults to babies. A newborn's cry elicits feelings in the people who hear it. It is hard to ignore. Crying becomes one of the infant's strongest signals to the people responsible for his or her care.

Another strong attachment behavior most babies have at birth is the ability to establish eye contact. When a newborn looks right into their eyes, most adults melt. And if you touch the little fingers, they are likely to curl around your big one. If you talk to alert newborns, they are likely to turn toward the sound of your voice. And if you move away from them slightly, their eyes will follow your face. All these behaviors promote attachment.

Studies indicate that babies react differently to the people they are attached to right from the beginning. Later this preferential response becomes obvious as babies cry when the object of attachment leaves the room. This is an important indication that **trust** is developing. They follow the person with whom they have the attachment, first with gaze alone, then, when they are mobile, by crawling after them.

Pause and review the scene at the beginning of this chapter involving the feeding experience and the interaction between the baby and caregiver. This is a special relationship. These two are a unit. Both feel that this is an intimate moment of a close relationship. This special form of communication—**interactional synchrony**—is like an "emotional dance." The caregiver and the baby send each other important signals. Both partners share emotions, especially positive ones.[6] The infant has the capacity to elicit delight from another; this in turn gives him pleasure. The example of the feeding experience illustrates some of the repertoire of behaviors involved in attachment. Through these mutually responsive behaviors, which include touching, fondling, and eye contact, as well as feeding, infants and adults form an extremely close relationship. Remember, too, that the information on the brain indicates that these early behaviors begin to form pathways in the brain and may stimulate mirror neurons. These pathways form the *physical foundation* of trust. Positive experiences stabilize the brain connections. Infants need this relationship because they cannot physically attach themselves to people to get nourished and cared for. They are dependent. Attachment is nature's way of ensuring that someone will care (in the emotional sense) and provide care (in the physical sense). *Remember principle 1: Involve infants and toddlers in things that concern them.* Don't work around them or distract them to get the job done faster.

Attachment Behavior: Seven to Eighteen Months

Once babies can distinguish their mother or caregiver from other people, two new worries begin. First, at about 8 to 10 months of age, babies begin to fear strangers. Second, now that they know who mother is, they worry about losing her. This latter fear usually appears by about 10 to 12 months. Both of these fears indicate the infant's ability to discriminate and recognize difference and therefore are obvious signs of mental growth. Corresponding to this second developmental fear is the baby's inability to understand that objects gone from sight still exist. Jean Piaget called this "object permanence"; it will be discussed further in Chapter 8. Infants' worry about losing their mother is understandable. They cannot foresee that a separation is only temporary. Knowing this, caregivers find it easier to understand a baby's desperate protest when he or she is left behind as a parent walks out the door.

It may be helpful to emphasize the interplay between dependency, mental development, and trust in this process of attachment. When an 18-month-old child is clinging to his mother and crying for her not to go (obvious dependent behavior), he is also saying "I *know* I need you" (a mental function). As his mental capacity grows, and his experiences teach him that he can trust his mother to return, from attachment comes trust as he learns that the world is basically a friendly place where he can get his needs met. From attachment also comes **autonomy**, or independence, as babies grow and begin to take over their caregiving by learning self-help skills. They also find it easier and easier to let go because they know that their parent will be back. This ability to trust a relationship is the foundation for independence—a focus of the toddler period.

This worry about leaving the parent or primary caregiver is called "separation anxiety." It is usually at its peak as the baby nears the end of the first year of life. If the child enters child care just at this time, the beginning can be very difficult. Children do better if they enter child care before or after the peak of separation anxiety.

Supporting Attachment in Quality Programs

In a quality infant-toddler child care program (center- or home-based), children gain courage to explore and participate (fostering mental and social skills) by using their parent or known caregiver as a home or trust base. Checking in periodically provides renewed energy to move out and continue exploration. It is important when the parent leaves that he or she not sneak away. By saying good-bye, the parent helps the child appreciate that the departure is predictable. Gradually a child learns that coming back is also part of saying good-bye. A sensitive caregiver can put into words what she perceives a potentially upset child to be feeling. Acceptance of these feelings, and not distraction from them, provides a young child with a secure base for emotional development.

The following suggestions may assist caregivers in helping parents with toddlers suffering from separation anxiety:

1. Help the parent understand that once the good-byes are said, the departure should be immediate. Help the parent know that you understand it is

Reflect

Remember Cameron in the Principles in Action box on page 98? What would you try to tell her mother about the developmental milestones of attachment? How can you help this mother better understand her child's crying?

hard to leave, but that it is easier on the child if departure is quick once the good-byes are said.

2. Allow the child his or her feelings, but don't get involved in them yourself. Avoid being a caregiver who distracts a child from his feelings or tries to minimize upset feelings.

3. Have an interesting, even enticing environment that calls out to children so that when they are ready, they can easily get involved with other people or simple activities.

Attachment is vital to infants' and toddlers' development and should be promoted in child care programs. At the same time, caregivers should realize that parents may fear their children may gain secondary attachments outside the

VIDEO OBSERVATION 5

Toddler "Checking in" While Playing with Chairs

See Video Observation 5: Toddler "Checking in" While Playing with Chairs for an illustration of how toddlers "touch home base" during free play. You'll see a child interrupt his play by going over to the caregiver, almost as if to recharge his batteries. This behavior is a sign of attachment.

Questions

1. If you were trying to explain behaviors that show the child is feeling attached to a caregiver, how would you describe this scene?

2. Have you ever seen a toddler "checking in" like this toddler did? If yes, think about how that scene was the same as or different from this one. If no, think about how it *might be* different. For example, sometimes the child just looks over at the adult instead of making physical contact.

To view this clip, go to www.mhhe.com/itc10e. Click on Student Edition, select Chapter 5, and click on Video Observations.

DEVELOPMENTAL PATHWAYS

Attachment

Preattachment: Indiscriminate Reactions (birth to approximately 12 weeks)

Early behaviors—crying, gazing, grasping—are designed to bring adults close to infants and to provide nurturance and comfort. The infant is not yet *attached*, because this care can be provided by any adult.

Making the Attachment: Focusing on Familiar People (10 weeks to 6–8 months)

Infants now begin to respond differently to different people. Social responses—cooing, smiling, babbling—are readily displayed with familiar caregivers. A stranger may receive a long stare and cause fear or distress. This stage is when trust begins to develop.

Clear Attachment: Active Closeness Is Sought (8 months to 18–24 months)

Now attachment to familiar people is clear. Young children show separation anxiety, becoming distressed when familiar people they trust leave them. Now young children *know they need* someone (a cognitive function) and send deliberate social signals, like clinging and resisting separation, to keep familiar people near them. The child is using her caregiver as a *secure base* from which to gradually explore a new environment and then return for emotional support.

A Reciprocal Relationship: Partnership Behavior (24 months on)

Young children now begin to understand an adult's coming and going. They are more able to let go and can be more flexible. Language helps them to process the separation experience (for example, "I'll be back after your nap").

home at the expense of their primary ones with parents. Caregivers can help ease parents' fears by letting them know they are unfounded. The secondary attachments are in addition to the primary ones, not replacements for them. Separation anxiety and all the feelings that go with being left in child care are also of concern to both parents and caregivers, who have to help children cope until they feel comfortable. It may comfort parents to know that these feelings are a sign that attachment is strong and that it will hold. Children will learn to cope with separation, and this skill will serve them for a lifetime. The various attachment behaviors and coping skills that develop in children indicate they are establishing trust in others and, at the same time, becoming self-reliant.

Measuring Attachment

What happens to the child who cannot get nurturing responses from people in her environment? And what about the child who seems indifferent or rejecting of the people around her? Developmental psychologist Mary Ainsworth created the **Strange Situation**, a sequence of staged situations, to answer such questions and to measure attachment strength between a mother and child. In this experiment the mother and infant enter a new environment and the baby is free to play. Then a stranger enters, and the mother leaves, and finally the stranger leaves and the mother returns. During this series of departures and reunions the reactions of infants can vary a great deal and are used to indicate a *pattern* of attachment behavior.

Securely attached infants and toddlers seem comfortable in the new setting and explore independently as long as the parent is present. Their degree of distress may vary when the parent leaves, but they immediately go to the mother when she returns and seek contact and comfort. Young children with an insecure avoidant attachment pattern do not seek closeness to the mother and do not seem distressed when the parent departs. They also seem to avoid the mother when she returns—they seem indifferent to the mother's behavior. Finally, young children with an insecure ambivalent (resistant) attachment pattern show positive and negative reactions to their parent. Initially, they seem very anxious, are reluctant to separate, and are in such close contact with their mother they hardly explore the new setting. They show great distress when their mother leaves and show ambivalent reactions when their mother returns (seeking closeness, but also hitting and kicking the mother in anger and remaining resistant to comforting). Secure attachment patterns were related to mothers who responded rapidly and positively to their babies. In contrast, insecurely attached infants were ignored or rejected, or were responded to inconsistently by their mothers.[7]

Some expansion of Ainsworth's research (especially work with abused and neglected children) indicates a fourth pattern called disorganized-disoriented. Young children with this attachment pattern show contradictory behavior by approaching the parent/caregiver but also looking away. They also show signs of fear, confusion, and disorientation, and they may be the least securely attached children of all.[8]

Early Research and Contemporary Issues

Most of the early research on attachment (especially that of John Bowlby, 1951, and Mary Ainsworth, 1978) focused on mothers and attachment. Things have changed since that research was done. Now there is more focus on men's roles in nurturance, sensitivity, and support, which leads to the attachment that used to be considered only mothers' territory. Fathers are not necessarily just the *other* parent; in some cases they are the *only* parent. Child care has made a difference in attachment patterns, as has the growing awareness of cultural diversity. Some children live in extended families or kinship networks and may have multiple attachments rather than a single strong one to just the mother. The mother, or even the father, may not be the primary person to whom the child is attached. Many more children from all kinds of backgrounds now are in early care and education settings starting from a few weeks old.

Imagine a child who is almost three years old and barely looks up from the sandbox when his mother arrives to pick him up. Is this indifference to the parent really a sign of insecure attachment? Could it be that he feels at home in the child care setting where he has been for most of his life? Maybe he is engaged in something interesting at the moment of her arrival. If he gets tested in the

Reflect

Have you observed a child in a new situation who did not react in the ways Ainsworth described? What might account for these different reactions?

Ainsworth Strange Situation, maybe he is so used to *separating* from his mother and going to other people that he just takes advantage of the toys in the room. He doesn't respond like Ainsworth's "securely attached" child when his mother leaves or when she comes back. We have to be careful about generalizing from research that was done in a certain time period, in different circumstances, and on different populations from the ones in child care today. Judging the degree or kind of attachment without understanding the bigger picture—including diversity, cultural awareness, and varied family lifestyles—can be harmful!

Attachment Issues

Not all babies enjoy an ideal relationship that fosters a secure attachment. The infant and caregiver may not respond to each other in ways that bring mutual delight and the quality care necessary for the infant.

Infants with Few Attachment Behaviors

Sometimes infants are born without a strong set of attachment behaviors. They may not be responsive or attractive. Adults may find it neither rewarding nor satisfying to interact with such babies or to meet their needs. Not only may these infants lack a set of pleasing behaviors, they may even reject any advances. They may constantly stiffen when cuddled or cry when touched. Some babies are just not responsive. They may be too active to attend, or too passive. In these cases, it is up to adults to promote attachment.

Caregivers can promote a secure attachment by being supportive, persistent, and not being put off by the baby. Sensitive caregivers find ways that cause less discomfort to hold the babies who reject them. They continue to touch and talk to these babies despite rejection. They use caregiving times to interact and pay attention to the child at other times as well. Sometimes just observing such babies regularly and in depth will help caregivers develop more positive and respectful feelings for them.

Caregivers also find ways to help too active and too passive babies attend. They discover ways to reduce stimulation or increase sensory input, depending on what is needed.

Center-based programs can provide for attachment needs through a primary-caregiver system in which babies are assigned to a particular caregiver. Group size is important if babies are to be responded to consistently and sensitively in order to promote attachment. More than about 12 babies works against such attachment.

Infants Who Experience Neglect or Indifference

Sometimes the attachment issues lie with the parents. The infant may be fully equipped with attachment behaviors, but the parent may fail to respond. Indifference or neglect, for whatever reason, can be devastating to an infant. The infant doesn't give up for a long time and may develop a set of behaviors that elicits a negative response from the adult, which is better than no response at all.

If the baby has no attachment or negative attachment, that is cause for alarm. Outside help is required. Child care workers may perceive the problem and refer the families for outside help, but it is beyond the caregiver's responsibility to solve attachment problems.

You may suspect this problem when a baby in your care does not thrive in the same way the other babies do. He or she may not be gaining weight or reaching milestones within a reasonable time. This attachment problem and failure to thrive may be related to a variety of other causes. You may see that the baby is unresponsive and resistant to everybody. Or perhaps you see him or her responding exactly the same to everyone—parent, caregiver, or stranger.

What happens if there is no attachment? A significant answer came from Harry Harlow, who learned something about attachment without even setting out to study it. He was interested in isolating rhesus monkeys so that they could live in a disease-free environment and not infect one another. He raised 56 newborn monkeys in separate cages, away from one another and their mothers. He was surprised to find that they grew to be very different adults from the rest of their species. They were more unsocial, indifferent, and aggressive than other rhesus monkeys, which are normally social and cooperative. None of the monkeys raised in isolation mated.[9]

Let's examine the implications for child rearing. Although virtually no one attempts to raise a child in total isolation, children are too frequently raised without enough human contact, without opportunities for interaction, and without consistent treatment. In such a situation, the problems are multiple. Though the infants have contact with adults who feed and change them, the adults may vary from day to day. The infants may be unable to distinguish one from the other or may find that their attachment behavior brings no consistent caregiving response. They find no one to call their own—no one whom they can influence. Eventually, such children give up and no longer try to influence anyone. Lacking not only attachment but also adequate physical contact, these infants are deprived of the variety of sensory input that comes with a healthy relationship. They become passive and noncomplaining, their development slows, and they may fail to thrive. Researchers believe it is important for babies to establish a consistent attachment to at least one person before four to six months of age.[10] *Remember principle 9: Build security by teaching trust.* Don't teach distrust by being undependable or often inconsistent.

Brain Growth and Attachment-Based Programs

Caregivers and home-based care providers who have some understanding of the attachment process can do a great deal to help parents recognize their importance and their impact on their infant. Offering labels for facial expressions and baby sounds and encouraging parents to slow down and observe their child's growing competence can go a long way toward fostering the vital, secure attachment relationship between an infant and parent.

This consistent and sensitive care is emphasized in the brain development research. When infants experience these secure attachments, hormones called **neurotransmitters** are secreted, and they induce a sense of well-being.

Trauma, and/or neglect, can reduce the secretion of these important hormones. Positive, nurturing experiences seem to reinforce certain pathways in the brain. There is a dynamic relationship between the *care* an infant receives and his or her brain *growth*. Healthy attachment develops when caregivers are consistent and responsive; relationships are primary to development.[11]

Studies of children in institutions where there was no attempt to promote attachment have kept many people from considering group care for infants. But infants in child care are different from infants in such institutions. They have parents (at least one). Most of them arrive in child care attached, and they remain attached. But we have learned from those studies of institutionalized babies who lacked attachment. We know now how vital attachment needs are. We know, too, that infants need ongoing, reciprocal, responsive interactions when they are outside their own home for significant periods during the day. We know that infants in child care retain their attachments to their parents.

Reflect

Think about what you have read concerning attachment and maybe anything that you have had the opportunity to observe. What can caregivers do to demonstrate their sensitivity to young children? What do infants and toddlers do to demonstrate their needs to caregivers?

Knowledge about caring relationships is transforming caregivers' work with very young children. Building and maintaining positive relationships that will continue over time, sometimes over several years, is a critical principle in "attachment-based" programs. This continuity of care begins with the creation of small groups of infants, each with its own qualified caregiver. Caregivers plan for each child, creating individualized portfolios for them. They plan for parents, too, encouraging them to observe the program and visit often. The caregiver-child relationship becomes an extension of the parent-child relationship. The environment is even organized with relationship continuity and secure attachments in mind; each group has its own room or space, and it is used exclusively by that group.[12] Research shows that infant care is not detrimental to development and to secure attachments if the *quality* of care is exemplary. Relationship-based programs appreciate that quality care is vital. Infants not only deserve but *must have* fine care, not just care that is good enough.

Children with Special Needs: The Importance of Early Intervention

Some infants and toddlers today may have attachment concerns because of developmental problems or delays. In the last thirty years much has been accomplished to support these young children and their families with an appropriate "service system" that contributes to their healthy growth and development. Responsive care and respectful family-centered interactions are key principles in this process of providing appropriate developmental support to young children with special needs.

What Is Early Intervention?

Early intervention is a process of identifying young children with disabilities, or "at risk" for developing disabilities, and creating a plan for supports so that they can achieve their full potential. The experience and opportunities outlined in the plan are based on the developmental needs of the child, looking specifically at their abilities within the cognitive, motor, communication, emotional-social, and adaptive areas of growth. Early intervention tends to be defined by an age range (before three years), as opposed to a specific disability or category, and it strives to illustrate or clarify a child's needs by use of observational detail, rather than the use of specific screening tools.

Early intervention encompasses a "multidisciplinary" approach in which a team of professionals works together to assess a child's unique strengths and needs. Team members include specialists from various fields or disciplines including health, psychology, medicine, early childhood, and special education. The team must include a family member or parent, and their questions and concerns are recognized as critical in order to determine the best plan for the child that is both comprehensive and culturally sensitive.

The Laws That Guide Early Intervention

It became clear over the years that specialized supports can increase the chances for a young child with a disability to achieve his full potential. Different states, however, addressed challenging issues differently, and a national agenda for an early intervention system was needed. In 1975 landmark legislation that set the stage for early intervention was passed, the Education for All Handicapped Children Act (Public Law 94-142). It stated that children with disabilities ages 6 to 21 years were entitled to free and appropriate public education, in the least restrictive environment (LRE), based on the child's needs and the family's preferences. Subsequent legislation, the Education of the Handicapped Act of 1986 (Public Law 99-457), extended services from birth to 21 years and the importance of an early intervention system for infants and toddlers was established.[13] Continuing refinements and amendments to this legislation, most recently the Individuals with Disabilities Education Improvement Act (IDEA, 2004, Public Law 108-446), have made clear the key principles related to early intervention. Services for very young children need to be in inclusive, not isolated, settings. The environment should be "natural," stressing everyday life, preferably a child's home or an early care and education program. Developmental assessment is mandated in Part C of IDEA 2004, and it must involve the family and reflect the unique strengths of the whole child. The process should be culturally sensitive, timely, comprehensive, and cost effective. Once the need for a referral is established, the Individualized Family Service Plan (IFSP) is developed. The IFSP is specific to children birth to three years old. The IEP (Individual Education Plan), also mentioned in Part C/IDEA 2004, is designed for children older than three years and its recommendations are primarily directed toward preschool and the public school system.

The Benefits and Challenges of Early Intervention

The major benefit of early intervention is that it can support young children with disabilities early in their development in overcoming many of the obstacles they face in their efforts to learn and to achieve their full developmental potential. It can also reduce the chance that a child will develop a secondary complication. For example, it is important to provide early support to a child with a motor disability so that a communication delay does not develop if his lack of physical coordination gets in the way of meaningful interactions that support language development. Early intervention programs also provide support to families to assist them in times of stress and to help them access relevant resources.

Recognizing which differences and/or delays may be temporary and which may persist is a major challenge. Finding a support resource "in time" versus assuming a child "will grow out of it" can make a huge difference in a child's long-term learning opportunities. Assisting families in their efforts to find the most appropriate resource and helping them to manage the stress often associated with the care of a child with special needs can be challenges to the most experienced caregivers.

Don't hesitate to get more information and find resources about early intervention and program support if you have questions concerning any child in your care. Remember that the primary focus of this chapter is attachment and intentional care, and it is vital to the development of all children. Responsive caregivers may be the first to intervene if they suspect that a child in their care has a disability. This early intervention can be key to establishing healthy growth in the long term, but it is critical to first recognize for any young child the importance of secure attachment.

NAEYC Program Standard 4
Assessment

DEVELOPMENTAL PATHWAYS

Attachment Behaviors

Attachment Behaviors

Young Infants (up to 8 months)	• Show they recognize their primary caregivers by sight, sound, and smell within the first two weeks of life • Respond with more animation and pleasure to the primary caregiver than to others • React to strangers with soberness or anxiety around the second half of the first year
Mobile infants (up to 18 months)	• May exhibit anxious behavior around unfamiliar adults • Actively show affection for a familiar person • May show anxiety at separation from the primary caregiver • Show intense feelings for parents
Toddlers (up to 3 years)	• May exhibit the same attachment behaviors as mobile infants but become increasingly aware of their own feelings and those of others • Express emotions with increasing control • May verbalize feelings once they start talking

Source: Carol Copple and Sue Bredekamp, eds., *Developmentally Appropriate Practice in Early Childhood Programs*, 3rd ed. (Washington, DC: National Association for the Education of Young Children, 2009).

Diverse Developmental Pathways

What you see	Opal, 14 months old, has been in child care for seven months. She still enters the infant/toddler program looking very anxious and clinging tightly to her mom, Joyce. Opal does not really *play* with any of the toys and expresses few emotions other than fear. Joyce does not seem able to comfort Opal; they rarely look directly at each other.
What you might think	This seems like insecure attachment, but Opal may just be slow to warm up to people. Her mom seems very remote and uncomfortable.
What you might not know	Joyce, Opal's mom, experienced four different foster homes before she was five years old. She was finally placed in the permanent care of her maternal grandmother when she was six. Joyce knows she has a hard time reading Opal's signals for care and nurturance, and it seems that she often feels overwhelmed by the parenting experience.
What you might do	Encourage Joyce to visit the program and, when you can, create a quiet, simple area where the three of you can play together. Watch Opal's facial expressions and try to label them for Joyce (especially the positive ones!). Joyce needs to develop trust in you and the program as much as Opal does.

Cultural Diversity and Developmental Pathways

What you see	Most mornings 22-month-old Kyoko is still carried into the child care setting by her mother (even though she is quite able to walk alone). She clings to her mother while her mom puts her jacket and various toys in her cubby. She often cries for a long period after her mother (reluctantly) leaves her, and she has little contact with the other children.
What you might think	Kyoko seems passive and too dependent on her mother. She should be doing more things for herself. She's been in the program for almost eight months. Why is separation still so hard?
What you might not know	It has been very difficult for Kyoko's mom to leave her in child care. She was raised to value close physical contact and intimacy between infants and mothers; in her culture this is important for close-knit family relations. Kyoko's father believes this program will help her become more independent, and since moving to this county four years ago he has been looking for ways to make sure that his children become "successful."
What you might do	Even though you've chatted with Kyoko's mother, try to make more contact with her. Try to find out more about her expectations for the program and share yours with her. Listen carefully before you make judgments about attachment and dependency.

Summary

Attachment is an ongoing interactive process influenced by the responsiveness of the caregiver and the characteristics of the infant or toddler.

Brain Research

- Current technology has provided insight into how the brain functions and the importance of early quality caregiving.
- Secure attachment relationships directly affect the way the brain gets "wired," and positive, warm interactions stabilize brain connections.
- Strong neural pathways support all areas of growth, especially cognitive and social development.

Milestones of Attachment

- Behaviors that promote the attachment experience—including crying, eye contact, and grasping—are present in an infant at birth.
- In the second half of the first year, infants usually indicate fear of strangers (8 to 10 months) and separation anxiety (10 to 12 months).
- Sensitive caregivers can assist toddlers and their parents/families in the process of establishing trust. This supportive care fosters self-reliance and exploration into a larger world.

Measuring Attachment

- The research of developmental psychologist Mary Ainsworth stands as a hallmark for the measurement of attachment strength between a parent and an infant or toddler.
- Secure infants respond with stress to a parent leaving them in a strange setting, but they seek closeness and are comforted when the parent returns. Insecure infants may or may not respond to a parent's exit, and they can respond in avoidant or ambivalent ways when the reunion takes place.
- Remember that fathers, as well as mothers, who provide sensitive, responsive care to their infants can create the secure base needed for healthy attachment. It is also important to appreciate cultural values and listen carefully before making judgments about attachment and dependency.

Children with Special Needs: The Importance of Early Intervention

- Early intervention encompasses a multidisciplinary approach to identifying and planning supports for young children with disabilities to help them achieve their full developmental potential.
- Landmark legislation in 1975, revised in 1986 and again in 2004, put early intervention on the national agenda and put forth key guidelines for assessment and intervention practices.
- Early intervention programs support families, as well as children, in finding relevant resources "in time" for healthy development and secure attachment.

Key Terms

attachment 94	interactional synchrony 99	Strange Situation 102
autonomy 100	mirror neurons 97	synapses 95
axon 95	neurons 95	trust 99
dendrites 95	neurotransmitters 105	

Thought/Activity Questions

1. Imagine a dialogue with a new parent concerning the topic of attachment. What would you like to share about this process? How would your comments change with the parent of a two-year-old?
2. Review Table 5.1, "Rethinking the Brain," on page 94. What points are the most important? Why? How might you share this information with a parent?
3. What happens to development if little or no attachment is made? Consider specifically emotional, social, and mental/cognitive growth.
4. Observe an infant-toddler program when the parent of a toddler is about to leave. What attachment behaviors do you see in the child? How does the parent respond? Consider what changes or additions you might like to see.
5. Describe the kinds of interactions that build a secure attachment. What obstacles might contribute to attachment concerns?

For Further Reading

Joni L. Baldwin and Patty Sorrell, "Collaborative Identification and Intervention in an Early Childhood Setting: Woody's Story," *Young Children* 68(2), May 2013, pp. 44–49.

MaryBeth Bruder, "Early Childhood Intervention: A Promise to Children and Families for Their Future," *Exceptional Children* 76(3), Spring 2010, pp. 339–355.

Robert M. Capuozzo, Bruce S. Sheppard, and Gregory Uba, "Boot Camp for New Dads: The Importance of Infant-Father Attachment," *Young Children* 65(3), May 2010, pp. 24–28.

Linda Gillespie and Amy Hunter, "Creating Healthy Attachments to the Babies in Your Care," *Young Children* 66(5), September 2011, pp. 62–64.

Carol Garhart Mooney, *Theories of Attachment* (St. Paul, MN: Redleaf, 2010).

Pam Schiller and Clarissa Willis, "Using Brain-Based Teaching Strategies to Create Supportive Early Childhood Environments That Address Learning Standards," *Young Children* 64(4), July 2008, pp. 52–55.

Perception

What Do You See?

Bea is exploring some beads. She looks at them, perhaps noting the different colors. She looks at the caregiver while touching the beads, exploring the shape and texture. She puts them in her mouth and then smiles at the caregiver when she hears, "You really seem to like those beads, Bea. How do they taste?" She keeps looking at the caregiver but then turns to the center of the room when she hears another caregiver comment about getting ready for a snack. She sniffs slightly and seems to be noting the smell of the cornbread baking—the smell that has been filling the room for the last 10 minutes. She drops the beads and crawls over to the area of the room being set up for the snack.

Did you notice how many different senses Bea was using to explore the beads? She also seemed to use the caregiver's words, the smells from the kitchen, and the setting up of the snack area to anticipate that food would be arriving soon.

Very young children are immediately involved in the process of gathering information and using it. Sensation is the stimulation of the sense organs (for example, eyes, ears, and taste buds), and **perception** is the ability to take in and organize this sensory information. It is an innate tendency to search for order and stability in the world, and it becomes increasingly fine-tuned as we age.[1] Sensory information provides an important link to all other areas of development. Learning in this area can be considered a *dynamic system*—"dynamic" in that it is an ever-changing process as we grow and mature, and "system" because it constantly influences other growth areas. Think about Bea in the opening scene of this chapter; she was obviously able to coordinate a great deal of sensory information! As infants and toddlers repeat experiences, they begin to make meaningful connections about the people and objects in their world. **Neural pathways**, or the dendrite connections between brain cells, are strengthened as they gather, apply, and benefit from their sensory encounters. This chapter reviews these perceptual, or sensory, abilities. It discusses the importance of outdoor, sensory-rich experiences in nature for very young children. It also includes some early warning signs for determining if a child might have a sensory impairment and the components of the IFSP for young children with special needs. Infants and toddlers are constantly exploring the world around them, and they make sense of things based on their discoveries and experiences.

Sensory Integration

The increasing public awareness of early brain development has validated what many parents and caregivers have known for a long time—learning for infants and toddlers is interrelated, and growth in one area influences growth in another. **Sensory integration** is the process of combining and integrating information across the senses and is critical to the development of perception. As infants become aware of their sensory experience, they can discriminate between people and make attachments. They learn to move their bodies in specific ways to accommodate new sensory information. They begin to relate what they have learned about an object or person through one sense (for example, sight) to what they have learned through another sense (maybe touch). This interrelatedness between sensory experience and motor experience is strong, and it provides the base for cognitive development. Young children need sensory experiences with opportunities for lots of repetition if they are to build healthy learning pathways in the brain. *Remember principle 4: Invest time and energy to build a total person.*

Initially, infants' sensory experiences and perceptions are direct and physical. The mouth is especially sensitive and should be considered a primary learning

Reflect

Think about Bea, the infant you met at the beginning of this chapter. How is she demonstrating sensory integration? How can her caregivers help her coordinate her sensory exploration?

Figure 6.1 Making Sense of the World. *Source:* Adapted from "World of Senses" by Joan Raymond, *Newsweek Special Issue*, Fall/Winter 2000, p. 18.

Infants come into the world wired to perceive it, and their early experiences complete their brain circuitry.

Touch: The primary sensory cortex is responsible for touch. This critical area of the brain can process tactile sensations by the fourth month *in utero*. By week 10, skin nerves appear.

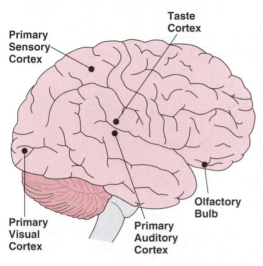

Primary Sensory Cortex

Taste Cortex

Primary Visual Cortex

Primary Auditory Cortex

Olfactory Bulb

Vision: Some simple signals in the visual cortex can be received from the fetus's eye at seven months *in utero*. But this is the slowest sense to develop, and the neurons in the vision pathway remain immature for several months after birth.

Taste: As early as seven weeks after conception, 10,000 taste buds on the tongue and soft palate begin to appear. The specific tastes that the fetus is exposed to before birth (what the mother eats) can shape later likes and dislikes in infancy.

Hearing: Prenatal exposure to sounds can have a lasting effect. By 28 weeks gestation, the auditory cortex can perceive loud noises. A newborn can usually recognize his or her mother's voice and prefers it to all others.

Smell: At birth, infants can distinguish their mother's smell. Even *in utero*, infants can detect the smell of amniotic fluid. The sense of smell seems closely linked to emotions and memories.

tool in the first months of life. As infants grow, they learn to *extend* themselves by tuning in to the senses that bring information from a distance. See Figure 6.1 for a summary of how and where senses develop in the brain. Current research related to brain development indicates that neurons, as they move around the brain, assume specialized functions. Review the visual and auditory areas again in Figure 6.1. If a neuron that would normally migrate to the visual area of the brain is instead moved to the hearing area, it will change to become an auditory neuron instead of a visual neuron. Individual neurons have the potential to serve any neural function . . . depending on where they end up![2]

This organizational process allows infants the ability to tune in to experience and to concentrate on certain aspects of it. The process is neurological—it cannot be seen. But we can see infants adjust to their experiences. Even though all the senses are operating, infants initially do not realize that the information they receive from these senses has continuity. They cannot yet perceive the repetiveness of events or interpret them. In a short time, however, connections between separate events are clarified. For example, crying infants will calm down as they realize that hearing a particular voice or seeing a particular face means that food or care is about to be given.

Researchers are reviewing more and more information about the value of outdoor environments for infants and toddlers and how multisensory experiences with nature can foster sensory integration. After we discuss each sensory domain, we will share positive strategies for fostering multisensory experiences *outdoors*.

This book talks about only **five senses** (hearing, taste, smell, touch, and vision), but it is interesting to speculate about possible other senses and whether infants may have many more sensory abilities than we retain as adults. Examine the following passage from *The Metaphoric Mind*, a book that argues that we have not five or six, but 20 or more senses.

> *Some human beings clearly detect minute changes in gravitational and magnetic fields. Others can detect the energy created by a flow of material in pipes, movement through soil, or electrostatic currents in the air. As adults these people are considered unique, mystical, or deviant in some other way. It may well be that these people have simply retained an awareness of senses they possessed as children.*[3]

Before reading about the development of each sensory or perceptual domain, pause and think about your own sensory awareness. Respectful caring, emphasized throughout this book, comes about as adults, caregivers, and parents slow down and become more empathic toward each other and very young children. In our busy, fast-paced lives we lose touch with our bodies and sensory abilities and how they are connected to everything we think and do. To become a better observer of young children and a more sensitive caregiver, think about and reconsider your own sensory awareness.

EXPLORE the following website for more information and resource material.

The Sensory Awareness Foundation, established by Charlotte Selver, a friend of Emmi Pikler, has developed a practice that encourages adults to rediscover their natural balance and self-confidence; activities encourage people to live in the moment.

www.sensoryawareness.org

Hearing

Newborns can hear at birth (and even before). They can sense the direction sound comes from as well as its frequency and duration. Researchers have found that sounds of 5 to 15 seconds seem to have the most effect on the infant's level of activity and heart rate (the two measures most frequently used to reflect an infant's awareness of a change in an event). If the sound lasts more than several minutes, the infant becomes less responsive. In other words, an infant is more attentive if you speak and then are quiet than if you make long speeches.[4]

VIDEO OBSERVATION 6

Boy Exploring Toy Car Using Touch and Sound

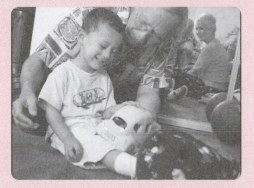

See Video Observation 6: Boy Exploring Toy Car Using Touch and Sound for an illustration of learning to coordinate sensory information. You see a boy who is being helped to use hearing and touch to learn about a toy car that he can't see.

Questions

- Why do you think the man chose to give the boy this particular toy?
- Are you aware of how many senses you use at once to explore a new object? What do you think is your strongest, most useful sense?
- In this example the adult is in more of a teaching role than in most other examples. Why do you think this is, and how do you feel about it? Would you feel differently if you knew this child became blind not long before the video was taken?

To view this clip, go to **www.mhhe.com/itc10e**. Click on Student Edition, select Chapter 6, and click on Video Observations.

Newborns recognize the sound of their mother's voice. Experiments have shown that infants only 20 weeks old can discriminate between the syllables "baw" and "gah." Listening to people's voices and noting differences seems to be an early skill. Young babies are especially responsive to a high-pitched, expressive voice, using a rising tone at the end of phrases. This describes a speech pattern now referred to as "parentese" (which is not the same as "baby talk"). Infants' early responsiveness to such sounds and patterns seems to encourage parents and caregivers to talk to them. This interaction strengthens both the emotional tie between them and the infants' readiness for the complex task of language development.[5] The way infants react to sounds or any other sensory stimulation, however, depends a great deal on the situation in which they experience them.

A loud or strange noise may be frightening, but the presence of a familiar, comforting caregiver transmits a sense of security and enables the infant to remain calm and open to learning. Young infants are also able to hear certain sounds that distinguish one language from another. By four and a half months, they are able to discriminate their own names from similar-sounding words. By five months, they can distinguish the difference between English and Spanish passages.[6]

Infants also know when someone is singing to them. Their behaviors are different when their mothers are singing to them as opposed to talking to them. When mothers sing, babies move less and stare more intently at them.[7] Certainly, infants need the opportunity to experience a variety of sounds, but remember that they need quiet times to appreciate the differences in sounds. If the noise level in the environment is too high, the infant spends a lot of energy tuning out and focusing. The optimum noise level varies with each child. Sensitive caregivers can determine what is more or less right for the individual after they get to know the child. Part of this awareness comes from knowing your own optimum noise level.

Some adults like background music, and others don't. However, a point to consider is this: if you want an infant to focus on a sound, that sound should be isolated and have a beginning and an end. For example, if a music box or CD player is constantly playing, the infant eventually stops listening because the sound is no longer interesting. Caregivers should be sure that mechanical toys and other noisemakers do not become substitutes for the human voice. Infants can determine a great deal from the inflection of a person's voice, and attending to the human voice and its inflections is the beginning of language development.

Toddlers have a greater ability to tolerate higher noise levels, so they can be in slightly larger groups than infants can. However, toddlers, too, vary individually, and some children are greatly overstimulated by multiple sounds. These children may be unable to focus when surrounded by noise. One way to help solve this problem is to have quiet spaces where one or two overstimulated children may retreat when they choose. We've seen pillow-lined closets, tents, and even large wooden boxes that babies can crawl into for this purpose.

NAEYC Program Standard 3

Teaching

Smell and Taste

Researchers know that smell and taste are present at birth, and they develop rapidly in the first few weeks. Newborns can distinguish the smell of their own mothers from that of other women who have just given birth, so smell obviously plays a role in attachment. (Mothers also often report that the smells of their babies are pleasing to them.)

Newborns respond to unpleasant strong odors such as ammonia or acetic acid (found in vinegar, for example) by turning away, but they seem insensitive to less interesting odors that are fainter. They respond positively to the odor of banana, somewhat negatively to fishy odors, and with disgust to rotten eggs.[8] An increase in breathing rate and activity level can be noted when odors are present in the air, and the greater the saturation of the odors, the greater the heart rate and activity level.

An environment rich in smells adds to a toddler program. They can be part of the daily program, such as food cooking, or they can be introduced by caregivers in such ways as "smell bottles." Be careful of making things that aren't edible smell delicious—such as chocolate shaving cream or peppermint flavoring in play dough—unless the toddlers are well conditioned to the idea that play dough and shaving cream are not for eating.

Some taste reactions are clearly developed at birth. Infants show disgust over bitter tastes and seem to have an innate sweet tooth.[9] Since breast milk is quite sweet, taste is another sense that may contribute to attachment. Salt taste is recognized soon after and will be accepted if the infant is hungry. A 10-day-old infant can show surprise if water is substituted for the expected milk, but there seems to be a correlation with whether the baby has been well fed; infants whose diets have been inadequate do not seem to notice taste differences rapidly.

Be careful not to condition infants to the taste of salt and other additives. There is no reason to spice food for the very young; they appreciate and enjoy the natural flavors if not covered. Most of us have learned that food in its plain state "needs something," and we are suffering for that acquired taste as people's blood pressures soar and many are on salt-restricted diets.

Tasting can be an important part of the toddlers' day as they are exposed to a variety of foods at meals and snack times. Of course, care should be taken to choose foods that don't present a choking hazard.

Reflect

How do you feel about infants and toddlers playing with their food? What might be the benefits? What possible cultural, and even gender, issues need to be acknowledged?

Touch

Sensitivity, or responsiveness to discomfort and pain, increases rapidly after birth. Some parts of the body are more sensitive than others. The head, for example, is more sensitive than the arms and legs. Individual babies vary in their sensitivity to touch, and for some, touch is unwelcome. Caregivers need to learn to handle those babies who are touch defensive in ways that cause minimal discomfort. One way is to lift such young infants on a pillow instead of picking them up as you would other babies. Some babies and toddlers respond better to strong touch than light touch, which seems to pain them.

Where and how we touch is related to culture. It is a good idea to find out what is forbidden or disrespectful in cultures different from your own if children from other cultures are in your program. For example, in some cultures children are never touched on the head, and to do so upsets parents. Consider the message mainstream America gives when one person touches or pats another on the head. How would you feel if your boss patted you on the head? Pats on the head are reserved for the very young or dogs, never for an equal or a superior. Though it seems very natural to most adults, perhaps it would be more respectful to restrain from patting babies and young children on the head.

Be aware if you are differentiating between boys and girls in the way you touch the children in your care. Sometimes people unconsciously touch one sex more than the other. Try to be equal in your treatment of both sexes.

Tactile perception (touch) relates to motor abilities (movement skills). As babies increase in their ability to move around, touch gives them more and more information about the world. And they seek this information almost emphatically. All environments for infants and toddlers should be touchable and mouthable (the mouth also gives the very young a good deal of information). While you are filling the environment with plastic toys (that are both touchable and mouthable), don't forget to provide some natural substances that the children can explore, such as wood or wool. (One educational approach, Waldorf education, believes that young children should experience only objects [toys] made from natural substances because artificial ones—things that look like something else—fool the senses.)

Give toddlers words for what they are feeling—soft, warm, fuzzy, rough, smooth. Be sure they have plenty of soft objects in their environment. Some programs occur in predominantly hard environments because hard surfaces and objects last longer and are more sanitary. Reducing softness is not a way to increase cost-effectiveness because a hard environment changes the whole program. Behavior tends to improve when an environment is softened.

Provide a variety of tactile (touching) experiences for toddlers. Even though they are up and around, they haven't outgrown their need to explore the world with their skin. Here are some ideas for offering toddlers tactile experiences that involve the entire body:

- A dress-up area filled with silky, slinky, furry, and other textured clothes
- A sensory tub filled with such things as plastic balls or yarn balls (securely fastened so children don't get tangled in loose ends) to climb into
- Swimming in plastic pools in the summer
- Sit-in sandboxes

If you're willing to let children wallow about getting whole body tactile experiences, be careful you don't tread on cultural values. Some cultures have strong prohibitions against children getting dirty or messy.

Other kinds of tactile experiences are designed mainly for the hands (or hands and arms). Some simple, one-step cooking allows children to have a tactile experience. Other possibilities include water play, sand play, play dough, and finger painting (which has several variations, such as shaving cream [not for the youngest toddlers]), cornstarch and water. Be sure you emphasize the process and not the product. The point of finger painting is to feel the paint and squish it around, not to make a pretty picture to take home.

Be careful not to exclude girls from these tactile activities because they might get messy. Some people tolerate messy boys more easily than they do messy girls.

Be aware that some toddlers do not want to get messy. Don't blame parents for this. It may be that the parent has discouraged messiness (for personal or cultural reasons). But sometimes the reluctance comes from the child's personality or stage of development. Many toddlers go through a period of refusing to get their hands messy.

Not all tactile experiences have to be messy. Many excellent programs for toddlers have very limited messy experiences. No one expects you to encourage children to muck around in mud unless you really want to set up that kind of experience. Some simpler but also valuable experiences include a pan of sand with spoons and sifters; a pan of birdseed (just to feel) or birdseed with pitchers, spoons, and cups; and a tray of salt to feel (and perhaps some little cars to run around in it). Just letting children go barefoot provides them with a variety of experiences as they encounter different textures underfoot.

NAEYC Program Standard 2
Curriculum

The Principles in Action

Principle 7 Model the behavior you want to teach. Don't preach.

Tyler is sitting up on the rug looking at his caregiver, who is close to him. She smiles. He smiles back. He gets up on all fours and takes off, stopping for a moment when he notices that he has left the soft thick rug. He crawls back and sits back down. He looks at his caregiver, who is idly poking her fingers into the rug. He also pokes his fingers into the rug. "Soft," she says, and he cocks his head to listen to her. Then Tyler gets up on all fours again, headed for a shelf of toys. Along the way he encounters an infant smaller than himself lying on her back on a blanket. He stops to investigate, and as he leans over to get a closer look, he notices a caregiver has come to sit beside him. He reaches for the baby's face, touching the smooth skin and patting the hair. He puts his lips on baby's head and looks up at the caregiver and smiles. She smiles back. He gets more vigorous in his investigations, and a hand comes down over his, touching him lightly. "Gently, gently," the caregiver says. He goes back to the original soft stroking.

1. Are these educational interactions?
2. What is the caregiver doing to encourage the child to touch and explore?
3. What relation does all that touching have to developing perception?
4. Can you tell how old this child is? What clues are you using?
5. Can you tell if this is a typically developing child? What clues are you using?
6. If the child hadn't responded to the caregiver's modeling of gentleness and had reached over to grab the baby's hair, what could the caregiver have done next?

Sight

We know more about sight than about the other senses, probably because most people depend so heavily on it. Infants can distinguish light and dark at birth. The pupillary reflex (the automatic narrowing of the pupil in bright light and widening in dim light) can be seen at birth, even in premature infants. Within a few hours infants are capable of visual pursuit. Their fixed focus seems to be about eight inches away. In other words, infants are equipped to see the mother's face while breastfeeding.

Within a few weeks, infants can discriminate among colors and prefer warm ones (red, orange, yellow) to cool ones (blue, green). Eye movements are somewhat erratic at first, but they rapidly become more refined. By the end of the second month, infants can focus both eyes to produce a single, though probably blurred, image. By the fourth month, they can see objects with clarity, and by six months, the average infant's vision is nearly 20/20.[10] Their ability to see is now comparable to that of an adult, though they have to learn to perceive and interpret what they are seeing.

Most newborns find all people and objects placed in front of them interesting—though some are more so than others. The human face is the most interesting of all (because newborns' visual abilities are clearly designed to promote attachment).

Infants of all ages need to be able to see interesting things. However, in the first weeks, eating and diaper changing provide sufficient visual input. As infants get older, a variety of visual material becomes more appropriate because it encourages them to move around in their world. Something interesting to see becomes something to reach for and eventually to move toward. Too much visual stimulation, however, can lead to a "circus effect." Infants become entertained observers rather than active participants and grow into passive toddlers who demand entertainment instead of inventing their own. Children used to outside entertainment are drawn toward television—the ultimate entertaining visual experience.

An entertained observer is quite different from a scientific observer. Entertained observers get hooked on a constant flow of novel visual stimulation. They get bored quickly and demand constant visual change. They may become television addicts. Because they experience such a strong assault on one sense (the visual), they ignore the fact that they are not actually involved physically or socially with the world around them. This eventual habit of observation and lack of involvement is detrimental to the development of a wide range of abilities.

Take cues from the infants themselves when setting up an environment that develops visual skills. Otherwise, it's hard to know how much sensory input is too much and when interesting new visual experiences will be welcome. If infants cry at certain things, too much may be going on, or they may not yet be ready to leave what they were paying attention to. If they are very quiet, they may be concentrating on something in particular or may be turned off by too many events. When infants find their world interesting and are allowed to explore it at their own pace, they learn to entertain themselves in the process of discovery. *Remember principle 7: Model the behavior you want to teach.*

Toddlers' visual worlds are larger, as they move around more. They also have a better understanding of what they are seeing. To get an idea of what toddlers' visual environments are like, get down at their level and look around. Things look very different from down there.

To cut down on visual stimulation for toddlers, put up low barricades to block areas of the room. Adults can see over the barriers to supervise, but children experience a visually calming room. (Barriers also can muffle sound to some extent.) Some rooms invite children to really focus on what's available; in others, toddlers get overexcited and have a hard time focusing.

Pictures add visual interest to a toddler's environment (though, of course, pictures also belong in an infant environment). Hang them low enough for the toddlers to see at their own eye level. One way to hang them is with clear contact paper that covers the picture and extends out beyond to stick to the wall. This way the picture is sealed in with no loose corners to pick at and tear and no tacks to swallow. Change pictures periodically, but not constantly, because toddlers appreciate seeing the familiar on a regular basis. Choose pictures that clearly depict familiar objects or other children in action. Be sure to represent different races in your picture display. Also be aware of the gender messages in the pictures you hang. Don't show pictures that are predominantly little girls looking pretty and doing nothing and little boys involved in engaging activities.

Aesthetics, or that which is judged beautiful, is a worthy but often unconsidered goal when designing an environment for infants and toddlers. Children are more apt to grow up with an appreciation for beauty if the adults around them demonstrate that they value aesthetics. Remember, too, that sensory integration is fostered *naturally* when young children can play outside in well-designed, aesthetically pleasing environments.

Multisensory Experiences and the Outdoor Environment

The sights and sounds of nature provide some of the most beautiful experiences and memories that many adults cherish. Yet for a growing number of young children, nature is increasingly becoming an abstraction—something seen in a picture or gazed at from a window. Some programs, even for infants and toddlers, still favor more indoor "learning-oriented" activities. But outdoor experiences, and the integration of the senses that they naturally provide, are extremely valuable and contribute a great deal to a well-balanced, quality early childhood setting.

Infants and toddlers benefit from being outdoors, where their choices for exploration, and especially their sensory opportunities, are expanded. All the sensory or perceptual domains discussed in this chapter—hearing, smell and taste, touch and sight—are positively supported by natural materials and activities in outdoor settings. Remember that outdoor multisensory experiences for very young children can create a unique ladder of learning. Natural light, fresh air, and the sights and sounds of nature contribute to a young child's sensory

Figure 6.2 Guidelines for Giving Children Multisensory Experiences Outdoors

1. Allow young children to experience information through movement, touch, taste, smell, hearing, and vision in a way that is unique for each individual. Let every child be successful and comfortable—one may sit quietly watching a butterfly, while another may roll in the grass.

2. Use some of the same indoor planning guides for outside space, providing a balance of low-activity/high-activity areas, wet/dry areas, soft/hard areas, and loud/quiet areas.

3. Encourage young children to observe changes in nature. Dry sand has a certain texture and can be poured from a bucket, but after a rain it feels quite different and has very different properties.

4. Plan sensorimotor activities that include whole-body experiences to foster sensory processing. Help young children lift, move, and build with rocks, logs, and sticks outdoors—such activities develop feelings of competence and body awareness.

5. Provide hands-on activities that use natural materials such as leaves, pinecones, sticks, and tree bark. Help young children to notice the details, smells, textures, and patterns of these materials.

6. Create outdoor spaces filled with natural vegetation that will encourage the presence of insects, birds, and animals (consider appropriate safety, of course). Young children are fascinated with bugs and animals, and watching them in their natural environments fosters children's natural sense of wonder!

Source: Some of these guidelines were adapted from "Beginnings Workshop: Sensory Integration," *Exchange* 177, September/October 2007, pp. 39–58.

integration in a way that can contribute to and expand any indoor experience. When sensory integration is *successful*, it allows young children to process information through all their senses in a way that is positive for each person. Natural outdoor spaces can provide the perfect setting for experiences that are challenging without being overwhelming. Figure 6.2 offers some tips on planning for more sensory experiences outdoors.

EXPLORE the following websites for more information and resource material.

Children and Nature Network provides access to news, research, and advice to support children's development in nature at home, at school, and in the community.

www.childrenandnature.org

Earthplay specializes in ideas and resources for enhancing outdoor play spaces.

www.planetearthplayscapes.com

The Edible Schoolyard shares descriptions of how to integrate gardening into all curriculum areas.

www.wedibleschoolyard.org

Outdoor, nature-based experiences provide the perfect place for young children to satisfy many of their sensory needs. If a young child has a unique sensory impairment, that child and his family can benefit from the development of an IFSP. It may include nature experiences to provide for his optimal sensory growth.

Children with Special Needs: Educating Families about the Individualized Family Service Plan

Early intervention is extremely important. The earlier a child is identified as having a disability, or is identified as being "at risk" for having one, the greater the likelihood that he and his family will benefit from early intervention services. According to the law, the early intervention services for young children under three years must be made available through the development of an **individualized family service plan (IFSP)**. This section discusses the requirements that are built into the IFSP and the important role that families play in the development of this written document that outlines early intervention services.

A key principle in the IFSP is that the family is a child's greatest resource and that a young child's needs are closely tied to the needs of his family. Also embedded in the IFSP are the beliefs that the best way to support a child is to build on the strengths of his family, and the family's priorities for a child evolve into the everyday routines and activities planned for that child. Respect for family privacy is essential; cultural diversity and family native language is always acknowledged in the planning process for the child.

The right to decline any service remains with the family. The cost of services depends on the policies of individual states, but no child can be denied services because his family cannot pay for them. The IFSP must include the following components:

- The infant/toddler's present levels of physical, cognitive, communication, emotional-social, and adaptive development
- Family information (with family consent) including resources, priorities, and concerns related to the infant/toddler's growth
- Major outcomes expected to be achieved by the infant/toddler (review periods are typically every six months)
- The specific early intervention services necessary to meet the infant/toddler's unique needs
- The natural environments (for example, home or an early care and education program) in which the early intervention services will be provided (or justification as to why services will not be provided in the natural environment)
- A written projected timeline for when services begin and how long they are expected to last
- The name of the services coordinator who will be responsible for the implementation of the plan and the coordination with other agencies
- The steps to be taken to support the infant/toddler's transition to preschool or other appropriate services[11]

All along the IFSP process, it is important for families and parents to write down the names and contacts of the persons and resources involved. Having this information can be very helpful if questions arise later. Early childhood caregivers can remind parents to do this and also keep track of the resources either of them may need as the young child's development progresses.

NAEYC Program Standard 7
Families

Table 6.1 Early Warning Signs of Sensory Impairment
Remember, any child may demonstrate some of these behaviors and *not* be having difficulty. Certain behaviors may be part of a particular child's personality or temperament and should be looked at in the light of *the whole child*.
• Frequently rubs eyes or complains that eyes hurt
• Avoids eye contact
• Easily distracted by visual or auditory stimuli
• Often bumps into things or falls frequently
• By six months does not turn toward source of sounds
• Talks/communicates in a very loud or very soft voice
• Shies away from touch
• Uses one side of the body more than the other
• Usually turns the same ear toward a sound to hear
• Reacts strongly to the feel of certain substances or textures

Source: Information adapted from the California Department of Education, the California Child Care Health Program, and the Portage Project TEACH, Region 5 Regional Access Project, 1999.

Reflect

Where would you go in your community to gather resource information related to sensory-impaired children? How would you organize it?—Topic folders? A notebook? A file box? How would you share this information with your staff? What guidelines would you give them when assessing children in your care?

Review Table 6.1; the focus is "Early Warning Signs of Sensory Impairment." How could this information be useful to caregivers, parents, and other resource specialists as they begin planning an IFSP?

It has already been stressed in this text that caregivers play a vital role in an infant's healthy growth and development. They are part of the team to help families find necessary supports and resources if they have questions or concerns about their child's development. If a caregiver has a developmental concern about a young child in her care, carefully selected resources should provide information to assist her and the parents to find the best support for the child.

DEVELOPMENTAL PATHWAYS

Behaviors Showing Development of Perception

Young infants (up to 8 months)	Show they recognize their primary caregivers by sight, sound, and smell within the first two weeks of life Look to the place on their body where they are being touched Begin to distinguish friends from strangers Hit or kick an object to make a pleasing sight or sound continue
Mobile infants (up to 18 months)	Push their foot into a shoe and their arm into a sleeve Actively show affection for a familiar person by hugging, smiling, running toward that person

	Understand more words than they can say
	Show heightened awareness of opportunities to make things happen
Toddlers (up to 3 years)	Identify self with children of same age or sex
	Classify, label, and sort objects by group (hard versus soft, large versus small)
	Identify a familiar object by touch when it is placed in a bag with two other objects
	When playing with a ring-stacking toy, ignore any forms that have no hole
	Stack only rings or other objects with holes

Source: Carol Copple and Sue Bredekamp, *Developmentally Appropriate Practice in Early Childhood Programs*, 3rd ed. (Washington, DC: National Association for the Education of Young Children, 2009).

Diverse Developmental Pathways

What you see	Zyana is a crawler; she does more sitting than crawling around. She's quiet and immobile much of the time, but it doesn't take much to entertain her: a sunbeam on the floor, a scrap of paper, the breeze from an open window. She seems to be able to float above the chaos that sometimes occurs in the infant room. She rarely demands attention.
What you might think	She needs to be more active. Some of the other children her age are 10 times more active than she is. Maybe she is depressed.
What you might not know	Zyana is very perceptive and she enjoys what she perceives. She is aware of her senses and finds them infinitely entertaining. Her temperament is such that she makes few demands. She's easygoing and able to concentrate on what's close to her without being disturbed by what else is going on in the room.
What you might do	Appreciate her as an individual. Be sure she gets enough attention. Just because she is easy to get along with doesn't mean that she should be ignored. Find out from her family what she is like at home and if they appreciate her or find her lacking in some way.
What you see	Seth, a toddler, cries a good deal. A lot of things bother him. For example, he fusses when you dress him and also when you undress him. He shies away when you touch him.
What you might think	This is simply his temperament. Or maybe they "spoil" him at home. Or maybe he doesn't like you. Or maybe he misses his mother.
What you might not know	Seth is hypersensitive. He is easily overstimulated and he is tactile-defensive. The textures of some clothing bother him, and he doesn't like the feeling of air on his arms and legs. The labels on clothing irritate his skin. Even your touch disturbs him.
What you might do	Find out what you can from his family about how to keep him comfortable. Observe carefully to see if you can figure out what bothers him and what doesn't. Cut the labels out of clothes or put them on wrong side out. Reduce excess stimulation. Don't quit touching him, but figure out what kind of touch is most acceptable. Try different things and watch for the effects.

Summary

Perception is the ability to take in and organize sensory experience.

Sensory Integration

- Sensory experiences are combined and integrated and influence other major growth areas.
- Specific sensory organs are located in particular areas of the brain and, as the brain matures, there is a constant interchange of action and reaction.

Hearing

- Newborns can hear at birth and are especially responsive to high-pitched familiar voices and sounds.
- Caregivers need to be aware of the unique preferences of young children; the optimum noise level varies with each child.

Smell and Taste

- Newborns can distinguish numerous smells and tastes and prefer pleasant smells and sweet tastes.
- An environment rich in smells adds to an infant-toddler program; be careful of making things that are not edible smell delicious.

Touch

- Newborns have a well-developed sense of touch; sensitivity to discomfort and pain increases rapidly after birth.
- Caregivers should be alert to potential cultural and gender issues related to touch.

Sight

- Newborns' vision is blurry (compared to that of adults); they can distinguish light and dark areas, and within a few weeks they can distinguish colors.
- Take cues from infants themselves when planning an environment to foster visual skills. Avoid the "circus effect"—more is not necessarily better.

Multisensory Experiences and the Outdoor Environment

- Outdoor experiences, and the integration of the senses that they naturally provide, can be extremely valuable to infants and toddlers.
- Guidelines for planning positive outdoor activities for infants and toddlers encourage hands-on experiences with a variety of natural (safe) materials.

Children with Special Needs: Educating Families about the Individual Family Service Plan

- The individual family service plan is a written document, created by a multi-disciplinary team, that outlines early intervention services for a young child with a disability (or "at risk" for a disability).
- A key principle in the IFSP is that the family is a child's greatest resource, and the best way to support a child with special needs is to build on the strengths of his family.

Key Terms

aesthetics 123
five senses 116
individualized family
  service plan (IFSP) 125

neural pathways 114
perception 114
sensitivity 119

sensory integration 114
tactile perception 120

Thought/Activity Questions

1. Look around an infant-toddler environment. Don't forget to go outside! List the experiences that you feel foster perceptual development. How can you determine when there is perhaps "too much of a good thing"?
2. Focus on one aspect of perceptual development (one of the senses). Create a toy to foster this area of growth. What do you need to consider?
3. Observe a child with a sensory impairment. What adaptations can you see the child making? How is the environment supporting his or her efforts? How is the family involved?
4. After reading this chapter, imagine that you are planning a parent meeting for your infant-toddler program. The topic is perceptual development. What key points about each sense would you want to share?
5. Think about your personal orientation to perceptual development—your sensitivity to your own senses. Which sense do you use the most? The least? Which one triggers the most memories? Are there any implications for your interactions with very young children?

For Further Reading

Jennifer Benson and Jennifer Miller, "Experiences in Nature: A Pathway to Standards," *Young Children* 63(4), July 2008, pp. 22–28.

Margaret Caspe, Andrew Seltzer, Joy L. Kennedy, Moria Cappio, and Christian DeLorenzo, "Engaging Families in the Child Assessment Process," *Young Children* 68(3), July 2013, pp. 8–14.

Gregory A. Cheatham and Rosa M. Santos, "Collaborating with Families from Diverse Cultural and Linguistic Backgrounds," *Young Children* 66(5), September 2011, pp. 76–82.

L. J. Miller, *Sensational Kids: Hope and Help for Children with Sensory Processing Disorders* (New York: Putnam/Penguin Press, 2006).

Trudi Schwartz and Julia Luckenbill, "Let's Get Messy! Exploring Sensory and Art Activities with Infants and Toddlers," *Young Children* 67(4), September 2012, pp. 26–34.

Mariana Souto-Manning, "Family Involvement: Challenges to Consider, Strengths to Build On," *Young Children* 65(2), March 2010, pp. 82–88.

chapter 7

Motor Skills

Focus Questions

After reading this chapter you should be able to answer the following questions:

1 How does the developing brain influence the growth of motor skills?

2 What is the function of reflex behaviors and why do they *change* during the early months?

3 What growth patterns are related to large motor skills and small motor skills during the first two years?

4 What can caregivers do to support families when seeking resources for young children with special needs?

What Do You See?

Anthony stands in the sandbox looking around the play yard. He bends over and picks up a sieve and spoon that are lying at his feet. He plops down, legs out straight, and starts spooning sand into the sieve and watching it pour out onto his knees. After several minutes he notices a tot bike that is sitting at the edge of the sandbox. He gets up and toddles toward the bike. When he reaches the edge of the sandbox, he concentrates his effort on getting his feet—first one, then the other—over the board that rims the sandbox. Once he gets to the bike, Anthony begins to move it away from the sandbox area. He alternates between standing and walking the bike, and sitting on it and scooting it with his feet (there are no pedals on the bike). He keeps on the walk, which is bumpy asphalt and slightly uphill. He allows the bike to coast down the slight incline and ends up near the gate. He starts to climb the gate, but an adult nearby walks over and gently redirects him to a climbing structure several yards away. As she moves toward a group of children washing dolls in dishpans on a low table, Anthony follows her. He grabs a sponge lying on the table and squeezes it, watching the soapy water drip out. He puts the sponge into the pan, holds it up dripping, and squeezes it again on the tabletop. He scrubs the tabletop briefly, then puts the sponge back into the water. He takes a doll out of another tub and puts it on top of the sponge in the tub in front of him. Another child reaches over and takes the doll back, and there is a slight tussle as Anthony tries to keep the doll. He lets go when he hears a call for snack time. He gives the sponge in the tub a pat, which splashes water onto his face. He smiles, pats it again, then races tripping across the yard to the snack table, where he is just in time to pour his own juice from a small, half-filled pitcher.

Movement is the natural, healthy experience of childhood. Most infants and toddlers move a lot. Anthony certainly demonstrated a great deal of movement! Very young children teach themselves when they are free to move on their own. It is through movement, muscular coordination, and the organization of perceptions that young children find out about and make sense of their world. Infants' motor skills may seem limited, but sensitive observation reveals competent abilities. Within a year and a half, most infants have learned many of the basic motor skills—arm-hand coordination, walking—that they will need throughout their lifetime. Their sensory experience has given them important feedback. They spend the next years perfecting, expanding, and refining the original postures and movements that they learned early on.

This chapter provides an overview of the progression of motor development. It includes major growth patterns, examines how the brain develops, and looks at how reflexive, large and small motor abilities all change and refine themselves in the first two and a half years. It includes guidelines for fostering motor development as well as some major resources for parents and caregivers to support children with special needs.

Physical Growth and Motor Skills

The average newborn weighs just over 7 pounds and is about 20 inches long. She is helpless and could not survive on her own. But growth occurs rapidly in a healthy, caring environment. By five months of age the infant's birth weight has doubled, and by her first birthday it has tripled. Even though the pace of weight gain slows during the second year, it has nearly quadrupled since birth.[1] Length also increases, and by the end of the second year, most children are about three feet tall. Physical growth is generally predictable. Numerous growth charts exist in books and doctors' offices, but each child is unique, and it is not unusual for growth during this time to occur in "spurts." The appearance of specific motor skills during this time can vary widely.

As a young child's overall size increases, parts of the body grow at different rates. At birth the head accounts for one-fourth of the newborn's entire body size, and the legs are only about one-third. By age two, the infant's head is only one-fifth of her body length, and her legs are almost one-half of her body length. This rapid growth provides a challenge; very young children must learn to coordinate the movements of bodies that are constantly changing. The way that infants learn to coordinate their bodies and refine their movements reflects amazingly well-organized growth patterns.

Stability of motor development can be explained by two major growth principles. The first is the **cephalocaudal** principle, which in Latin means "head to tail." This principle states that growth follows a pattern that begins with the head and moves down the rest of the body. For example, children generally lift their heads before they sit up and before they stand. The second principle is the **proximodistal** principle, which is also from Latin and means "near to far." It indicates that development moves from the center of the body outward. For example, young children generally use large, sweeping movements of their arms before they use their hands and fingers. Overall, you can see young children use their heads (and their sensory skills, like vision) before they walk. And you can see them move their arms in circling patterns before they have the ability to pick up that potato bug hiding in the corner of the sandbox (pincer grasp).

Growth is not just a process of getting bigger; although as discussed previously, that certainly happens. The brain matures and growth within it moves from the brain stem at the base of the neck to the cortex in the frontal area. Movement becomes less reflexive and more voluntary. Growth is also the process in which motor skills, both large and small, are refined. As motor skills grow and expand, young children are better able to clarify their needs and explore the world.

Brain Growth and Motor Development

Motor development is largely observable; we can see infants make voluntary movements and refine their physical skills. Now, thanks to neuroscience technology, we can also see how the brain changes and grows as young children develop. At birth the brain weighs only about 25 percent of its eventual mature adult weight of three and a half pounds. It reaches nearly 90 percent of that weight by age three. By age six the brain is almost adult size, although specific skills continue to develop into adulthood.[2] Everyday behaviors that are observable also give us insight into brain growth. The development of reflexes is a good example (see Table 7.1).

Table 7.1 Some Basic Reflexes in Infants	
Reflexes at Birth	
Rooting	Head turns toward things that touch the cheek.
Sucking	Tendency to suck things that touch the lips.
Stepping	Legs move when infant held upright with feet touching floor.
Palmar grasp	Hands curl around object placed in them.
Babinski	Toes fan out if sole of the foot is stroked.
Moro	If head support released, arms fling out and seem to grasp.
Startle	Arms fling out in response to sudden noise.
Tonic neck (fencing)	Head turns to one side and arm extends while other arm flexes.
Swimming	Swimming movements occur when infant placed in water.
Reflexes after Birth	
Reciprocal kicking	If infant held outward, kicks legs alternate (bicycling).
Neck righting	If head turns, the body follows.
Parachute	If infant is falling, arms go forward.
Landau	If infant placed on stomach, arms and legs extend in "U" position.

It is important first to acknowledge that the number of neurons (brain cells) a child is born with does not increase throughout life. What changes is the increase in the number of connections between the brain cells. What also happens is something called **myelinization**, a process by which brain fat (myelin) coats and insulates the neural fibers. It accounts for the rapid gain in overall brain size after birth. These neural fibers, or axons, are then better able to transmit electrical impulses (synapses) and make more stable "learning connections."[3] Brain growth in the first year is primarily a process of insulating neural fibers and expanding, or growing, "dendrite trees." In addition, the neurons in the brain move around and become arranged by function. Some move into the upper layer of the brain—the **cerebral cortex**—and others move below this area to subcortical levels. The subcortical levels are fully developed at birth and regulate most of the reflexes and such fundamental activities as breathing and heart rate. As growth continues, cells in the cerebral cortex become more mature and interconnected. These cells will become responsible for complex motor skills and higher-order processes such as cognition and language.

This activity can be measured by an EEG, or electroencephalogram, which detects and measures brain wave activity, and growth in the first year can be seen as surges in brain activity. For example, there is a surge in activity at 3 to 4 months, when infants are doing voluntary reaching; at 8 months, when they crawl and search for objects; and also at 12 months, when they are walking.[4] Surges are related to the massive production of synaptic connections; the brain is busy making sense of experience. There seems to be clear evidence now that what forms the brain circuitry early in life is *experience*.

Importance of Free Movement, Observation, and Imitation

Current research on brain development has provided more understanding of the importance of *free* movement and the growth of motor skills. As infants repeat and practice simple sensorimotor patterns (turning their head or reaching for an object), they are maintaining important synaptic linkages. An interesting environment that allows movement and encourages active engagement with people and objects may improve the quality of brain functioning (density of synapses) and strengthen synaptic connections (increased myelinization).[5]

The mirror neurons bring to light the whole interesting role of observation and imitation of movement and how that affects brain development. As humans observe a task, the motor cortex of the brain becomes active in the same area needed to *perform* the task. We know that infants and toddlers certainly watch others and then repeat what they have seen (often complex tasks without teaching). Mirror neurons may give more insight into *how* motor experiences link to cognitive and social skills. A key thing to remember is that new experiences give young children the opportunity to interpret the world and expand neural connections. This, of course, makes it all the more important to identify and treat young children with early motor or sensory delays so that they reach their full developmental ability.

Current brain research continues to emphasize the following key points:

- Movement develops as a result of nature (the child's biology) and nurture (experience) and begins as early as six weeks' gestation.
- More neural connections and experience foster more coordination and stronger muscles.
- Increased myelinization in the brain influences the development of fine motor skills.
- What forms brain circuitry early in life is *experience*, and it is essential in "fine-tuning" the young brain's ability to respond to the environment.

Brain research also has clearly indicated that there are *sensitive periods* for development. But there is also tremendous **brain plasticity**—that is, the brain's tendency to remain somewhat flexible. Plasticity is greatest before age two when the new synapses are still expanding and have not yet been pruned. The brain is amazingly adaptable. In some cases of early trauma, regions of the brain will take over the function of a damaged area of the brain. Although we are still in the process of appreciating more about the vital "windows of opportunity" for learning, don't forget that it is never too late to provide quality experiences for a young child.

Reflexes

Newborns can make few voluntary movements beyond gross random arm and leg movements. Most of the first movements are **reflexes**, which are unlearned, organized, involuntary responses that occur in the presence of different kinds of stimuli. The muscles seem to react automatically.

Reflexes serve several functions. Some, like blinking, swallowing, and clearing the face for breathing, are protective. Others, such as kicking the legs alternately (reciprocal kicking), are precursors of later skills—in this case, walking. Pediatricians and other infant specialists pay attention to reflexes because they indicate brain growth. As the growth of the brain shifts from the brain stem to the cortex, reflexes change or disappear. Healthy babies have the same breathing reflex that adults have, as well as a cough and gag reflex that keeps the breathing passage clear. Their eyes blink and squint, and their pupils narrow just like those of adults. They coordinate sucking and swallowing, and they pull away from painful stimuli. These are all common reflexes that are present at birth and remain throughout a person's lifetime.

Some reflexes are specific to newborns and change or disappear as the child grows. Other reflexes make their appearance during the first few months. As the new reflexes appear, some of the ones present at birth begin to disappear. Some of the most visually obvious reflexes—and those most often assessed by physicians—are summarized in Table 7.1 on page 133. The reflexes are grouped into those present at birth, and those that appear after birth.

Not only is it interesting to see how reflexes serve as the basis for later movement, it is useful for caregivers to know what reflexes indicate about infants' behavior and development. It is useful to know that babies have not chosen to move in a certain way (for example, rooting before starting to suck), but that they

Reflect

Do you think infancy might be an ideal time to teach swimming? Why or why not? Why might some people think it would be an ideal time? What are some reasons *not* to teach infants to swim?

have to do so. The appearance of certain reflexes, the lingering of reflexes, and the absence of others can indicate differences in development. This aspect of development is complex. When parents or caregivers notice that a baby is showing what seems to be inappropriate reflexive behavior, they may want to discuss what they have noticed with a developmental expert or a doctor.

The Principles in Action

Principle 10 Be concerned about the *quality* of development in each stage. Don't rush infants and toddlers to reach developmental milestones.

An infant-toddler center treats all children as individuals. It never pushes development but instead watches its babies reach developmental milestones, each on his or her own schedule. One child in the program was born prematurely, and another one has been determined to be developmentally delayed, so the idea of each on his or her own schedule has even more meaning in this program. The child with the developmental delays is being carefully monitored by an infant interventionist and has an individualized family service plan (IFSP) that has been carefully thought out. All the children see pediatricians regularly. Recently this program received a notice that its continued funding will depend on its ability to get all children in the program to developmental milestones on time, except for any children officially identified with special needs. The staff has been mandated to take training on a diagnosis and prescription method of using activities and exercises to bring all children closer in their abilities to reach the milestones. The staff and director are horrified. Their motto (which they got from Magda Gerber's work) is "*in* time; not *on* time."

1. What is your reaction to this situation?
2. Is there value in allowing children to develop at their own pace? Explain your answer.
3. Are there disadvantages to allowing children to develop at their own pace? If yes, what are they?
4. Do you think the activities and exercises make a difference? Explain your answer.
5. Do you have experience with being pushed to achieve? If yes, does your experience relate to infants and toddlers? If it does, how?

Large Motor Skills and Locomotion

Eventually, infants make movements that are voluntary instead of reflexive. These movements are generally divided into two broad types: large or gross motor skills, which have to do with large muscles and big movements, and small or fine motor skills, which have to do with small muscles and more delicate movements.

The brain, the body, and the environment all contribute to move an infant toward increased strength and **locomotion**, or the ability to move from one place to another. Various developmental areas work together to advance a child to more complex and refined levels of growth.

Large muscles contribute to an infant's ability to move in two directions: up (to an upright position) and around (on a horizontal plane). The two are intertwined because the child needs to get up to move around and needs to move around to get up. Little by little, babies gain control over these muscles. The first muscles to develop are those that control head movements. As babies perfect the skills involved in turning the head from side to side and lifting it up, they strengthen the shoulder muscles. As they begin to move around and squirm, lifting their arms and legs, they develop the trunk muscles. All this preparation is for turning over, just as turning over is preparation for (that is, strengthens the muscles necessary for) sitting up. A child will learn to come to a sitting position without ever having been propped up. The ability to sit comes from developing the muscles prerequisite to the upright position. Infants get ready to sit by learning to move the head and by turning over. The building of the muscle systems is vital; practice at sitting is not.

Research from the Pikler Institute

According to Emmi Pikler's research and experience at the Pikler Institute in Budapest, if no one interferes by praising or otherwise motivating children, they will develop movement skills in a predictably sequential manner. If children are put on their backs from the beginning of life and no one manipulates them by putting them into positions they can't get into by themselves, they will learn to turn over, roll, creep, crawl, sit, stand, and walk on their own. They accomplish all this by playing with each movement over and over and becoming absorbed in each little detail. They are scientists studying movement and patiently experimenting. Infants are born ready to learn. Through their fascination with their bodies and strong motivation to develop movement, they prove to be highly competent, independent learners. Their persistence to increase movement skills sets a theme for later learning.

Pikler's approach to keeping babies on their backs and unrestricted in the first few months is a strength-based approach. Babies placed on their stomachs before they can roll over by themselves are relatively helpless. On their backs they can see much more, use their arms and hands, and kick freely. On their stomachs they can only see by holding up their heads, which is a strain on them, as noted by the number of babies who complain loudly during what is known as "tummy time" in the United States.

At the Pikler Institute in Budapest, thousands of babies have spent their first months only on their backs until they can roll over on their own. The problems plaguing babies in the United States, such as flat or misshapen heads or weak neck and chest muscles, were not an issue at the Pikler Institute during its 65 years of existence. The difference is that Pikler babies are never propped up; are never put in high chairs, swings, or infant carriers; and are never seated in strollers. They aren't even carried in positions they can't get into by themselves. Their development is natural and remarkable.[6]

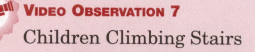

VIDEO OBSERVATION 7

Children Climbing Stairs

See Video Observation 7: Children Climbing Stairs for examples of children using gross motor skills by practicing stair climbing. Notice how each child goes about it in a slightly different way.

Questions

• How many different ways did these children use to get on and off this low platform? Describe each way.
• What other environmental features might give children an opportunity to practice stepping up and down safely?
• What does this scene tell you about the program's philosophy?

To view this clip, go to **www.mhhe.com/itc10e**. Click on Student Edition, select Chapter 7, and click on Video Observations.

A general principle involved in motor development is that *stability is the means to mobility.* Infants cannot move until they gain a good, solid base from which to move—whether the movement is vertical, as in sitting and standing, or horizontal, as in crawling and walking. This same principle operates on another level as well. Exploration (mobility) is related to psychological stability (trust in attachment).

The plan for developing muscular stability is a part of the infant's makeup—as is the plan for mobility. Nobody has to "teach" either sitting or walking. When typically developing babies have gone through the necessary muscle development, they will be able to sit and walk without any lessons or practice.

Early motor experiences also can be described from the dynamic systems approach. Each action is made up of bits and pieces of experience, and motor skills change each time they are used.[7] As infants' muscles grow, they achieve strength and balance, their brains mature, and they put together the necessary skills that lead to mature movement and walking. Each skill is a construction of

Reflect

What experience do you have with developmental charts? Do you have any feelings about them?

Table 7.2 The Bayley Chart: Major Milestones of Gross Motor Development (ages 1 to 40 months)

Skill	Month When 50% of Infants Have Mastered the Skill	Month When 90% of Infants Have Mastered the Skill
Lifts head 90 degrees while on stomach	2.2	3.2
Rolls over	2.8	4.7
Sits without support	5.5	7.8
Stands holding on	5.8	10.0
Crawls	7.0	9.0
Walks holding on	9.2	12.7
Stands alone	11.5	13.9
Walks	12.1	14.3
Walks up steps	17.0	22.0
Kicks ball forward	20.0	24.0

Note: Norms based on European American, Latino, and African American children in the United States.

Source: Maureen Black and Kathleen Matula, *Essentials of Bayley Scales of Infant Development Assessment* (New York: Wiley, 2000); selection of items from D. R. Shaffer and K. Kipp, *Developmental Psychology: Childhood and Adolescence*, 7th ed. (Belmont, CA: Wadsworth, 2007), Table 6.1, p. 205.

abilities that emerges as infants actively reorganize existing motor capabilities into new and more complex skills. New motor patterns are modified and refined until all components work together smoothly.

Table 7.2, "The Bayley Chart," is based on the *Bayley Scales of Infant Development*, created by Nancy Bayley.[8] The Bayley chart shows some major milestones of gross motor development and locomotion widely used in the United States to assess the development of children from the ages of 1 to 40 months. Children are individually assessed to see how they perform age-appropriate tasks.

Another way of looking at development in the first three years comes from Emmi Pikler's research (see Table 7.3, "The Pikler Chart"). There are several differences between the Bayley and the Pikler charts. One is that items on the Pikler chart are not based on a test situation and are not intended to be used for diagnostic purposes. The Pikler chart was created with an educational aim to guide caregivers (originally at the Pikler Institute in Budapest) in their work with children under three years of age.[9]

Not only do the purposes of the two charts differ, the items and the timetables differ as well. For example, look at the first item on the Bayley chart (Table 7.2): "lifts head 90 degrees while on stomach." Lifting the head is a part of the first stage of gross motor development. The person giving the Bayley

Table 7.3 The Pikler Chart: Ages at Which Children's Gross Motor Activity Is Observed in Everyday Life *(ages 3 weeks to 36 months)*

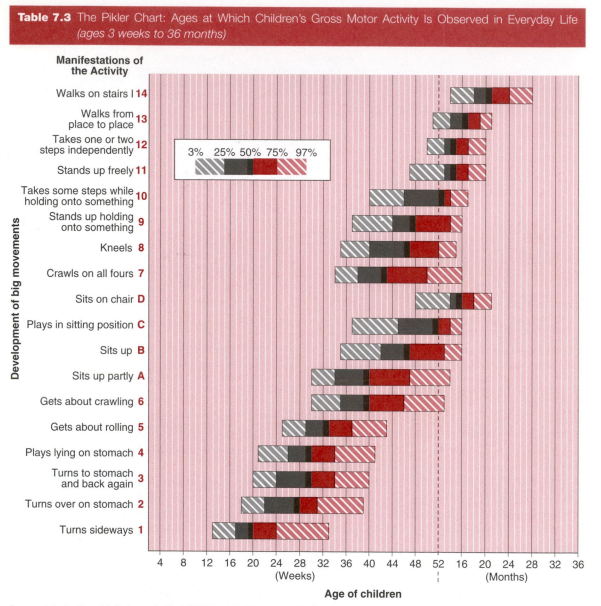

Development of big movements

Manifestations of the Activity

Walks on stairs I **14**
Walks from place to place **13**
Takes one or two steps independently **12**
Stands up freely **11**
Takes some steps while holding onto something **10**
Stands up holding onto something **9**
Kneels **8**
Crawls on all fours **7**
Sits on chair **D**
Plays in sitting position **C**
Sits up **B**
Sits up partly **A**
Gets about crawling **6**
Gets about rolling **5**
Plays lying on stomach **4**
Turns to stomach and back again **3**
Turns over on stomach **2**
Turns sideways **1**

3%   25% 50% 75%   97%

4 8 12 16 20 24 28 32 36 40 44 48 52   16 20 24 28 32 36
(Weeks)   (Months)

Age of children

Source: Adapted from M. Gerber, ed., *The RIE Manual for Parents and Professionals* (Los Angeles: Resources for Infant Educarers, 1979).

assessment places the baby on her stomach and watches how well she holds her head up. How the baby does depends to some extent on whether she has had what's called tummy time. In the 1960s, when the *Bayley Scales* were first designed, most U.S. babies were placed on their stomachs for sleeping, so they had plenty of opportunity to lift their heads and develop the muscles needed to do so. The "back to sleep" campaign, introduced in the 1990s to reduce the risk of sudden infant death syndrome, or SIDS, changed parents' and caregivers' former practice of putting babies in a prone position for sleeping. Now most babies are put to sleep on their backs (as Pikler advocated in the late 1930s).

An unforeseen consequence of putting babies to sleep on their backs, however, is that infants who aren't free to move during their waking hours (after the first weeks of life) don't do as well on the first item on the Bayley chart because of poorly developed neck and chest muscles. Thus there is now is a campaign to teach parents and caregivers about giving babies waking time on their stomachs, known as "tummy time." Many infant experts now strongly recommend (or even mandate) daily tummy time starting at birth. However, tummy time advocates are not necessarily advocates for the freedom-of-movement approach. Babies with weak neck and chest muscles may have spent most of their waking hours strapped into various devices such as car seats, strollers, and other kinds of baby carriers. That kind of restriction is what makes the muscles weak, not lack of tummy time.

Pediatricians regularly test babies' neck muscles by grabbing their hands and pulling them to a sitting position to see how far back their heads lag. Pikler never did that, nor do any of the people following her approach or Gerber's philosophy. Pediatricians wouldn't do so either if they understood how freedom of movement relates to the development of *all* the muscle systems, including the neck and chest. They would recommend minimizing the use of baby "containers" and instead tell parents to put their babies on a firm surface on their backs and let them move freely during their waking hours. That way the muscle systems develop in a natural order so that when ready, babies roll onto their sides, and eventually turn over on their stomachs by themselves. They then create their own tummy time, and anyone can see how strong their neck and chest muscles are.

The Pikler chart (Table 7.3) has no item related to lifting the head. Pikler used her research and theories with babies in residential care. Since 1946 the Pikler Institute has put all babies on their backs, asleep and awake. They remain on their backs until they can turn themselves over, so the first motor activity milestone is turning on the side, not lifting the head. Lifting the head occurs once babies roll over on their own, and by then their neck and chest muscles have developed adequately. No one at the Pikler Institute tests babies by pulling them up by the arms to see the strength of their neck muscles. Instead, they observe the babies closely during their everyday life and pay close attention to all of the preliminary movements the baby accomplishes before actually achieving the first motor activity milestone listed on the Pikler chart. Caregivers make continual observations and do daily recording on the babies for whom they are primary caregivers. It's important to realize that Pikler looked at more than just major milestones, because she was as interested in what it took to get to those milestones as she was in the milestones themselves. The staff at the Pikler Institute, including the current director, Pikler's daughter Anna Tardos, are still carrying on Pikler's work in infant-toddler care programs and parenting classes, but the residential care program terminated in 2011. Tardos and her staff also provide training for professionals and others, both at the Pikler Institute in Budapest and elsewhere in Europe, the United States, and South America. Magda Gerber's approach to gross motor development was similar, and her associates continue to work with parents and professionals in the United States and Germany, and recently have expanded to Singapore and Beijing.

Look at another difference between the Bayley and the Pikler charts. The item "sits without support" on the Bayley chart (Table 7.2) is assessed in a situation in which the baby is placed in a sitting position, after which the adult lets go and observes to see how long it takes the baby to start to fall over. Pikler would never do that, though the Pikler chart shows plenty of interest in the milestones related to sitting. Four "sitting" items appear on the Pikler chart (Table 7.3). The first relates to how the baby gets into a sitting position. The baby is not tested, but rather just observed as he begins to move into what will eventually become a sitting position. That item is called "sits up partly." Once the baby gets into a sitting position ("sits up"), the next observations focus on what he can do in a sitting position. That relates to the item called "plays in sitting position." The fourth item in that group, "sits on chair," is significant for a reason that may not be obvious to everybody. Sitting on a chair is something babies must do on their own. No adult ever puts a baby on a chair. A basic rule of the Pikler approach is that babies are never put into a position that they cannot get into themselves. That means they aren't stood up or sat up until they stand up or sit up on their own. Babies put themselves on a chair when they are ready. This accomplishment signals the beginning of eating at a table with others. Before that time, babies are held for feeding.

Remember principle 10: Be concerned about the quality of development in each stage. Don't rush infants and toddlers to reach developmental milestones.

Small Motor Skills and Manipulation

The small muscles that an infant gradually begins to control include those of the eyes, mouth, speech organs, bladder, rectum, feet, toes, hands, and fingers. We focus here on the development of the hands and fingers, known as **manipulation**. The achievements within this area are not isolated skills; they are organized and combine themselves in an increasingly refined manner.

The sequence in which infants learn to manipulate objects shows how complex this ability is. Figure 7.1 illustrates the developmental sequence. At first, newborns generally hold their hands in tight fists (although the clenched fist is more relaxed in those babies who were treated to gentle birth procedures). They hold on to any object put into their hands, gripping so tightly that they can, if held up, support their own weight. But they have no control over their grasp and cannot let go, no matter how much they want to. That's why Pikler and Gerber taught parents and caregivers not to put anything into a baby's hand. At some time before six months (usually at a little over two and a half months), the tight fists remain relaxed most of the time, and the hands are open.

During the first three months, more of the hand and arm movements become voluntary. Infants begin to reach for objects, first with their eyes, then with open hands. By around three and a half months, they can often close on an object within reach.

Figure 7.1 Fine motor development: manipulative skills, birth to 21 months

Source: Bayley Scales of Infant Development, Second Edition (BSID-II). Copyright © 1993 by NCS Pearson, Inc. Reproduced with permission. All rights reserved. *Bayley Scales of Infant Development* is a trademark, in the US and/or other countries, of Pearson Education, Inc. or its affiliates..

Grasps and holds ring
0.8 month
(range 0.3–3 months)

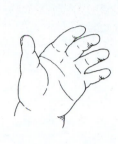

Hands predominantly
open and relaxed
2.7 months
(range 0.7–6 months)

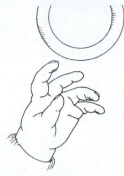

Reaches for dangling ring
3.1 months
(range 1–5 months)

Closes on dangling ring
3.8 months
(range 2–6 months)

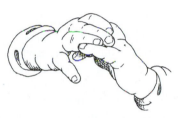

Fingers hand in play
3.2 months
(range 1–6 months)

Palmar grasp
3.7 months
(range 2–7 months)

Neat pincer grasp
8.9 months
(range 7–12 months)

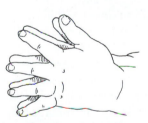

Pattycake (midline skills)
9.7 months
(range 7–15 months)

Scribbles spontaneously
14 months
(range 10–21 months)

Much fine motor development comes from encouraging children in self-help skills.

The observations of manipulative skills in the Pikler Institute are much more refined than just whether the child is reaching or grasping. Staff give much attention to what kinds of play objects children need at what stage to encourage specific manipulative skills, and make regular observations on how the children handle these objects. At the beginning, babies in the institute aren't given toys or other things to grasp until they discover their own hands (called hand regard). According to Éva Kálló and Györgyi Balog, writing about a young baby in their book *The Origins of Free Play*, "The observation of his hands, as well as the interplay between them, precedes and prepares him for manipulation."[10] When babies aren't distracted from their own hands, they can concentrate for long periods on just moving their hands and fingers and watching them.

Eventually babies can grab an object within reach. At the Pikler Institute, that first play object is a scarf made from a piece of cotton fabric. Babies go from using a palmar grasp to pick up objects (see Figure 7.1 on page 143) to using a pincer grasp with the thumb and forefinger. As they learn to manipulate objects with more skill and a variety of motions, they work on their pincer grasp by picking up small objects. They go on to use their forefingers to poke, hook, and probe. Of course, all these skills are valuable for playing—putting smaller bowls in larger ones, taking covers off objects, and exploring the properties of play objects (balls roll, blocks do not).

Encouraging Self-Help Skills

Much fine motor development in toddlers comes from encouraging them in self-help tasks. As they get more adept at eating with utensils, pouring their own milk, taking off their own shoes, and zipping up their jackets (with a start from an adult), their ability to use their hands and fingers grows.

Toys and materials add to their chances to practice as they play with what you provide them (such as dress-up clothes, dolls and doll clothes, play dough, button and zipper boards, latch boards, stringing beads, nesting toys, simple shape sorters, snap-together blocks, telephones, water and paintbrushes, crayons, felt pens, scissors, simple paper puzzles, blocks, small figures, cars, and trucks). Be sure that you encourage boys and girls to engage equally in fine motor activities.

Remember Anthony in the scenario at the beginning of the chapter. He was encountering many chances to build his skills in walking, running, climbing, and balancing just by being in an environment with equipment and choices. He was also building fine motor skills as he practiced grasping, holding, scooping, pouring, and squeezing with the toys and materials available to him. These experiences not only helped him develop his perceptual skills but also contributed to cognitive development. *Remember principle 8: Recognize problems as learning opportunities, and let infants and toddlers try to solve their own. Don't rescue them, constantly make life easy for them, or try to protect them from all problems.*

Fostering Motor Development

Caregivers can do several things to foster motor development in infants. Try to keep children in the position in which they are freest and least helpless during their waking hours. Emmi Pikler's research shows that even the youngest babies change position an average of once a minute.[11] So, if they are strapped into an infant seat or a swing, they are not able to do what they would do naturally if free. Avoid contraptions that confine infants. (Car seats are, of course, a necessary exception.)

Encourage infants to practice what they know how to do. Babies get ready for the next stage by doing thoroughly whatever it is they are doing in the present stage. Trying to teach babies to roll over or walk keeps them from fully exploring and perfecting the skills they already have. They reach each milestone just when they are ready, and their own inner timetable dictates when that will be.

Allow babies to move into positions by themselves. The process of *getting into* a position is more important than *being in* the position—the process promotes development. Babies get ready for standing by sitting and crawling, not by being stood up.

The body needs a certain amount of stress to grow. Avoid rescuing babies when they get in an uncomfortable position, but wait and see if they can get out of it on their own. Obviously, you don't leave babies in great distress alone and unsupported, but you don't want to always make everything easy for them either. Reasonable, or optimum, stress stimulates growth, increases motivation, and strengthens the body as well as the psyche.

Above all, *facilitate* development in all motor areas, but there's no need to *push* it. Because we live in a "hurry-up" culture, some people are most anxious for babies to reach milestones "on time" or even early. "In time" is a better guide for milestones. Each baby has his or her own timetable. There is no reason to impose

Large muscle activity cannot be saved for outdoor times but must be allowed and encouraged indoors.

someone else's. The question to ask is, how well is this baby using the skills he has, and is he progressing in his use of those skills? With these two concepts in mind, you will not have to be so concerned about where babies fit on the chart. *Remember principle 2: Invest in quality time, when you are totally available to individual infants and toddlers. Don't settle for supervising groups without focusing (more than just briefly) on individual children.*

Promoting motor development in toddlers follows the same principles as those for infants. Toddlers need freedom to move and experience a variety of ways of using the skills they possess. Large-muscle activity cannot be saved for outdoor time but must be both allowed and encouraged inside. A soft environment—pillows, mattresses, foam blocks, and thick rugs (indoors), and grass, sand, pads, and mats (outdoors)—helps toddlers roll, tumble, and bounce around. Various kinds of scaled-down climbing and sliding equipment (both indoors and outdoors) allow the toddler to experience a variety of skills. Wheel toys (these can be saved for outdoors for the older toddler) give a whole different kind of experience as toddlers learn first to walk them and later to pedal them. Large lightweight blocks encourage building skills as toddlers carry them around; form them into walks, houses, and abstract structures; and then practice gross motor skills on them.

Wandering, carrying, and dumping are gross motor skills that toddlers practice a great deal. Rather than seeing these as negative, caregivers can provide for them in the curriculum. Some programs have things available to dump (and put back). One center even suspends from the ceiling a bucket of objects whose sole purpose is dumping (and refilling). Wandering usually involves picking up objects, carrying them to another location, and putting them down. Sometimes they are actively discarded, and sometimes just dropped—abandoned as if forgotten. The map in Figure 7.2 shows the path of a two-year-old over a period of 20 minutes. The black dots represent each time the child picked up or put down an object. Notice the territory he covered and the number of times he picked up

NAEYC Program Standard 2
Curriculum

Figure 7.2 Map tracing the movements of a two-year-old

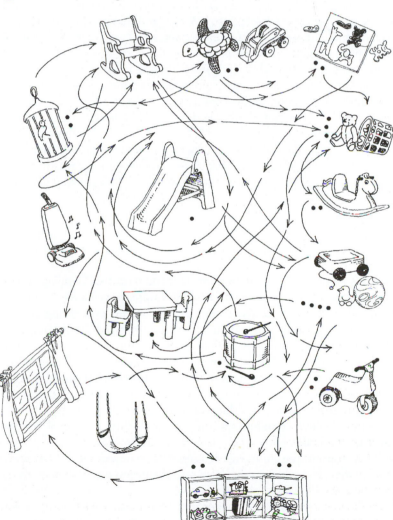

and put down objects. This is not unusual two-year-old behavior. Typically, as children get older, they are able to spend more and more time with specific activities. The closer they get to three, the less likely toddlers are to spend good parts of the day moving from one place to another. But early in toddlerhood, this constant movement is part of gross motor development, and the environment, both indoors and outdoors, should be set up to accommodate that need.

Remember, too, that poor nutrition contributes to malnourished children who lack the muscle and bone strength necessary for typical motor development and activity. Malnourished children may also have central nervous system concerns, which can limit coordination and motor control. Overweight babies may have limited development too. When infants have excess weight to move, they may not be motivated or able to develop needed motor skills.

A word of caution concerning the brain development information: be alert to any marketing that uses brain research to sell toys and materials. Natural everyday experience and interactions are the best ways to foster significant neural connections. Interpretation of research must be done with care and sensitivity, and the uniqueness of each child should always be preserved.

Notice whether you are encouraging gross motor movement more in boys than in girls. Girls need strong, skillful bodies as much as boys do. Both sexes in toddlerhood enjoy running-and-chasing games. The freedom to roll around on the floor, jump onto pillow piles, wrestle, and somersault is just as appropriate for girls as for boys. Music and movement, dance, and circle games encourage all young children to move and have fun. Take walks and examine interesting things along the way. Just remember to give children a choice and keep group size small.

Reflect

How do you think environment influences motor development? (Don't forget to include nutrition and practice.)

Children with Special Needs: Finding Resources

This chapter has focused on how physical growth and motor skills change during the first three years. Knowing about healthy development remains the primary guide for early intervention and assessment when working with young children with special needs. Reflexes, for example, were acknowledged as significant because they indicate brain growth. Helping the parents and families of young children with special needs find relevant guides and resources is particularly important if their children are to achieve their full potential. This section lists some national resources related to early childhood special education and suggests guides for sharing resources with parents and families.

Resources usually encompass the specific services a child may need, but they also can connect the family and caregiver with the appropriate services that *they* may need to best support the child and each other. If resources are to be effective, they must be current and relevant; they also must be timely and individualized to the issues of each family.

Early childhood caregivers and teachers are in a unique position to provide resources to the families of young children with special needs. They know about developmental milestones, and they know and have observed the children in their care. As already mentioned, their notes and observations play an important role in the development of the IFSP. Sharing questions and concerns with families who may have children with a disability is the first step in the early intervention process. Finding support information and resources for them can help families realize that they are not alone in their efforts to find the best for their child.

It is important for caregivers and teachers to develop a *library* of resources, and to keep them current it is important check websites frequently for accuracy. These resources should be shared openly—for example, at the entrance or drop-off site of the early care and education program. Some families do not want to identify themselves as having questions or needing help, but they may be very grateful to seek answers in private. Once they gain some information, and confidence, they may seek more resources publicly. Try to share two or three resources at any one time as they can have overlapping value. This also lets families know that there may not be just one approach to a question or concern.

A good resource is easy to access; the contact information is clear and complete whether it is a physical address or a website. A good resource also takes into account cultural diversity, providing information in more than one language. Good resources do not contain "alarming" information, but provide material that is concrete, developmentally based, and professionally referenced.

The benefit of a timely resource is that it can help families and caregivers feel emotionally strengthened by the support, and they in turn become knowledgeable because of the information. Another benefit is that a good resource should provide a "sense of direction" for the care of a child with special needs. As the needs of families and children change, access to resources needs to expand. Often one good resource leads to another!

The following list of resources represents a variety of agencies and a variety of disabilities. They were selected because their information base is extensive and broad; more resources continue to be available in the area of early childhood special education. The descriptions are brief and caregivers should review the sites before referring families to them. These sites were available at the time of publication, but websites change their content frequently. All informational resources need to be reviewed often for relevance and accuracy.

EARLY CHILDHOOD SPECIAL EDUCATION RESOURCES

Arc of the United States

http://www.thearc.org
Here is the website of the national organization of and for people with mental retardation and related disabilities and their families. It includes governmental affairs, services, position statements, FAQs, publications, and related links.

Association to Benefit Children (ABC)

http://www.a-b-c.org
ABC presents a network of programs that includes child advocacy, education for disabled children, care for HIV-positive children, employment, housing, foster care, and day care.

Consortium for Citizens with Disabilities (CCD)

http://www.c-c-d.org
Included in this coalition is an Education Task Force that follows issues of early childhood special education, the President's Commission on Excellence in Special Education, issues of rethinking special education, 2001 IDEA principles, and many other related issues.

Disability-Related Sources on the Web

http://www.arcarizona.org
This resource's many links include grant resources, federally funded projects and deferral agencies, assistive technology, national and international organizations, and educational resources and directories.

Division for Early Childhood (DEC)

http://www.dec-sped.org
A division of the Council for Exceptional Children, the DEC advocates for the improvement of conditions for young children with special needs. Child development theory, programming data, parenting data, research, and links to other sites can be found on this site.

Institute on Community Integration Projects (ICI)

http://ici.umn.edu
Research projects related to early childhood and early intervention services for special education area described here.

Learning Disabilities Association of America (LDA)

http://www.ldaamerica.org
The purpose of the LDA is to advance the education and general welfare of children with normal intelligence who show disabilities of a perceptual, conceptual, or motor coordination nature.

National Association for Child Development (NACD)

**NAEYC Program
Standard 4**
Assessment

http://www.nacd.org
The home page of this international organization provides links to various programs, research, and resources into such topics as learning disabilities, ADD/ADHD, brain injuries, autism, gifted, and other related topics.

National Dissemination Center for Children with Disabilities (NICHCY)

http://www.nichcy.org
This organization provides information and makes referrals related to specific disabilities, early intervention, special education, individualized

education programs, and a listing of parent's guides to resources for children with disabilities.

Special Education News

http://www.specialednews.com
This site discusses the problems of coping with both poverty and disabilities, including topics related to behavior management, conflict resolution, early intervention, and specific disabilities.

Special Education Resources on the Internet (SERI)

http://www.seriweb.com
SERI offers information in all areas of special education in early childhood, including disabilities, developmental delays, behavioral disorders, and autism.

The Family Center on Technology and Disability

http://www.fctd.info
This national center works with children and families with disabilities that use assistive technology; information on technological aids is free.

The National Center for Learning Disabilities (NCLD)

http://www.ncld.org
NCLD works with individuals with LDs, their families, educators, and researchers; it promotes research and disseminates information, and advocates for policies to protect the rights of individuals with LDs.

Council for Exceptional Children (CEC)

http://www.cec.sped.org
CEC is the largest professional organization for improving the educational experience for individuals with all exceptionalities, including giftedness.

Supporting Emotional Needs of the Gifted (SENG)

http://www.sengifted.org
SENG is directed to parents and educators and has information on identification and emotional development of children who are gifted.

Center on the Social and Emotional Foundations for Early Learning (CSEFEL)

http://csefel.vanderbilt.edu
CSEFEL focuses on promoting the social-emotional development and school readiness of children from birth through age five.

Technical Assistance Center on Social Emotional Intervention for Young Children (TACSEI)

http://www.challengingbehavior.org
TACSEI creates free, research-based resources to assist families and agencies when working with children who are at risk for delays or disabilities.

DEVELOPMENTAL PATHWAYS

Behaviors Showing Development of Motor Skills

Young infants (up to 8 months)	• Use many complex reflexes: search for something to suck; hold on when falling; turn head to avoid obstruction of breathing; avoid brightness, strong smells, and pain • Reach, grasp • Lift head, hold head up, roll over, transfer and manipulate objects
Mobile infants (up to 18 months)	• Sit up • Crawl and pull up to stand • Walk, stoop, trot, walk backward • Throw objects • Use marker on paper
Toddlers (up to 3 years)	• Walk up and down stairs, can jump off one step • Kick a ball, stand on one foot • Thread beads, scribble with marker, handle scissors • Draw a circle

Source: Carol Copple and Sue Bredekamp, eds., *Developmentally Appropriate Practice in Early Childhood Programs,* 3rd ed. (Washington, DC: National Association for the Education of Young Children, 2009).

Diverse Developmental Pathways

What you see	Morgan hasn't been walking very long, but she is all over the place. She not only walks but climbs everything in sight. This child is never still for a minute unless she is sleeping, and she does sleep well. No wonder. She uses a lot of energy with all the moving she does.
What you might think	This is a hyperactive child. She's the kind they give medication to when they get in school.
What you might not know	Morgan is a lot like her father. They both have a good deal of energy. Her father is an athlete, and he has a job that is physically demanding, so he's glad he has all that energy. He's glad his daughter does too. He isn't worried that she is hyperactive, because he has seen hyperactive children and they are different from Morgan. For one thing, they don't seem to sleep much, and Morgan sleeps very well.
What you might do	Give her room to move and make sure she is safe. Arrange the environment so she can't climb up things that aren't safe. Make sure she spends enough time outdoors to get the fresh air and the feeling of space that keeps her able to use her energy in positive ways. Help her appreciate quiet activities as well. Even though she is not drawn to the book area, you can probably find some ways to get her over there.

(continued)

What you see	Vincent arrives all dressed up and is obviously inhibited by his clothes. His shoes have slippery leather soles, making him afraid to run. He never climbs outdoors. Indoors he is inhibited too, because he avoids all the sensory experiences (like water, sand, play dough, and even using felt pens) that might dirty his clothes.
What you might think	This family puts their child's appearance before his developmental needs. They are limiting his ability to develop physically and obviously don't understand the importance of freedom of movement and sensory experiences.
What you might not know	This family is from another country where going to school is an important privilege, and they consider your program to be school. They have strong ideas about children being properly dressed, and they wonder why the other children are dressed in jeans and old clothes. They feel that Vincent's appearance is a reflection of their family's caring for him.
What you might do	Get to know this family and what their perceptions are. Establish a relationship that is based on trust. Don't push them to change, but help Vincent develop his physical skills within the confines of the situation. Eventually you may be able to figure out together with the parent(s) how the child can gain more freedom to get involved physically and still be a positive reflection of his family.

Summary

The progression of physical growth and motor skills follows a generally stable pattern of development.

Physical Growth and Motor Skills

- Infants learn to coordinate the movements of their bodies as they are constantly changing; numerous factors influence the *rate* of motor development.
- Stability of motor development is fostered by the cephalocaudal and proximo-distal principles.

Brain Growth and Motor Development

- Myelinization and expanding dendrite connections account for brain growth after birth.
- Motor development is influenced by neurons moving into the cerebral cortex and surrounding area of the brain.

Reflexes

- Reflexes are unlearned, involuntary responses to different stimuli; some are present at birth, and some appear several weeks or months later.
- Reflexes change and/or disappear as brain growth occurs.

Large Motor Skills and Locomotion

- Large, gross motor skills progress as an infant practices generalized movement.
- Milestones for large motor development exist but should be used with caution; each child is unique and growth rates may vary.

Small Motor Skills and Manipulation

- Small, fine motor skills related to hand and finger movements advance rapidly during the first 18 months.
- Self-help tasks are some of the best activities to foster small motor skills.

Fostering Motor Development

- Encourage infants and toddlers to practice what they know how to do; avoid "teaching" motor skills.
- Everyday experiences and interactions are the best ways to foster brain growth and neural connections, and thus influence motor development.

Children with Special Needs: Finding Resources

- Relevant and timely resources assist caregivers and families in finding appropriate early intervention services for young children with special needs.
- A "good" resource is easy to access, culturally sensitive, developmentally appropriate, and professionally referenced.

Key Terms

brain plasticity 135
cephalocaudal 132
cerebral cortex 134

locomotion 136
manipulation 142
myelinization 134

proximodistal 132
reflexes 135

Thought/Activity Questions

1. Review Table 7.2 on page 139. Suppose the mother of a child in your care found this information in a popular magazine. She wants to discuss its meaning with you. Consider the following and what you would say:
   A. Her child is healthy and motor growth seems very normal. What would you say?
   B. You have some concerns about some lags in motor development and have been waiting for such an opportunity. What would you say?
   C. The father brings you this chart instead of the mother. What would you say?

2. Invent a toy to foster motor development in infants. Think about and discuss how this toy promotes physical growth.
3. Pretend that you are going to conduct a parent meeting. Outline the details of a discussion regarding how to set up an environment to promote gross motor development. Consider the following:
   A. Promoting safety
   B. Fostering development, not *pushing* it
   C. Teaching parents about developmentally appropriate environments
4. Discuss how relevant resources can help families who have a child with special needs. What are the components of a "good" resource?

For Further Reading

Frances M. Carlson, *Big Body Play* (Washington, DC: National Association for the Education of Young Children, 2011).

J. Gonzalez-Mena, E. Chahin, and L. Briley, "The Pikler Institute: A Unique Approach to Caring for Children," *Exchange* 166, November/December 2005, pp. 49–51.

Dan Gartrell and Kathleen Sonsteng, "Promote Physical Activity—It's Proactive Guidance," *Young Children* 63(2), March 2008, pp. 51–53.

É. Kálló and G. Balog, *The Origins of Free Play* (Budapest: Association Pikler-Lóczy for Young Children, 2005).

Rea Pica, "Babies on the Move," *Young Children* 65(4), July 2010, pp. 48–50.

Emmi Pikler, "Give Me Time: Gross Motor Development Under Conditions at Loczy," *Bringing up and Providing Care for Infants and Toddlers in an Institution*, ed. A. Tardos, pp. 135–150 (Budapest: Association Pikler-Lóczy for Young Children, 2007).

Anna Tardos, "The Child as an Active Participant In His Own Development," *Bringing up and Providing Care for Infants and Toddlers in an Institution*, ed. A. Tardos, pp. 127–134 (Budapest: Association Pikler-Lóczy for Young Children, 2007).

chapter 8

Cognition

Focus Questions

After reading this chapter you should be able to answer the following questions:

1 Describe what is meant by "the cognitive experience." How does it change from infancy to toddlerhood?

2 How would you compare and contrast the theories of Piaget and Vygotsky?

3 What are appropriate guidelines for adults to foster cognitive development in young children?

4 How do brain-based learning principles support infant-toddler cognition?

5 What are the key components of a high-quality early childhood inclusion program?

What Do You See?

Nick stands holding an empty pitcher in his hand. He goes over to a box of toys, reaches in, and brings out a small plastic bowl, an egg carton, and the lid to a peanut butter jar. He sets these in a row on a low table and pretends to pour something in them from his pitcher. He is careful in his actions and methodically fills each container, including each compartment of the egg carton. Then, seemingly satisfied that the task is done, he tosses the pitcher aside with a joyous shout. He starts across the room in another direction when he notices a plant standing on a table. He immediately runs back to where he left the pitcher and rummages through the pile of dolls and blankets hiding it from his view. He finds it, carries it over to the plant, and carefully pours pretend water into the pot. He abandons the pitcher again and picks up a doll. He scolds the doll, bangs it on the floor several times, wraps it in a blanket, and then lovingly puts it to bed in a box of toys. As he bends over the box, he spies a picture book with fire engines on the cover. He looks at the pictures for a moment, puts the book on his head, and races around the room screaming in what seems to be an imitation of a siren. As he passes by a toy shelf, he sees a wooden fire truck. He pulls it out and proceeds to push it around on the floor. He stops and looks at the holes on the truck where the little firefighters are supposed to sit. No little firefighters are in sight. He pauses for a moment, looks around, and goes to the pitcher once more. Nick carefully fills each hole in the fire truck with whatever pretend liquid the pitcher contains.

Knowing and understanding the world come from active involvement with people and things. Infants and toddlers are naturally active and interactive. Nick is a good example of a young child who is actively involved in his world. His previous experiences are clearly reflected in his ability to combine known things in new ways. He seeks experiences that are interesting to him, and he shows that he can make adaptations that lead to problem solving. These skills and others related to cognition, or mental development, are the focus of this chapter. Some of the work of Jean Piaget, the leading Swiss cognitive psychologist, and Lev Vygotsky, the Russian developmental psychologist, are discussed. The information on early brain development is confirming how young children learn, and implications of that understanding are included. The chapter concludes by reviewing the benefits of early childhood inclusion programs for young children with and without disabilities.

The Cognitive Experience

The process of gathering information, organizing it, and finally using it to adapt to the world is the essence of the **cognitive experience.** Whenever a topic such as cognition or mental growth is discussed, it is easy to also include such terms as *intellect*, *learning*, and maybe eventually *academics* as related concepts. Most people think of the cognitive process as it relates to IQ scores and school-type experiences (including grades!). A quality infant-toddler program will promote cognitive and intellectual growth in young children, but it will not look the same as a traditional classroom setting. Understanding *how* children grow and learn is basic to planning a developmentally appropriate setting that will foster cognitive development.

How do infants develop knowing and understanding? Initially, they perceive experiences directly with the senses. For infants to acquire the ability to comprehend this sensory information, they must be able to distinguish between the familiar and the unknown; later they will begin to consider, to formulate, and eventually to form mental images in this process of experiencing and clarifying the environment.

This process is primarily unseen; therefore certain assumptions concerning cognition must be inferred by observing obvious physical movements. Infants begin by exploring the world with their bodies. They internalize what they take in through their senses and display it in their physical movements. Infants gather vital information through such simple acts as mouthing, grasping, and reaching. You can see infants practicing these acts, repeating them over and over, and they refine them rather quickly. For example, when newborns first bring the mouth toward a nipple, the mouth opens wide and ready. With only a few trials, they learn just what size opening the nipple requires and adjust the mouth accordingly in anticipation of what will go into it. They have refined a simple action. Soon they will judge how far to reach and what shape the fingers must take to pick up a cup or a toy. Much later, as adults, they may refine their actions further to reach without looking and strike a particular chord on the piano or input data on a computer keyboard. All these muscular refinements had their beginnings in that tiny mouth adjusting itself to the appropriate size for the nipple. In this example, cognition has been tied to fine motor development. You can think of other examples in which cognition is tied to gross motor development, social development, and emotional development. Learning and thinking support all areas of development.

The knowing process—cognition—also involves language abilities. As young children use their senses to experience the world, they need labels to categorize and remember these experiences. By creating these labels, children increase their ability to communicate and begin to control and regulate their own behavior. These expanded abilities give young children additional opportunities to understand the world.

Sensorimotor Experience: Piaget

The theorist who has contributed much to our understanding of cognitive development in infants and toddlers is Jean Piaget. He was most interested in how children come to know about their world. He was not so much interested in how much a child knows (that is, quantity, or IQ), but rather in the quality of a child's understanding and how the child can eventually justify or explain it. He named the first stage—birth to two years of age—the **sensorimotor stage**. This name, which means the coordination of sense perception and muscle movements, is appropriate because that coordination is the beginning of thinking. Table 8.1 lists the components of the sensorimotor stage.

Table 8.1 The Sensorimotor Stage		
Age	**Sensorimotor Behaviors**	**Examples**
Birth–1 month	Reflexes, simple inborn behaviors	Crying, sucking, grasping
1–4 months	Refines simple behaviors, repeats and combines them	Reaching, grasping, sucking on hands/fingers
4–8 months	Repeats activity using objects, begins limited imitation	Accidentally makes a mobile in the crib move, notices it, tries to make it happen again
8–12 months	Intentionality: plans a movement to make something happen	Pulls a string to bring a toy closer
12–18 months	Experiments with objects to create new events	If a ball rolled from the table will bounce, what will a book do?
18–24 months	Imagines events and solves problems, invents through mental combination, begins to use words	Pretends to throw a ball, calls to a caregiver or parent, "Here ball"

Gradually, infants come to know that they can control the interaction between themselves and objects. They like this new piece of knowledge, and they keep testing it. This process of taking in new information and processing it (or *playing* with it), is what Piaget called **assimilation**. This process allows infants to make information their own and to incorporate new experience into previously developed mental concepts or categories. Piaget used the term **accommodation** to describe what happens when this new information refines or expands previous mental categories. Initially the senses assimilate everything, but then they begin to accommodate to particular sights and sounds (focusing on a face, for example, and ignoring the bright light). It is through the ongoing dynamic system of assimilation (taking in experience) and accommodation (adjusting to it) that young children adapt to the world, and it is a lifelong process.

When babies are practicing and combining these first actions, they are in love with their own bodies—fascinated by what they are feeling and doing. Eventually that fascination moves from their own bodies to the effects their actions have on the environment. They get interested in what happens when they shove their arm out and hit a toy. A new understanding develops with this shift of focus from self to environment, from action to consequence. Babies begin to realize that they and the objects in the world are separate.

You can see this same progression of development a bit later in toddlers having art experiences. At first, children are most interested in what it feels like when they scribble or scrub with a paintbrush on paper. Later they start looking at the product of their action—the drawing or painting. Some children don't focus on the product until after three years of age.

Knowing they are in a world full of objects and part of it, but not the whole of it, is a great step forward in understanding for infants. Nevertheless, their ideas of objects differ greatly from those of adults. Infants acknowledge the existence only of things they can see, touch, or otherwise know with their senses. When you hide her favorite toy, the young infant does not look for it because she believes it no longer exists. "Out of sight, out of mind as the saying goes." If you bring the toy out of hiding, it has been re-created for her. This understanding of the world makes a game of peekaboo extremely exciting: What power—to create and uncreate a person in an instant. No wonder peekaboo has universal fascination. What the young infant lacks is what Piaget called **object permanence**, or the ability to remember an object or person even though they cannot be seen, touched, or heard. Eventually, infants become aware that objects continue to exist even when they can't see them. But gaining this awareness is a gradual process.

At about one year of age, children begin to think in a more sophisticated way and to use tools. Give them a stick and they will use it to gain an out-of-reach toy. Give them a string with something they want at the end and they know just what to do. Novelty becomes an end in itself. Children will deliberately manipulate the environment to find out what happens.

Table 8.2 Piaget's Stages of Cognitive Development	
Stage	**General Description**
Sensorimotor stage (0–2 years)	Child progresses from reflexive action to symbolic activities; has ability to separate self from objects; has limited awareness of cause and effect.
Preoperational stage (2–7 years)	Child is able to use symbols, such as words; has better reasoning skills but is still perceptually bound in the here and now.
Concrete operational stage (7–11 years)	Child has logical thought, but only in regard to concrete objects; has ability to order things by number, size, or class; also has ability to relate time and space.
Formal operational stage (11 years and older)	Child has abstract, logical thought; has ability to consider alternatives in problem solving.

With all this experimenting, children develop some new abilities: the ability to anticipate where an object will be when they drop it, the ability to remember an action after a short interruption, and the ability to predict. Watch an 18-month-old child who has had experience with a ball. He may roll the ball off a table and turn his head to the place where it will land. Or if the ball rolls under a chair, he may look for a way to get it out again. Or if he rolls a ball toward a hole, he will run to the hole to watch the ball drop into it.

The next step in the development of understanding comes when infants can find solutions mentally. After enough experience using their sense perceptions and muscles, they can begin to think of ways of acting and try them out in their head before doing them. This is a big step in the process toward self-regulation. They can think of past and future events. You can see they are using mental images and connecting thoughts to experiences and objects that are not present. They can throw an imaginary ball or contemplate the solution to a problem before they begin to tackle it.

Table 8.2 provides a brief overview of all four of Piaget's stages of cognitive development. The focus of this chapter is stage one—sensorimotor—and a small part of stage two—preoperational.

Sociocultural Influences: Vygotsky and Piaget

The beginning of language and the ability to pretend signal the end of the sensorimotor stage and the beginning of what Piaget called the **preoperational stage**. Piaget was not alone in his appreciation of thought and language and their impact on how children come to understand their world. Recently, numerous developmentalists have looked more closely at infant-toddler cognitive growth.

The work by Lev Vygotsky gives another perspective on the importance of language and how young children acquire problem-solving skills.

The findings by Piaget and Vygotsky suggest that infants and toddlers are competent in problem solving and that their cognitive skills develop rapidly. A comparison of Piaget and Vygotsky can help caregivers and parents understand cognitive growth and developmentally appropriate practices, especially as to how they pertain to a child's sociocultural world. By highlighting the skills of preoperational children and by reviewing the ideas of Piaget and Vygotsky, we can better understand how young children become independent, self-regulating learners.

Preoperational children can use mental images for their thinking processes. Thinking, though still tied to the concrete, is not limited to sense perceptions and body movements. Although toddlers don't practice this very much, they *can* think while standing or even sitting still. (However, they still need to be gathering a great number of concrete experiences *to think about*, so don't let anyone pressure you into sitting toddlers down in order to educate them.) Because of their increased ability to hold and store mental images, toddlers entering the preoperational stage have increased **memory**, or recall, of past events. Although the word *yesterday* may not yet be in their vocabulary, they *can* remember yesterday—and the day before.

Reflect

What problem-solving skills have you observed in infants? How do those skills expand in toddlerhood?

Self-Regulating Learners

Young children's sense of the future also increases as their **ability to predict** grows with their experience in the world. They continue to use trial and error to strengthen this skill, not only in the concrete world ("I wonder what will happen if I pour sand in the sink"), but also in the social one ("I wonder what will happen if I pour sand in Jamie's hair"). Sometimes these experiments are both social and physical and are thought out on the conscious level ("If I pinch the baby, will he cry?"). Sometimes children don't make such clear decisions, but they are still problem solving in a trial-and-error way ("I wonder if hitting Erin will get an adult over here to pay attention to me," or "If I break enough limits, can I get my caregiver and mother to quit talking to each other so we can go home?"). What appears to be naughty behavior may in reality be this scientific testing that eventually leads to self-regulation.

Pause for a moment and review some of Piaget's major points. Piaget believed:

- Knowledge is *functional*—it leads to something
- Information gained from experience helps an individual *adapt* to the world
- Significant knowledge can be used to accomplish something (important when considering children's *play* experience)

Piaget's view of the young child's cognitive growth contains four key assumptions. First, interaction with people and the environment is essential. As young children grow and mature, they use experience to build, or **construct new**

knowledge. The child's action on objects (sucking, pulling, pushing) is the central force for cognitive development.

Second, Piaget viewed the growth of the young child as gradual and continuous. The concept that objects are permanent grows slowly from the first few days of a child's life. As the "quality" of that concept matures, it provides the memory base, and the language, from which the toddler can create "pretend" play experiences.

Piaget believed that there is a connection between successive periods of development. This third assumption indicates the importance of the *quality* of development in *each* stage of a child's life. A skill or ability later in life depends on the maturing and improving of earlier achievements. In other words, don't push infants and toddlers to be "smarter." The "growth of mental structures," according to Piaget, will foster natural (appropriate) learning.

A fourth basic point Piaget made involves the young child's *ability to construct a plan*. He believed that this is one of the major competencies to develop during the first two years, and he referred to this ability as **intentionality**. Intentionality gradually emerges as a child selects objects, plays with them, repeats actions on them, and creates a plan. This experience often involves a great deal of absorption; the young child may appear to be "lost in thought."[1]

Take a moment to think about the complexity of creating and using mental images and the ability to construct a plan for thinking. Thinking is not limited to sense perceptions and body movements. It is also a social experience. While infants and toddlers actively explore things in their world, they are often also interacting with other people.

Social Interaction and Cognition

Vygotsky believed that cognitive activities have their origins in these social interactions. His work emphasizes the importance of social interaction and adds a significant piece to Piaget's view that mental development occurs only in stages (the child is capable only because biological growth has occurred). By comparing the perspectives of Piaget and Vygotsky, one can better understand how infant-toddler thinking emerges (see Table 8.3).

Vygotsky, like Piaget, believed that children *construct* their understanding of the world. Infants and toddlers gather and practice important learning constantly. Vygotsky would agree with Piaget that knowledge is functional in that it helps individuals adapt to the world. However, Vygotsky would emphasize that this learning is *co-constructed*. Young children acquire important skills (especially those skills unique to people, such as specific memory and symbolic thought) with the help of another, more experienced learner. This help is certainly not always in the form of a lesson. Caregivers who work with infants and toddlers often provide appropriate prompts to help children think about their own experiences. If caregivers step in too early or too late, valuable learning may be lost. Vygotsky's views on **assisted learning**, and how learning can lead to development, differ from Piaget's. Vygotsky's focus is that social interaction

Table 8.3 Comparison of Piaget's and Vygotsky's Approaches to Cognitive Development	
Similarities	

- Both believed that young children *construct* their knowledge—they build their information base from experience.

- Both believed that young children acquire abilities when they are *ready*—previous skills serve as a base for new learning.

- Both believed that *play* provides an important opportunity to learn and practice life skills.

- Both believed that language is significant for cognitive development to advance.

- Both believed that cognition was fostered by "nature and nurture."

Differences

• Piaget believed that knowledge is primarily *self-constructed* and discovery oriented.	• Vygotsky placed emphasis on the importance of *co-constructed* knowledge and assisted discovery.
• Piaget believed that *maturation* (moving through stages) allows for cognition to advance; development leads to learning.	• Vygotsky believed that learning can be "advanced" (not pushed) with the *assistance of an expert* (adult or peer); learning can lead to development.
• Piaget believed that hands-on, *sensory-rich play* provides valuable practice for later adultlike behavior.	• Vygotsky was more specific and emphasized *pretend play* that allows children to distinguish between objects and their meaning and to experiment with new cause-and-effect relationships.
• Piaget believed that language provides labels for many previous experiences (egocentric speech), and that it is the primary means through which children interact.	• Vygotsky believed that language is absolutely essential for mental growth; *self-talk* is eventually internalized into higher levels of mental development and self-directive behavior.
• Piaget's stages are universal and apply to children around the world; the nature of thinking is largely independent of cultural context.	• Vygotsky stressed the importance of culture and society for fostering mental growth; cultures influence the course of cognitive development (reasoning skills may not appear at the same age in different cultures).

is a prerequisite for children to develop problem-solving skills and that early language experience is critical to this process. Vygotsky believes that children, through assisted learning, are constantly learning from others and then they make that learning their own, through play. For Piaget, children *discover* learning through their play experiences, and then take that learning into their social interactions with others. Piaget believed that development precedes learning ("that mental structures" mature and foster learning). The **zone of proximal development** (ZPD) is the phrase used by Vygotsky to describe how adults can appropriately assist children's learning. ZPD is the difference between what children can do on their own (independent performance) and what they can do with further guidance (assisted performance).

Consider an infant who, after crawling under a very low table, tries to sit up. There's no room. He continues to try to lift his head until he realizes that he is stuck. He starts screaming. His caregiver peers under the table, lending her quiet presence. While maneuvering the infant's head, the caregiver talks to him so that he stays low and in a crawling position. She uses verbal and physical cues to guide him out from under the table.

Vygotsky would label the head bumping and squirming the child experienced as the child's "level of independent performance." The way the child got out from under the table was what Vygotsky would call the "level of assisted performance." You might ask yourself, why go to all the trouble? Why not just lift the table off? According to Vygotsky, if caregivers appropriately assist children in problem solving, children stay with the situation longer and learn more. (*Note:* The Reggio Emilia schools are proving what Magda Gerber has been saying for years about problem solving. Problem solving and learning work best when in a positive, responsive environment that encourages interactions. The adult, taking cues from the child, assists the child only until he or she can work independently. If the child doesn't need or want help, the adult backs off.)

Appropriate is a key word for understanding the concept of helping and guiding children. Appropriate help has to do with being respectful and sensitively responsive and always takes into consideration what is best for the child. *Remember principle 8: Recognize problems as learning opportunities, and let infants and toddlers try to solve their own. Don't rescue them, constantly make life easy for them, or try to protect them from all problems.*

Language and Cognition

A "guided," or socially shared, cognition is at the root of Vygotsky's theory regarding the mental development of children. When caregivers and parents interact with children in collaborative ways, they provide the tools for mental growth that are important to language development. Language, according to Vygotsky, plays a central role in cognition. Language is the first type of communication between infants and adults. Caregiving experiences provide the opportunity for infants and adults to experience these communication opportunities. Gradually, during infancy and toddlerhood, all the gestures, words, and symbols of social interaction that a young child experiences become internalized. It is this eventual communication with self (internalized language) that Vygotsky believed was so important to self-regulation and cognition. Vygotsky's theory acknowledges that cognition and language develop separately, but that they begin to merge within a social communication context. The language of others helps a young child organize and regulate her own behavior verbally.[2] How many times have you heard a young child repeat (maybe in abbreviated form) what she has just heard or been told? Vygotsky stressed the importance of this private speech (and, later, make-believe play) to cognitive development more than did Piaget.

Today much thought is being given to the importance of a child's cultural background and how these early social interactions contribute to mental development. In his sociocultural theory, Vygotsky focused on how social interaction

NAEYC Program Standard 7
Families

helps children acquire the important skills and ways of behaving native to their culture. He believed that the sharing of cultural activities (e.g., cooking) between child and adult contributes significantly to the child's understanding of his or her world. Although some of Vygotsky's ideas may seem obvious to most parents and caregivers, misinterpretations do occur. Some people force children to learn things inappropriate for their age—for example, math flash cards at three years of age—and use the work of Vygotsky to justify it. After reviewing some of Vygotsky's concepts, we can't help but appreciate how much he valued the uniqueness of each child and that child's cultural history.

Piaget and Vygotsky have both contributed to our knowledge of the mental growth of young children. Piaget focused on the biological changes that contribute to cognition. Vygotsky stressed how social interaction might transform a child's thinking and problem-solving abilities. Today neither theory by itself would be enough to completely explain cognitive development. As they grow and mature, children need the support of sensitive adults.

Look now at the behavior and play of three children and see how they relate to the biological and social perspectives of Piaget and Vygotsky. Try to determine what might be going on for each child and how the environment might be influencing them. By being able to discuss the ideas of Piaget and Vygotsky, we can resist the pressure to apply inappropriate school-like academic experiences to the education of infants and toddlers. Remember, both Piaget and Vygotsky believed that play is extremely important to the child's learning and that pushing a child does not foster real understanding of the world.

The first child is lying on his back on a rug surrounded by a few toys. He turns slightly toward a ball lying near his arm. He stretches, and the movement causes him to accidentally touch the ball. It moves, making a sound. He startles at the sound and looks toward the ball. He lies still again; his gaze wanders. Then he moves his arms again—a big, sweeping gesture—and the ball moves again, making the same jingling sound. He again startles, and a look of surprise comes on his face. You can almost hear his question, "Who did that?" He looks at the ball, looks around, and looks at the ball again. Then he lies still. A few moments later his arms come up and out again, this time tentatively waving. He misses the ball. Nothing happens. He lies still again. He repeats the action, again tentatively. This time his hand passes in front of his eyes, and a spark of interest comes over his face. He looks intently at his hand, and you can almost hear him asking, "What's that thing? Where did it come from?" He moves his fingers, and delight comes into his eyes. "Hey, it works!" he seems to say. His arms continue to wave, taking the fascinating fingers out of his line of vision. He breezes by the ball again, causing it to make just a whisper of sound. His eyes search for the source of the sound.

The second child is sitting on a rug near the first, but they are separated by a low fence. She has a rubber toy in her hand and is banging it up and down on the floor, giggling at the squeaks issuing forth. The toy bounces across the rug as she lets go, and she crawls happily after it. She stops to explore a string with a large bead on the end, but glances to see where the other end is. The string disappears into a pile of toys on the lowest shelf at the edge of the rug. She expectantly pulls the string and laughs delightedly. Then she catches sight of a bright red ball that has rolled out from the pile of toys that fell off the shelf. She crawls over to it and begins to smack it with her hand, making noises while doing so. She seems to expect the ball to move. When it doesn't, she tries again with more force. The ball moves slightly, and she moves after it. She is getting more and more excited, and as she approaches the ball, one hand accidentally swipes it so that it rolls some distance and disappears under a couch in the corner of the room. She watches it roll, starts after it, but stops when it disappears. Looking puzzled, she crawls over to the edge of the couch but does not lift up the ruffle at the bottom to check underneath. She looks a little disappointed, but then she crawls back to the rug and the squeaky rubber toy. As the scene closes, she is once again banging the toy against the floor and laughing at the noise it makes.

The third child is sitting at a table putting puzzle pieces in a three-piece puzzle. When she gets stuck, she looks to a nearby adult, who gives her verbal hints about how to turn the pieces. When she completes the puzzle, she turns it upside down and smiles at the clatter of wooden pieces hitting the tabletop. She works the puzzle again, faster this time, with no help from the adult. When she finishes the puzzle, she puts it back on a low shelf and moves to another table where several other children are poking and squeezing play dough. She asks for a piece, and when none is forthcoming, an adult intervenes, helping each child give her a bit off the hunks they are playing with. She sits contentedly poking and prodding her play dough, periodically conversing with the other children about what she is doing. Her monologue is not in direct response to anything they are saying. There is little interaction at the table, though there is lots of talking. The child we are focusing on rolls her play dough into a ball, then sits looking at it for a minute. Then she begins to pat and shape it, obviously with purpose in her actions. When she has produced a lopsided lump, she sits back, satisfied, and announces to no one in particular that she is finished. She gets up and walks away. As she leaves the table, another child grabs her piece and incorporates it into his own. This act goes unnoticed. The girl, seeing a cart of food being wheeled into the room, runs to the corner to a row of sinks and begins to wash her hands. We leave her thoroughly soaping her hands and arms and obviously enjoying the experience.

Play and Cognition

It is essential to recognize the importance of play to a young child and how it contributes to his or her cognitive development. When observing children, it is difficult to infer from their physical behaviors and play what they are thinking. By using Piaget's and Vygotsky's ideas of early cognitive development, we can attempt to guess what these children are thinking and how they are being influenced by their environment. We can begin to see the transition from unintentional, even accidental, behavior to purposeful and directed behavior that manifests through problem solving, mental images, representational thought, and pretend play. We can also see how appropriate adult support can help children learn how to foster cooperation among themselves.

By the second year, children can think about their world even when they are not directly experiencing it. They also begin to represent things by the use of symbols. Engaging in **pretend play** marks an important step in a child's thinking, and it usually is joined by the beginning of language. Pretend play is when children can represent things through symbols and have the ability to think of their world when not directly experiencing it.

Take the time to observe a two-year-old and a three-year-old involved in pretend play. You may be able to see three different changes or trends that have come about as a result of cognitive growth.

**NAEYC Program
Standard 2**
Curriculum

The younger a child is, the more apt he is to be the center of his own pretend play. As he gets older, he gradually acquires the ability to remove himself from center stage. He is then ready to take the role of other imaginary characters. Notice a one-year-old pretending to feed himself. When he gets a little older, he will pretend to feed his doll rather than himself. His doll, however, remains very quiet. By about two years, the child has the ability to make the doll "wake up." Now he can make his doll feed itself. The child can now assume the role of others in his play. He can stand back and consider the other's feelings and one role in relation to another. (Is the doll hungry? How much "food" should he supply for his doll?) As he gets older, pretend play becomes more complex and involves other people (for example, several four-year-olds "grocery shopping" in a dramatic play area).

Another change in pretend play can be appreciated when a child begins to substitute one object for another. A very young child needs a real object, or realistic replica, for pretend play. If she is feeding herself, she needs a real cup or real spoon (or plastic replica). As a child gets older (closer to about 22 months), she acquires the ability to substitute one object for another. Now perhaps a stick can be used as a spoon, especially when feeding a doll.

At first this substitution is quite limited. Objects need to look like the real thing, and the child may not be able to substitute too many things at one time. Young children need to have available objects to enhance their play. It is important to appreciate that as children get older (closer to four years), it may be difficult for them to substitute a well-known object for something else.

As pretend play continues to develop, a child can invent several actions and combine them. These combinations expand and become more complex as the child gets older. A young child may initially just pretend to feed himself. As he combines actions and integrates them into other experiences, he may eventually pretend to "open a restaurant" and feed several dolls (and no doubt any people who will cooperate).

A toddler's cognitive growth is visible in numerous areas. Pretend play, however, is one of the most dramatic abilities to be observed in a young child. The development of purposeful behavior needs to be planned for and respected by adults.

The Principles in Action

Principle 8 Recognize problems as learning opportunities, and let infants and toddlers try to solve their own. Don't rescue them, constantly make life easy for them, or try to protect them from all problems.

Caitlin and Ian are two 18-month-olds in your family child care home; they have been with you since they were 6 months old. Caitlin is spirited and alive with activity; Ian is not as active and tends to observe Caitlin a lot or follow her lead. This morning Caitlin is busy dropping shapes through holes in a plastic box. When a shape does not fit readily into a hole, she pounds it vigorously with her hand to make it fit and then quickly turns the box to find another hole. She giggles with delight at the sound of each shape dropping into the box. Ian is watching her from a slight distance holding his stuffed dog; he seems interested but makes no attempt to approach Caitlin and her activity. Caitlin is suddenly finished with the plastic box. She moves over to the block area where you have arranged a few blocks on the floor and added a new small red car. She immediately notices the new car and says, "Car!" This attracts Ian's attention, and he moves over to the block area too. Caitlin gives the new car a push, and it rolls (faster than she realized) under a nearby bookshelf and is out of sight. Caitlin rushes over to the bookshelf intent on retrieving the car even though it has probably rolled too far under the shelving for her to reach it. Ian looks over to you with an expression that seems to say, "Now what?"

1. How would you describe each child's approach to exploration and problem solving?
2. How would you interact with each one to foster their individual learning opportunities?
3. Are you at all concerned with Ian's approach to problem solving? Or with Caitlin's approach? Why or why not?
4. What would you do about helping the children retrieve the red car?
5. What would you try to provide in an environment to foster problem solving in young children?

Supporting Cognitive Development

The prerequisite for promoting cognitive development is security and attachment. Through the attachment process, infants develop skills such as *differentiation* as they distinguish the person(s) they are attached to from others in their world. Attachment also shows *intentionality* as infants and toddlers use all their behaviors to bring the attached person(s) close and keep them there. Clinging, crying infants or toddlers are exhibiting strong intentionality (a mark of early cognitive behavior) as they try to get the parent to remain. This may be annoying, and it is not usually recognized as cognitive behavior; yet in truth it is very purposeful and intelligent.

Responding to other needs is also one of the prerequisites for promoting cognitive development. Children with unmet needs put their energies into trying to get someone to meet them, which focuses their cognitive development in a narrow way. Children whose needs are met consistently will feel trusting and comfortable. Children who feel comfortable will *explore the environment*. From continual exploration comes cognitive development.

Cognitive development is promoted by inviting and encouraging exploration in an environment rich in sensory experience. When given the opportunity to play with objects in any way they wish, children encounter problems. Remember that problem solving is the basis of infant-toddler education as it is outlined in this book. Allowing infants and toddlers to solve the kinds of problems they run into during the course of a day promotes their cognitive development. Free choice ensures that children find problems that are meaningful to them. Solving someone else's problem is not nearly as interesting to most of us as solving the ones that are related to something that really matters to us.

It helps problem solving if adults do such things as adding words (labeling sensory input—"That rabbit feels soft and warm," or "That was a loud noise," or "That sponge is soaking wet"). In addition, adults can help by asking questions, pointing out relationships, reflecting feelings, and generally supporting a child.

Encourage children to interact with one another during problem solving. The input infants and toddlers get from their peers can be useful and can also offer more than one way to a solution. Remember, both Piaget and Vygotsky believe that interaction—with objects and with other people, especially peers—promotes cognitive development. Include dramatic play props for toddlers. Through pretend, they build the mental images that are so important for the thought process.

The Importance of Real-Life Experiences

Reflect

Have you seen caregivers do too much for young children? What effect do you think this has over time?

NAEYC Program Standard 3
Teaching

There is no need to create "academic" experiences for young children. They learn significant concepts that are embedded in real-life, everyday activities. Normal conversations can *teach* colors and shapes—for example, "Please bring me the red pillow," or "Do you want a round cracker or a square one?" Number concepts, including size and weight comparisons, happen naturally as young children play with blocks and sand. Key ways to support cognitive growth include providing experiences with a variety of materials, supplying the opportunity to figure out relationships, and fostering the feeling that you can make things happen in your world.

Outdoor experiences also provide wonderful ways to encourage cognitive development in young children. When they have had the experience of planting beans, for example—and then watering, picking, snapping, washing, and eating them—they really understand what the word *bean* means. Because of these many associations, by the time they see the written word for bean and have listened to related stories, they are ready to *decode* the word itself. Such "emergent literacy" experiences begin to build in children an appreciation of what the idea of reading is all about. There is no need to teach the alphabet to infants and toddlers. Provide experiences that build concepts and lead (on the literacy continuum) to the eventual joy of reading itself.

Infants and toddlers are naturally creative. If you don't hinder them with restrictive limits and an impoverished environment, they will give you lessons in how to use toys and materials in ways you never imagined. Curiosity is part of this push for creativity and needs to be valued and nurtured. Infants and toddlers are newcomers to the world, and they want to know how everything works. They don't want to be told; they want to find out on their own. They are scientists. They don't take anything for granted but rather must prove each hypothesis. Nurture this quality in them! *Remember principle 4: Invest time and energy to build the total person (concentrate on the "whole child"). Don't focus on cognitive development alone or look at it as separate from total development.*

It can be helpful to remind yourself that according to both Piaget and Vygotsky, infants and toddlers

- Are involved in the process of creating knowledge from experience
- Are the builders of their own understanding
- Use a creative construction process to make sense of their experience

In this active process, young children learn to combine known things in their world in new ways. Think about the development of pretend play. As a result of exploring and manipulating things, toddlers experiment with new combinations and recombining known elements in new ways. This is the essence of creativity—the process of combining known things in new ways.

The appreciation of creativity as part of cognitive development emphasizes the importance of planning for it and for allowing it to develop. When a young child has opportunity to explore and experiment, understanding is fostered. Once children understand how something works (usually as a result of playing with it), they seem naturally to start using it creatively. Exploration is not the same as creativity. Exploration is the beginning point. When promoting cognitive development, try to follow some of the suggestions given in this section. Then step back and watch for the creative, problem-solving process.

Brain-Based Learning

The research on early brain development that has gotten so much attention nationwide may confirm what many parents and caregivers already know about how young children learn. It may also cause many misinterpretations about development and may fuel marketing strategies for "smart toys," "screen time," and "super-stimulating" environments. This is an important time to think about young children and to care about how they learn and grow. No doubt, in the next few years many questions about brain development and learning will be answered. Right now, however, some significant things do seem clear about how the brain learns.

Reflect

Have you noticed "smart toys" in stores or shopping areas? What are their claims? What do you think of such marketing?
(Hint: "Smart Toys" are usually those props advertised as making your child smarter or raising his or her IQ.)

VIDEO OBSERVATION 8

Father Diapering Toddler

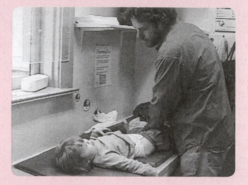

See Video Observation 8: Father Diapering Toddler for an example of an activity that relates to cognitive development.

Questions

- Why do you think we picked a diapering scene instead of one that showed a child in a more obviously intellectual pursuit of some sort?
- Do you see evidence that the child and man have a relationship? What part do relationships play in cognitive development?
- Can you explain how the child was showing that potty training is more than a physical issue and has cognitive connections?
- Explain how this scene illustrates a child learning language in context.

To view this clip, go to **www.mhhe.com/itc10e.** Click on Student Edition, select Chapter 8, and click on Video Observations.

Attachments are primary to development, and learning takes place best in trusting, responsive relationships. The brain functions as an integrated whole; all the developmental areas are involved. Infants are active learners, and the brain becomes more active when adults respond to infants' cues and signals for attention. Environments are powerful; learning context is as important as learning content. Routines need to be sensitive to relationships (be aware of group size, ratio, and time spent caring for an infant). Meaningfulness of an experience increases the possibility that it will be remembered. Experience and repetition strengthen neural pathways in the brain's circuitry, but don't confuse drill with repetition. Repetition is child-sensitive and comes from the child; drill is adult directed and adult needs (not the child's) are being addressed.[3]

It is brain density (or neural connections) and myelinization rather than brain size that contributes most to learning. The brain circuits and neuropathways that have been reinforced and refined translate experience into learning. These branching dendrites in the cortex allow for specific measurement thanks to today's advanced technology. Growth spurts, reflected by increased brain activity, in the first two years actually align themselves with the sensorimotor experiences of Piaget's theory.[4]

More and more we realize that no one theory completely explains how children learn. The theories of Piaget and Vygotsky can be combined to help appreciate cognitive development in the early years. Brain-based learning principles—hands-on, discovery-oriented, collaborative, open-ended experiences—very similar to Piaget's and Vygotsky's ideas and developmentally appropriate practice also help us appreciate the essential interconnectedness of young children's learning.[5]

Brain-based learning provides evidence that strong neuropathways are created through early experience, and early brain development research reinforces the following key points:

- Inborn abilities and active curiosity interact with various experiences to develop early problem-solving skills.
- During the first six months, infants focus on developing a sense of security.
- During the second six months (and beyond), infants and toddlers turn toward exploration and new discoveries, and active movement maintains the synaptic connections.
- Cognitive development emerges from a foundation of emotional security and social stability.

Go back and take another look at the three children playing in the scenario on pages 166–167. Try to be sensitive to what might be happening in their brains. Can you see neural circuitry being strengthened? Can you see the "magic trees of the mind" (*Magic Trees of the Mind* is the title of Marion Diamond's book on brain growth.) growing more dense? Allow yourself to imagine, to wonder. *Remember principle 5: Respect infants and toddlers as worthy people. Don't treat them as objects or cute little empty-headed people to be manipulated.*

EXPLORE the following websites for more information and resource material.

The Program for Infant/Toddler Care promotes responsive care to ensure infants receive a rich and positive beginning; various resources are available.

www.pitc.org

Project Construct is a constructivist approach to learning based on the idea that children develop knowledge by interacting with their environment; through hands-on experiences, children gain understanding of their world and learn to work collaboratively.

www.projectconstruct.org

Children with Special Needs: Early Childhood Inclusion

How children begin to understand and learn about the world has been the focus of this chapter. And learning about the world in a natural setting, or as *least restrictive* as possible, is significant for the development and learning of the young child with special needs. Today an increasing number of infants and toddlers, with and without disabilities, learn and play together in homes and early care and education programs that reflect a *sense of belonging* for every child. The reaction against educational practices that separate and isolate children with disabilities is at the core of early childhood inclusion programs.

The federal legislation enacted over the last 30 years has been fundamental in shaping the changes in which services and inclusion programs are now organized for young children with special needs. Inclusion can take different forms, so having a basic understanding of what it means and looks like is important in order to achieve high-quality early childhood inclusion programming.

Early childhood inclusion supports the right of every infant and young child and his family to participate in a broad range of activities as full members of programs, communities, and society. The desired results of inclusive experiences, regardless of a child's ability, include a sense of accomplishment, positive social relationships and friendships, and the opportunity to learn and reach one's full potential.[6]

Access to a wide range of learning opportunities and play-based activities and environments is a key characteristic of high-quality early childhood inclusion programs. Adults in these settings promote participation, engagement, and belonging for all children. When specific intervention is required for the child with special needs, activities are routine-based and never ignore the whole child.

Collaboration among families, caregivers, and specialists, as required by the individualized family service plan (IFSP), is the cornerstone for planning and implementing high-quality early childhood inclusion. A system of supports needs to be in place for families and organizations so that their efforts are successful. Resources, policies, research, and funding should provide a quality framework that reflects and guides positive inclusion practices.

EXPLORE the following websites for more information and resource material.

The National Professional Development Center on Inclusion works with states to offer professional assistance to support inclusion; resources are available for families, early intervention providers, schools, and agencies.

http://npdci.fpg.unc.edu/

Pyramid Plus: The Colorado Center for Social Emotional Competence and Inclusion seeks to increase the use of inclusive practices in early care education settings by integrating nationally recognized inclusive practices.

www.pyramidplus.org

DEVELOPMENTAL PATHWAYS

Behaviors Showing Development of Cognition

Young infants (up to 8 months)	• Respond to human voices, gaze at faces • Look for dropped toy • Try to cause things to happen • Identify objects from various viewpoints and find a toy hidden under a blanket when placed there while watching
Mobile infants (up to 18 months)	• Try to build with blocks • Persist in a search for a desired toy when toy is hidden under other objects (e.g., a blanket or pillows) • Use a stick as a tool to obtain a toy • Push away someone or something not wanted
Toddlers (up to 3 years)	• Help dress and undress themselves • Define use of many household items • Use names of self and others • Begin to realize others have rights and privileges

Source: Carol Copple and Sue Bredekamp, eds., *Developmentally Appropriate Practice in Early Childhood Programs* 3rd ed. (Washington, DC: National Association for the Education of Young Children, 2009).

Diverse Developmental Pathways

What you see	Madison often asserts her independence (lots of "Me do it!" in her vocabulary). At two-and-a-half years old, she enjoys sorting objects, and you've heard her "teaching" the other children specific labels like "hard," "soft," and even names of colors. She loves to listen to stories and often comments about the characters she knows. She prefers indoor activities and *working* alone. She often has a problem cooperating with the other children.
What you might think	Madison is one smart little girl! She is not at all empathic with her peers, and she often seems bored with them. She should play outside more in group activities. How long will it be before she is bored with the whole program?
What you might not know	Madison is the only child of a professional couple. They spend a lot of time with her—usually reading stories and playing language games. They'd like to see her have more friends (the reason they are sending her to your program), but future academics will be much more important.

(continued)

DEVELOPMENTAL PATHWAYS

Behaviors Showing Development of Cognition *(continued)*

What you might do	Continue to support Madison's love of stories. When she's with a small group of children at story time, let her hold the book and even tell part of the story. Use "feeling" words (*happy, sad, surprised*) related to the story and to the other children. When you can, read stories outside and plan "extension" activities in the play yard supporting her interactions with others. Encourage Madison's parents to observe the program. Try to find out more about their goals for her development.
What you see	Devon is a gentle little boy; he doesn't protest about anything! He usually just watches the other children and makes no effort to interact. When you *give* him a toy to play with, he simply looks at it, then drops it. At almost three, he uses very little language and seems content to have you do all his talking. When his mother drops him off, she usually leaves quickly.
What you might think	You are worried because Devon should be *doing* more things. His mother is avoiding something. What is going on?
What you might not know	Devon's mom had a long and difficult delivery with him; there was some concern of mild oxygen deprivation to the brain, but no specifics were provided. She is worried about Devon's lack of responsiveness too. She has talked with Devon's pediatrician and is doing some simple games at home with Devon. She really wants to talk to you—she's feeling guilty about the situation—but she just doesn't know where to start.
What you might do	Continue to interact with Devon without overwhelming him. Offer him sensory-rich experiences—lots of sand and water play—and *demonstrate* the steps of an activity. ("Here is the soap, put it in your hand. Now reach for the water.") Plan to be really available to Devon's mom at arrival and departure times. As soon as possible, make a time to talk with her.

Today we know that quality early childhood inclusion benefits children, with and without disabilities, caregivers, and families. For children with disabilities, inclusion programs provide better developmental outcomes; skills learned in a natural setting are better generalized to other learning experiences. Also, social competence and social interactions are enhanced by peer models. For children without disabilities, inclusion programs provide a greater understanding of differences and the opportunity for diverse friendships. Sometimes modifications made for the *included* child can result in more creative problem solving for other children. For caregivers and teachers, inclusion programs provide the opportunity to be a crucial member of a team, gather valuable information, and reinforce their solid understanding of early childhood development and learning. For families, inclusion programs provide objective information about disabilities, the chance to teach their child about acceptance, and the opportunity to appreciate that they are not isolated, but part of the community.[7]

Communities that support inclusion programs better allocate their early childhood resources by limiting the need for separate special education programs. Everyone has the opportunity to learn something new, and everyone has the chance to problem solve.

Remember that early childhood inclusion is not accomplished by simply placing a child with disabilities in a setting with his typically developing peers. Meaningful participation, and not mere closeness to activities, is necessary for a child to achieve his full potential. Always appreciate the uniqueness of each child and allow him to express his competence to the best of his ability.

Think about what inclusion might *look like* while reading about Peter, a developmentally delayed toddler. He is 20 months old. He is still crawling and has made no attempt to stand. For unknown reasons, Peter experienced anoxia (reduced oxygen) at birth. As part of his IFSP he attends a toddler early childhood inclusion program three mornings a week.

Peter is sitting on the floor watching two other toddlers and an adult roll a ball to each other. He has been interested in the ball game for several minutes. His eyes carefully follow the ball as it rolls from one person to another, and if the ball leaves the circle, he turns his head to watch one of the toddlers run to retrieve it. He makes no other indication of involvement.

"Peter, would you like to join our ball game?" the teacher asks. (This teacher was involved in the development of Peter's IFSP and understands that ball play is a valuable experience for him.) Peter does not look at her, but continues to watch the ball.

"We can move closer to you so that you can play, too." The teacher rolls the ball toward Peter. It stops at the edge of his foot. He makes no movement toward the ball, but has visually followed it constantly.

"The ball touched you, didn't it, Peter? Would you like to touch it?" the teacher says encouragingly. He slowly looks up at her and then to the ball. Peter points at the ball with one finger and "pokes" at it. It moves slightly, and he smiles with pleasure.

Suddenly the toddler sitting next to Peter reaches across his lap and gives the ball a swipe. It rolls back to the teacher.

"David must want us to continue our ball game. He has rolled the ball back to me," the teacher comments. "Marissa, open your hand a little more this time when the ball comes to you." The teacher demonstrates with her palm up and her fingers curled. "Peter, watch Marissa push the ball away." Marissa rolls the ball toward Peter. This time it stops near his knee. Peter looks at the ball. This time he does not poke at it but attempts to swing at it with his palm up. Even though his movement is slow and deliberate, he misses hitting the ball.

"Good try, Peter. Do it again," says the teacher. After two more swings, Peter connects with the ball, and it rolls out of the circle. He follows it with his eyes but makes no attempt to crawl after it.

David jumps up to get the ball. On his way back he notices a bug nearby on the floor and drops the ball. Marissa by this time has wandered toward the block area. The teacher reaches the ball. "Peter, would you like me to roll the ball to you?" Peter, who was watching David and the bug, looks back to her and opens and closes and opens his hands.

"You look ready. Here it comes." The ball rolls to Peter. He stops it and holds on to it tightly. He does not lift it or attempt to roll it back to the teacher. Gradually, he moves the ball in a back and forth motion between his hands. After several minutes he lets the ball roll away and turns to watch David, who has joined Marissa in the block area. "Would you like to continue playing with David and Marissa? You can move into the block area." Peter looks at the teacher. Then he slowly gets into his crawling position and proceeds toward the block section.

Peter will no doubt have plenty of opportunities to play with the ball—and with David and Marissa. The teacher is providing him encouragement and some demonstration, but she does not push him. Like all children, children with special needs need time and opportunities to practice activities, and inclusion programs can provide valuable learning opportunities.

Remember that motor development and problem solving combine for young explorers, with or without disabilities, and limit setting and childproofing are real safety issues for parents, caregivers, and teachers. Magda Gerber refers to motor skills as an infant's growing **body wisdom**. In any early care and education program, whether practicing inclusion principles or not, providing for basic needs and supporting early attachment are critical for healthy growth. As young children develop and learn, exploration should be supported and sometimes for children with special needs, it has to be encouraged. Provide choices and play opportunities in a safe setting. Parents, caregivers, and teachers need a lot of energy to keep up with young children! Freedom with guidance is the motto.

Summary

Cognition refers to thinking and mental skills, and it includes the ability to receive, process, and use information.

Cognitive Experience

- Knowing and understanding come from active involvement with people and things.

- The ability to adapt to the larger world begins with processing sensory information and matures to include language abilities and problem-solving skills.

Sensorimotor Experience: Piaget

- The beginning of cognition, as described by Piaget, is the coordination of sense perception and muscle movements.
- The six substages of the sensorimotor period gradually move from simple reflexes at birth to inventing mental images and beginning to use language by age two.

Sociocultural Influence: Vygotsky and Piaget

- Both Vygotsky and Piaget believed that young children use experience to construct or build new knowledge, but for Vygotsky this was primarily a co-constructed experience—the assistance of another person was significant.
- Vygotsky emphasized the importance of a child's social and cultural world, and that cognition grew rapidly after the second year because of language and the advent of pretend play.

Supporting Cognitive Development

- Cognitive growth is best supported by inviting and encouraging infant-toddler exploration in an environment that is rich in sensory experience.
- Mathematical concepts, emergent literacy, and creativity are all fostered when young children have the opportunity to explore, experiment, and problem solve in a safe, appropriate environment.

Brain-Based Learning

- Learning for young children is holistic, and it takes place best within trusting, responsive relationships.
- Brain-based learning principles are very similar to the ideas of Piaget and Vygotsky concerning cognitive development; the principles also align with developmentally appropriate practice.

Children with Special Needs: Early Childhood Inclusion

- Early childhood inclusion programs allow young children, with and without disabilities, to learn and play together; federal legislation supports reactions against educational practices that isolate and separate children with special needs.

- Young children, with and without disabilities, caregivers, teachers, and families all benefit from early childhood inclusion programs; everyone has the opportunity to appreciate differences and learn something new.

Key Terms

ability to predict 162
accommodation 160
assimilation 160
assisted learning 163
body wisdom 178
cognitive experience 158

construct new
   knowledge 162
intentionality 163
memory 162
object permanence 160

preoperational stage 161
pretend play 168
sensorimotor stage 159
zone of proximal
   development 164

Thought/Activity Questions

1. What behaviors indicate that a child is developing cognition? Describe at least three of them.
2. Discuss Piaget's and Vygotsky's major views about the mental development of children. What guidelines would you share with parents and caregivers concerning each approach?
3. Design a toy for an infant or a toddler that would foster cognitive growth. Include reasons why the toy would be good for this.
4. You are the guest speaker at a parent meeting for an infant-toddler program. The topic is cognitive development. What main points do you want to share?
5. How do early childhood inclusion programs benefit both children with disabilities and children without disabilities?

For Further Reading

Elena Bedrova and Deborah J. Leong, *Tools of the Mind: The Vygotskian Approach to Early Childhood Education*, 2nd ed. (Upper Saddle River, NJ: Pearson/Merrill Prentice Hall, 2007).

Deb Curtis, Kasondra L. Brown, Lorrie Baird, and Annie Marie Coughlin, "Planning Environments and Materials That Respond to Young Children's Lively Minds," *Young Children* 68(4), September 2013, pp. 26–31.

Carol Copple, *Growing Minds: Building Strong Cognitive Foundations in Early Childhood* (Washington, DC: National Association for the Education of Young Children, (2012).

Jennifer B. Ganz and Margaret M. Flores, "Implementing Visual Cues for Young Children with Autism Spectrum Disorders and Their Classmates," *Young Children* 65(3), May 2010, pp. 78–83.

Gabriel Guyton, "Using Toys to Support Infant-Toddler Learning and Development," *Young Children* 66(5), September 2011, pp. 50–56.

Maria Hamlin and Debora B. Wisneski, "Supporting the Scientific Thinking and Inquiry of Toddlers and Preschoolers through Play," *Young Children* 67(3), May 2012, pp. 82–88.

Diane E. Levin, *Beyond Remote-Controlled Childhood: Teaching Young Children in the Media Age* (Washington, DC: National Association for the Education of Young Children, 2013).

Rebecca Parlakian, "Inclusion in Infant/Toddler Child Development Settings: More Than Just Including," *Young Children* 67(4), September 2012, pp. 66–71.

Sandra Petersen, "School Readiness for Infants and Toddlers? Really? Yes, Really!" *Young Children* 67(4), September 2012, pp. 10–13.

chapter 9

Language

Focus Questions

After reading this chapter you should be able to answer the following questions:

1 What happens during the *receptive* language period and during the *expressive* language period?

2 What does language allow a child to do? How does it affect thought and cognition?

3 How does brain growth influence language development?

4 Compare guidelines for fostering language development and early literacy development. How are they similar and/or different?

5 What is bilingualism and how does it influence language development?

6 What are some important attitudes to keep in mind when working with parents and families of children with special needs?

What Do You See?

A caregiver is seated at a low table with a baby; they are sharing a snack. "Do you want a drink of milk, Aidan?" he asks.

The child answers, "Mmmmmmm mmm, ooo, milk!" and reaches for the cup.

Mike pours a small amount of milk into the cup for Aidan. The child lifts it to his lips and takes a sip. Then he says, "Mimimimimi, burrrr, burr" into the cup, delighted with the effect of the movement of his lips on the milk. Milk splashes on his face. Mike says, "I want to wipe your face," and reaches for a wet washcloth. Aidan sets the cup down, and it tips over making a puddle on the table. "Oooooo milk . . . ," he says, pointing to the puddle.

Mike says, "Yes, the milk spilled. We need a sponge." He reaches for a sponge with one hand and puts it on the puddle; with the other hand he begins wiping Aidan's face with the washcloth. "Eeeeeeee." Squeals of protest accompany the face cleaning. When all is in order again, Mike reaches for the milk carton, holds it out, and asks, "Do you want more milk?"

Aidan answers, "Uhuh, milk!" emphatically, with a vigorous shake of his head while shoving the cup toward his caregiver.

In this brief scene Aidan conveyed a variety of meanings through a few sounds and a single word. In a short time, this same scene might include a verbal sequence that could look something like:

"Me milk" (meaning, "Yes, please, I'd like some milk").
"Milk spill" (meaning, "Hey, somebody spilled the milk!").
"Me, no" (meaning, "No, thank you, I don't want any more milk").

And by the time Aidan is a toddler, he will be saying this same thing using longer phrases, such as:
"Give me milk" (perhaps with a "please").
"Oh, oh, Mike, me spill milk."
"Me no want more."
Without ever being corrected, Aidan will eventually say:

"I want some milk (please)."
"Oh, oh, Mike. I spilled my milk."
"I don't want any more, thank you."

This exchange between Aidan and his caregiver represents the early ability to learn to talk and use language, and it is an amazingly complex process. Very early in life infants begin to coordinate their gestures and make meaningful sounds. They begin to organize their experiences to make themselves understood—to communicate. This ability to develop language involves all the other areas of growth and is influenced by emotional and social development. Through language young children learn to coordinate their experiences (just as Aidan did in the introductory scene), and give and receive feedback on them.

This chapter examines the foundations of language growth and what a person needs for language to develop. We review what language allows an individual to do, and how the environment may influence language, brain growth, and early literacy. Guides for fostering language development, bilingualism, and supporting parents and families of children with special needs are also discussed.

The Progression of Language Development

Language represents experiences and events through abstract symbols or words. Although there are rules for combining words, young children begin putting them together in creative and unique ways. We define **language** as the systematic arrangement of arbitrary symbols that has generalized meaning. It allows us to communicate about things that are not visible, and those that are past or future. It is important to remember that these sounds, symbols, and interactions that we begin to experience early in life are tied to the way we think about and understand the world.

Infants are born with communication intent; they are not born with language. It is not clearly understood how children acquire the ability to use language. Usually language development is discussed in terms of *what* tends to happen *when* (see Table 9.1). No one theory or approach completely explains the development of this ability. It may be more helpful to combine several approaches in an effort to appreciate how language develops. We have already discussed the importance of attachment for infants. Within this responsive relationship, infants learn about **social interaction**—the back-and-forth imitative and caring exchange between a caregiver and an infant. This is a critical component of language growth. When they are cared for and find pleasure in this caring, infants imitate their caregivers, and their caregivers, in turn, continue to respond to them. This back-and-forth behavior seems almost to reinforce itself.

Infants all over the world begin to develop language in very similar ways. The *ability* to acquire language seems to be inborn, or *innate*. Certain mental and physical skills have to be present for language to progress. As infants grow, *maturation* contributes to the ability to develop words (or labels) and understand symbols. Piaget noted that object permanence sets the stage for language development. Young children have to be able to make sense of, or interpret, their world before using their first words. Vygotsky stressed the sociocultural context of language development. Social interaction helps young children understand the relationship between experiences and appropriate labels for them.[1]

In essence, several important things seem to happen at the same time when children acquire language. Thinking of them as the "three I's" may help. *Innate* abilities have to be present; a child has to have certain cognitive skills and mental structures to develop language. A child also needs the opportunity to *interact* with others in a responsive way in order to *imitate* them. This process of imitation, involving interaction and based on innate abilities, should be viewed in a bit more detail. Looking at two developmental levels of language—receptive (birth to one year) and expressive (end of first year to beginning first words)—gives more insight into the progression of language.

Receptive Language

Infants share their pleasure in making sounds with their parent or caregiver. They come to associate language with a social occasion. As they coo and babble, they find that they are responded to, which in turn encourages them to respond to and imitate their partner. They become aware of rhythms, pitches, and sounds of words. Language can become a way to excite or to soothe a baby.

Eventually, babies begin to make connections between sounds or sound patterns and events or objects. They notice, for example, that when they are handed a particular object (such as a teddy bear), the same sound pattern occurs time after time. Their storybooks have the same sounds with the same pictures. They notice that whenever their diapers are changed, they hear one of the same sounds and patterns. What the infant takes in and understands is called **receptive language**.

From the beginning, of course, infants react to being spoken to, but it is the voice—pitch and tone—rather than the meaning of the words that they respond to. Later, when they begin to respond to the meaning behind the words, this

Table 9.1　Language Development: What Happens When

Age	Hearing/Understanding	Talking
Birth–3 months	• Child will awaken at loud sounds, startle, or cry.	• Child will make pleasure sounds.
	• Child will listen to speech, turn to you when you speak.	• Child will repeat same sounds a lot (cooing, gooing).
	• Child will smile when spoken to.	• Child will cry differently for different needs.
	• Child will recognize your voice and quiet down if crying.	• Child will smile when he or she sees you.
4–6 months	• Child will respond to tone of voice (loud or soft).	• Child will make gurgling sounds when alone.
	• Child will look around for sound (e.g., phone ringing, dog barking).	• Child will tell you (by sound or gesture) to repeat something. May be a form of play.
	• Child will notice noise or sound from toys.	• Child will use speech or noncrying sounds to get and keep your attention.
7–12 months	• Child enjoys games like peekaboo and patty-cake.	• Child will use speech or noncrying sounds to get and keep your attention.
	• Child will listen when spoken to.	• Child will imitate different speech sounds.
	• Child will recognize words for common items like juice, cup, doll.	• Child's babbling will have both long and short groups of sounds such as "tata," "upup," "bibibibi."
		• Child will have one or two words ("bye-bye," "no," "dada"), although they may not be clear.
12–24 months	• Child will follow simple commands and understand simple questions ("Roll the ball," "Where is the doll?").	• Child can use many different consonant sounds at the beginning of words.
	• Child will point to a few body parts when asked.	• Child can put two words together ("no juice," "more milk").
	• Child will point to pictures in a book when they are named.	• Child can use one- to two-word questions ("Where kitty?" "Go bye-bye?").
24–36 months	• Child can follow two requests combined ("Get the ball and put it on the table").	• Child will ask for or direct your attention to objects by naming them.
	• Child will continue to notice sounds (telephone ringing, TV sound, knocking at the door).	• Child's speech is understood most of the time.
	• Child will understand differences in meaning ("go/stop," "in/on," "big/little," "up/down").	• Child uses two- to three-word "sentences" to talk about and ask for things.
		• Child has words for almost everything.

Source: Adapted from *How Does Your Child Hear and Talk?* American Speech-Language-Hearing Association (10801 Rockville Pike, Rockville, MD 20852), 1988. Reprinted with permission.

response is true receptive language. Caregivers are sometimes surprised to discover that receptive language is so advanced. When children are spoken to in meaningful ways, they understand what is being said to them much earlier than might be expected.

Expressive Language

As their early cries and vocalizations are responded to, infants learn to refine them, eventually sending more specialized vocal signals. The more they know that their signals or messages are received, the more skilled they become in sending them. From their partnership with a caregiver or two, they learn to convey a variety of clear feelings—hunger, discomfort, anger, and pleasure. This first clear expression, or use of a word, is called **expressive language**. The key to infants beginning to connect sounds with meaning is the adult's responsiveness. If no one responded to their initial cries and vocalizations, infants would have no reason to strive to make signals.

The actual moment a child utters her first word may be quite a surprise to the person who is present to hear it. One day a little girl may see a banana on a counter and reach for it, saying "nana." She may be surprised by the reaction—a flutter and flurry of smiles, hugs, and pats, followed by a piece of banana being placed in her hand. She will probably smile back and say her new word two or three more times. Later on she may be asked to repeat her performance when the late shift of caregivers arrives. Perhaps the caregivers, so pleased with this new accomplishment, will report it to the parent. Or maybe they'll keep their pleasure to themselves and let the parent discover this special event and be the one to report the first word when he or she hears it.

Most young children acquire these first words, and their meanings, amazingly quickly. Certainly the words they hear most frequently from their parents and caregivers influence their vocabularies. But young children, sometimes by about 18 months, use a process called **fast mapping** to acquire language rapidly. Fast mapping is a process in which a young child uses context cues to make a quick and reasonably accurate guess about the meaning of an unfamiliar word. This partial understanding of a word can happen after hearing it only one time.[2] For example, a young child can quickly learn new animal names because the brain has already "mapped" known (or familiar) animal names. *Dog* is easy if you already know *cat* (and have made some assumptions about fur, four legs, and a tail). This mental charting of new words occurs relatively quickly because the young child does not stop to figure out the exact definition. She uses familiar contexts and repetition to *generalize* the meaning of the new word. Sometimes, of course, errors do occur and a child's understanding of words may be limited. The time in which the adult and the child focus on the same experience can help a toddler learn word meanings appropriately. "Dogs" and "cats" get sorted out quickly, and we're on to "birds" and "airplanes"!

Children refine their language and develop grammatical rules on their own. They don't need corrections or language lessons. They learn by being part of

**NAEYC Program
Standard 3**
Teaching

real conversations—ones that move forward. Sometimes conversations just go around in circles when the adult tries to teach by repeating everything the child says in a more correct form. If nothing the adult says adds to the content, these merry-go-round conversations are meaningless. It is more important for adults to realize that as children begin to use longer phrases to communicate, they are also using language as an important tool for thinking.

What Language Allows a Child to Do: The Cognitive Link

There is an obvious increase in the ability to communicate as a child moves into and through toddlerhood. This ability to clarify needs and gather information is expanded as a young child acquires language. In addition to facilitating communication, language has a dramatic impact on self-regulation, thought, and cognition.

Infants and toddlers can "think" before they acquire language, but when children really begin to use language, their cognitive abilities take a major step forward. The ability to label experiences, indicating object permanence, enables children to enter into a symbolic realm. As noted in the definition of *language*, experiences do not have to be "in the moment"; they can be remembered, and a word can stand for an object. As children gather labels for experiences, their memories also grow. This memory bank will soon have categories within it. And the categories will eventually allow for a complex classification system. The experience of seeing a cat and learning that label gradually moves into a child's understanding that there are many breeds of cat and that this particular four-legged creature also belongs to a larger category of "animals." Information can be generalized from this understanding, but it all began with the label "cat."

Reasoning and the ability to order experiences are developed as a result of language. Watch (and listen) to a toddler as she plays. You may often overhear her actually telling herself what to do ("Now I'm going to the sandbox. Then I'm going to make a road"). This "verbal instruction," or private speech, allows a child to plan her own behavior (**self-regulation**) and to move her learning experiences from one situation to another. This ability to focus and to organize information eventually allows for abstraction and more formal cognitive thinking. Language increases our adaptation and coping skills. It provides us with the skills to be more clearly understood by others and to more concretely understand events around us. In a world with ever-increasing demands, appreciating how children cope effectively would be a significant goal for parents and caregivers.

The Brain and Early Language Development

What is happening in the brain while a young child is trying to acquire language? Some of the brain research in this area is the most fascinating, and the most specific. Several key findings should be noted and reviewed. Genes and

Children Eating at Table with Caregiver

See Video Observation 9: Children Eating at Table with Caregiver for an example of how children gain meaning from context.

Questions

- What was the adult doing that helped the children expand their language skills?
- Do you think special "language lessons" would be more effective than what you saw here?
- If someone asked you to explain how feeding is curriculum, could you use this scene to illustrate your answer?

To view this clip, go to **www.mhhe.com/itc10e**. Click on Student Edition, select Chapter 9, and click on Video Observations.

experiences (nature and nurture) work together for healthy brain growth. As already noted in this chapter, an infant may be physically capable of producing sound, but without nurturing interactions a language delay is likely. These early interactions influence the circuitry, or wiring, in the brain. Language development is dependent on the early neural connections (synapses) that are stimulated through responsive interactions with others. And these early experiences seem to be linked to prime times, or optimal periods, for particular aspects of language learning to occur.

During the first few months, a child's brain has **neuroplasticity**—that is, it is very flexible and responsive. This is no doubt why young infants initially respond to all the sounds of all languages. But this plasticity lessens with age. Early in brain growth, neurons seem to cluster around particular sound patterns called *phonemes* (the smallest units of sound in a language). When these patterns (for example, "pa" or "ma") are repeated, "auditory maps" are formed; neural pathways are reinforced, and brain circuitry is made more permanent.[3] This allows an infant to organize patterns of sounds within her native language. By the end of the first year, if certain sound patterns are not heard with regularity, it is very difficult for a child to construct new pathways. This is why it is so difficult to learn another language after we get older. Those pathways will never be as easily formed as they are in the first 12 months.

The recent research of Dr. Patricia Kuhl, Professor of Speech and Hearing Sciences and Co-Director of the Institute for Learning and Brain Sciences at the University of Washington, reinforces several key points in early brain development. Early exposure to language alters the brain, and this information has further expanded our understanding of auditory mapping. Between 8 and 10 months infants move from being "citizens of the world" (responding to all sounds) to listening more carefully to sound distinctions. Brain activity increases, and infants organize "sound statistics" that are particular to their native language. Their responses are more specific to those sounds only. Social interaction and face-to-face time play a critical role in this process.[4]

Another view of how auditory maps are formed comes from the brain research looking at the role mirror neurons play in language development. Mirror neurons were first discussed in relation to movement imitation patterns; these neurons were activated to repeat or imitate the exact actions observed in someone else. (Remember: infants will imitate an action made by another person but will fail to imitate the same movement if made by a robot.) This imitation pattern we now know also holds true for sounds. Infants older than nine months can learn new speech sounds they have never heard before (mirror neurons activated), but only if the new sounds come from a real person. Learning new sounds doesn't occur at this age if the infant hears the same word on a tape recorder or video.[5] Remember, too, that the mirror neurons seem to be influenced by a goal or intention (food was often the goal in the original research). Repeating sounds and learning language need to be embedded in meaningful, everyday experiences. This is especially relevant when considering early literacy.

Brain Activity and Language Competency

As young children acquire language, their brains become increasingly specialized for this complex task. Increased electrical activity tends to be concentrated in the left hemisphere of the cortex. Increased brain activity and increased language competency are linked in the second half of the first year. It is at about 7 to 12 months that infants join phonemes to syllables and syllables to words.[6] Look back at Table 9.1 and at Aidan and his caregiver at the beginning of the chapter. Try to imagine brain dendrites, those "magic trees of the mind," expanding rapidly as a young child makes sense of sounds as a result of experience. The first word, usually at the end of the first year, is just the beginning of the language explosion.

Experience also relates to vocabulary. A toddler's vocabulary is strongly correlated to how much interaction she experiences. Infants need to hear words, and these words need to be linked to real events. These are the kinds of experiences that create permanent neural connections. Meaning fosters connecting! Television doesn't do it; TV is just noise to a very young child. The emotional context of language seems to influence neural circuitry too. Connecting words to pleasant experiences (or negative ones) affects memory. A young child is more apt to remember the label for her special toy or favorite food.

Some debate exists about prime times, or optimal periods, particularly as they relate to language development. Do those "windows of opportunity" slam shut? Probably not. But more is said in the brain research about the specific timing of language than about any other developmental area. Two particular events that are critical to brain development happen in the first two years. The sensorimotor systems are strengthened through myelinization, and attachment relationships are established. These events dramatically influence brain functioning and growth, and because brain growth is holistic, they must also play a dramatic role in early language acquisition. These two events (myelinization and attachment) may be most significant to our understanding of critical periods of brain growth.

Fostering Language Development

Caregivers and parents can foster language development in infants by using language with them from the start. *Talk* with them long before they can talk to you. Use real, adult talk and include them in conversations with other people. Listen to infants and encourage them to listen too. Parents may be helpful in providing caregivers with their infant's unique patterns of communicating. Even very young infants are responsive to language, and the rhythm of their body movements will correspond to the rhythm of early language dialogues.

Remember to use these early dialogues during caregiving times and during playtime (when appropriate). Most adults seem to engage in this activity naturally; they imitate a baby's sounds as well as initiating their own sounds. It is important at these times to use real labels for an infant's experiences. When an infant responds, turn what may have been your monologue into a dialogue.

Discuss the past and future with very young children, as well as the present. "Now" may be the primary experience for infants, but as they move toward toddlerhood, yesterday, last week, and tomorrow can be part of your conversations. Knowing what is about to happen helps infants and toddlers predict events and begin to understand the labels for things, events, and people.

Play games with sounds and words. Tell stories, sing songs, and recite or create rhymes and poems. Be sure to value and make room for young children's participation—many of them have a wonderful ability to create playful sounds and words. This needs to start early with cooing and babbling and continue until children are creating their own nonsense rhymes and sound games. Remember, too, to put language into gross motor activities. When statements are made like "I see you *on top* of the steps, Jason," Jason learns about spatial relationships and the prepositions that go with them.

Play games with songs
and words.

Be sure that older toddlers have plenty of experiences to talk about as their world begins to expand (infants find enough *conversation* in caregiving routines and day-to-day play). A short field trip or walk around the block can provide conversation material for some time. Pictures, novel objects, and bits of science and nature can spark a child's interest and result in fun extemporaneous discussions and dialogues.

Questions can be important tools to foster language. Ask questions that require a choice: "Do you want a piece of apple or a piece of banana?" Ask open-ended questions (those that have no right answer): "What did you see on your walk?" Closed questions (those with one right answer—for example, "You saw a dog on the walk, didn't you?") are fine, too, as long as the child enjoys them and doesn't feel interrogated. Encourage young children to clarify what they don't understand by asking questions themselves. They sometimes like to ask the questions as well as answer them, thus collecting and practicing labels for objects.

Read books aloud to children beginning in infancy. Read to children individually or in small groups when there is an interest. Make this time frequent, short, and spontaneous—a fun activity accompanied by lots of cuddling and snuggles. Story or book time for infants and toddlers should resemble what parents do at home more than what preschool teachers do at circle time. This pleasurable association with books is one of the key correlates to early literacy.

These suggested guidelines for supporting early language development are summarized in Figure 9.1.

Figure 9.1 Guidelines for Fostering Early Language Development

1. Engage young children in dialogue during daily caregiving and play times.

2. Describe what is happening as it occurs; use the labels that children need to learn.

3. Talk *with* young children and interact with them; slow down and encourage them to think about what they are saying.

4. Play games with sounds; tell stories and sing songs.

5. Provide young children with interesting experiences that in turn can provide conversation material; really listen to them.

6. Offer older toddlers new experiences to talk about that relate to their expanding world.

7. Share new and novel objects (for example, bits of science and nature) to engage children's interest and to encourage fun dialogue about those objects.

8. Use questions as important language tools and encourage children to ask questions when they need more information.

9. Make book experiences pleasurable for children; point out pictures, rhyming sounds, and fun characters.

10. READ to your baby! (National Library Association slogan)

Early Literacy

Young children learn literacy skills much the same way they learn language skills, and the rapid brain growth that is going on to facilitate language is also setting the stage for literacy. The attachment relationships that are being established,

The Principles in Action

Principle 3 Learn each child's unique ways of communicating (cries, words, movements, gestures, facial expressions, body positions) and teach yours. Don't underestimate children's ability to communicate even though their verbal language skills may be nonexistent or minimal.

You have just been hired as a child care provider in a new infant-toddler program. The director suggests that you spend your first few days gradually getting to know the children. On your first morning you observe the following interactions. A volunteer mom is happily playing peekaboo with her 14-month-old daughter. The little girl is obviously delighting in the turn-taking pattern of conversation; there are lots of giggles from both of them. One of the caregivers is changing a child; she is talking to him about the clean diaper she is going to put on him. He is looking at her intently and reaches for the diaper while she is talking. Another child is crying softly near the entrance; her mom has just left. A caregiver is sitting beside her offering comforting words ("I can see you are feeling sad." "Your mommy will be back after lunch"). The sobbing toddler is leaning against the caregiver but does not seem to want to sit on her lap. Over in the far corner of the room you can see two toddlers playing with small blocks; a caregiver is sitting near them. One child is using a few Spanish words; the other is using only English. You can hear the caregiver repeating some of each of the toddlers' words, easily using both Spanish and English.

1. Describe the language and communication patterns you see.
2. How are the children's unique ways of communicating being acknowledged by the adults?
3. Clarify how each child is being shown respect.
4. Would you do anything differently from any of the adults you were observing?
5. What do you find most challenging when trying to communicate with young children?

the perceptual-motor experiences that are being organized, and the cognitive events that are being processed all contribute to emerging literacy during infancy and toddlerhood.

Literacy—the ability to listen and speak, and eventually to read and write—has its beginnings in a variety of early, everyday experiences. Becoming literate is a process that starts in the context of the family. Infants and toddlers listen to the voices around them, and they engage in vocal interactions with their caregivers. They observe the facial expressions of the people near them, and they look at the detail on objects that interest them. They enjoy rhymes and songs and hearing spoken language with rich intonations. Once they start using words themselves, they gradually realize that those words can be written down and read back to them. Young children develop an awareness of oral and written language in an interrelated and holistic way rather than in a series of stages. This ongoing process of becoming literate is referred to as **emergent literacy**, and it starts at birth. Meaningful experiences and interactions with others are key to communication and to literacy skills.

This *meaningfulness of interactions* has been documented further by Professor Amy Wetherby at Florida State University. Her First Words Project examined what early literacy looks like. The project found that predictors of emergent literacy skills in preschoolers could be traced back to early interactions between infants and toddlers and their caregivers. Early sharing behaviors, such as sharing attention, sharing feelings, and sharing intentions, were significant to the development of language and later literacy. Infants who had a wide range of gestures and sounds and began understanding and using words early became preschoolers who showed clear and stable emergent literacy skills. Toddlers who enjoyed the use of a variety of objects in their play and who demonstrated book knowledge (for example, how to hold a book, how to turn pages) became preschoolers who enjoyed and displayed preliteracy skills.[7]

All these interactions with infants and toddlers have emphasized a respectful and responsive environment with adults who enjoyed sharing language and literacy activities. Conversations were meaningful and had a sense of direction or intention. *Intentionality* in this literacy context means that caregivers support everyday experiences that lead to developmentally appropriate skills in early literacy. A caregiver, for example, may intentionally provide a 13-month-old the opportunity to pick up small items by himself (building fine motor skills critical for writing) and then later offer the same child crayons to play with (providing direct experience with drawing and writing). The adult recognizes the relationship between these experiences and *offers* them intentionally to the child, thus supporting an important developmental goal.[8]

Early Literacy and School Readiness

Fostering the growth of literacy is a big topic today. Many people are very interested in making sure that all children know how to read at least by third grade. That in and of itself is a relevant goal. But *how we do what we do* is critical—especially when dealing with very young children. Early literacy, or emergent literacy, is different from reading readiness, which focuses more on teaching shapes and colors and using writing tools. New approaches involve making sure young children have appropriate books and relevant experiences related to listening, speaking, reading, and writing.

Some current research is particularly focused on picture book sharing as a way we can assist young children with *observing* and *exploring* written language. When caregivers and parents share picture books with young children, they are showing them that written language and illustrations are used to communicate meaning. Young children's comments and questions about picture books provide a context for oral language development. And, as the story is read to them, they begin to realize that words can be written down. Such book sharing involves *oral* language that supports the *written* story. Implications of this research indicate that young children who have had frequent opportunities to be involved with picture book sharing have progressively more verbal and nonverbal emergent literacy behaviors.[9] These behaviors are defined as shared gaze (looking at pictures with caregivers); facial expressions indicating understanding of book content; attempts to turn pages and hold the book; memory of story content (predicting upcoming events); and participation in labeling objects or actions within the story.[10]

Research on picture book sharing points to the importance of providing opportunities for young children to observe and explore picture books independently and with adults. However, it also brings up questions. Should we expect all infants and toddlers to show these emergent literacy skills? No, probably not. Additional research needs to focus on larger groups of infants and toddlers and look at more diverse settings. Also, young children vary in their interests in picture book sharing; not all will show the same interest in books! Providing time for picture book sharing is important—and more research is needed to understand and foster key emergent literacy behaviors.[11]

Current emergent literacy research reminds caregivers and parents of the following:

- Be sensitive to literacy and language interactions that are child initiated and not just adult initiated.
- Storybook/picture book sharing is an important tool for fostering emergent literacy.
- More research is needed with toddlers from diverse linguistic and cultural settings, especially related to toddlers' early writing attempts.
- The family setting (where parents express *pleasure* in reading and writing) plays an important role in providing emergent literacy-related activities for infants and toddlers.
- Caregivers of bilingual infants and toddlers should be especially sensitive to establishing rapport with families, focusing on oral language development, and providing materials in the home language and culture.

Remember that development cannot be hurried. Take your cues from the young child. Overstimulating environments and adult expectations that exceed infant-toddler capabilities get in the way of healthy growth. In confusing and overwhelming settings, young children become stressed and even depressed. Oral language is fundamental to literacy, so have frequent one-to-one conversations with infants and toddlers and maintain eye contact. As noted, when coos and babbled sounds give way to words, repeat and elaborate those words back to the toddler. Much of the literacy research that exists today is focused on the importance of early interactions that are responsive and interactive.

Principle 7, *Model the behavior you want to teach*, deserves specific emphasis when considering early literacy. Allow very young children to see you engaged with language and environmental print. Let them see you reading and enjoying books and using print for everyday experiences (adding an item to your grocery list, writing yourself a reminder note). Several more guidelines for fostering literacy in infants and toddlers are listed in Figure 9.2. As you read them, think about how you are fostering literacy in very young children and how you are ensuring their future enjoyment of their own literacy skills.

EXPLORE the following websites for more information and resource material.

The Frank Porter Graham Child Development Institute at the University of North Carolina at Chapel Hill shares knowledge to enhance early development and to influence public policy.

www.fpg.unc.edu

The Center for Prevention and Early Intervention Policy focuses on maternal and child health and early childhood issues; numerous downloadable resources are available.

www.cpeip.fsu.edu

Figure 9.2 Guidelines for Fostering Literacy in Infants and Toddlers

1. Provide a sensory-rich environment, including vocal and verbal interactions, singing, shared baby books, cheerful surroundings, and simple pictures on the wall.

2. Provide an enriched social environment that allows opportunities for infants and toddlers to watch and interact with others.

3. Periodically change the scenery: move furniture, change pictures or the carpet in the play area.

4. Explore the environment with a young child, look out the window, gaze into the mirror, play with water in the sink.

5. Take infants and toddlers on outings. Talk about where you are going and what you are doing, and name objects you see along the way.

6. Have fun with infants and toddlers when they initiate playfulness, and express your interest in and enthusiasm for their new accomplishments.

7. Respect linguistic, sociocultural, and economic differences among young children and their families.

8. Remind yourself that each child is unique in her or his literacy development (just as in any other area of growth).

9. Provide an interesting variety of materials to allow talking, listening, drawing, and reading.

10. Demonstrate your own interest in and curiosity about the world.

Even babies can enjoy books.

🌸 Cultural Differences, Bilingualism and Dual Language Learners

All these guidelines are culturally bound. Some cultures view language practices and the language socialization process differently from the way we have presented them here. They may have different goals for their children regarding language and literacy. They may also use different methods from the beginning. You may or may not approve of the cultural approach to language that some of the parents in your program use, but you must respect cultural differences and try to understand how values and approaches other than your own may serve the individual in the particular culture.

An example of a cultural difference in language is provided by Shirley Brice Heath, who describes a culture in which babies are made a part of everything that is going on by being held continually but are rarely talked to during the first year. They pick up language by being immersed in it, not by having it directed at them. This shows later in their use of language. They have a holistic view of objects in context. They have difficulty talking about an object out of context, such as sorting out the attributes of that object and comparing them with those of another object out of context. When shown flash card pictures of a red ball and a blue ball and asked, "Is the red ball or the blue ball bigger?" children from this culture would have difficulty sorting out the attributes of color and size, though in a real-life situation they could determine the larger ball and throw it when asked to do so. Rather than teaching the concepts accepted as important by the mainstream Canadian and U.S. culture (such as color, shape, and size), this culture values the creative use of language, including metaphors. These children show great skill at creative verbal play and use of imagery.[12]

Children in child care are influenced by the caregiver's culture. Children who grow up in two cultures and incorporate both are said to be *bicultural*. Whether or not those two cultures conflict and cause the child to feel torn between them depends on the child, the parents, the caregiver, and the cultures themselves. Sometimes children seem to get caught *between* two cultures and experience a lot of pain in their upbringing. A child can be bicultural and still be English speaking, as are many children in this country and other parts of the world. Many bicultural people, however, speak more than one language.

Infants can learn two languages from day one, and by the time they are toddlers, they can be very skilled at switching back and forth between them to different people and in different contexts. **Bilingualism** is a skill to be valued and nurtured. Child care can provide excellent opportunities for this skill to develop as children of one language background come into contact with caregivers of another. Take advantage of any chance you have to help children become bilingual (with the parents' permission, of course). You can do this by talking to children in your own language (if their family speaks a different one) or another language (if you are bilingual yourself).

Keep in mind the "language relationship." The language relationship is established without fanfare when two people meet for the first time. For two monolingual English-speaking people, there is no option; the language of their relationship is English, and they never even think about it. But when two bilingual persons meet, the situation is different. There is a choice, and once the choice is made, the two feel most comfortable when they speak the language of their relationship to each other, though both may be fully capable of speaking the second language.

When a bilingual caregiver meets a young infant, the choice of language is present to some extent because the baby is not yet a full-fledged member of a language community. If bilingualism is a goal, establishing a relationship in the target language from the beginning is quite simple.

Goals of the "Language Relationship"

Establishing this relationship is a little more difficult with a child who is already partway along in his or her language development because of the difficulty in communicating until the child learns the second language. The strength of the bilingual goal and the extent to which children feel secure and are able to get their needs met should determine whether to establish a language relationship in a language other than the child's own with the primary caregiver. When both caregiver and child are skilled at nonverbal communication, the choice isn't so difficult. Once the language relationship is established, there is a motivation to learn the second language, and it isn't long before verbal communication is established. It is important, however, to remember that, although some children seem to "pick up" language fast, language acquisition doesn't happen overnight. Communication is necessarily weak at the beginning and often for a long time afterward. It's very hard on some older babies and toddlers to be put into situations where they can't understand what is said to them. Just imagine how you would feel being totally dependent on someone who didn't speak your language.

When bilingualism is a strong goal and the child is liable to suffer from the initial lack of communication, it is best to have two caregivers to relate to the child. One can then establish a relationship in the second language while another is present to establish a language relationship in the child's own language. Thus the child can become bilingual in a secure situation. This way of ensuring bilingualism is common practice in many families in different parts of the world.

Be careful that you don't ask bilingual or limited-English-speaking parents to speak English to their children when their inclination is otherwise. If you do, you are disregarding the language relationship. And you may be impairing the communication between parent and child. Magda Gerber, a bilingual person herself, said that it is natural for parents to speak to their children in the language they themselves were spoken to in infancy and toddlerhood. Even parents who have become proficient in English may find that the words of caring come more easily in the language of their own beginnings. Be careful not to hinder parents' ability to communicate caring and tenderness to their children.

Be concerned about the quality of verbal communication in your environment or program if bilingualism is a goal. Unless you are proficient in the

NAEYC Program Standard 1
Relationships

language you are using to communicate with the child, the goal of bilingualism may get in the way of communication. If your ability to express yourself in the target language is limited, you should weigh communication and the child's language development against the goal of bilingualism.

As already mentioned, a solution to this problem, if there is more than one adult and bilingualism is a goal, is for one adult to establish relationships in one language and the other to establish them in the second language. In this way, children establish a relationship with someone who is proficient in one language and are assured of good communication while they progress in a second language. Without someone to communicate with who is proficient, the child misses out. With one proficient speaker and one less-than-proficient one, the child can gain some added benefits without losing out on first-language development. This scene shows how bilingualism can work in a family child care home.

It's late in the afternoon, and a woman is heating tortillas on the stove. A three-year-old watches her from the kitchen table. He tells her that he is hungry—in Spanish. She smiles and answers him in Spanish, at the same time handing him a warm, soft, rolled-up tortilla. Another three-year-old appears at the doorway, requesting a tortilla in English. She obliges with a second tortilla and again answers in Spanish. Both children stand by the table chewing their tortillas, obviously relishing the flavor.

A man enters the kitchen. "Ummm, something smells good," he comments.

"Yes," replies the woman. "Guess what?"

"Tortilla. It's yummy," says the first child, holding his out to show the man.

"Want a bite?" asks the second child.

"Here's one for you," says the woman, handing the man his own fresh, hot tortilla.

All three chew contentedly. Then the man says, "How about Grandma? Go ask her if she wants a tortilla."

The first child runs from the room, calling, "Abuelita, Abuelita, quieres tortilla?"

This child, only three years old, is managing to learn two languages and, further, is learning when to use each one. The other child is getting exposure to a second language and developing his receptive language skills. Depending on the circumstances, he may begin to use it himself one day. In the meantime, he's in a situation where he can use and be understood in his own language while learning another one.

The skill of using language appropriate to the situation is not limited to children using two languages. All speakers learn early to distinguish between language styles. Listen carefully to the difference between the way two three-year-olds talk to each other and the way they talk to adults. Listen, for example, to the way children "play house." The one playing the mother talks the way she perceives adults talk; the one playing the baby speaks in a different way altogether. Clearly, they have learned that there is one style for talking to peers and another for talking to adults. Children also distinguish among the adults with whom they speak. The way they talk to their mother may be different from the way they talk to their father, a caregiver, or a stranger on the streets.

Reflect

Why are bilingualism and bilingual education such an important topic today? What are the implications for programs for infants and toddlers?

Language is culturally bound and influences our lives immeasurably. Infants and toddlers learn to use language in natural settings when they are spoken to, responded to, and listened to. Language influences how they perceive the world, organize their experience, and communicate with others.

Children with Special Needs: Supporting Parents and Families

The importance of communicating effectively with parents and families has been mentioned several times in this chapter related to language development and dual language learners. We know that the family is the young child's greatest resource, and building on the strengths of the family directly supports the development and learning of the young child. This is particularly relevant when working with children with special needs and their families.

The birth of a child is an exciting, amazing, and life-changing event. Parents and family members most always have wonderful expectations for this new person and harbor dreams about their future. What happens if this new child has a disability? Who can answer the numerous questions about the care of this child and help find the resources necessary for assistance and information? All expectations can be quickly replaced by fear, denial, guilt, and anger.

It may be helpful for caregivers and teachers working with families who have children with special needs to keep some key principles in mind before trying to offer specific support strategies. Foremost, the family is the single most important influence on the development and learning of any young child, and early intervention approaches recognize the critical role of the family. Effective partnerships with families develop over time and are based on mutual trust. Every family has unique strengths and each family should be seen as an active participant and decision maker in the plans for their child. Culture, home language, and differences among families need to be respected; intervention services need to be individualized, flexible, and responsive. Family activities should be supported and encouraged; teachable moments, especially for young children with special needs, occur in everyday routines and in a variety of settings. Coordination and cooperation among agencies, caregivers, and families create early intervention services that are comprehensive, easily accessed, and cost effective.[13]

The following support strategies deal with helping families with the *emotional* impact of caring for their child with special needs. Grief is often viewed as the common reaction of a family to the diagnosis that their child has a disability. Denial and anger may follow, and acceptance of the diagnosis can take years. Not all families, however, experience a grief reaction; they may become "experts" in their child's condition or try to "normalize" and downplay the diagnosis. Be aware of patronizing their experience or "feeling sorry" for them. Many parents may certainly not realize the full impact of their child's disability, and helping them to find relevant support resources is crucial.

Families can feel strengthened by concrete information. Caregivers should provide observational detail and documentation to parents so that they can "see" their child's progress. Respect family privacy when sharing information; create time and private space "just to talk." It is also important for caregivers and teachers to remember that although they are vital members of the early intervention team, they are not therapists.

Review Figure 9.3, "Communication Milestones and Warning Signs for Communication Disorders" and the "Developmental Pathways" box that follows. How might caregivers and teachers share such information with parents in a way that can strengthen their knowledge base and encourage mutual understanding?

Reflect

Imagine that you have a child with a communication disorder in your program. What would you need to consider? List several appropriate language activities.

Figure 9.3 Communication Milestones and Warning Signs for Communication Disorders

Young infants (birth to 8 months): Young infants communicate initially to get their needs met and then expand their communication to include playful exchanges, learning the rhythms of interacting with their caregivers. Warning signs for the young infant include the following:

- A general lack of interest in social contact (infant avoids eye contact, holds body rigidly).
- Lack of response to the human voice or other sounds.

Mobile infants (6 to 18 months): Mobile infants playfully experiment with language and communicate with purpose. At this stage, infants often speak their first words. Mobile infants will practice newly acquired words over and over and try to use them whenever they can. Warning signs for the mobile infant include the following:

- At 8 to 9 months, the child stops babbling (infants who are deaf babble at first and then stop).
- The child does not show interest in interacting with objects and caregivers in familiar environments.
- At 9 to 10 months, the child does not follow direction of point.
- At 11 to 12 months, the child does not give, show, or point at objects.
- At 11 to 12 months, the child does not play games such as patty-cake or peekaboo.

Older infants (16 to 36 months): There is typically a language explosion at the beginning of the older infant stage. The number of words that toddlers know increases rapidly, and they start to use simple grammar. Warning signs for the older infant include the following:

By 24 months, the child
- Uses 25 or fewer words

By 36 months, the child
- Has a limited vocabulary
- Uses only short, simple sentences
- Makes many more grammatical errors than other children at the same age
- Has difficulty talking about the future
- Misunderstands questions most of the time
- Is often misunderstood by others
- Displays fewer forms of social play than other children at the same age
- Has difficulty carrying on a conversation

Source: Adapted from "Early Messages," *Child Care Video* magazine, Fall 2002. Reprinted by permission of J. Ronald Lally, Far West Laboratory for Educational Research and Development and California Department of Education.

DEVELOPMENTAL PATHWAYS

Behaviors Showing Development of Language

Young infants (up to 8 months)	• Use vocal and nonvocal communication to express interest and exert influence (cry to signal distress, smile to initiate social contact) • Babble using all types of sounds • Combine babbles; understand names of familiar people and objects • Listen to conversations
Mobile infants (up to 18 months)	• Create long, babbled sentences • Look at picture books with interest, point to objects • Begin to use *me, you*, and *I* • Shake head no, say two or three clear words • Demonstrate intense attention to adult language
Toddlers (up to 3 years)	• Combine words • Listen to stories for a short while • Have a speaking vocabulary that may reach 200 words • Develop fantasy in language, begin to play pretend games • Use *tomorrow* and *yesterday*

Source: Carol Copple and Sue Bredekamp, eds., *Developmentally Appropriate Practice in Early Childhood Programs*, 3rd ed. (Washington, DC: National Association for the Education of Young Children, 2009).

Diverse Developmental Pathways

What you see	Jai always lets everyone know when he has arrived! He runs into the room, leaving his mom to put his things in his cubby, and immediately begins to order the children about in a loud voice. His language is clear and most always *command oriented* ("Get car," "Come now"). He likes vigorous toddler play but always seems to need to be boss and gets frustrated quickly if he is *not* the boss. He still expresses most of his feelings in actions (hitting and grabbing) and not words.
What you might think	Jai is an aggressive little boy. He doesn't have much language to express his feelings. He's beginning to be a *problem*!
What you might not know	Jai is the youngest of three boys. His two older brothers boss him around a lot and often tease him. They enjoy television and include him in some of their games based on television, often using a lot of pretend hitting and fighting (which sometimes gets out of control).
What you might do	Give Jai some space and time to vent when he arrives; let him get some of his apparent frustrations out. Providing some water and sand play, before any specific activities, is a good idea. Let him know that he is safe with you and that you will help him (by modeling with words) to get what he needs—he doesn't always have to be boss. Encourage his friends to use their words, too, especially if you can see that they don't want to follow Jai's *orders*. You have observed that sometimes

(continued)

Behaviors Showing Development of Language (*continued*)

	in the afternoons he does enjoy listening to books. Make the most of this time by using books about feelings and his interests (cars!). You might want to send some of these books home with his mom. Ask her if the children watch much television at their house, and be ready to provide some alternative activities for young children.
What you see	Hema is a very quiet little girl; English is her second language. When she arrives with her mother, her mother does all the talking. She says that her daughter talks a lot at home, and she thinks that she should be reading books by now (Hema is not yet three). Hema usually plays by herself in the doll area and in the quiet (book) area. She doesn't avoid other children, but she does nothing to initiate contact.
What you might think	Hema's parents are very demanding. They are creating too much stress for her, and this is causing her to withdraw from social contact with the other children.
What you might not know	In Hema's culture, a child is considered a special gift to a family. Everything is done for her; she has little opportunity to express her needs. Conversations with children are not valued, but academics and school achievements are very important. It is assumed by Hema's parents that she will be successful in school.
What you might do	Get to know Hema's parents more and appreciate what they value. Encourage them to come and visit your program. Let them see you interacting and having conversations with children. Encourage Hema to use the words she knows and gradually involve other children in her play (maybe just one at a time). Let the family know that you value literacy, too, but share more information with them about its *emergent* qualities.

Supporting the parents and families of children with special needs takes time and energy. Building a quality relationship in which real teamwork exists, and adults truly cooperate with each other, requires effort and the sharing of authentic feelings. Recognizing challenges and problems as learning opportunities requires trust and mutual respect. Caregivers and families communicating with honesty and sensitivity provide the base for quality service systems for young children with special needs. Such efforts can have a lasting positive effect!

Summary

Language is a symbol system that has generalized meaning.

The Progression of Language Development

- Social interaction is critical to *what* happens *when* concerning language development.

- Interactions, the opportunity to imitate, and the maturation of innate abilities, combine to move language forward.
- *Receptive language* (birth to one year) is the time in which infants *take in*, organize, and understand experience.
- *Expressive language* (end of the first year to beginning of first words) is the time in which young children refine and *send* more specialized sounds and words.

What Language Allows a Child to Do: The Cognitive Link

- With language a child can label experiences, indicate object permanence, and enter into a *symbolic* realm.
- Cognition and language together foster the ability to reason and develop the ability to order experiences and expand adaptation and coping skills.

The Brain and Early Language Development

- Language development is dependent on early neural connections (synapses), which become more permanent pathways as frequently heard sounds are "mapped" in the brain.
- Two events that are critical to brain development (and to language development) happen in the first two years—myelinization and attachment.

Fostering Language Development

- Guidelines for language growth focus on interactions *with* young children, not *at* them.
- Interesting, relevant experiences give young children a variety of things to listen to and talk about.

Early Literacy

- Young children learn early literacy skills in much the same way as they acquire language skills—all developmental areas work together in a meaningful, relationship-oriented context.
- Guides related to early literacy revolve around sensory-rich experiences in which young children see adults engaged with and sharing language and print.

Cultural Differences and Bilingualism

- Bilingualism exists when a child has been exposed to and has learned two languages; this can start right from birth but doesn't have to.
- Establishing a "language relationship" requires sensitivity, understanding, and respect; *quality* verbal communication in caregiving is the goal.

Children with Special Needs: Supporting Parents and Families

- The core message for supporting parents is to recognize that the family is the child's greatest resource; building on family strengths directly

supports the development and learning of the young child with special needs.
- Every family experiences the emotional impact of caring for their child with disabilities in unique ways; take time to learn when documentation, resources, and privacy "just to talk" are most appreciated.

Key Terms

bilingualism 198
emergent literacy 194
expressive language 187
fast mapping 187
language 184

literacy 194
neuroplasticity 189
receptive language 185
self-regulation 188
social interaction 185

Thought/Activity Questions

1. Review Table 9.1 (page 186). A parent asks you about her eight-month-old child's language growth. How might the information in this chart help you? How might it be used inappropriately?
2. Visit the library in your area and review the children's section. Select at least five books that you think are appropriate for toddlers. Justify your choices.
3. Observe a child under three years of age. What language behaviors do you see? What emergent literacy behaviors do you see? What does language allow him or her to do?
4. Compare the guidelines for language development (Figure 9.1, page 193) with the guidelines for literacy development (Figure 9.2, page 197). What similarities and differences do you see? How are the two areas of development linked?
5. Imagine that you have a young child in your program who speaks another language. What would you do to communicate with this child and facilitate her interactions with the other children?
6. What support would you try to provide for parents and families of children with special needs? What considerations would you want to keep in mind?

For Further Reading

Jennifer J. Chen and Suzanne H. Shire, "Strategic Teaching: Fostering Communication Skills in Diverse Young Learners," *Young Children* 66(2), March 2011, pp. 20–28.

M. Gerber, "Babies Understanding Words," *Educaring* 3(4), 1982, pp. 5–6.

J. Gonzalez-Mena, "Caregiving Routines and Literacy," in *Learning to Read the World: Language and Literacy in the First Three Years* ed. S. E. Rosenkoetter and J. Knapp-Philo (Washington, DC: Zero to Three, 2006), pp. 248–261.

Beverly Kovach and Denise Da Ros-Voseles, "Communicating with Babies," *Young Children* 66(2), March 2011, pp. 48–50.

Karen N. Nemeth, *Basics of Supporting Dual Language Learners: An Introduction for Educators of Children from Birth through Age 8* (Washington, DC: National Association for the Education of Young Children, 2012).

Karen N. Nemeth and Valeria Erdosi, "Enhancing Practice with Infants and Toddlers from Diverse Language and Cultural Backgrounds," *Young Children* 67(4), September 2012, pp. 49–57.

Mari Riojas-Cortes, "Culture, Play and Family: Supporting Children on the Autism Spectrum." *Young Children* 66(5), September 2011, pp. 94–99.

Judith A. Schickedanz and Molly F. Collins, *More than the ABCs: The Early Phases of Reading and Writing* (Washington, DC: National Association for the Education of Young Children, 2013).

Nancy S. Stockall and Lindsay R. Dennis, "The Daily Dozen: Strategies for Enhancing Social Communication of Infants with Language Delays," *Young Children* 67(4), September 2012, pp. 36–41.

chapter 10

Emotions

Focus Questions

After reading this chapter you should be able to answer the following questions:

1 Describe emotional development in very young children. How does it change from the first year (infancy) to the second year (toddlerhood)?

2 How would you define *temperament* and *resiliency*? How is research related to these two developmental concepts helpful to caregivers of very young children?

3 Compare fear and anger in young children. What caregiving strategies can adults use with very young children to help them cope with these two strong emotions?

4 How can adults support a child's sense of self-direction and self-regulation? How might such adult behavior also support early brain development?

5 Describe five challenges faced by the field of early childhood intervention. What similar challenges exist in infant-toddler care and education?

What Do You See?

The scene is a family child care home. Sofia, a two-year-old, is taking the toys off a low shelf and putting them in a cardboard box. She wanders off from this activity and stops briefly to look out the window, touching her tongue to the cold glass. Then she meanders over to a three-month-old who is lying on a blanket beside a caregiver. Dropping down heavily, she reaches for the baby's head. The caregiver reaches out and touches the toddler's head softly, saying, "Gently, gently, Sofia. You may touch, but you have to be gentle." Her abrupt motion turns into a light touch, and she strokes the infant for a minute the way she has just been stroked. But then she gets more energetic, and her stroking becomes a heavy pat. The caregiver holds her hand back and once more says, "Gently, gently," as she strokes her head again and holds her hand. But this time Sofia's response is different, and she lifts her free hand to hit the infant, an expression of determination crossing her face. The caregiver stops her, firmly grasping her hand. Thwarted in her attempt, Sofia turns on the adult, eyes flashing, and begins to struggle. At the same time, she starts to make protesting noises. The scene ends with a very angry little girl being removed from the vicinity of the helpless infant. The last thing you hear is the caregiver's calm voice saying, "I know you're angry, Sofia, but I can't let you hurt little Trung."

Sofia will learn over time to manage her emotions, and the adults in her life are helping her by accepting her strong feelings and respecting her right to have them. They are also, of course, *not* allowing her to hurt others or herself. She will learn that strong feelings can be expressed in socially acceptable ways and that coping skills will help her to manage her very real, everyday frustrations.

Emotions and feelings are linked early in a child's development. What they are and where they come from can be of special interest to caregivers and parents. The word **emotion** comes from a Latin word meaning to move away and to disturb or excite. Emotions are the affective response to an event, and they come from within an individual, though they may be triggered by an external event. The word **feeling** refers to a physical sense of, or an awareness of, an emotional state. It also involves the capacity to respond to that emotional state.

The point is that emotions and feelings are real. They may be triggered from the outside (for example, by someone else), but the feelings themselves belong to the person experiencing them. You should never discount another's feelings. A young child may be in distress over something you consider very minor. But his or her feeling is real and should be acknowledged and accepted. From this acceptance base, young children can learn to value their own emotions and feelings, to calm themselves, and to act in ways that are considered socially acceptable. When caregivers and parents help infants and toddlers recognize their own feelings and cope with them, they are contributing to children's inner sense of self-direction and competence.

This chapter focuses on emotional development and how feelings in the very young change over time. It discusses factors that influence this development, the importance of appreciating individual temperament, and how to foster resiliency. Specific attention is given to helping infants and toddlers (like Sofia in the opening scenario) cope with fear and anger. It covers the fact that strong (stress-related) emotions can affect the neurochemistry of the brain. It also highlights some challenges faced by the field of early childhood intervention and how these challenges may be similar to those faced in infant and toddler care and education programs.

The Development of Emotions and Feelings

Feelings and emotions develop and change over time. Newborns' emotions are related to immediate experiences and sensations. Newborns' emotional responses are not very defined but are rather a general stirred-up or calmed-down response. Refined responses depend on development that occurs after birth. Memory and the ability to understand and anticipate are examples of how emotional expression evolves through the cognitive development that occurs gradually during the first two years.

Gentle-birth advocates, such as Frederick Leboyer, the French obstetrician, share a concern that infants do have emotions from the first moments of life. Until Leboyer advertised his gentle-birth techniques, it was widely believed that babies did not feel much at birth. If they had sensations, the possibility that they had emotional responses was discounted. Research shows that infants do have the

This baby sees somebody new and isn't sure how to respond. Looking at the caregiver's face will likely provide reassurance. That reassurance comes from "social referencing."
Source: Photo courtesy of Frank Gonzalez-Mena.

use of their senses at birth. Consequently, researchers and caregivers are not questioning the emotional aspects of what infants feel. Although infants cannot talk about what they experience emotionally at birth, their physical reactions can be observed. Evidence exists that they react to harsh stimulation with tenseness. We once thought that the panicky birth cry and the tightly clenched fists were normal and even necessary. Now that Leboyer and others have demonstrated what happens when you reduce such harsh stimuli as bright lights, loud noises, and abrupt changes in temperature, we know that a newborn can be relaxed and peaceful. Some babies born under Leboyer's method even smile right after birth.[1]

In the first weeks of life, infants' emotional responses are not very refined. Either very young infants are in a stirred-up state or they are not. They may cry with great intensity, but it is hard to put any labels on what they are feeling. As they mature, however, the stirred-up states begin to differentiate into familiar adultlike emotions such as pleasure, fear, and anger. By the second year, you can see most of the finer variations of these basic emotions. Toddlers express pride, embarrassment, shame, and empathy.

Research indicates that late in the first year of life, infants can *link* information about another person's emotional expression with environmental cues. For example, a 12-month-old faced with a potentially fearful event—a stranger or a new situation—may look first at a trusted caregiver's face to check for that adult's emotional expression. If the caregiver looks pleased or comfortable, the baby is more likely to be at ease and accept the situation. The opposite is also true—if the caregiver is concerned, the baby reacts with concern. This "checking in" in the emotional domain is called **social referencing**.[2] Infants use the emotions of others to guide their own emotions. They can use this information and experience to begin to calm themselves. Self-calming techniques are discussed later in this chapter.

Sometimes people want to divide feelings into two categories: good and bad. However, all feelings are good; they carry energy, have purpose, and provide us with messages that are important to our sense of self-direction. A better way to divide them is into "yes!" feelings and "no!" feelings. Some examples of "yes!" feelings are joy, pleasure, delight, contentment, satisfaction, and power. Infants and toddlers should experience plenty of these kinds of feelings. Power is a feeling you might not expect to find in a list of "yes!" feelings in infants and toddlers, yet it is vital to very young children. Power comes as they discover they can make things happen in their world—they can influence the objects and, most especially, the people around them. Attachment, and the sense of trust that comes with it, is one means of ensuring a sense of power in infants.

The "no!" feelings, especially fear and anger, are the ones that command the most attention, and we discuss them here at length. It is important for caregivers to understand how to support children in their efforts to learn to use coping techniques. Equally important is knowing about temperament and how to foster resiliency. The healthy establishment and understanding of these two developmental concepts—temperament and resiliency—directly relates to a child's positive sense of self-direction and self-esteem.

Temperament and Resiliency

Temperament is an individual's behavioral style and unique way of responding to the world. It involves a set of personality characteristics that are influenced by nature (genetics) and by nurture (interactions). These unique patterns of emotional and motor reactions begin with numerous genetic instructions that guide brain development and then are affected by the prenatal and postnatal environment. As an individual infant continues to develop, the specific experiences she has and the social context of her life influence the nature and expression of her temperament.

Trying to assess temperament and measure how individual traits are shaped has proven to be a challenge. The longest and most comprehensive study of young children's temperament began decades ago with the work of Alexander Thomas and Stella Chess. Their research inspired a growing body of information related to temperament, including its stability, its biological roots, and how it can *change* based on child-rearing and caregiver interactions. The nine temperament traits described by Thomas and Chess are summarized in Figure 10.1. They are often measured along a continuum of "low" to "high," depending on the individual trait.

The traits discussed by Thomas and Chess were grouped into three temperamental types. The easy, flexible baby (about 40 percent of the population) is adaptable, approachable, and positive in mood. The slow-to-warm baby

Figure 10.1 Nine Characteristics of Temperament

1. **Activity level:** Some infants and toddlers move around a lot and seem to be constantly doing something; others tend to stay in one place and move very little.

2. **Rhythmicity:** Some infants and toddlers eat, eliminate, and sleep on a schedule almost from birth; others do not and are unpredictable.

3. **Approach-withdrawal:** Some infants and toddlers enjoy everything new and approach easily; others withdraw from almost every new experience.

4. **Adaptability:** Some infants and toddlers adjust quickly and easily to new experiences; others do not.

5. **Attention span:** Some infants and toddlers play happily with one object for a long time; others wander from one thing to another.

6. **Intensity of reaction:** Some infants and toddlers laugh loudly and howl when they cry; others simply smile or whimper.

7. **Threshold of responsiveness:** Some infants and toddlers sense every light, sound, and touch and react to it, usually with distress; others seem not to notice changes.

8. **Distractibility:** Some infants and toddlers can be distracted easily from an interesting (or perhaps dangerous) experience; others cannot be sidetracked.

9. **Quality of mood:** Some infants and toddlers seem to be always smiling and in a pleasant mood; others are often irritable.

Source: Adapted from S. Chess, A. Thomas, and H. Birsch, "The Origins of Personality," *Scientific American* 223, 1970, pp. 102–109.

(about 15 percent) is at first negative in new situations but with time and patience, eventually adapts. The feisty, spirited, difficult baby (about 10 percent) is often in a negative mood, is unpredictable (especially related to eating and sleeping), and has intense and irritable reactions related to new settings and people.[3] Notice that about 35 percent of the young children did not fit any specific category, but instead they displayed unique *blends* of temperamental characteristics.

Understanding temperament can help parents and caregivers a great deal in their efforts to foster positive interactions with young children—even when the children's dispositions are quite different. The Goodness of Fit model (again the work of Thomas and Chess) clarifies how to do this by creating caregiving environments that acknowledge each child's temperament while encouraging more *adaptive* interaction. Caregivers of slow-to-warm children are encouraged to give them time to adapt and draw them in slowly to new situations. Allow independence to unfold. Caregivers of happy, curious children need to make sure that they are safe while exploring and set aside special time to interact with them. Sensitive attention is always appreciated, even by easy, flexible children who do not demand it. Caregivers of feisty, intense, and moody children need to be flexible, prepare them ahead of time for change, and provide for vigorous play. Patiently guide them and build positive interactions.[4]

NAEYC Program Standard 3
Teaching

These boys have discovered a snail. Each has a different emotional reaction. Is it their temperament that makes a difference?

Recognizing and appreciating individual differences can help adults respond to the challenges of young children's temperaments in caring, supportive ways. Caregivers need to be aware and cautious, however, when *applying* categories and labels. Self-fulfilling prophecies can occur if adult expectations begin to inappropriately shape the way children behave. If "difficult" children are treated as such, the behavior may be set regardless of the child's *real* temperament.

So, how real is an infant's temperament? Is temperament stable at birth or not? Some behaviors do seem to have what researchers call "long-term stability." Infants and toddlers who scored low or high on irritability, sociability, or shyness, for example, are likely to respond similarly when assessed years later. Thomas and Chess believed that temperament was well established by three months of age. Much of our information today states, however, that there is more stability in temperament after two years of age. Temperament itself may develop with age—early behaviors change and reorganize themselves into new, more complex reactions.[5] The *predisposition* a young child has to behave a certain way gets molded and modified by experience. Cultural diversity plays a tremendous role in how children are responded to and socialized. Each family is unique.

Resiliency and Healthy Emotional Development

What contributes to the stability of certain temperament patterns has led numerous developmental specialists to examine the trait of **resiliency** and how it contributes to healthy emotional growth. Resiliency is the ability to overcome adversity in an adaptive manner. Much of the research in this area has been done with troubled youths, especially young adolescents. These youths were also often identified as *already* in problem situations, the most obvious being poverty. Some of the current information on resiliency shifts the approach from a "bounce back from adversity" focus to a focus on competency and inner strength. The idea of fostering inner strength and competency early in development is a valuable goal in an effort to prevent later concerns. Fostering resiliency in a person and showing respect are approaches that share the same goal of healthy emotional development.

Resiliency is the ability some people seem to have to *thrive* despite adverse environmental conditions. Today it is viewed as a dynamic process and not as a stable trait. Children may not be resilient in all situations, but they can learn to cope with problems and comfort themselves. It is impossible to shield a child from all stress (and the research on resiliency usually examines multiple stressors—poverty, high-risk conditions, absent parents), but fostering resiliency can bolster a positive adaptation to some stress, resulting in new strengths.[6] We apply this later in the chapter in the discussion on fear and anger.

Resilient children have several specific characteristics. They have an *active approach* to life's challenges; they look for resolutions to problems. They also seem to understand cause and effect; things usually happen for a reason. Resilient children are able to gain positive attention; they are appealing and sociable, with an easygoing disposition. Finally, they see the world as a positive place, and they believe in a meaningful life.

EXPLORE the following websites for more information and resource material.

ResilienceNet provides comprehensive information about human resilience; a panel of experts monitors resources to ensure quality.

http://resilnet.uiuc.edu

Search Institute is an independent, nonprofit organization that has created a framework of developmental assets associated with resilience in children; resources are also available.

www.search-institute.org

Research on resiliency tells us that there are protective factors that can enhance its development. Caregivers of young children can incorporate these protective factors when they plan curriculum and design environments. Very young children can learn early in their lives that they are competent people and that the world is an interesting place. Such early learning promotes emotional stability and health and fosters lifelong coping skills. Examine the list of strategies presented in Figure 10.2. What strategies that foster resiliency can you add?

Figure 10.2 Caregiving Strategies to Promote Resiliency

1. Know the children in your care (developmentally, individually, and culturally) and build a positive, caring relationship with each child.

2. Build a sense of community in your program in which each child experiences a sense of belonging while appreciating the rights and needs of others.

3. Build strong relationships with families that foster trust and mutual respect.

4. Create a clear and consistent program structure so that children can predict routines and feel safe.

5. Make learning meaningful and relevant so that each child can see connections and experience his or her own competence.

6. Use authentic assessment procedures, like portfolios, so that families can appreciate and take pride in their child's unique development.

Source: Adapted from Bonnie Bernard, *Turning the Corner: From Risk to Resiliency* (Portland, OR: Western Regional Center for Drug Free Schools and Communities, Far West Laboratory, 1993).

Helping Infants and Toddlers Cope with Fears

A baby is sitting on the floor playing with a soft rubber ball. She stops playing for a moment and looks around the room, searching. She finds her mother close by, a look of relief passes over her face, she gives a big smile, and she continues to play. She hears a door open and sounds coming from the other room. Two people enter. The baby freezes. One of the people, a caregiver, approaches her enthusiastically—holding out her arms, talking warmly and excitedly. The baby stiffens. As the individual moves nearer, the baby's whole body attitude is one of moving back, away. She remains in suspended animation until the moment the person's face arrives close to hers. She then lets out an enormous howl. She continues to scream and stiffen even though the person talks soothingly and moves away slightly. She stops only when the caregiver moves away and her mother comes in close to soothe and comfort her. She clings to her mother, swallowing her last sobs while keeping a suspicious eye on the stranger.

"I'm sorry I scared you," says the caregiver, gently keeping her distance. "I see that you are really afraid of me." She continues to talk in a quiet, calm, reassuring voice.

This child is obviously attached and experiencing strong feelings of fear that result from her cognitive ability to distinguish her mother from strangers. Stranger anxiety is a common and perfectly normal fear. The caregiver in this scene found it effective to back off from the infant. Next time she will probably approach more cautiously and slowly, allowing the child time to "warm up to her." She will discover what it takes for this particular child to accept her. Some children will allow a direct approach; others do better when the stranger ignores them but remains near enough so that the child can decide to approach when he or she is ready to do so.

The causes of fear change as infants grow into toddlers. After the first year or two, the fears of noise, strange objects, unfamiliar people, pain, falling, and sudden movements decrease. However, new sources of fear take their place (for instance, imaginary creatures, the dark, animals, and the threat of physical harm). Notice that the movement is from immediate events and sensations to more internal events, imagined, remembered, or predicted. This change is related to the child's growing ability to think and consequently understand potential dangers. Consider the caregiver's response in the following scene.

The toddler room is full of activity. A jack-o-lantern on the shelf gives a clue as to the time of year. Three children are on a low loft in a dramatic play area putting on hats and shawls and other dress-up clothes. A child enters the room, holding on to his father's hand. He is wearing a mask. He sees the three children in the loft and immediately comes up to join them. Two children go about their business, but the third one takes one look at the mask and begins to cry quietly. He backs off and tries to hide behind the box of dress-up clothes. He keeps his eyes on the masked face. A caregiver, seeing his distress, approaches quickly.

She speaks matter-of-factly to the masked child. "Kevin, Josh doesn't like your mask. He needs to see your face." She takes the mask off Kevin and holds it out toward Josh. "See, Josh, it's Kevin. He had a mask on. That's what scared you." Josh still looks nervous as he glances from the mask in the caregiver's hand to Kevin's face and back to the mask. "Here, do you want to see it?" She offers to hand it to him. Kevin protests, grabs the mask, and puts it back on. Josh looks terrified again. The teacher firmly removes the mask. "I won't let you wear that, Kevin, because Josh is scared." She hands the mask to another caregiver and asks him to put it away. Kevin protests mildly and then gets occupied trying on a furry hat and admiring himself in the mirror. Josh then crawls out from behind the box, watches the mask disappear across the room, and looks at Kevin's face. Then he picks a hard hat out of the box, puts it on, and goes to stand by Kevin to look in the mirror. The caregiver, seeing the situation is over, leaves to mop up a spill at the drinking fountain.

This caregiver, like the first one, understood and accepted the child's fear. Acceptance is vital if children are to eventually recognize, identify, and accept their own feelings. It is important to provide security and to help young children find their own way of coping. Comforting can be done in a way that leads children toward learning to comfort themselves and knowing when to ask for help.

Sometimes it helps if an infant can "relearn" a situation that was once frightening. This relearning is called **conditioning**. For example, a particular object or activity that provokes fear can be proved harmless if it is presented along with something that is pleasant or if a loved person is present to explain the situation. It may take several introductions. Stop if the child seems highly anxious and try again in a few months. For a summary of guidelines to help infants and toddlers cope with their fears, see Figure 10.3.

Consider the following situations. Would knowledge of your own coping techniques help you respond to these children? How would knowledge of the children's temperament help you?

Figure 10.3 Caregiving Strategies for Helping Young Children to Cope with Their Fears

1. Accept children's fears as valid; acknowledge their fears as being real to them.

2. Give children support and show confidence that they can find ways to cope.

3. Use foresight to prevent fearful situations when possible; encourage strangers to approach young children slowly, especially if strangers are dressed in an unfamiliar way.

4. Prepare toddlers for potentially frightening situations; tell them what to expect.

5. Break frightening situations into manageable parts.

6. Couple the unfamiliar situation (for example, going on a field trip) with a familiar object (for example, holding a special toy).

7. Give young children time to adjust to something new.

A nine-month-old child has just been left at the center by his mother, who is late to work. Although she did stay with her son for a few minutes before handing him over to the caregiver, who happens to be a substitute and new, he started screaming when she hastily said good-bye to him and hurried out the door. He is now sitting on the floor, terrified, alternately screaming and sobbing. What is the probable meaning of this child's behavior? How would you respond if you were the substitute?

A two-year-old is looking through a stack of books lying near at hand. She is on a soft cushion looking very relaxed. Next to her is a caregiver holding another child who is also holding a book and looking at the pictures. The child on the cushion picks a book and flips through it. She comes to a picture of a clown, slams the book shut, and sits looking terrified. How would you interpret this child's behavior? How would you respond if you were the caregiver?

A two-and-a-half-year-old is making an enclosure out of large plastic blocks. She stands inside looking very proud of herself, saying, "Look at my house, teacher." A siren screams outside in the street. She freezes. Then she races to the stack of cots and crawls under the bottom one, squeezing her body almost out of sight. What do you make of this behavior? How would you respond if you were the caregiver?

In your responses, did you acknowledge the children's feelings? Did you have the urge to rescue them, or could you find ways to give them some help in discovering their own methods for relieving their feelings? Can you see what purpose the fear might serve in each of these situations?

In general, fear protects the individual from danger. In infants, it is fairly easy to see how fear functions, because infants react to falling, to harsh assaults on their senses, and to separation from the person primarily responsible for their well-being. Fear can protect them from danger. Toddlers have more complex fears because their cognitive development has expanded. When they are frightened, both infants and toddlers often protect themselves by withdrawing, as contrasted to angry infants and toddlers, who more often lash out.

Helping Infants and Toddlers Cope with Anger

Anger, like fear, may make life hard for caregivers. Take another look at the opening scenario of this chapter. Remember Sofia and her frustrations with the infant and with her caregiver? Review how the adult dealt respectively with both children. The caregiver protected the infant, but in doing so made Sofia angry. Nevertheless, the adult treated her anger with respect by accepting the fact that she was angry and by acknowledging that fact to her. However she did not allow Sofia to act on her anger by hurting Trung.

Although the cause of this toddler's anger seemed to be being thwarted, causes are sometimes not related to the immediate situation and come from some deeper place. It is harder to accept a young child's feelings as real and valid when *you* do not see any good reason for them. When the cause for anger is not as obvious or is not considered valid by adults, they tend to make remarks like "Oh, that's nothing to get mad about" or "Oh, come on now, you're not really mad." But feelings are real even when the cause isn't obvious or doesn't seem valid. Respectful caregivers do not contradict the feelings an infant or a toddler expresses. They *pay attention* and try to *reflect* what they perceive coming from the child. This approach says to the child, "What you feel is important." Nothing is done to discount or minimize the importance of recognizing and accepting feelings. One should not have to justify feelings—that they are present is enough.

Caregivers must manage somehow to be serene, tolerant, and self-controlled if they are to accept and reflect feelings. They must be able to be empathetic. But, at the same time, they must not deny their own feelings. Just as principle 6 states, *caregivers should be honest about how they feel* and be able to decide when it is appropriate to express their feelings. Competent caregivers also learn how to set aside their own feelings when appropriate in order to understand what a child is feeling. This is the empathetic relationship. It is important to help children recognize, accept, and then cope with their own feelings. Remember that this is also an important way to foster self-regulation.

In addition to accepting a child's feelings and expressing their own when appropriate (which teaches by modeling), caregivers can deal with infants' and toddlers' anger in several other ways. Prevention, of course, needs to be considered first. Be sure that infants and toddlers do not confront too many frustrating problems during their day. Toys should be age-appropriate and should also be in good repair. Toys that don't work or have missing parts can be frustrating. No need to remove all sources of frustration, however, because that eliminates problem solving. Remember to provide for infants' and toddlers' physical needs. A tired or hungry child is more easily angered than one who is rested and full. Short tempers hinder problem solving because the child gives up in unproductive anger.

Young infants have limited resources for expression. Crying may be their only option, and crying is a good release for infants because it involves both sound and physical activity. The early crying can later become refined physical activity and

Reflect

How do you express your anger? Do you do it in different ways? Do you find that you often do not express anger when you feel it, especially when you cannot act on it?

words as infants grow in their ability to use their body and language. Caregivers who allow infants to cry in anger are also able to direct angry toddlers' energy to pounding clay, throwing beanbags, and telling people how they feel. This way neither infants nor toddlers learn to deny or cover up their anger in an unhealthy way.

Look at the following situations and think about how the caregiver might respond. Here's a situation with an angry two-year-old:

The boy is playing with a plastic rake next to a low fence in the yard of an infant-toddler center. He sticks the rake through the fence and twists it. When he tries to pull it out again, he finds it stuck. He pulls and twists, but the rake doesn't come loose. He shows frustration on his face. His little knuckles are white from holding on to the rake handle. His face is getting red with anger. He kicks the fence, then sits down and cries.

VIDEO OBSERVATION 10

Child Trying to Get Her Turn in a Swing

See Video Observation 10: Child Trying to Get Her Turn in a Swing for an example of a child who wants something and has some feelings about not getting it. Pay attention to your own feelings as you watch this scene. Are you affected by what you perceive the child's feelings to be?

Questions

- What do you think this child is feeling? What tells you? How do you know?
- What would you feel if you were in this child's situation?
- Is she coping well with her feelings? If yes, how? How would you cope in this situation?
- What does the use of the swing tell you about this program's philosophy on independence or interdependence?

To view this clip, go to **www.mhhe.com/itc10e**. Click on Student Edition, select Chapter 10, and click on Video Observation.

Here is another two-year-old who is angry for a different reason:

> The girl is dragged into the center screaming and kicking. Her exasperated mother gives the unwilling little hand to a caregiver, tells her daughter good-bye, and walks briskly out the door. The child runs after her mother, begging her not to go. As the door shuts, she grabs the handle and tries to open it. When she finds she cannot, she lies on the floor right in front of it screaming and kicking.

Sometimes anger mobilizes extra energy for problem solving or provides motivation to keep on trying. Not all problems have satisfactory solutions, and in such cases anger may be the only way to express the frustration that is felt. This expression can be seen as an aspect of asserting independence. It takes time and a trustworthy environment to learn to regulate difficult emotions.

A Caution: Some cultures have different ideas about expressing anger and do not see independence as a goal. It is important to consider what each parent wants for his or her child.

The Principles in Action

Principle 6 Be honest about your feelings around infants and toddlers. Don't pretend to feel something that you don't or not to feel something that you do.

The caregiver believes part of her job is to help children with their feelings. She models being congruent—that is, showing what she really feels rather than pretending everything is OK when it's not. Not that she shows strong feelings in such a way that babies are frightened, but she believes that if you are annoyed you shouldn't pretend not to be. One of the mothers in the program who is of a different culture from that of the caregiver always has a little smile on her face no matter what happens. The caregiver never can tell what she is feeling. The caregiver tells her about principle 6 and asks if she believes in it. She explains that in her culture equanimity is always the goal. Showing emotions is bad because it disrupts group harmony. She says that she wants her baby to learn to control expression of feelings and she's working on teaching him. The caregiver worries that she might be doing harm to the baby, but at the same time she believes in cultural sensitivity. The caregiver's goal is to bridge cultures. She seeks to understand the mother's point of view so they can together figure out what is best for the baby.

1. What do you think?
2. Is there a way you can see both points of view—the caregiver's and the mother's?
3. Is there one point of view that is more comfortable than the other for you?
4. Do you think these two will be able to understand each other and figure out what's best for this baby in this situation? What would it take for that to happen?
5. Can the baby learn both ways of expressing his feelings and eventually operate in two cultures equally well? If yes, what would it take for that to happen? If no, why not?

Self-Calming Techniques

Most infants discover ways to calm themselves and use these devices into tod-dlerhood and beyond. It is important that children not rely solely on others to settle their emotional upsets. Most infants are born with varying degrees of abilities called **self-calming devices**. At first the techniques are quite simple, just as the infants' emotions are also simple (though intense). The most com-monly seen self-calming device is thumb sucking, which may start at birth (or even before). As infants' emotions become more complicated, so do their abilities to deal with them. The variety of self-calming behaviors that can be observed in an infant-toddler child care setting will give you an idea of how these behaviors work.

Twelve children are engaged in various activities. Two infants are asleep in their cribs in a blocked-off corner of the room. One six-month-old is on the lap of a caregiver, taking her bottle. Two three-month-olds are lying on their backs in a fenced-off corner of the room watching two toddlers who are poking toys through the slats of the fence. These children are being watched by one adult, who also has her eye on a toddler who is headed for the door, apparently intent on some outdoor activity. In another corner of the room, four toddlers are eating a snack, seated at a table with another adult. Suddenly, a loud bang from the next room interrupts all activity.

One infant wakes up, starts to cry, then finds her thumb, turns her head down into the blanket, and goes back to sleep. The other sleeping infant startles without waking up, twists around slightly, and then is quiet.

The six-month-old taking her bottle stops, looks intensely at the caregiver, gropes with her free hand for something to hang on to, and hangs on tight.

The two infants on their backs start to cry. One struggles to change his position, gets involved in his effort, and stops crying. The other continues to cry.

The two toddlers who have been watching them stop their activity. One sits down and starts twisting her hair. The other heads for his cubby, where he knows he will find his special blanket. The child who was headed to the door runs to the caregiver, picking up a doll on the way. He stands by the caregiver, stroking the smooth satin dress of the doll.

Of the children who were having a snack, one cries and cannot comfort himself until the caregiver's voice soothes him saying, "Yes, that was a loud noise, and it scared you." One cries for more food, one cries for mommy, and one climbs under the table, whimpering.

Some self-calming behaviors are learned; others, like thumb sucking, appear to be innate. A newborn who is tired or frustrated will suck even when no nipple is present. When children are a bit older, thumb or finger sucking still calms in times of stress. Knowing that someone they trust is nearby and checking in with them (glancing toward them or calling) helps children calm themselves. This growth of self-calming behaviors, from one as simple as sucking to one as complex as sharing important feelings, is a process influenced and supported by social relationships.

Developing Self-Direction and Self-Regulation

When adults help very young children recognize their own feelings, and support their efforts to calm themselves, they contribute to children's inner sense of self-direction and self-regulation. As young children learn to *regulate* their sensory input, motor skills, problem-solving abilities, and language, they become better able to *direct*, or make things happen around them. They are also more influenced by others—parents, caregivers, and peers—as they learn how to appropriately respond to the demands of their environment. Remember Sofia at the beginning of this chapter. With her caregiver's help she is learning how to manage strong emotions in more socially acceptable ways. This complex process of self-regulation takes time and persistence; everyday experiences provide opportunities to practice. Don't forget that each culture may define emotions and their regulation differently. What may be acceptable in one family or culture may not be appropriate in another.

Responding to and respecting young children's basic needs sets the stage for them to coordinate their own sense of self-direction and self-regulation. Abraham Maslow, in his classic hierarchy of needs theory, recognized this self-directing, persistent effort; he saw it as a process he called **self-actualization**. He noted that healthy people are always in the *process* of self-actualizing. They are aware of their potential and strive to make choices that move them toward it. Maslow said that self-actualized people perceive reality clearly, are open and spontaneous, have a sense of aliveness, are able to be objective and creative, have the ability to love, and above all have a strong sense of self.[7] Maslow made it clear that people acquire these characteristics only when their physical, emotional, and intellectual needs have been met. He sets out five levels of needs (Figure 10.4) and emphasizes that the needs on one level need to be satisfied before an individual can move on to the next level.

What are the implications of Maslow's levels of needs for caregivers? Levels 1 and 2 are of primary concern in infant-toddler programs and are usually regulated by licensing requirements. Levels 3, 4, and 5, the primary focus of this book, emphasize the importance of establishing emotional support and maintaining caring relationships if an individual is to realize her full potential. It is important to meet young children's basic needs in a way that responds to higher needs at the same time. Respectful caregiving in infancy encourages young children to be engaged learners eventually able to regulate their own needs and interactions.

Although Maslow stressed the importance of meeting needs, he also pointed out that overindulgence is not good. If children's needs are met promptly most of the time, sometimes they can wait a bit. Maslow said, "The young child needs

Figure 10.4 Maslow's Hierarchy of Physical, Emotional, and Intellectual Needs

Source: Abraham H. Maslow, *Motivation and Personality* (New York: Harper & Row, 1970), p. 72.

LEVEL 5

Self-Actualization

(Needs that relate to achievement and self-expression, to realize one's potential)

LEVEL 4

Esteem   **Self-Esteem**

(Needs that relate to maintaining satisfying relationships with others—to be valued, accepted, and appreciated, and to have status)

LEVEL 3

Love   **Closeness**

(Needs that relate to love, affection, care, attention, and emotional support by another)

LEVEL 2

Safety   **Security**   **Protection**

(Needs that relate to physical safety to avoid external dangers or anything that might harm the individual)

LEVEL 1

Sex   **Activity**   **Exploration**   **Manipulation**   **Novelty**
Food   **Air**   **Water**   **Temperature**   **Elimination**   **Rest**

(Needs that are essential body needs—to have access to food, water, air, sexual gratification, warmth, etc.)

not only gratification; he needs also to learn the limitations that the physical world puts upon his gratifications. . . . This means control, delay, limits, renunciation, frustration-tolerance, and discipline."[8]

All creatures have a need for stress and even for problems. *Optimal* (not maximal or minimal) stress gives children an opportunity to try out their own powers and to develop their strength and will by pushing them *against* something. Problems, obstacles, even pain and grief, can be beneficial for the development of a sense of self-direction. The guidelines given in Figure 10.5 can assist caregivers in fostering self-direction and self-regulation in young children. A child's sense of self-direction is nourished by the respectful child-adult relationships these strategies promote.

NAEYC Program Standard 1
Relationships

Figure 10.5 Strategies for Fostering Self-Direction and Self-Regulation

1. Help young children pay attention to their perceptions; use words for their experiences: "That soup is hot." "That loud noise scared you."

2. Allow quiet times so that young children can focus on their own experiences and emotions, especially when they are deeply involved in an activity.

3. Provide an appropriate environment and stable relationships, then allow young children's sense of self-direction to move them toward what they *need* to do developmentally (tasks like crawling, walking or talking); when they are *ready* to move on, they will.

4. Provide choices: when a person (at any age) is given a choice, he or she is more apt to learn from that experience, thus becoming more competent and eventually becoming a more confident decision maker.

5. Encourage independence: be present and provide a trusting base from which to take reasonable risks; respectful, caring relationships allow for holding on *and* letting go.

6. Help young children understand the perspectives and feelings of others; support them in handling limits as you redirect behavior in a positive manner.

The Emotional Brain

Many of the findings related to brain development clearly validate the caregiving principles that are the philosophical core of this book. Understanding what is happening to the brain from an early developmental perspective can sharpen our awareness of just how important sensitive, responsive care is to a young child's healthy growth. We know that the brain is impressionable; it has plasticity and clearly responds to a variety of experiences. The brain is resilient; it can compensate for some negative experiences if they are not unduly prolonged. And the brain is *emotional*! It reacts to, and processes, emotions.

Before language develops, early emotional exchanges between infants and their parents or caregivers serve as the basis for communication. These early emotional exchanges actually foster brain growth. When a responsive relationship has been established, an infant experiences delight in seeing that person. Visual emotional information is processed through the neurons in the right hemisphere of the cortex, and brain activity increases. This arousal in the brain usually causes an increase in the infant's physical activity. And if the cues that result from this behavior are responded to correctly by the parent or caregiver, brain growth is encouraged. A sensitive adult influences not only an infant's expression of emotion, but also the neurochemistry of that young brain.[9]

Current brain research has provided more insight related to this early brain specialization. The right side of the brain seems to be more responsible for processing intense negative emotions and for creativity. Greater growth is experienced in this area during the first 18 months, and it dominates brain functioning for the first three years. The left side of the brain, which matures more slowly during this period, is more responsible for language, positive emotions, and interest in new experiences.[10] Because the right side of the brain is developing more rapidly and is responsible for regulating *intense* emotions, the role caregivers play in assisting young children's emotional regulation becomes very important!

Stress and Early Brain Development

The significance of stable relationships in young children's lives has been cited numerous times in this text. In light of what is now known about the *emotional* brain, sensitive and comforting support in reaction to young children's stress is key to fostering self-regulation. When caregivers accept children's emotions, create a safe place for emotional expression, and teach coping strategies, young children learn to deal with life's ongoing frustrations and challenges.

Additional research has indicated a link between what happens when language develops and what happens when we experience stressful emotions. Brain technology, especially use of magnetic resonance imaging (MRI), has shown that the amygdala, in the central part of the brain, is the significant structure for processing fear, anxiety, and other potentially negative emotions. The work of Golnaz Tabibnia, a neuroscientist at the University of California at Los Angeles, has shown that our emotional responses can be reduced if we identify and label our emotions. Tabibnia discovered that the language processing that activates the frontal areas of the brain leads to a decreased response from the amygdala.[11] Giving young children words to label their feelings, especially the negative ones, has *real meaning* for brain development. The frontal cortex areas of the brain are able to regulate the emotional centers. That's why emotion labeling and using emotion words may help children regulate emotional responses as they experience them, and in the long term.

Earlier in this chapter it was noted that optimum stress can provide growth opportunities for young children. Stress may be necessary for development, but how much is too much? Frequent and intense early stress experiences (poverty, abuse, neglect, or sensory deprivation) actually cause an infant's brain to reorganize itself. The infant's "stress regulation mechanism" is set to a higher level to help him or her cope more effectively (related to the "fight or flight" experience often referred to in psychology), and certain chemicals are released in the brain. One of the best understood neurochemicals is the steroid hormone called cortisol. It can be measured in saliva. During times of stress, cortisol is released in the brain. It alters brain functioning by reducing the number of synapses in certain parts of the brain. If these neural connections continue to be destroyed by cortisol, developmental delays in cognitive, motor, and social behavior result. The good news is that very young children who have warm, nurturing care in the first year of life are less likely to produce high levels of cortisol in times of stress.[12] The attachment experience acts as a protective buffer against stress.

EXPLORE the following website for more information and resource material.

The National Child Traumatic Stress Network (NCTSN) is a unique collaboration of experts whose goal is to increase access to services for traumatized and stressed children and their families.

www.nctsnet.org

The Impact of Neglect

Much of the current information about the brain emphasizes the importance of attachment and nurturing responsive care for healthy neural development. We've acknowledged what can happen if a child receives too much stimulation, or too much stress. But what happens when a baby is with a depressed parent, and the infant's cues for emotional interactions are ignored? Over time the baby also develops depressive behavior and is less active and more withdrawn. The young child may also begin to turn inward for self-stimulation and self-soothing. When tested, these babies had elevated heart rates, elevated cortisol levels, and reduced brain activity. Infants whose parent(s) are depressed and neglectful are at greatest risk for long-term developmental delays from the age of 6 to 18 months. This is also the prime time for emotional attachments. An important note to add is that when the parent was treated and went into remission, the baby's brain activity returned to normal.[13] This is clearly an example of how important family support is when considering the overall healthy development of young children.

The brain research currently available highlights the following points related to emotional development in very young children:

- Emotional (and social) development is vitally connected to cognition and language.
- Too much stress, and the release of related hormones, over a long period can lead to problems with self-regulation, learning, and adapting to everyday circumstances.
- Brain specialization during the first three years plays a significant role related to self-regulation and emotional growth.
- Brain growth and neural development inform and support developmentally appropriate practice in early childhood.

For all of us, and especially for young infants, emotions amplify experience. Strong troublesome emotions need a supportive context if an infant is to learn to tolerate and adapt to such feelings. Don't forget that joy and delight are also strong emotions and can create an attitude that the world is full of wonderful things to discover. Respectful relationships are prerequisites for healthy emotional growth.

Children with Special Needs: Challenges and Trends

Early childhood intervention has a complex history, and providing quality support services to young children with special needs and their families is a challenging task. Even with the legislative mandate that exists for multiagency cooperation, there is still a lack of consistency for planning and program implementation in many areas across the country. In this section, five specific challenges and trends in early intervention are examined; the impact of these challenges and trends on infant-toddler care and education is also included.

The first challenge is the importance of recognizing that basic child development principles are key to effective early intervention services and program practices. A developmental framework challenges caregivers, teachers, parents, and the community to remember that all children are special. Understanding child development fosters an appreciation of the *uniqueness* of each child, and their special needs, while at the same time appreciating the *abilities* of the whole child. This principle has been mentioned numerous times in this book. True partnerships with families center on the knowledge that the child's most important resource, his attachment base, is his family. Responsive child-parent interaction is key to a child's development and learning.

The challenge remains, however, that many persons and agencies involved in early intervention come from varied disciplines that do not have a strong background in childhood development. Assisting families, especially with a young child with special needs, to find appropriate supports and resources is enhanced when caregivers, teachers, and specialists have an understanding of the early years. Fortunately, evidence exists that supports the finding that a *developmental approach* in early intervention is growing.[14] The trend to expand this understanding across agencies relates to the second challenge to be discussed—workforce development.

There is a major challenge in early intervention, and in early care and education, to create and adopt an effective training model to build a competent workforce. "Effective" means that the teaching practices that are encouraged are consistent across teacher education programs and that they have measurable outcomes. States need to develop clear professional standards for training and develop comprehensive career pathways. This is especially true in the fields of early care and education and early intervention because numerous exciting career opportunities *do* exist for caregivers and teachers. The early years in a child's life have a long-range impact; quality trained educators can make a big difference!

Caregivers and teachers may well have the *knowledge* of what to do with young children, but sometimes *doing* it presents the challenge. For example, an Individual Family Service Plan (IFSP) may not outline for the caregiver just "how many times" a specific activity may need to be presented to a child with a disability before it is effective. Knowing what to do and understanding the *developmental outcome* can be very challenging! Teacher training programs need to be expanded in both preservice (prior to completing a certificate or degree) and inservice (ongoing job-related training) areas of education. The trend in teacher education programs needs to be an understanding that adults learn best when what is taught (information), and why it is taught (understanding), merges with what competence *looks like*. Being part of an IFSP team and creating the elements of an effective early inclusion classroom definitely require a variety of skills.

The third challenge in early intervention is related to teacher education and workforce development—there is a lack of measurable research data to support best practices in education. The research-to-practice gap also exists in early care and education. Finding enough valid research that supports teacher behaviors and program practices, and demonstrates positive outcomes for children and families, remains a challenge in many areas of education. But it is especially crucial and needed in early intervention because of the increased vulnerability of the very young child with special needs. The *timing* of intervention activities, grounded in well-documented research, is critical for a young child to reach his full growth potential.

The Pikler approach and the Gerber philosophy of respectful, responsive curriculum, a major trend in infant-toddler care and education, may be a bright spot in teacher-caregiver education for both early intervention and early care and education. Research from programs using this approach and philosophy, both in this country and internationally, is being gathered and the authors of this book believe it is already informing teacher education programs. A key element in this approach is that caregivers and teachers are concerned about the quality of growth at each stage of infant-toddler development and learning.

The fourth challenge in early intervention relates to the early intervention service system itself. The early intervention process involving multiple agencies cooperating with each other to provide assessment, diagnosis, and program planning for a child with special needs often lacks integration and coordination. Team collaboration and group problem solving frequently have challenges in and of themselves. Add to that families in stress and limited community resources, and it is easy to see why the early intervention system overall may need a more comprehensive approach to be consistently effective with young children and their families.

Related to the challenge of coordination within the early intervention service system is the need for more evaluation and feedback. Measurable outcomes and teaching practices need to be stated clearly. Careful attention to details at every level of the service system is vital if the young children involved, and their families, are to have positive experiences related to development and learning. The trends toward greater family involvement and sensitivity to cultural differences, as well as a more educated workforce, should create a group of parents and caregivers better *informed* to ask questions in the early intervention process. Parents and caregivers giving their input early (for example, in the IFSP) will contribute to more well-documented, clearly understood interventions within the system.[15]

The fifth and final challenge to be discussed in this section is funding. The national legislative mandate of thirty years ago to provide services for young children with special needs has never been fully funded. States can vary dramatically in distribution of their education funds in order to include children with special needs. Families often struggle to find adequate and appropriate supports for their children. Some practices have resulted in "reverse" inclusion in order to obtain public school funds. In some cases, services are defined and provided for only the most disabled children, and those children that might do well in an inclusive program are isolated in special education settings in order to receive any services at all.[16]

Early care and education, infant-toddler care, and early intervention have all contributed to the growing public awareness of the importance of the first three years in a child's life. The trend toward these three fields combining their efforts in a more defined and collaborative way should result in more state and national funding initiatives. The strength provided by the three fields to "pool" their documented research and best practices could result in more funding and program sustainability for all of them!

NAEYC Program Standard 4
Assessment

Reflect

Think for a moment about an infant or toddler in your care who was *difficult*. Describe the child's behavior. What were your reactions? What would you try to do if you were in the same situation today?

The challenges within early childhood intervention may seem varied and complex, but the recognition of the critical importance of the early years is well documented and growing. Current trends are fostering increased public awareness and support. Visionary leadership is needed to implement research-based, best practices for the early care and education workforce. Informed collaboration between families and community agencies is needed to implement natural and inclusive settings in a cost-effective and sustainable way. This is an exciting time to be involved in early childhood intervention—and in the care of infants and toddlers. Principles are becoming clear that the best way to support the needs of all young children and their families is to provide responsive and respectful care.

DEVELOPMENTAL PATHWAYS

Behavior Showing Development of Emotions

Young infants (up to 8 months)	• Express discomfort and comfort or pleasure unambiguously • Can usually be comforted by a familiar adult when distressed • Laugh aloud (belly laugh) • Show displeasure or disappointment at loss of toy • Express several emotions clearly: pleasure, anger, anxiety or fear, sadness, joy, excitement
Mobile infants (up to 18 months)	• Show pride and pleasure in new accomplishments • Express negative feelings • Continue to show pleasure in mastery • Assert self, indicating strong sense of self
Toddlers (up to 3 years)	• Frequently display aggressive feelings and behaviors • Exhibit contrasting states and mood shifts (stubborn versus compliant) • Show increased fearfulness (of the dark, monsters, etc.) • Are aware of their own feelings and those of others • Verbalize feelings more often, express feelings in symbolic play

Source: Carol Copple and Sue Bredekamp, eds., *Developmentally Appropriate Practice in Early Childhood Programs*, 3rd ed. (Washington, DC: National Association for the Education of Young Children, 2009).

Diverse Developmental Pathways

What you see	Jacob always arrives with a smile on his face. He's flexible and easygoing—even when things don't seem to go his way. He enjoys playing in small groups, and you've even seen him being empathic with others (patting and comforting a crying child).
What you might think	At almost three years of age, Jacob is a pleasure to be around, but on busy days you almost forget about him. Sometimes you feel guilty that you don't spend more time with him.

What you might not know	Jacob is a middle child—he has a brother two years older, and there is a new baby at his house. There is some financial stress at home—his dad is working two jobs, and his mom is doing a catering business out of the home (while caring for the new baby). There isn't much attention time at home for Jacob.
What you might do	Try to check in more with Jacob—it may be just a smile when you catch his eye, or sitting near him while holding another child. Try to set aside some special time with him doing his favorite things. Let him *help* you put the napkins out for snack. Remember that all children need special attention. Just because Jacob doesn't demand it doesn't mean he doesn't enjoy it. Don't allow yourself to overlook him because you are busy.
What you see	Megan is an active and intense two-and-a-half-year-old. She lets everyone know when she is happy or not! She's fussy and often gets into conflicts with other children over a toy or other object.
What you might think	Megan is a handful! You appreciate her zesty temperament, but you don't like her aggressive tendencies. She often seems frustrated, even *before* she begins activities.
What you might not know	Megan is a feisty child. She loves the rough-and-tumble play she often gets into with her five-year-old brother. She does receive subtle and not-so-subtle mixed messages from her parents: her father (from another culture) disapproves of her active behavior and often reprimands her; her mother has just started working outside the home and loves her new job—she sees Megan's behavior as a sign of her daughter's growing independence.
What you might do	Help Megan with her intense reactions. Empathize with her when things don't go her way, but place firm limits on any aggressive behavior. Try to give her extra time for transitions; let her know that a snack is coming and that then she will be going outside. Help her manage her frustrations better by providing lots of active play opportunities. Remember that her feisty behavior today could set the stage for leadership skills tomorrow.

Summary

Emotions are the affective response to an event.

The Development of Emotions and Feelings

- Young infants have emotional responses that are not very refined; stirred-up states begin to differentiate themselves in a few months into the emotions of pleasure, fear, and anger.
- Toddlers express pride, embarrassment, shame, and empathy; adults need to support toddlers' efforts to learn to use coping techniques to deal with everyday frustrations.

Temperament and Resiliency

- Temperament, or an individual's behavioral style, can be discussed in terms of *traits*, and understanding these traits can help caregivers respond to children in caring, supportive ways.
- Resiliency, or the ability to overcome adversity, is viewed as a dynamic process; research related to it indicates that there are caregiving strategies to promote its development and to foster lifelong coping skills.

Helping Infants and Toddlers Cope with Fear

- A common fear in the first year is stranger anxiety. Fears become more complex in toddlerhood and can be related to imaginary creatures, animals, the dark, and threat of harm.
- It is important to accept fears as valid and to give young children time to adjust to new experiences.

Helping Infants and Toddlers Cope with Anger

- Respectful caregivers accept and reflect a young child's anger; they do not contradict what the child is feeling while they protect the child (and others) as she learns to develop coping skills.
- Anger can mobilize extra energy to solve problems or release frustration. It is important to remember that some cultures have different ideas about expressing anger.

Self-Calming Techniques

- Learning to settle personal emotional upsets is an important skill. Some of these *self-calming* behaviors may be innate (for example, thumb sucking) and others can be learned (for example, sharing feelings).
- The growth of self-calming behaviors is influenced by the development of trust and supported by caring, social relationships.

Developing Self Direction and Self-Regulation

- Implications from the work of Abraham Maslow and others indicate how important it is for caregivers to meet the primary needs of very young children in respectful ways if higher-level needs are to be fulfilled.
- A child's sense of self direction and self-regulation is nourished by respectful adult-child relationships.

The Emotional Brain

- Early emotional exchanges (before language) between infants and their caregivers foster brain growth. Respectful relationships strengthen brain pathways and are the prerequisites for healthy emotional growth.
- Frequent and intense early stress experiences can cause an infant's brain to reorganize itself. Stress hormones are released, causing a reduction of the number of synapses in certain areas of the brain.

Children with Special Needs: Challenges and Trends

- Five major challenges exist within the early intervention field: the need for a stronger knowledge base in child development, expansion of the early intervention workforce, more valid research related to early intervention, more collaboration and evaluation within the service system, and more sustainable funding.
- Early intervention, early care and education, and infant-toddler care have contributed to a major trend—the growing public awareness of the importance of the first three years in a child's life. The combined strength of these fields should result in more funding initiatives and program sustainability.

Key Terms

conditioning 217	resiliency 214	social referencing 211
emotion 210	self-actualization 223	temperament 212
feeling 210	self-calming devices 222	

Thought/Activity Questions

1. Review your definition of attachment. What role does it play in emotional development?
2. How does knowing about temperament help you interact more effectively with very young children? How might you encourage resiliency?
3. How would you help calm a fearful eight-month-old infant? How would your behavior change if a two-year-old was fearful?
4. How would you help a toddler cope with anger? Describe a recent experience with an angry toddler and what you did in response.
5. How would you describe your own temperament? Do you think you are a resilient person? Consider how the answers to these questions influence your interactions with very young children.
6. What challenges exist in the field of early childhood intervention? How do current trends also influence infant-toddler care and education programs?

For Further Reading

Emily J. Adams, "Teaching Children to Name their Feelings," *Young Children* 66(3), May 2011, pp. 66–68.

J. J. Baumgartner and T. Buchanan, "Supporting Each Child's Spirit," *Young Children* 65(2), March 2010, pp. 90–95.

Enid Elliot and Janet Gonzalez-Mena, "Babies' Self-Regulation: Taking a Broad Perspective," *Young Children* 66(1), January 2011, pp. 28–33.

Ida R. Florez, "Developing Young Children's Self-Regulation through Everyday Experiences," *Young Children* 66(4), July 2011, pp. 46–51.

Dan Gartrell, "Aggression, the Prequel: Preventing the Need," *Young Children* 66(6), November 2011, pp. 62–64.

M. Gerber, "Helping Baby Feel Secure, Self-Confident and Relaxed," *Educaring* 1(4), Fall 1980, pp. 4–5.

Jamilah R. Jordan, Kathy G. Wolf, and Anne Douglass, "Increasing Family Engagement in Early Childhood Programs," *Young Children* 67(5), November 2012, pp. 18–22.

chapter 11

Social Skills

Focus Questions

After reading this chapter you should be able to answer the following questions:

1 What are some examples of early social behaviors?

2 Describe Erikson's first three stages of psychosocial development. What do you think of his view concerning how social skills develop in young children?

3 Why is learning to cope with fears and other feelings around separation considered an important social skill?

4 How do guidance and discipline support the development of social skills?

5 A major component of discipline involves teaching prosocial behavior. What are some examples of prosocial behaviors and why are they important to encourage in young children?

6 What seven gifts can adults give infants and toddlers to promote healthy brain growth?

What Do You See?

A mother enters the infant center carrying a child who has a tense look on her face. The child has both arms around her mother's neck and is hanging on tight. Her mother puts her diaper bag into a cubby by the entrance, speaks briefly to the caregiver, then says to her daughter, "I have to go pretty soon, Rebecca. You're going to stay here with Maria. She'll take care of you while I'm gone." She bends over to try to put her daughter down. Maria has come over near the couple and kneels down, waiting. Rebecca clings tighter and refuses to be put down, so her mother sits down on the floor with Rebecca still in her arms. They both sit there for several minutes. The child begins to relax a bit. She reaches for and takes hold of the handle of a push toy and rolls it back and forth across the rug while still in her mother's arms. She gets absorbed in this and gets off her mother's lap and moves slightly away. With that, her mother gets up, leans down, and kisses her daughter. She says, "It's time for me to go now. Good-bye." She walks over to the door. Rebecca follows, looking distressed. At the door her mother turns once briefly, waves, throws a kiss, turns back, opens the door, and is gone. At the sound of the door closing, Rebecca lets out a wail, then collapses in a heap, sobbing.

NAEYC Program Standard 1
Relationships

One of the most important sets of social skills that all people have to learn is how to separate from those they care about. Rebecca is working on this skill. Later in this chapter you'll see how Maria helped Rebecca handle her feelings about being left behind.

Social skills, the focus of this chapter, define the range of appropriate behaviors for interacting and connecting with others. These behaviors contribute to *socialization*, which is the process of learning the standards and expectations of a specific culture. Social development underlies and is supported by all other areas of development. As very young children learn to manage their bodies, they are more able to control their actions around other people. As their cognitive abilities expand and allow them to take the perspective of another, they can use the words they know to cooperate and share ideas and feelings. Emotional self-regulation contributes to young children's growing independence, and it is this expanding ability to control and regulate one's own behavior that eventually enables a child to become a participating member of a group. Learning social skills as part of the socialization process takes time, and young children need the caring support of trusted adults.

It is important to appreciate social skills from a developmental perspective. Infants and toddlers, especially toddlers in this society, have some specific tasks to accomplish. A secure attachment base allows a child to generalize trust and therefore *separate* from their parents with some degree of ease. Muscle and motor development provide for social skills that range from *toilet learning* to *self-feeding*. Cognitive and language skills combine to help young children *solve problems* and *make their needs clearly known* to others. A sense of self and a growing ability to manage feelings provide the base for the development of *empathy*. And it is through empathy, this feeling with another, that we develop interdependent relationships and become a caring society.

Parents, of course, are a child's first teachers and play a major role in the development of social skills. It is important for child care providers to understand and appreciate what social skills are emphasized at home so that a child does not experience contradictory messages. Caregiver-family partnerships are obviously very important. The significant thing to appreciate is that young children learn social skills from responsible adults who care about them, who model the behaviors the culture values, and who consistently show them respect.

This chapter looks at the progression of social skills from infancy through toddlerhood. We give special emphasis to the theory of Erik Erikson, covering the stages of trust, autonomy, and initiative. We also discuss how guidance and discipline support young children's social growth and lead to the development of prosocial behavior. The importance of promoting healthy brain growth and fostering self-esteem for all children are the concluding topics for the chapter.

At no time in history has the development of social skills been so important. We can't afford to raise a generation to believe that might is right. We need to teach young children how to resolve conflicts without resorting to force. This teaching starts with infants. Emmi Pikler's first book, *Peaceful Babies, Contented Mothers* (printed in Hungarian in 1940), focused on the issue of raising peaceful people. She carried that theme over into her work in setting up and maintaining the Pikler Institute, where children were reared in a residential setting. Indeed, observers are surprised at the social skills such young children show.

Another significant socialization issue is illustrated in the Principles in Action feature. When adults focus so heavily on intellectual skills that they don't notice a child's lack of social skills, development can be lopsided and the child gravely disadvantaged. Pikler's and Gerber's approaches stress the importance of focusing on the whole child.

The Principles in Action

Principle 4 Invest time and energy to build a total person (concentrate on the "whole child"). Don't focus on cognitive development alone or look at it as separate from total development.

Cody is 26 months old and the caregivers in his toddler program marvel at him. As the only child of two professional parents, he talks like an adult, using big words and complex sentences. He knows the words to many songs he has heard on the radio and enjoys telling everybody about the latest video he has seen. He seems to be trying to teach himself to read, and he is already a whiz at number concepts. He seldom pays attention to the other children and spends most of his time showing off his many skills to adults or else by himself. He doesn't seem to know how to enter into the play of others or even how to play close to them in a parallel way. He has so entranced the caregivers that they seem blind to his need to learn social skills so he can connect with his peers. Nobody is worried about Cody.

1. Do you see a reason to worry?
2. If you worked in that program, what might you do to help Cody become interested in other children and want to learn to relate to them?
3. If you see Cody's development as lopsided, how might you approach the parents to talk about what you perceive?
4. Why do you think Cody seems to need so much attention from the adults?
5. What other ideas do you have about Cody?
6. What else would you like to know?

Early Social Behaviors

Attachment is the prime factor in the development of social skills. Right from the beginning, infants interact with *synchrony* by moving their bodies to the rhythm and body movements of those who talk with them. These dancelike movements are minute, but they are present—even if a speaker is unaware of them. They occur only in response to language (any language, not necessarily that of the infant's family), and do not show up in response to other kinds of rhythms.[1]

Imitation is another early social behavior we can observe. In the first few weeks, infants will imitate such behavior as opening their eyes wide or sticking out their tongues. Early smiling by infants is also a social behavior designed to involve the adults around them in social exchanges. Whether the first smiles are *real* social smiles is debated, but they usually elicit a social response!

Within a few months, most infants are effective at nonverbal communication and have become attached to specific people. They show fear reactions, or **stranger anxiety**, when people they don't know are present. This reaction seems to be strongest in infants who have excellent communication with their parents. Often it is lessened when the stranger remains silent and noncommunicative. During this period, generally the second half of the first year, separation anxiety is also present. Infants become distressed when their key people move away from them or leave them. Establishing trust is the major way to ease this concern for very young children, but it is a *process*, and we will discuss it in more detail.

By the second year of life, infants are already making nonverbal social gestures that predict to some extent which of them will be well-liked preschoolers and which will have difficulty with peer relationships. The infants who will probably become well-liked preschoolers already have a number of *friendly* gestures that they exhibit regularly, such as offering toys, clapping hands, and smiling. Infants who regularly use threatening or aggressive gestures, or a mixture of friendly and unfriendly gestures to their peers, are more likely to grow into less-liked preschoolers.[2]

Stages of Psychosocial Development

Erik Erikson was one of the first theorists to consider social development. In his major work, *Childhood and Society*, he noted that at each stage of life conflicts emerge between individual needs and the ability to satisfy those needs. These *conflicts* tended to be socially based—other people were seen as able to help the individual resolve issues. When "resolution" occurred, then positive growth ensued and the individual moved on to the next stage. Erikson took a life-span perspective and outlined eight separate stages; in this chapter we discuss only the first three stages (information applying to children under three years). (See Table 11.1 for details.)

Reflect

Are you a person who has a basic sense of trust? What do you think gave you that trust?

Trust

The first stage of psychosocial development is **trust**. Sometime during the first year of life, if infants find that their needs are met consistently and gently, they decide that the world is a good place. They develop what Erikson called a "sense of basic trust." If infants' needs are not met consistently, or are met in a harsh

Table 11.1 Erikson's First Three Psychosocial Stages of Development (*Bold stages relate to children under three years of age*)		
Age	**Stage**	**Description**
0–1 years	**Trust versus mistrust**	**Children come to trust the world if their needs are met and they are cared for in sensitive ways. Otherwise they see the world as a cold and hostile place and develop a basic sense of mistrust.**
1–3 years	**Autonomy versus shame and doubt**	**Children work at becoming independent in areas such as feeding and toileting. They can talk and assert themselves. If they don't learn some degree of self-sufficiency, they come to doubt their own abilities and feel shame.**
3–6 years	Initiative versus guilt	Children thrust themselves into the world, trying new activities and exploring new directions. If their boundaries are too tight and they continually overstep them, they experience a sense of guilt about these inner urges that keep leading them into trouble.

manner, they may decide that the world is unfriendly and develop mistrust instead of trust. Such infants can carry this outlook into adulthood if nothing happens to change their view of life.

If infants are in child care, the adults in the program have some responsibility for ensuring that the children in their care gain a sense of basic trust. The infant's *needs* must be a primary concern of everyone in the program. There is no way to run an infant program that emphasizes anything but individual needs. The importance of developing a sense of basic trust also means that infants in child care need small groups with consistent caregivers. Stability in programs contributes to the infants' well-being and building sense of trust.

Part of developing trust means coping with separation. As attachment strengthens, so does the pain of being away from the person(s) to whom the child is attached. Child care providers spend a lot of time and energy helping children manage the feelings separation brings forth. The opening scene at the beginning of the chapter provides an example. Review that scene again. There is Rebecca, collapsed on the floor in a heap, sobbing.

She looks up as a hand touches her shoulder. She sees, kneeling beside her, Maria, the caregiver. She moves away from the touch. Maria continues to stay close by her. "I see you're upset that your mom left," Maria says. Rebecca begins to scream again.

Maria remains close, but silent. Rebecca's screams subside, and she goes back to quiet sobbing. She continues to sob for a while; then she spots her diaper bag where her mother left it in her cubby. She reaches for it; her tear-stained face has a look of expectancy on it. Maria gets it out for her. Rebecca clings to it. Maria reaches inside

NAEYC Program Standard 1
Relationships

and pulls out a stuffed bear wrapped in a scarf. Rebecca grabs the bear, hugging it fiercely. She strokes the scarf, holding it to her nose periodically and smelling it. Her face gets more and more relaxed.

Maria moves away from her. Rebecca doesn't seem to notice. Maria comes back with a box of dolls and blankets, which she arranges on the floor near Rebecca. Rebecca crawls over immediately, tips the box over, and crawls inside. The scene closes as Rebecca is wrapping a doll in a blanket and putting it to bed in the box next to her bear, which is covered with the scarf.

Notice how Maria helped Rebecca cope with separation. She stated the situation and the feelings. She was available but not pushy. She was sensitive to Rebecca's responses to her touch and to her words. She encouraged Rebecca to find solace in familiar belongings. She set up the environment to entice and support Rebecca.

NAEYC Program Standards 2 and 3
Curriculum and Teaching

Helping Children through Separation　Because separation is such an important issue and social skill in infancy and toddlerhood, it deserves consideration and planning on the part of adults. Always try to be honest; state the facts and include labels for emotional feelings ("Your mom had to go to work and you are feeling unhappy about being left"). Handle the separation experience with the appropriate degree of seriousness and avoid underplaying the importance of and degree of suffering the child may be experiencing. It takes time for a very young child to establish trust; in the meantime, if the child is afraid, accept that fact. Offer support and help the child develop coping skills. Remind yourself that some children appreciate the closeness of others, and some move away and prefer a toy or other interesting material.

Welcome things from home that the family may provide for comfort. A special blanket, stuffed toy, or even Mom's old purse may be just the special attachment object that provides the temporary support a child needs. Allow young children individual ways of feeling comforted; some children may want to leave a special sweater on even if it is a warm day. Remember, too, that it is important to deal with separation with a child who *seems* not terribly upset. Coping with separation and loss is a lifetime task; throughout our lives we lose those we are close to, and life events change our circumstances. The coping skills we develop in the first three years should serve us for a long time. When young children learn to cope with the fears of separation, they gather feelings of mastery, and trust expands to include others in social relationships.

Reflect

What do you remember about a time in your life that you were separated from someone you were attached to? What feelings do you remember? What helped you cope with them? Did someone help you cope?

Caregiver Issues with Separation　Sometimes it is difficult for caregivers to deal with infants' and toddlers' feelings related to separation because of their own experiences. They may have lingering feelings about their own past separations and may prefer to not reopen old wounds. In such cases, they may be uncomfortable around children who are suffering a sense of loss. Instead of trying to understand what is going on, caregivers may want to distract the young children and just get the feelings to go away. But the pain of separation doesn't just "go away," and children need to learn to cope with such feelings. Separation, in fact, is part of the curriculum, and caregivers need to be able to plan for it and focus on it.

It is also important for caregivers to recognize infants' and toddlers' range of feelings around separation. Feelings of loss may range from mild discomfort to anxiety, loneliness, sadness, and even grief. A child may experience one, or all at once. Although infants and toddlers are not necessarily competent at describing feelings, it is easy to detect that they feel the same range of emotions that adults feel.

Caregivers need to be ready to face the fact that parents have separation issues too. Sometimes it seems that parents magnify separation problems and even create additional ones because of their own pain at leaving their children. It is difficult to deal with a parent who sneaks out because he or she hates to say good-bye. Some good-byes are prolonged and too complicated, and the child who was ready to separate decides not to! Some parents suffer because their child cries when they leave; others suffer because their child *doesn't* cry. Be sensitive to parents' feelings; encourage them to call during the day and check on how their child is doing. Some parents may feel a sense of guilt about leaving their children—they need support and compassion too.

Remember there are also separation issues *within* a child care program. As shifts change, adults come and go. Infants and toddlers may have to deal with separation from a beloved caregiver before they say hello once again to a beloved parent. Some of the comings and goings can be lessened in a family child care home, because the group size tends to be smaller and fewer adults are in the program.

Autonomy

Erikson's second stage of psychosocial development, **autonomy**, occurs as the growing infant reaches the second year and begins to move around in the environment. When infants become toddlers, they begin to perceive themselves as separate individuals, not just a part of the person(s) to whom they are attached. They discover the power they possess, and they push toward independence. At the same time, their developing capabilities allow them to do more for themselves. They learn self-help skills.

Readiness for toilet learning is an example of the coming together of increased capabilities and the push for independence. The necessary capabilities lie in three separate domains—the physical (control), the cognitive (understanding), and the emotional (willingness). The goal is to get the movement toward independence working for you. Be thoughtful and avoid power struggles. It is best for the child to see you as a support to her own developing capabilities and independence.

Language provides clues about another area of autonomy. The "NO!" for which toddlers are so famous is a further clue to the push for separateness and independence. They differentiate themselves from others by what seems to be defiance. If you want them to go in, they want to stay out. If you want them to stop, they want to start. If you're serving milk, they want juice.

Caregivers don't usually see as much of this kind of behavior as do parents. The tie between parent and child is a much stronger, more passionate one. Many children feel more secure and therefore more free to express themselves in words

Reflect

Are you a person with issues around separation? Do children's feelings upset you more than other people you know? If yes, what can you do about your own separation issues? If no, how do you think you learned to cope with separation?

Reflect

Do you react strongly to the behaviors toddlers show when working on issues of autonomy? If yes, why? If no, why not? Do you think your culture has anything to do with your answer?

and actions at home than they do in child care. It is important not to make parents feel they are doing something wrong because more defiant and rebellious behavior comes out when they are present. Rejecting behaviors are normal, and even good, for toddlers to exhibit. These behaviors show that the child's growing sense of autonomy and separateness is strong.

Language provides additional information about autonomy. "Me do it!" shows that drive for independence. By capitalizing on this drive, you promote the development of self-help skills. When children want to "do it," set up the situation so they *can*.

Sometimes, in the name of fairness, children are constantly asked to give up a turn or to share a toy before they are finished with it. When this occurs in an environment where there are no private possessions, rather than learning to be a sharing person, some children learn just not to care. It doesn't matter to them whether they play with this toy or that one or for how long. They learn to stay uninvolved rather than face the pain of being constantly interrupted and sidetracked. Think what it would be like to be a child who never gets a chance to play out a fantasy or reach a point of satisfaction by being allowed to have a toy in your possession until you are really through with it. How would this situation affect attention span? Do some children learn to have short attention spans because some caregivers overstress sharing? Programs need to give young children opportunities to finish tasks, and allow them private spaces where sharing isn't always required.

Initiative

Erikson's term for the stage of older toddlers as they approach preschool age is **initiative**. The focus on autonomy eventually passes. The energy that has previously gone into separating and striving for independence, and which often results in defiance and rebellion, is now available for new themes. This energy pushes children to create, invent, and explore as they seek out new activities. At this new stage, toddlers become the initiators of what happens in their lives and gain enthusiasm from their newfound power.

The caregiver should respond to this need to initiate by providing information, resources, freedom, and encouragement. Although older toddlers still very much need limits, the caregiver can set and keep the limits in such a way that toddlers don't feel guilty about this powerful push they feel to take initiative. People with initiative make valuable citizens. They gain this quality early in life when the people around them encourage them to be *explorers, thinkers,* and *doers.*

Guidance and Discipline: Teaching Social Skills

Guidance and discipline are part of the ongoing process of teaching social skills to children—and it is sometimes a challenging and frustrating process. It may be helpful to pause and define this process, and to consider the long-range goals of self-reliance and self-esteem. (This might come in handy when you are trying to support a screaming toddler determined to grab a toy away from another child!) *Guidance* is the philosophical approach to teaching the standards and expectations of your culture, and *discipline* means the specific techniques used to accomplish this task. Your guidance philosophy determines your discipline techniques; no one technique always works, but your philosophy should remain constant and support children's ongoing growth toward positive socialization.

NAEYC Program Standard 3
Teaching

Security and Control for Infants

In the first three years, young children learn many social skills, and helping them to deal with frustrations, solve problems, and establish a sense of security requires caregivers who value and respect children's uniqueness. Guidance during the first year needs to be accepting and trust building. Infants require no discipline because limits come naturally from their own limitations. Guidance for infants means providing security and responsive care; caregiving needs to provide the control that infants lack. An example of providing control when an infant needs it occurs when newborns cry in distress that is not hunger. Sometimes being wrapped tightly in a blanket helps them to calm down, and the blanket seems to provide the control they do not have in their arms and legs.

This same theme—tightness providing the control the infant lacks—looks different in the toddler stage. Toddlers may also appreciate a "feeling of tightness" (control from the outside) in situations where their own underdeveloped ability to control themselves gives way. Holding out-of-control toddlers tightly, and at the same time soothing them, usually enables them to regain inner control.

Limits for Toddlers

Toddlers need to feel that there are **limits** even when they do not need the tightness of outside control. Think of limits—rules of behavior—as invisible fences or boundaries. Because they can't see these boundaries, children need to test in order to discover them. Just as many of us are compelled to touch the surface behind the "wet paint" sign, so are toddlers compelled to bump up against a limit to see if it is really there and to make sure it will hold. Some children do more testing than others, perhaps a factor related to temperament, but all children need to know that there are limits. The limits provide a sense of security, just as the tight blanket does for the newborn.

To illustrate the security that limits provide, think of yourself driving across a high bridge. You probably have done that more than once in your life. The limits on the bridge are the rails on the sides. Can you imagine yourself driving across that bridge if the rails were removed? You don't physically need those rails, you know. After all, how often have you actually bumped the rails while driving across a bridge? Yet the thought of the bridge without the rails is terrifying. The rails provide a sense of security, just as the limits set for toddlers provide security in their lives.

Any discussion of limits, guidance, and discipline in toddlers quickly brings forth a discussion of what to do about such behaviors as biting, hitting, throwing things, and negativism. No single answer covers all behaviors in all situations with all children. The only single answer that applies is "It depends. . . ."

Biting   Let's look at biting. Start by asking, "Why is this child biting? What is behind the behavior?" If children are very young, they may be biting out of love. Sometimes when adults model playful nibbling, chewing, or "eating up" as a way of demonstrating affection, infants imitate their actions by biting those they love. Mouths are expressive organs, and when a child is too small to convey the intensity of a feeling with words, biting may do it.

Not all biting, of course, is done for love; some is done for power. When a child is small, physical power is minimal. But the jaws have powerful muscles, and little teeth are sharp. Even a very young child can do real damage with a bite. Some children learn this as a means of getting their own way with children who are bigger than they are. Biting can also be done out of curiosity, out of anger, or in an effort to gain attention.

The way to stop biting is to prevent it, not try to deal with it after it happens. Biting is too powerful a behavior to allow to continue. It's too painful for the person bitten, and it's too frightening for the biter to have that much power to do harm. A useful technique after waylaying the biting is to redirect the urge. Give these children something to bite on that is made for biting—teething rings, cloth, or rubber or plastic objects. Offer these as choices, saying something like, "I can't let you bite Craig, but you can bite the plastic ring or this wet washcloth."

What else you do besides controlling the behavior and offering biting alternatives depends on the origins of the biting. If it is being modeled, try to cut off the modeling. If it is an expression of a feeling (love, frustration, or anger), teach alternative means of expression. Help children redirect their energy into positive ways of expressing the feelings. If a power issue is involved, teach children other techniques for getting what they need and want. If it is an attention issue, find ways to give children attention without biting being the trigger. There is no easy solution, and it may take a good deal of brainstorming, discussion, cooperation, and teamwork even to identify the origins of the behavior and the appropriate approach.

Biting is an example of an aggressive (intent-to-harm) behavior. Other aggressive behaviors that cause toddler caregivers problems are hitting, kicking, shoving, pulling hair, throwing objects, and destroying toys and materials. To figure out what to do about these behaviors, you must go through a problem-solving process, looking at the particular child, the possible origins of the behavior, the message behind the behavior, the way the environment may contribute to the behavior, the way adult behavior may trigger the aggression, and the resources the child has for expressing feelings. Beware of advice that advocates any one simple solution. Behavior is complex, as are children. No one approach is right for everyone all the time.

Figure 11.1 Guidance and Discipline Techniques Supportive of Social Growth

1. Plan the child care environment to avoid *trouble spots*; provide enough time, space, and materials to support the developmental needs of infants and toddlers.

2. Appreciate the temperament and uniqueness of each child; some young children can use language to express their upset feelings, but others need to vent frustrations in more physical ways.

3. Be aware that sometimes natural consequences may be the best teacher (for example, "When you hit him, he doesn't want to play with you" can be very effective); always be aware of safety-related issues and be available to *explain* consequences.

4. Always avoid any discipline technique that inflicts pain—physical or psychological; pain fosters aggression.

5. When you set a limit, explain *why*—young children are more apt to comply if they understand why they are being asked to do something; don't expect agreement immediately, and remain available to repeat an explanation.

6. Cultivate a family-caregiver partnership in your program; discipline practices are deeply embedded in the beliefs of the family.

7. Model the behavior you want to teach; remember that the word *discipline* comes from a Latin word meaning "teaching," and lead the way by showing a child what to do.

Negativism   Negativism is another category of difficult behaviors that caregivers of toddlers must try to understand. A frequent complaint from caregivers is "They won't do what I say." Part of the problem may be that toddlers can't always translate word messages into physical control, even when they understand what you want. Another part of the problem is that when toddlers are faced with demands or commands, they often do the opposite.

The secret to dealing with negativism is to avoid challenges. Stay out of power struggles. If you approach a toddler who is outside a limit—say, a girl climbing on a table—start by being calm and matter-of-fact rather than confrontive. State the limit in positive terms, such as "The ramp is for climbing" or "Feet belong on the floor." One particularly talented teacher simply says, "You can put your feet right here," patting the appropriate place. Nine times out of ten the feet go directly to where they belong! Something about the way she says it conveys such a confident and positive attitude that there is no challenge issued.[3]

Figure 11.1 highlights some general considerations related to guidance and discipline for very young children.

Teaching Prosocial Skills

Prosocial behavior is a significant social skill. It includes actions toward or interactions with another person with no thought of reward for oneself. There is no gene for it; it has to be planned for and taught. Some of the prosocial or altruistic behaviors we typically think of include empathy (feeling *with* another),

NAEYC Program Standard 3
Teaching

Prosocial behavior includes helping another person.
Source: Photo courtesy of Jude Rose.

sympathy (feeling *sad* for another), friendliness, compassion, cooperation, caring, comforting, sharing, taking turns, and conflict resolution.

It is probably clear from this list that these are not the typical behaviors of very young children. Some children *do* have natural inclinations, or a temperament, toward friendliness and cooperation. But most of the time adults and caregivers need to support, encourage, and model prosocial skills. Helping young children see the value of prosocial skills, and guiding them to use those skills, promotes successful peer interaction in the present and (we hope) a more peaceful world in the future. Figure 11.2 gives suggestions for promoting and teaching prosocial skills.

EXPLORE the following websites for more information and resource material.

The Center for the Social and Emotional Foundations for Early Learning (CSEFEL) is focused on promoting the social-emotional development and school readiness of young children from birth to age five; it is a national resource center designed to share best practices in early childhood programs across the country.

www.csefel.vanderbilt.edu

The Incredible Years: Parents, Teachers and Children Social Skills Training Series is an evidence-based program whose goal is to prevent and treat children's behavior concerns and to promote social and emotional competence; the programs work across cultures and socioeconomic groups.

www.incredibleyears.com

Figure 11.2 Guidelines for Promoting and Teaching Prosocial Skills

1. Create an environment that fosters self-help skills; follow a consistent daily routine and use pictures to label areas so young children can find and use (and eventually return) materials on their own.

2. Encourage young children's ideas; welcome their contributions and support their efforts to share, care for, and help each other.

3. Model the behaviors you want young children to acquire; show concern for those who are upset, and say "Thank you" when someone shares something with you.

4. Acknowledge and support young children's efforts to cooperate; create cooperative activities—for example, an art project in which children can work together to create a "group picture."

5. Develop a sense of community and establish an atmosphere in which young children are expected to be supportive and kind to each other; use phrases like "Our group," "All our friends are here," and "Look at what we did together."

6. Pay attention to any child who is constantly picked on or rejected; both aggressors and victims need extra attention and support to become self-reliant and to have good feelings about themselves.

7. Plant the seeds of conflict resolution (but do not expect them to truly flower until middle childhood); encourage young children to talk to each other, give them the words they may need, help them to see one another's point of view, help them to decide on some kind of conclusion, and praise their efforts.

Promoting social development and prosocial skills is a challenge. It takes time and thought . . . and lots of repetition and patience. Adults and caregivers have to be committed to the task and recognize that as they foster skills like kindness and forgiveness, they may learn more about their own capacity for sensitivity and empathy.

Promoting Healthy Brain Growth

The importance of early social contact has been emphasized a great deal by the current brain research. Social development discussed in this chapter has its beginnings in the early attachment experiences, and these experiences cause an amazing sequence of activity related to brain function.

J. Ronald Lally, a pioneer in planning environments for infants and toddlers, has been a leader in interpreting brain research as it relates to quality care for very young children. He has identified seven "gifts" that are vital for healthy brain growth and social development.

1. *Nurturance* is caring and giving. Because each infant is unique, nurturance means responding to every infant individually. When an infant feels a caregiver's responsive nurturance, comfort and security are established. It is the comfort of this connection that is vital for attachment and social growth.

VIDEO OBSERVATION 11

Girls Playing Together

See Video Observation 11: Girls Playing Together for an example of children socializing with each other and enjoying each other's company as they move around through a play structure setup. Note that the adult is not teaching them or interfering in any way. She remains quietly nearby in case they need her.

Questions

- Are you surprised to see children this young interact so positively with each other? Why or why not?
- What is your experience with children interacting in the early toddler stage?
- What social skills are these children showing?

To view this clip, go to **www.mhhe.com/itc10e**. Click on Student Edition, select Chapter 11, and click on Video Observations.

2. *Support* is the context of care that a child receives. To support a young child means that the caregiver must respect a child's various feelings. Caregivers offer support by acknowledging a child's frustrations, by encouraging curiosity, and by enforcing rules that promote social interactions with others.
3. *Security* is related to both nurturance and support, and it is what makes a child feel safe. Caregivers provide security when they provide reliable, responsive care and when they enforce safety rules consistently.
4. *Predictability* is the "gift" that is vital for a child's sense of security and mental growth. Predictability is both social and environmental. A child needs to be able to rely on people and to be able to find things and places. Predictability avoids both confusion and rigidity. It allows a child to feel secure and to seek challenges.

NAEYC Program Standard 9
Physical Environment

5. *Focus* supports very young children's attention in their environment. An infant or toddler's attention span will increase if there are not too many toys, too many interruptions, or too many other people. Their opportunity to focus on meaningful experiences needs to be respected. Vital brain circuitry is being formed.

6. *Encouragement* from a knowledgeable caregiver tells a young child, "I appreciate your efforts; you are becoming a competent person." A child's own learning is reinforced through encouragement. It is a response that understands the importance of a child's imitation, experimentation, and discovery as critical links to learning.

7. *Expansion* of a child's experience involves "bathing (not drowning) the child in language." Watch for the young child's cues and build on his or her unique experiences. Involvement in fantasy play, talking along with a child, and responding to activities are all ways to demonstrate to young children the value of learning.[4]

The child care setting that offers these seven gifts provides a base for the practical application of brain research and for the secure social development of a child. Current research has emphasized just how early neural circuitry is formed and how critical social development is to that formation. The healthy brain is a social brain!

The Special Need of All Children: Self-Esteem

All children need loving relationships, stable environments, and the opportunity to see the world as an interesting place. These values not only set the stage for prosocial skills, as discussed in this chapter, but they underlie the healthy growth of all areas of development and learning. Assisting young children with special needs in the process of reaching their full potential requires a setting that is caring, stable, authentic, and encouraging.

Caregivers, teachers, parents, and the community need to be aware of the importance of positive messages that support a young child's self-esteem. For example, disability "labels," which tend to devalue the uniqueness of each child, need to be replaced with *descriptive profiles* when early intervention is being considered for an individual child. Family involvement that centers on the strength-based skills of the family needs to be seen as vital to the effective creation of an individualized family service plan. And looking at what children can do versus what they cannot do is crucial for a child's placement in an inclusion program.

Today we recognize that children with special needs and their families need to get messages within a supportive service system that are positive about their *abilities*. All of us need messages about what we can do! The resulting sense of inner positiveness that is created by such feedback is the prerequisite for emotional health and competent social interaction. How this develops is important to understand and appreciate.

Social skills and the socialization process have been the focus of this chapter. The foundation for interacting with others is attachment. From a nurturing attachment experience, children learn to value themselves and others. This valuing of self is called **self-esteem**. Self-esteem is vital for *all* children. It is important for caregivers creating quality experiences for children to appreciate this need.

The definition of self-esteem is complex. As children grow and develop, their self-esteem is constantly being reshaped as they interact and experience the world. It is a personal assessment of positive worth. But it is not the "me, my, mine" sense of worth. An individual with self-esteem is confident, optimistic, and sensitive to the feelings and needs of others. The roots of this lifelong process are clearly taking hold in infancy and toddlerhood.

Experiences That Foster Self-Esteem

Two types of experiences are most significant to the development of self-esteem. As an infant experiences attachment that is secure and nurturing, his self-concept begins to develop. Self-concept is formed by the infant's feelings about himself as they are reflected in his interactions with others. When an infant is responded to and is part of a loving relationship, his self-concept is positive and trusting.

The second important experience that contributes to self-esteem is the successful accomplishment of tasks. As a toddler explores and interacts with her world, her self-image is growing. Self-image is a more personal assessment of an individual's experience. If a toddler lives in a world with lots of "no's" and has little opportunity to test her skills, her image of herself may be low. Her inexperience limits her view of her own competence.

Very young children need secure relationships (with others) and opportunities to actively explore the world (on their own). When the self-concept is positive and trusting and the self-image is vital and active, children experience life as accepting and meaningful. This is the beginning of self-esteem. Children's ability to feel themselves as loving and competent allows them eventually to see others in a similar way.

Pause for a moment and think about how the work of Erikson, Piaget, and Vygotsky relates to children's positive feelings about themselves. Erikson emphasized the establishment of trust (through relationships with others) and autonomy (through experiences with everyday events) as vital to healthy development. Piaget and Vygotsky viewed children as active participants in their own world. This physical activity leads to cognitive activity, eventually resulting in coping skills. Individuals with self-esteem tend to have good coping skills.

As young children experience the challenges and limits of life, they need the stability of a personal base within themselves. This is important for all children; it may be even more important for children with special needs. We all need a place to "come home to," a place that is accepting and renewing. The ability to create such a place is the essence of self-esteem.

How can adults help children develop self-esteem? The importance of a secure attachment has already been mentioned. Adults who feel good about themselves tend to pass that feeling on to their children. It is important that caregivers and parents see self-esteem as a lifelong process and that they are contributing to their own needs for nurturance and challenge.

DEVELOPMENTAL PATHWAYS

Behaviors Showing Development of Social Skills

Young infants (up to 8 months)	• See adults as objects of interest and novelty; seek out adults for play • Smile or vocalize to initiate social contact • Anticipate being lifted or fed and move body to participate • Try to resume a knee ride by bouncing to get adult started again
Mobile infants (up to 18 months)	• Enjoy exploring objects with another as the basis for establishing relationship • Get others to do things for their pleasure (wind up toys, read books) • Show considerable interest in peers • Indicate a strong sense of self through assertiveness; direct actions of others (for example, "Sit here!")
Toddlers (up to 3 years)	• Gain greater enjoyment from peer play and joint exploration • Begin to see benefits of cooperation • Identify self with children of the same age or sex • Exhibit more impulse control and self-regulation in relation to others • Enjoy small group activities; show empathic concern for others

Source: Carol Copple and Sue Bredekamp, eds., *Developmentally Appropriate Practice in Early Childhood Programs*, 3rd ed. (Washington, DC: National Association for the Education of Young Children, 2009).

Diverse Developmental Pathways

What you see	Makayla spends a lot of time getting very close to children's faces, which annoys them and gets in the way of her making connections. At 18 months she doesn't move around as much as the other children her age, and when she does she sometimes trips and falls.
What you might think	She lacks social skills. She needs more practice with using her motor skills.
What you might not know	The parents have been hearing concerns from their pediatrician and yet are hesitant to follow up on the testing that she advises.
What you might do	Observe Makayla to see if she just needs to learn social and motor skills or if there is something else going on. Build a relationship with the parents. If they come to trust you, you may be able to support them in ways that will bring them around to following the pediatrician's advice.

(continued)

DEVELOPMENTAL PATHWAYS

Behaviors Showing Development of Social Skills (*continued*)

Cultural Diversity and Developmental Pathways

What you see	Xavier, 14 months old, is crying and clinging to his mother as she is trying to walk out the door.
What you might think	This is typical behavior and to be expected. This is a step toward Xavier becoming an independent individual. He is expressing his feelings openly.
What his mother might think	This is embarrassing because it shows a lack of proper upbringing.
What you might not know	This family is not interested in their child becoming an independent individual; instead, they are more worried that he is unmannerly and is disrespecting his elders, both of which are moral mandates for the group-oriented behavior they want their child to learn.
What you might do	Learn more about the family's perspective and share yours, but not in a "parent education mode." Work on supporting Xavier and helping him develop the behaviors his family expects.

Adult feedback to children should be authentic. Persistently positive information, like persistently negative information, does not prepare children for the *real* world. They will not be ready for the challenges of peers and school if caregivers and parents have not given them honest information. Remember to trust their competence and encourage their resiliency. Remember also that it is attachment that initially fosters competence and resiliency, and it remains the prime factor in the development of social skills and self-esteem.

Summary

Social skills are learned behaviors that connect us, help us to be independent, and foster cooperation and interdependent relationships.

Early Social Behaviors

- Attachment is the prime factor in the development of social skills.
- Infants imitate adult social behavior; toddlers demonstrate stranger and separation fears.

Stages of Psychosocial Development

- Erikson's stages of psychosocial development are stated in terms of social issues that young children need to resolve.
- The first three stages are discussed: trust versus mistrust, autonomy versus shame and doubt, and initiative versus guilt.

Guidance and Discipline

- These two concepts combine to foster the ongoing process of teaching social skills to young children.
- Security and caring control are required for infants.
- Toddlers need limits that support them and help them to control their frustrations and challenges.

Teaching Prosocial Skills

- Prosocial skills involve interactions with others with no thought of reward for oneself; prosocial skills promote positive socialization.

Promoting Healthy Brain Growth

- J. Ronald Lally, a leader in interpreting brain research, has identified seven "gifts" to promote healthy brain growth and social development.

The Special Need of All Children: Self-Esteem

- All children need adults who respond to their attachment needs and respect them for their unique growth patterns.

Key Terms

autonomy 241	self-esteem 250
initiative 242	stranger anxiety 238
limits 243	trust 238
prosocial behavior 245	

Thought/Activity Questions

1. What do you think are the most important social skills in our society? How would you begin to teach them to infants and toddlers?
2. What are the early challenges (first three years) and social skills discussed in Erik Erikson's theory? What makes this "classic" theory relevant for the early care education field today?
3. Discuss what "guidance" and "discipline" mean to you. How would your guidance approach differ when caring for infants versus when caring for toddlers?

4. List behaviors that you think indicate positive social development. How can caregivers and parents encourage these behaviors in the first three years?
5. Why do you think teaching prosocial skills to young children is a significant part of early childhood curriculum today?

For Further Reading

Amy L. Dombro, Judy Jablon, and Charlotte Stetson, *Powerful Interactions: How to Connect with Children to Extend Their Learning* (Washington, DC: National Association for the Education of Young Children, 2011).

L. G. Gillespie and A. Hunter, "Believe, Watch, Act! Promoting Social Behavior in Infants and Toddlers," *Young Children* 65(1), January 2010, pp. 42–43.

Marylou H. Hyson and Jackie L. Taylor, "Caring about Caring: What Adults Can Do to Promote Young Children's Pro-social Skills," *Young Children* 66(4), July 2011, pp. 74–84.

J. R. Lally and P. Mangione, "The Uniqueness of Infancy Demands a Responsive Approach to Care," *Young Children* 61(4), July 2006, pp. 14–20.

Rosa M. Santos, Angel Fettig, and LaShorage Shaffer, "Helping Families Connect Early Literacy with Social-Emotional Development," *Young Children* 67(2), March 2012, pp. 88–93.

Gay Ward and Crystal Dahlmeier, "Rediscovering Joyfulness," *Young Children* 66(6), November 2011, pp. 94–98.

Donna Wittmer, "The Wonder and Complexity of Infant and Toddler Peer Relation ships," *Young Children* 67(4), September 2012, pp. 16–26.

chapter 12

The Physical Environment

Focus Questions

After reading this chapter you should be able to answer the following questions:

1 What needs to be done to make a safe environment for infants and toddlers?

2 How can you create a healthy environment for infants and toddlers?

3 What areas need to be provided for in the layout of an infant-toddler program?

4 How does the developmental appropriateness of the environment relate to safety and to learning?

5 What should be in the play environment?

6 When assessing the quality of an infant-toddler environment, what five dimensions should you consider? What are four other considerations?

What Do You See?

Olivia is sitting on the floor next to Kai, who is lying on his back. He turns onto his side, and then onto his stomach. He stops, pushes up, and smiles at Olivia, who smiles back and then squeals. Kai rolls onto his side again and over quickly onto his back. He looks around for Olivia and discovers he has moved to a new place. He looks pleased with himself. Olivia now throws herself onto all fours and is crawling toward a low platform nearby. She climbs up easily and sits back down, looking at the room from her new vantage point. She watches Kai continuing to roll until he is almost on the other side of the room. She quickly crawls down from the platform and over to Kai, who is now lying on his back waving a cotton scarf in the air. Olivia crawls over to another scarf and brings it to him, and now he has one in each hand. She settles back into a sitting position and picks up a soft ball that is close to her foot. She squeezes it several times, then crawls over and puts it in a bucket, which already has another ball in it. She empties both out onto the floor and watches them roll in opposite directions. Kai laughs out loud at the sight.

Compare that scene to this one.

Savannah is the same age as Olivia, and Travis is Kai's age. Savannah is strapped into a baby swing and Travis is on the floor strapped into an infant seat. When the swing stops, Savannah fusses until a caregiver comes over and gives her another push. Travis has a toy in his hand, but he drops it and now he can't reach it. He cries and a caregiver comes over and gives it to him. She puts three more toys on his lap and leaves. He throws all the toys on the floor and cries again. In the meantime Savannah has stopped swinging and started fussing. On her way over to push Savannah, the caregiver says to her teammate, "I think we should get one of those motorized swings." Then she walks over to Travis, who is screaming now. "Young man," she says. "I think you are throwing those toys out on purpose just to get me over here to pick them up." She brings a frame of hanging toys and sets them across Travis, who reaches out and grabs a ring and tries to pull it off. "Now those toys are going to stay put!" she says as she goes off to push Savannah again.

What did you see? Did you notice that Olivia and Kai were able to move around and experience the environment on their own? They were absorbed in what they were doing and also able to interact with each other. What about Savannah and Travis? They could see what was in the environment, but they couldn't get to anything. They were dependent on the caregiver to interact with them and keep them interested.

Both environments were safe—a primary consideration. We'll return to these two scenes later in the chapter to explore other environmental qualities they exhibit. The Child Development Associate (CDA) assessment process defines quality settings for infant and toddler care as those that are safe environments that promote health and learning.

This chapter examines each of those components and then goes on to use an assessment tool called "dimensions of teaching/learning environments" created by Betty Jones and Liz Prescott.[1]

A Safe Environment

NAEYC Program Standard 9
Physical Environment

Safety is a first consideration in planning for infants and toddlers. Group size and adult-child ratio are important factors in creating a safe environment. The WestEd Center for Child and Family Studies, in conjunction with the California Department of Education, has created the guidelines shown in Table 12.1.

Creating a Safe Physical Environment: A Checklist

- Cover all electrical outlets.
- Cover all heaters so children are kept well away from them.
- Protect children from all windows and mirrors that aren't shatterproof.
- Remove or tie up all drapery cords. (Long strings, cords, and ties of any kind should be eliminated to prevent strangling.)
- Get rid of all slippery throw rugs.
- Get some instructions from your local fire department on how to put together a plan in case of fire. Consider the number and location of fire extinguishers, easy exit, and methods for carrying children who can't walk. Then schedule periodic fire drills.

Table 12.1 Guidelines for Group Size and Adult-Child Ratios

Group Size Guidelines (Same-Age Groups)			
Age	Adult-Child Ratio	Total Sizes	Minimum Number of Square Feet per Group*
0–8 months	1:3	6	350
8–18 months	1:3	9	500
18–36 months	1:4	12	600
Mixed-Age Guidelines (Family Child Care)			
Age	Adult-Child Ratio	Group Size	Minimum Number of Square Feet per Group*
0–36+ months	1:4**	8	600

*The space guidelines represent minimum standards of adequate square footage per group; the amounts shown do not include space used for entrance areas, hallways, diapering areas, or napping areas.

**Of the four infants assigned to a caregiver, only two should be under 24 months of age.

Source: Developed by the Far West Laboratory for Educational Research and Development and the California Department of Education.

- Make sure there are no poisonous plants in the environment. (Many common house and garden plants contain deadly poisons. If you don't know which ones, find out!)
- Make sure all furniture is stable and in good repair.
- Remove lids from toy storage boxes to prevent accidents.
- Make sure all cribs and other baby furniture meet consumer protection safety standards—that is, slats are close together so babies can't get their heads stuck, and crib mattresses fit tightly so babies can't get wedged between mattress and side and smother.
- Keep all medicines and cleaning materials well out of reach of children at all times.
- Beware of toys with small parts that can come loose and go into mouths (such as button eyes on stuffed animals).
- Remove all broken, damaged toys and materials.
- Be sure no toys or materials are painted with or contain toxic substances.
- Know first aid and cardiopulmonary resuscitation (CPR).
- Keep a first aid kit at hand.
- Keep emergency numbers by the phone along with parent emergency information. Update parent emergency numbers frequently.
- Make sure the equipment you have is appropriate for the age group served. For example, climbing structures should be scaled down for toddlers.
- Supervise children well and allow them to take only minor risks but not risks with grave consequences. (Don't differentiate between boys and girls in the degree of risk you allow.)

If you have children with special needs in your program, you need to do a safety check that includes their special circumstances or disabilities. Are there ramps of an appropriate degree of slant for wheelchairs? Is some equipment safely adaptable for their special needs?

A Healthful Environment

A healthful environment is as important as a safe one. Good light, comfortable air temperature, and ventilation contribute to the health and well-being of the infants and toddlers in the environment.

Creating a Healthful and Sanitary Environment: A Checklist

- Wash hands often. Hand washing is the best way to keep infections from spreading. Wash after coughing, sneezing, wiping noses, and changing diapers and before preparing food. Use dispenser soap instead of bar soap and paper towels instead of cloth. Avoid touching faucets and waste receptacles after washing. (Foot-controlled faucets and trash cans with a foot-controlled lid opener eliminate the probability of recontaminating clean hands.)
- Wash children's hands regularly also, especially before eating and after diapering or using the bathroom.
- Do not allow children to share washcloths or any other personal items.
- Clean toys and play equipment daily for any group of children who are young enough to mouth objects.
- Wear socks or slippers rather than street shoes in areas where infants lie on the floor.
- Vacuum rugs and mop floors regularly.
- Be sure each child has his or her own bed, cot, or pad, and change sheets regularly.
- Take routine precautions in changing diapers to prevent the spread of illness. Provide a clean surface for each changing by washing down the waterproof diaper changing area with disinfectant solution and/or provide fresh paper each time. Wash hands carefully after each changing.
- Take routine precautions in food preparation, serving, and cleaning up. Wash hands before handling food. Store food and bottles in refrigerator until right before using them. To wash dishes and bottles, use extra-hot water. (Dishwashers with the hot water heater turned to high help eliminate germs.) Use a weak bleach solution if you don't have a dishwasher. Date all stored food. Clean out the refrigerator regularly, and throw away old food.
- Be sure all children in your care are up to date on their immunizations.
- Learn to recognize the signs of common illnesses.

- Make clear policies about which symptoms indicate when a child is too sick to be in your program. Parents' and caregivers' ideas and needs often differ when it comes to this subject.
- Require permission slips before you administer any medicine, and then be sure to give prescriptions only to the child with his or her name on the bottle.

Although you do not want to compromise health practices, be aware that cultural differences may arise concerning health matters. Try to be sensitive to parents who have ideas different from accepted practice about the paths to good health.

Also be sensitive to the special needs of chronically ill children, who sometimes have immunity problems. They may need extra protection from the spread of virus and bacteria that other children in your program carry. Examine your health and sanitary practices carefully to be sure you give these children the protection they need. Resist criticism from those who accuse you of being overprotective.

Nutrition

Caregivers must pay careful attention to what to feed infants and toddlers and how. Food must be appropriate to the child's age, physical condition, and cultural or religious traditions. The tastes and habits children develop in the first three years can influence them throughout their lifetimes. Because obesity is such a concern in the United States, child care programs should be concerned about dietary habits. Feeding a well-rounded variety of wholesome foods can make a difference, especially if the program also has discussions with families. The goal should be for children to grow up eating mostly wholesome and nutritional food and to eat sugary or fatty foods as only an occasional treat, not an everyday menu. French fries, donuts, and candy are not appropriate foods for children. The eating environment and interactions with caregivers can create a warm, comfortable feeling about eating that encourages good eating habits and a positive attitude toward food.

Feeding Infants

Babies go through many stages as they move from taking only liquids, to learning to chew and swallow solid food, to feeding themselves table food. Babies' first food is either breast milk or formula. Although caregivers don't make the decision about which to use, what they do can encourage or discourage mothers to continue breastfeeding after the child enters child care. Because breast milk has the advantage of being uniquely suited to human infants' growing needs and offers protection against infections, caregivers should make an effort to support breastfeeding mothers. Such a simple device as a comfortable chair in a quiet, private corner for mothers to nurse gives a supportive message. Being aware of arranging for the baby to be hungry when the mother arrives is another way to support breastfeeding. Knowing the details of how to store breast milk safely helps a mother feel secure about continuing to nurse her baby (see Table 12.2).

Table 12.2 Storing and Using Breast Milk
• Expressed breast milk should arrive cold in a clean and sanitary bottle.
• It should be stored immediately in the refrigerator or in the freezer if it arrives frozen.
• All bottles should be clearly labeled with the date of collection and the child's name.
• Any milk remaining after a feeding should be discarded and not used again.
• Refrigerated breast milk should be discarded after 48 hours.
• When warming bottles, use running tap water or place the bottle in a container of warm water for five minutes or less.
• Do not let milk sit at room temperature because bacteria can grow.
• Do not use a microwave to warm breast milk.

For detailed instructions about how to keep food for infants sanitary and safe, see Susan Aronson and Patricia Spahr's *Healthy Young Children: A Manual for Programs*.[2] This manual has sample meal patterns for infants in the first year, giving examples of what they can eat and when. It includes such information as how to introduce solid foods, when to introduce cow's milk, how to avoid baby-bottle tooth decay, how to wean, and many more details. Of course, understanding each family's approach to feeding infants is vital, especially if there are cultural differences, food restrictions, or pertinent taboos. Infants with special needs may have a specific diet or ways of being fed that caregivers need to know about. Parents are the source for this information.

Offer good individualized infant nutrition, or ask parents to provide nutritious food and bottles. Some guidelines agreed on by most pediatricians are to wait on solids until the child is three to six months old, then introduce them slowly, one at a time, working up from a spoonful to a reasonably sized infant helping. Most pediatricians have a favorite order in which they advise introducing solids, starting with cereal. Most advise waiting to introduce foods that may trigger allergies, such as egg white, orange juice, and especially nuts and nut butters such as peanut butter. Stay away from mixtures like casseroles that contain several foods, because if one ingredient causes an allergic reaction, you won't know which one. Stay away from all additives—salt, sugar, and artificial colors and flavors. Infants need pure, natural, unseasoned food. Don't serve honey or corn syrup to infants under a year old, because these foods may contain a certain kind of spore that causes a food poisoning only infants are susceptible to. Avoid foods that infants can choke on, such as raw carrots and popcorn.

Feeding Toddlers

Infants who opened their mouths so happily for whatever the caregiver wanted to put into it can sometimes become toddlers who are picky eaters. The growth

VIDEO OBSERVATION 12

Feeding Routine

See Video Observation 12: Feeding Routine for an example of an environment that is developmentally appropriate and works well for the children in it. Watch this remarkably calm and civilized feeding scene.

Questions

- Why do you think this program has children sitting together in low chairs at the table instead of in high chairs? Does the environment tell you anything about the philosophy of the program?
- How safe does this environment seem to be? Can you see any hazards?
- How comfortable and secure do the children seem to feel in this environment? What might be contributing to their comfort and sense of security?

To view this clip, go to **www.mhhe.com/itc10e**. Click on Student Edition, select Chapter 12, and click on Video Observations.

rate in the first year of life is so great that food intake must be plentiful. Toddlers' growth rate takes a plunge and, often, so do their appetites. If adults aren't aware of the change, their worries or behavior can create eating problems. It's common for worried adults to urge and cajole in ways that fan the flames of toddlers' natural resistance. It's important to offer a nutritious variety of foods, but it's also important to let toddlers decide how much and what they will eat. Small portions help encourage toddlers to eat up! It's surprising how much fresh air and exercise can affect a toddler's appetite. All children should get as much of both as possible. Watching the toddlers at the Pikler Institute eat is truly eye-opening. Because fresh air and exercise are priorities in that program, all toddlers get a lot of these every day. When they sit down at mealtimes, they are *hungry*. It's a pleasure to see children this age enjoy their food so much. No games are ever used to get them to eat. They relish food.

Many of the guidelines for infant feeding also apply to toddlers. Choose food that is pure and natural—not processed with additives. Toddlers (and infants too) enjoy finger food, but remember that not all cultures see finger food as appropriate. If families do not object, consider what you give for finger food. Think in terms of fruit or vegetable snacks rather than cookies or highly salted crackers. Give crunchy foods like apple slices and carrot sticks only when children have enough teeth and the ability to chew them. Avoid such foods as popcorn, nuts, peanut butter, hotdog rounds, grapes, and other foods on which toddlers might choke. Cut hotdogs lengthwise and then in small pieces—avoid rounds! Cut grapes at least in half, and cut big ones in fourths. This particular caution goes double for those children with special needs whose reflexes may not be totally developed and who may be more prone to choking or breathing difficulties.

The Learning Environment

NAEYC Program Standards 2 and 3
Curriculum and Teaching

Much of the **structure** of an infant-toddler program comes from a well-planned environment. According to Louis Torelli, "A well-designed environment . . . supports infants' and toddlers' emotional well-being, stimulates their senses and challenges their motor skills. A well-designed group care environment promotes children's individual and social development."[3]

If you think about how learning at this age depends on emotional well-being, sensory experiences, and free movement, you may wonder about the environment that Savannah and Travis are in at the beginning of the chapter. Go back to the two scenes that open this chapter. Read them again and recall what you read in Part 2 about motor development and its connection to perception and cognition. Think about the experiences of Olivia and Kai, who were moving all over the environment in the first scene, as compared with those of Savannah and Travis, who were strapped in a swing and an infant seat. What discoveries are they making? They are learning how to attract adult attention, but that's about all. Olivia and Kai don't need adult attention while they are exploring and learning many other things, including their own increasing capabilities.

Research shows that behavior is influenced by environment.[4] A structured environment gives us clues about how to behave in it. Just compare the library with the workout room in the gym. Or think of how the grocery store communicates what's expected, with carts at the door and open shelves and checkout stands, compared with a jewelry store, where you sit at a glass counter and someone offers you things from behind lock and key.

Infants and toddlers also get messages from the environment if it is well planned and consistent. In fact, learning to receive those messages is an important part of their socialization process as they learn about expectations for various behavior settings.[5]

Children with physical limitations will get specific messages if the learning environment isn't adapted to their special needs. For example, if a child in a

Reflect
Look around the environment you are in right now. What messages does it send about the way you are supposed to behave in it? Think about a contrasting environment you have been in recently. What different messages did it send?

The learning environment can be outdoors as well as indoors. Many infants and toddlers today need to get outdoors more often, especially in places where there are still elements of nature around—like a dirt hill for toddlers in this program to climb.

wheelchair isn't able to go outside or across a thick carpet, his experiences in the program will be limited. If toys or equipment aren't at his level, he gets the message that they're not for him to play with. Make accommodations in the environment for *all* the children in the program, including those with special needs.

Although much learning goes on in the play area of the infant-toddler environment, it is not confined to that space. The whole environment, including caregiving areas, is the learning environment in an infant-toddler program. See the sample classrooms in Figures 12.1, 12.2, and 12.3.

Layout

There are some general rules for setting up an environment for infant-toddler care, whether in a center or family child care home. You should have a designated place for arrivals and departures. Near this area should be storage for children's belongings. The sleeping area should be apart from the play area and should have a subdued atmosphere that has restful colors and is quiet and nonstimulating. The eating area also should be somewhat separate from the play area, though the two may overlap at times because you use eating tables for various other kinds of activities. The eating area should, of course, be close to a kitchen or other warming or cooking facility. The diaper area should be away from the eating area and close to a bathroom, or at least a sink. The indoor play area should be cheerful and well lighted and should invite exploration. There should be an outdoor play area as well that is equally inviting to explore. At the Pikler Institute in Budapest, eating and sleeping are also done outdoors, and the environment is set up appropriately for these two activities. The children have two sets of beds—one set that stays outdoors. Storage and office space (at least a desk and phone) are also usually a part of the environment. Infants and toddlers come to learn what is expected in each space if the spaces are distinct from one another.

The furniture, equipment, and materials for caregiving activities vary somewhat with the philosophy and goals of the program. The following corresponds to the philosophy of this book.

Figure 12.1 Infant Classroom

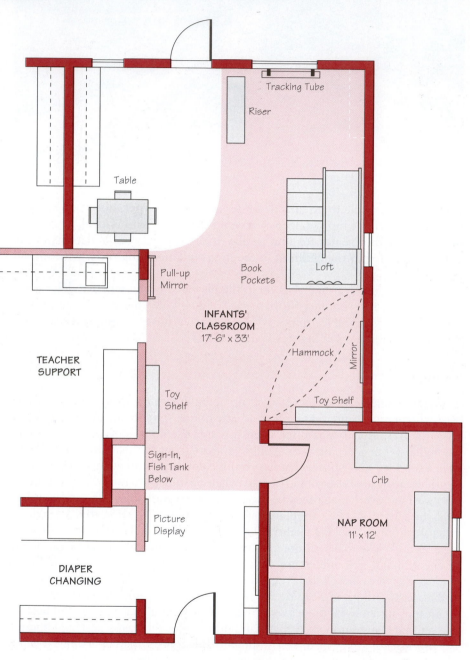

Tracking Tube

Riser

Table

Pull-up
Mirror

Book
Pockets

Loft

INFANTS'
CLASSROOM
17'-6" x 33'

TEACHER
SUPPORT

Hammock

Mirror

Toy
Shelf

Toy Shelf

Sign-In,
Fish Tank
Below

Crib

Picture
Display

NAP ROOM
11' x 12'

DIAPER
CHANGING

Figure 12.2 Toddler Classroom

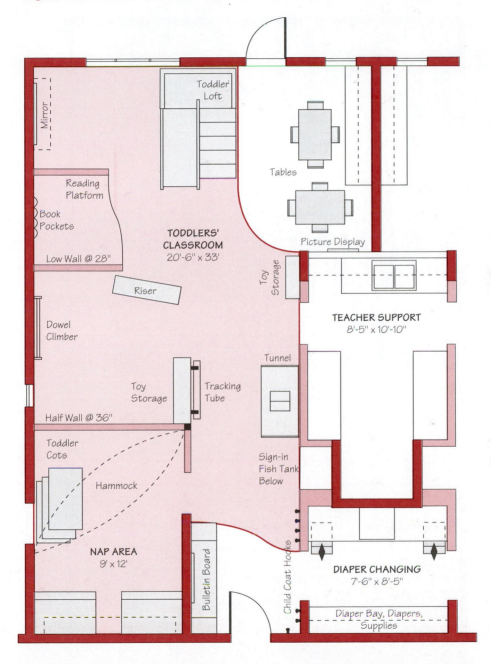

Toddler Loft

Mirror

Reading Platform

Book Pockets

Low Wall @ 28"

TODDLERS' CLASSROOM
20'-6" x 33'

Riser

Dowel Climber

Toy Storage

Tracking Tube

Half Wall @ 36"

Toddler Cots

Hammock

NAP AREA
9' x 12'

Bulletin Board

Tables

Picture Display

Toy Storage

Tunnel

Sign-in Fish Tank Below

Child Coat Hooks

TEACHER SUPPORT
8'-5" x 10'-10"

DIAPER CHANGING
7'-6" x 8'-5"

Diaper Bay, Diapers, Supplies

Figure 12.3 Infant-Toddler Classroom

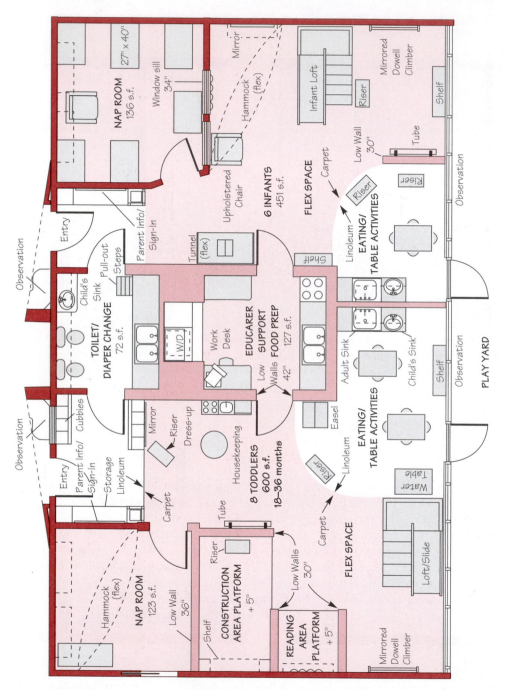

Eating

A refrigerator and provision for warming food either in the room or very nearby are essential. A sink and counter also are essential. A dishwasher is handy. Tools and utensils for food preparation are needed as well as unbreakable dishes, cups, and spoons, in addition to bottles and nipples (which the parents may send with the children). The eating and food preparation area needs storage for food, dishes, and utensils. Small, low tables and chairs that children can get in and out of themselves add to feelings of independence. (Some children eat better in smaller groups because small groups are less stimulating, which is something to consider when choosing tables.) Although some programs feel high chairs are a necessity, we advocate using low tables and chairs for children who are able to get into them themselves, and holding babies to feed them if they can't get into chairs by themselves. It takes some training on the part of the caregivers to get children to eat at the table if they have a choice to leave. Provision should be made for adults to eat in comfort—whether in the room or somewhere else—so they feel more at home than if they always have to stand at a counter or squat in tiny chairs.

Sleeping

The sleeping furniture depends on the ages of the children. The youngest infants are more secure in bassinets or cradles; older infants need cribs. Toddlers can sleep on cots or pads on the floor. Children should not share cribs, cots, or bedding; each child should have his or her own.

Although sleeping separately is standard practice in infant-toddler care, for cultural reasons and for health considerations, it is important to recognize that some cultures do not consider separate sleeping arrangements for infants or toddlers either normal or healthy.

Diapering

The diapering area needs counters or tables to change diapers. Diapering counters usually have children lying sideways to the adult. At the Pikler Institute, the diapering areas are arranged so that the child lies perpendicular to the open edge and facing the adult. The adult then bends straight over instead of twisting to one side. All supplies needed for diapering should be stored within arm's reach of the diapering counter. Supplies include diapers, cleaning products for disinfecting the changing surface after each diapering, and sanitary storage or disposal for soiled diapers. A sink with warm water, soap, and towels must be in the diapering area and cannot be located where food is prepared or dishes are washed.

Toileting

Toddlers appreciate child-size toilets, and they need access to sinks with soap and paper towels (or a sanitary way to use cloth towels). This area should be convenient to play space, both indoors and outdoors.

Developmental Appropriateness

The most important factor in a learning environment is that it be developmentally appropriate for the age group. Infants are not served in an environment planned only for toddlers, just as toddlers do not behave the same in an environment designed solely for infants or for preschoolers. Developmental appropriateness is vital.

Often you have to be extremely flexible when you have infants and toddlers in the same room. The environment not only has to respond to the needs of the particular age constellation but must also respond to changes as the children grow and develop over time.

Appropriate Environments for Infants

How is the environment different for the infant and for the toddler? Partly it is size. The younger the child, the smaller the group and the space around should be. For the newborn, space can be frightening, and very confined space is appropriate—like a bassinet. Older immobile babies need expanded space, but not enormous space. They need to be on the floor but protected from walking feet that might step on or trip over the helpless infants. This is the age for which playpens are most appropriate. As babies begin to move around, by either rolling or crawling, they need even more space. The standard playpen is too small. When they first get upright, children need support for cruising—rails or furniture to hang onto. In a home environment, coffee tables, end tables, chairs, and couches provide this support. An infant center must have other provisions. (The *outside* of the playpen will work for this purpose.)

A word about cribs: Cribs are not good learning environments; they are sleeping environments. When the message is consistent about what cribs are for, some babies learn early to associate them with sleeping and have less difficulty going to sleep when put down. But if the crib is lined with toys and hung with mobiles and music boxes, a mixed message is given. The environment is stimulating, not conducive to sleep. It is better to give the message that playing happens outside the crib. Cribs are too small for all but the youngest babies to play in anyway. It is better to use them only to confine tired children, not alert, awake ones. Awake children need a different environment.

Appropriate Environments for Toddlers

Toddlers, of course, need even more space and gross motor challenges appropriate to their age level. They also need an environment that encourages independence—steps up to the sink so they can wash their hands, pitchers to pour their own milk and juice, cloths so they can wipe up their own spills, a dishpan at hand so they can bus their own dishes. Toddlers also need an environment that invites them to explore using gross and fine motor skills and all their senses.

The play space should contain a variety of age-appropriate toys and equipment that encourage active, creative, whole-body play as well as manipulative skills. It should suit the mood of all children at any given time on any given day—those who feel energetic, those who feel mellow, those who want to be alone, and those who feel sociable.

Family Child Care and Mixed-Age Groups

Setting up a child care environment for children of varying ages in a home differs from setting up an environment in a center-based program where children are grouped by age. Family child care homes have some distinct advantages that centers find hard to come by. There is less likely to be an "institutional feel" to them. The small scale of a home environment can be a great comfort to children who are easily overstimulated. There is a richness in a home that results from the greater variety found in an environment set up for mixed-age groups as well as adult family members. A home naturally provides a variety of textures, sounds, and activities as life in the home continues in the presence of the children. Some of the advantages of being in a home are also some of the challenges that providers face as they try to make their homes safe, comfortable learning and care environments for children. Seeing how family members use their time may be a wonderful experience for children as they watch the teenage family member fix her car or grandma sort her stamp collection. But the activities the family members engage in may not necessarily be good for children. For example, if the same teenager comes in and plops down in front of the television, that may be a problem the provider will have to deal with.

The Principles in Action

Principle 8 Recognize problems as learning opportunities, and let infants and toddlers try to solve their own. Don't rescue them, constantly make life easy for them, or try to protect them from all problems.

A family child care provider has her home set up so that children can explore freely. She's pleased at the way they make discoveries, run into problems, and take steps to solve them. Recently she enrolled a two-year-old named Austin who is physically challenged, and she's trying to provide opportunities for him to explore, make discoveries, and solve problems. Austin is not able to move from one place to another, so the provider helps him experience new sights and orientations by changing him from place to place in the room. He can reach out if he is securely positioned so he's not in danger of falling over. The provider has figured out ways to get him close enough to the toys so that he can make his own choices about what to play with. She either puts him close to the shelves or takes one of the baskets of toys and lays it on its side so he can reach in. She also has modified some of the toys so they work more easily. She watched him try to turn the pages of a cardboard book, and he struggled so hard that he finally gave up. That time she rescued him, put him in her lap, and turned the pages for him as they read the book together. Later she came up with the idea of gluing Popsicle sticks to the pages, so he can get his hand around a stick and open up the cover. Using the sticks on the other pages, he can go through the whole book. He's delighted that he can do it himself, though he still looks to her to enjoy books with him. She's investigating how to provide even more opportunities for Austin to play with toys that he can easily have an effect on. Making something happen is one of the inner urges of all toddlers, and Austin, too, is intrigued with creating an effect. The provider is working hard to give him many opportunities.

1. What other ideas do you have to help this child explore in the environment even though he can't get around by himself?
2. Imagine yourself at this moment physically challenged in the environment where you are right now. What kind of help would you need to make use of your limited reach and grasp if you had a strong desire to make an effect on something in this environment?
3. Think about the various ways this caregiver could move Austin from place to place in her home or make it possible for him to move himself.
4. What might be some barriers in the average home that would prevent this child from exploring the environment more fully?

Unlike the carefully designed center layouts shown in Figures 12.1, 12.2, and 12.3, family child care in a home depends on a preexisting floor plan that is for family living rather than specifically for child care (see Figure 12.4). Providers make choices about which rooms to use for children's activities. Some choices are obvious, like bathrooms for washing and toileting, kitchens for cooking and perhaps eating. In the other chosen rooms, furniture may need to be rearranged to make space for play. Some providers create play spaces in the living room, family room, dining room, a spare room, a basement, a converted garage, or a combination of rooms. Furniture may be moved back to make room for children to move around, or it may be rearranged as dividers to create sections for storage and use of specific children's toys and materials. Area rugs also can be used to define **play spaces**. Good use can be made of loft beds as spaces where older children can go to be away from younger ones. On the other hand, cutting off the legs of a loft bed to a safe height makes a low climbing space for younger children as well as perhaps a small area to crawl under. **Mixed-age groups** present a special set of challenges. The provider must be diligent about providing a safe environment that allows play and exploration for all ages. That means putting things at different levels for different age groups. Low shelves make toys accessible to everybody, so in mixed-age groups, care must be taken to put only appropriate and safe toys and materials on them that are suitable for even the very youngest child. Infants and toddlers who still explore by mouthing must be protected from small

Figure 12.4 Family Child Care Setting

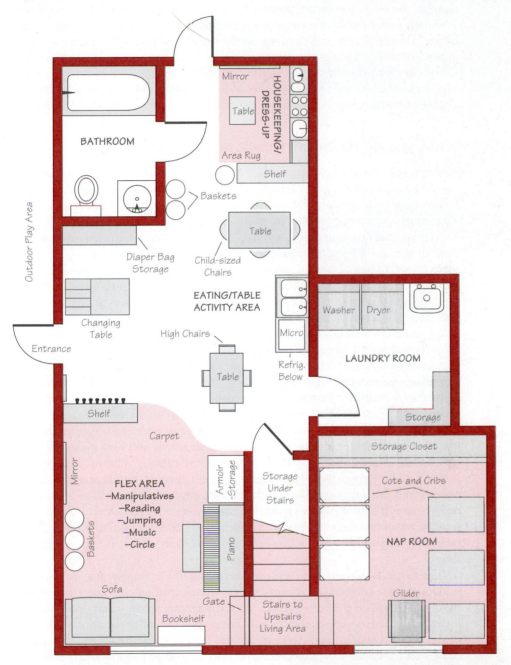

parts and fragile toys. Activities not suitable for the youngest children can be done at the kitchen table or counter to keep them out of reach of little hands. The materials must be stored up high. Nobody wants a toddler pulling out the hundred-piece puzzle and chewing on the cardboard pieces. Storage for toys is important so everything isn't out every day. Rotating toys ensures novelty when stored toys are brought out for use, and creates new interest in old things. Some toys should be rotated and others should be left out all the time to give children a sense of consistency.

What Should Be in the Play Environment

NAEYC Program Standard 2
Curriculum

Age appropriateness is again the key to what toys, equipment, and materials should be in the play environment (see Appendix B). Newborns and very young infants need little in their play environment. A few things to look at are enough. The most interesting object in their environment is the live human face. Recognize that fact, and don't try to replace it with toys, pictures, or even television. Infants need responsive people more than they need any animate or inanimate object. (They also need lots of peace and quiet and minimal stimulation.)

When infants discover their hands and spend time thoroughly exploring them, they are then ready for some simple play objects. At first they see their own hands as fascinating objects, but eventually they learn that their hands belong to them, can be controlled, and can be used to explore other objects. It's important that children not be distracted from hand exploration because it's the first step to using the hands to explore other things. The progress is from exploring to experimenting to building. This information comes from the research at the Pikler Institute and has also been observed by one of the coauthors of this book. That's an unusual situation in the United States, where infants are bombarded from birth by a multitude of multisensory toys that are visually stimulating with bright colors and movement and also make noises or play music. These toys are entertaining, but they move babies from enjoying self-entertainment to becoming dependent on outside entertainment. When one toy gets boring, it's replaced with another, or an adult steps in to provide the amusement. It's the author's experience that babies who get used to this pattern tend to spend less time exploring the simple toys advocated by the Pikler Institute and taught by Magda Gerber's RIE (Resources for Infant Educarers) Associates.

The first play object used by those who follow Pikler's approach and Gerber's philosophy is a cotton scarf, about 14 × 14 inches. Instead of laying the scarf flat on the floor within the baby's reach, the adult arranges it so it stands up, making it easier for the baby to see and grab at. That's one reason for the scarf to be made of cotton—it's stiff enough to stand up by itself. Also it's heavy enough so the baby won't breathe it in, which is the danger of a silk or nylon scarf. The baby lying on her back on a firm surface can turn her head from side to side, so when she spies the scarf, she reaches for it. It's easy to grab even without much finger control. The lightweight scarf can be waved, fingered, clutched, and dropped.

Some babies discover peekaboo by dropping the scarf on their face and removing it. They can also create the effect of dark and light without any outside help.

Notice that the scarf doesn't do anything on its own. It needs the baby. A favorite saying of Magda Gerber was, "Active toys make passive babies; passive toys make active babies."

The next play materials introduced at the Pikler Institute and the RIE trainings are also simple, lightweight things that babies can grasp, mouth, drop, turn, bang, poke, and explore in a number of ways. None of these dangle over the baby but rather are on the floor within reach so the baby can do more than just look at them and perhaps bat them. The amount and variety of play materials increase as the infants get older, but they remain simple. At the Pikler Institute, babies' play objects are, among other things, bowls (plastic and metal), wooden spoons, and plastic glasses that stack; these are similar to those the children use at meals, but not exactly the same. Babies thus learn to distinguish between play objects and the real thing.

By toddlerhood, the play objects change and the variety increases. One simple idea observed by the author at the Pikler Institute was a basket of neatly folded children's shirts and pants—clothing for the children to explore, try on, and take off themselves and one another. The clothes were a little on the large side, so they were easy to put on. It was such a simple idea to allow the children to explore something they were familiar with, but in a playful way—without any adult goal in mind. That's what real play is about.

There are several secrets to the success of these simple play materials. One is a safe environment where the children can move around and interact with each other. Another is one-on-one time during the essential activities of daily living so that children get plenty of individual attention each day. Because the children get their need for adult attention satisfied through these personal, focused activities, they are free to explore and play on their own without adult attention. Caregivers at the Pikler Institute are taught not to interrupt or distract children at play.

Pikler was clear that her approach was about helping infants find out, from the beginning, that they are competent learners, capable of exploring the world around them and learning about it. They become capable problem solvers. They feel powerful. They are motivated to learn and need no outside rewards for their examinations and explorations. Children who play with simple toys under the conditions summarized above develop long attention spans and learn to focus with concentration. All these are the kinds of skills that make for later success in school. Of course, children also develop cognitive skills, learn concepts, and gain manipulative and other physical skills in this environment that is so carefully thought out and arranged for play.

Toys and Materials for Inside

The list of appropriate toys and materials in the inside environment can be almost endless. Practically anything you can think of that is safe and interesting can become a **learning tool** for toddlers. Here are a few things for the inside environment you might not have thought of:

- Plastic margarine tubs.
- Blocks of various sizes, especially large, lightweight, plastic-covered foam ones that allow even toddlers to build, stack, and produce structures and enclosures with them.
- Shoe boxes with lids. Children love to take lids off and put them on again. You can put a surprise inside.
- Scarves are fun for all ages, but don't give silk ones to infants.
- Books, books, books.
- Muffin pans with a ball in each cup (a beginner's "puzzle" that even the very youngest child can be successful with).
- Flannel boards with felt pieces. Make them available to toddlers, and watch them explore, experiment, and talk as they move the pieces around.
- Paper to tear. Toddlers have very long attention spans when paper tearing is an activity.[6]

Toys and Materials for Outside

The outside environment should receive as much attention as the indoor one. It should give infants a feeling of being safe and should give toddlers plenty to do. Younger infants need a shaded, grassy, protected place to lie on a blanket. Crawlers need safe spaces to crawl and explore, with textures to feel that don't hurt their knees. A hint for protecting knees comes from a reviewer of this text. Take adult-size tube socks and cut off the toes. Double them and pull them up over crawlers' knees to create instant, cheap, knee pads! Crawlers need safe objects to manipulate and mouth. Beginning walkers need smooth surfaces that aren't too challenging as well as push-and-pull toys. Wheel toys are good for this age group too.

Here are some ideas of what to have in the outside environment for toddlers:

- Truck inner tubes. These are usually free. Don't inflate fully. They make great bouncers.
- Knotted ropes to swing on.
- Trapezes made of a dowel suspended from ropes. Wrap the ends of the dowel with duct tape.
- Sling swings hung very low for the child to swing on belly-down.
- Milk crates, big wooden boxes, thick planks, and sawhorses to make climbing structures.
- Wheel toys, including riding toys, push toys, and wheelbarrows and wagons to haul things around in.
- Small slides toddlers can go down headfirst if they want to.
- Various elevations—especially a hill. A hill is always fairly dry, even after a rain, and it's a challenge to walk up and down it. If you can get grass to grow on the hill, it makes a good place to roll.

- Rocking toys that children can get off and on by themselves.
- A sandbox with all sorts of containers and shovels and funnels, big and small.
- Water in all sorts of containers—little plastic swimming pools, big saucers, cement-mixing pans, baby bathtubs. Supply containers, funnels, hoses, sponges, cloths, and paintbrushes. Painting with water is always a favorite. Remember to always watch children around water—even a small amount can be dangerous.
- Straw provides additional softness for outside. Children can jump into it and haul it around.[7]

Assessing the Quality of an Infant-Toddler Environment

Besides looking at age appropriateness, there are other ways of assessing the quality of a learning environment.

In their book *Dimensions of Teaching-Learning Environments II: Focus on Day Care*, Elizabeth Jones and Elizabeth Prescott defined five dimensions of a learning environment: soft-hard, intrusion-seclusion, high mobility–low mobility, open-closed, and simple-complex.[8]

NAEYC Program Standard 4
Assessment

Balancing Soft and Hard

The soft-hard dimension is fairly self-explanatory. Assess this dimension of an infant-toddler environment by asking the question, Is the learning environment full of softness? In their indoor environment, infants and toddlers need soft blankets, stuffed animals, cozy furniture, mattresses, pads, cushions, and laps. In the outside environment, they need grass, sand, water, soft balls, pads, and laps. A soft environment is *responsive*. Many centers tend to have less softness than infants and toddlers need—partly because it is harder to clean soft materials and surfaces and partly because they tend to wear out. Child care homes usually do better than centers regarding providing enough softness, because a home usually has the stuffed furniture and curtains that centers lack.

Is there also some hardness, or is there carpet on every inch of the floor and grass on every inch of the yard? Infants need to be placed on firm surfaces both asleep and awake. A firm mattress lowers the risk factors of SIDS, and hardness on the floor or other play surface provides the resistance infants need for good posture and for them to learn to move their bodies. Hard floors and smooth cement present a different feel to the crawler, are easier to walk on for the beginning walker, and make nice noises for the older toddler. Some hard surfaces and hard play objects and materials belong in infant-toddler care, but the emphasis should be on softness.

Providing for Intrusion and Seclusion

The environment should provide for both optimum intrusion and seclusion. Desirable intrusion comes as the outdoor environment comes inside, providing interest and novelty. Low windows allow children to see what is happening outside, in back, or on the street but protect them from the dangers and noise. Desirable intrusion also occurs as outsiders come into the infants' and toddlers' environment—the telephone repair person, parents picking up children, visitors. Caregivers should maintain an optimum level of intrusion.

Seclusion should be provided so children who need to be alone or with one other child can find spaces to do that. Of course, supervision must always be a concern, but there are ways to make private spaces that adults can still see into. One simple way is to move a couch out from the wall. One center has a series of topless wooden boxes against one wall, with holes to crawl into. The sides screen the crawlers and toddlers from the rest of the room, but adults can see into them.

Louis Torelli talks about the importance of being able to break away from the larger group:

> A multi-level design, for example, varies the floor height with appropriately scaled platforms, lofts, "nests" and canopies. These mini learning environments set up a landscape for safe exploration in which infants can handle a toy, look at a book, stack blocks, crawl up steps, or simply watch the adults and other children from a cozy, semi-enclosed "private space."[9]

For some children with special needs, a place to escape what may be for them too much stimulation is imperative. Be aware of these children's needs for seclusion and minimal stimulation and provide for those needs.

Encouraging Mobility

High mobility and low mobility should both be encouraged in an environment for infants and toddlers. Children who are old enough should be able to move around freely. Children should not have to wait for outdoor time to engage in vigorous movement. That means, of course, that group size must be on the small side. Eight is big enough for an infant-toddler group. Two- to three-year-olds can manage in a slightly larger group—12, if the environment is well planned. Children with special needs may benefit from being in even smaller groups.

The Open-Closed Dimension

The open-closed dimension has to do with choices. An example of openness in the environment is low open shelves that display toys to choose from. Closed storage is also appropriate to regulate or reduce choices and to get rid of a cluttered atmosphere.

Openness also has to do with the arrangement of furniture and dividers. A good arrangement is to have openness from your waist up so you can supervise, but some feeling of closed space below so infants and toddlers aren't overwhelmed by large expanses.

This is a complex activity with soils, utensils, pots, and eventually seeds.

The open-closed dimension also has to do with whether a play object or material has one right way to do it (like a puzzle, form board, or graduated stacking rings) or whether it encourages all kinds of exploration. A stuffed animal and play dough are both open, as is water play. Children under three need many more open materials and toys than closed ones. Older toddlers may enjoy some closed materials and tasks, but younger ones and infants disregard their intended use and make everything open. They find ways to use all play objects and materials (closed ones as well as open ones) that adults never dreamed of. For an infant, the concept of the wrong way to use a play object doesn't exist.

The Simple-Complex Dimension

Simple play objects and materials are the best for infants. Ruth Money in "The RIE Early Years 'Curriculum'" says, "We offer simple objects such as empty plastic bottles or lightweight colanders that an infant can lift and look through."[10]

The complex end of the simple-complex dimension has to do with combining play objects and materials. Sand, water, and utensils combined present lots more possibilities for action than any one of the three by itself. Caregivers who explore this dimension find that attention spans increase when complexity is introduced into toddlers' environments.

Those who remember Jim Greenman heard him talk about four other dimensions of good environmental planning for infants and toddlers: scale, aesthetics, acoustics, and order.[11]

Scale

Think about how you feel in places like cathedrals and other buildings designed to make you feel small. That's the way infants and toddlers feel in any environment designed for other age groups. Even a preschool environment will add to infants' and toddlers' feelings of smallness. When they sit in chairs that leave feet dangling, swing in swings they can't get into or out of, or play at chest-high tables, they feel smaller than they need to feel. Infants and toddlers need rooms, ceilings, furniture, and spaces scaled down for them. You want them to feel big and capable, not small and inadequate. The physical environment can make a difference in their self-concept.

Aesthetics

Infants and toddlers should spend their time in a place that is visually appealing. Lighting is an important factor in visual appeal. If possible, avoid the overlit and even effect of fluorescent lighting. Natural lighting gives variety and adds warmth. Color and its different emotional qualities should be considered, as should visual noise. In most infant-toddler environments, there is so much going on—so much to see—that the background should be calm, warm, and neutral. Greenman suggests avoiding the usual riots of color and design when planning walls, surfaces, curtains, and other fabrics. With a neutral backdrop, the people, toys, and materials stand out better, allowing children to find them and focus on them. The children are less distracted.

Acoustics

Reflect

Think about the place where you are most comfortable and happy. What are the characteristics of this place? Can you learn anything from your own experience about how to set up an environment for infants and toddlers? Would any of those characteristics be appropriate for that age group?

Noise can be a real problem where infants and toddlers are together in a group. Every effort should be made to lower the noise level and protect the children who need quiet from those who are shouting, crying, or engaging in noisy activities. Group size has a lot to do with noise level, which is an important reason to keep groups small. Dividing the space helps, too, as does providing plenty of softness to absorb sound (carpets, stuffed furniture, pads and cushions, curtains, and acoustical ceilings). Be aware of background noises and their effect on the children and adults as a group and individually. Some lights emit a high-pitched sound that irritates sensitive ears. Noise from fans or other machinery can be soothing or irritating, depending on the sound and the room. When the group contains one or more children with hearing impairments, even greater attention must be given to acoustics if those children are to be able to use whatever residual hearing they have.

Order

Relating to both aesthetics and acoustics is a sense of order. Because infants and toddlers create constant disorder as they spread toys and materials around, pull things apart, and dump and rearrange everything they can get their hands on, the environment needs to provide a sense of basic order that is in contrast to the constant mess on the floor. Room arrangement should contribute to the sense of order. Using furniture, shelves, and screens to divide play space into small modules just large enough for two or three children (or slightly more for older toddlers) helps them focus and cuts down on noise (visual as well as auditory). Clear pathways should lead to these play spaces, and each space should contain shelves of toys. In addition, if entrances to spaces offer some motor challenge, such as stepping up or crawling through, children spend less time wandering.

Of course, the room only needs to be divided below the three-foot level so the whole room is in view at the adult level. That's an important point to make: there are two environments in the room—below three feet and above three feet. To fully understand the children's environment, you need to get down at their level. When you're down there, you'll discover things like baseboards, of which you are probably totally unaware. It is good to get low and take the children's perspective regularly when planning and maintaining an environment for them.

Order relates to a sense of aesthetics. Infants and toddlers get messages from the environment if it is well planned and consistent.

Order and accompanying consistency are vital qualities of an environment in which children with visual impairments are served. If the walking paths are cluttered, or the furniture is moved around, a child who has memorized the environment will feel insecure and hesitate to move around in it.

Throughout this chapter, you may have noticed a huge missing piece is screens! Television, videos, and handheld electronic devices that are now part of most young children's lives at home and away have no place in play environments set up for infants and toddlers.[12]

The environment is never determined once and for all. Planning, arranging, evaluating, and rearranging is an ongoing process as caregivers strive for quality and find what works best for them and for the children as they grow and change.

Appropriate Practice

Overview of Development

According to the National Association for the Education of Young Children, a feeling of security allows young babies to use their senses and physical abilities to explore and learn about what's around them, including objects and people. For young infants, security has to do with attachment and trust. The same is true for mobile infants; however, safety becomes a huge concern for babies constantly on the move, spurred on by curiosity. They need a safe and rich environment for their quest to learn all they can about the world. Toddlers too need a safe and interesting environment for their explorations, which take on new dimensions as they are constantly trying to discover who they are, what they can do, and who is in charge. Throughout the first three years, the sense of security that was a major issue in early infancy combines with the urge to explore, and children develop increasing purposefulness in their explorations.

Developmentally Appropriate Practice

Following are samples of developmentally appropriate practices that relate to the physical environment:

Health and Safety

- Adults follow health and safety procedures, including proper hand washing methods

and universal precautions to limit the spread of infectious disease. There are clearly written sanitation procedures specific to each area. Instructions on the proper diapering sequence (including use of protective gloves), cleaning cribs and play areas, and food storage and preparation (including dish washing) are displayed on the walls as visual reminders to adults.

- Health records on infants' well-baby checkups, immunizations, and particular health problems are filed separately and confidentially for every infant. Clear policies alert parents to when infants must be excluded from child care for health reasons.
- Caregivers do safety checks of all areas, inside and out, several times a day.
- Emergency evacuation plans are posted on the wall near the infants' daily record charts; a bag of emergency supplies and child emergency forms are immediately accessible. Evacuation drills are practiced on a regular basis.

For Infants

- Adults provide infants with an auditory environment that is not overstimulating or distracting. They choose music and other recordings that infants enjoy.

- Space is arranged so children can enjoy moments of quiet play by themselves, have ample space to roll over and move freely, and can crawl toward interesting objects. Areas for younger infants are separated from those for crawlers to promote the safe interactions of infants in similar stages of development.
- A variety of safe household items that infants can use as play materials are available, including measuring cups, wooden spoons, unbreakable bowls, and cardboard boxes.
- Mobile infants have an open area where balls, push-and-pull toys, wagons, and other equipment encourage free movement and testing of large-muscle skills and coordination. Low climbing structures, ramps, and steps are provided. Structures are well padded and safe for exploration.
- Open shelves within infants' reach contain toys of similar types, spaced so that infants can make choices. Caregivers group materials for related activities on different shelves.
- An outside play space adjacent to the infant area includes sunny and shaded areas. It is enclosed by protective fencing. The ground around climbing structures and in some of the open space is covered with resilient, stable surfacing for safety, making it easy for mobile infants to push wagons and ride on toys. There are soft areas where young infants can lie on quilts.

For Toddlers

- The environment and schedule have enough predictability and repetition to allow toddlers to form expectations, repeatedly practice emerging skills, and feel the security of a familiar routine.
- Caregivers organize the space into interest or activity areas, including areas for concentrated small-group play, being alone, art/water/sand

and other messy activities, dramatic play, and construction. The activity areas are separated by low partitions, shelves, or sitting benches, making it difficult for running toddlers to disturb toddlers engaged in concentrated play, and creating clear traffic patterns.
- Children have daily opportunities for exploratory activity.
- A child-size sink with paper towels is located near areas designated for messy activities, so toddlers learn that cleaning up and washing their hands follow any messy activity.
- Children have many opportunities for active, large-muscle play, both indoors and outdoors.
- Each toddler has a cot and bedding that are personally labeled. Getting his or her own blanket or special stuffed toy is part of the child's nap routine.

Individually Appropriate Practice

Following are samples of individually appropriate practices that relate to the physical environment:

- Adults ensure that every child receives nurturing, responsive care.
- Adults create an "inclusive" classroom, making sure that spatial organization, materials, and activities enable all children to participate actively.

Individualizing is a vital requirement if each and every child is to receive what he or she needs from the environment and people in it. For some children, environmental adaptations and adult interventions are necessary for caregiving routines, and also for encouraging free play.

Culturally Appropriate Practice

Following are samples of culturally appropriate practices that relate to the physical environment:

- Caregivers work in partnership with parents, communicating daily to build mutual

(continued)

Appropriate Practice *(continued)*

understanding and trust and to ensure the welfare and optimal development of the infant.

- Caregivers listen carefully to what parents say about their children, seek to understand parents' goals and preferences, and are respectful of cultural and family differences.
- Caregivers and parents confer in making decisions about how best to support children's development or handle problems or differences of opinion as they arise.

Much of the way the environment is set up in this chapter has to do with stressing independent exploration and self-help skills. In families where interdependence is more important than independence, the setup of the environment may not make much sense. It is not OK to just use parent education to get parents to see the approach in this book as the only right way. Remember that developmentally appropriate practice mandates that professionals work in partnership with parents and work to build mutual understanding and trust. The goal is to ensure the welfare and optimal development of the child. Identity issues can be at stake, so it is imperative that caregivers seek to understand and respect cultural differences as well as involve parents in decisions about what's best for their child.

Source: Carol Copple and Sue Bredekamp, eds., *Developmentally Appropriate Practice in Early Childhood Programs,* 3rd ed. (Washington, DC: National Association for the Education of Young Children, 2009.).

Appropriate Practice in Action

Look back on the Principles in Action scene on page 271 in terms of appropriate practice.

- Go through the items under the "Developmentally Appropriate Practice" section for toddlers in the Appropriate Practice box and think about the scene. Obviously you don't have the whole picture, but from what you have read, which practices are compatible with what the family child care provider is doing?
- What about the items under the "Individually Appropriate Practice" section? How many of those are compatible with what you read the provider is doing?
- After reading the last paragraph under the "Culturally Appropriate Practice" section, consider that all parents may not have the same goals as the family child care provider for free exploration, making discoveries, and problem solving as independently as possible. If Austin's parents don't have the same goals, what can or should the provider do?

Summary

Creating a safe, healthy, developmentally appropriate physical environment both indoors and outdoors for infants and toddlers supports learning and development as well as making meeting needs a cooperative venture.

A safe and healthful environment

- A number of factors need to be considered to create a safe and healthy environment for infants and toddlers, including:
  - o Nutrition
  - o Feeding infants
  - o Feeding toddlers

The learning environment

- The learning environment is made up of a play area plus the spaces for care-giving activities such as:
  - o Eating
  - o Sleeping
  - o Diapering
  - o Toileting

Development appropriateness

- Developmental appropriateness is important for safety reasons but also to facilitate learning.
  - o What is appropriate for infants is different from what is appropriate for toddlers.
  - o Mixed-age groups in centers and family child care homes provide a special set of challenges for making the environment work for everybody.
  - o The toys and materials that are developmentally appropriate vary for each age group.
  - o What should be in the play environment?

Assessing the quality of an infant-toddler environment

- Assessment of any infant-toddler environment is an ongoing process and requires taking into consideration the factors already mentioned plus looking at five dimensions and four additional considerations, including:
  - o Soft-hard dimension
  - o Intrusion-seclusion dimension
  - o High mobility–low mobility dimension
  - o Open-closed dimension
  - o Simple-complex dimension
  - o Scale
  - o Aesthetics
  - o Acoustics
  - o Order

Key Terms

learning tool 276   play spaces 272
mixed-age groups 272   structure 264

Thought/Activity Questions

1. Using the checklists in this chapter, evaluate an infant-toddler environment.
2. Make your own checklist using the key points under the section on assessing the quality of an infant-toddler environment. Use that checklist to observe an infant-toddler program.

3. Figures 12.1, 12.2, and 12.3 show center-based program environments. Draw a layout of a home (it could be your own home) and design spaces in it that would accommodate a group of children of varying ages, including infants and toddlers.

For Further Reading

Deb Curtis, "What's the Risk of No Risk?" *Exchange,* No. 192, March/April 2010, pp. 52–56.

Jennifer B. Ganz and Margaret M. Flores, "Implementing Visual Cues for Young Children with Autism Spectrum Disorders and Their Classmates," *Young Children* 65(3), May 2010, pp. 78–83.

Janet Gonzalez-Mena, "What Works? Assessing Infant and Toddler Play Environments," *Young Children* 68(4), September 2013, pp. 22–25.

Éva Kálló and Györgyi Balog, *The Origins of Free Play*, trans. Maureen Holm (Budapest: Association Pikler-Lóczy for Young Children, 2005).

Ruth Anne Hammond, *Respecting Babies: A New Look at Magda Gerber's RIE Approach* (Washington, DC: Zero to Three, 2009).

Irene Van der Zande, *1, 2, 3. . . The Toddler Years* (Santa Cruz, CA: Santa Cruz Infant Toddler Care Center, 2012).

Ruth A. Wilson, "Aesthetics and a Sense of Wonder," *Exchange*, No. 132, May/June 2010, pp. 24–26.

chapter 13

The Social Environment

What Do You See?

The caregiver is new to the early childhood field and this is her first day in the infant room. She goes around and introduces herself to the children starting with Brian. "Oh, what a big strong boy you are," she says and she picks him up and holds him high in the air. When she notices that he doesn't look scared, she compliments his bravery. Next she approaches Brianna and leans over her, smiling gently. "What a pretty little girl," she says, lightly stroking her cheek. "And look at that outfit you have on!" The teacher watching her wonders what she will say when she approaches the next baby, who is dressed in green and there is no way to tell gender.

Maybe you too are wondering. What did you notice about the interactions this adult had with these two babies? She is tremendously focused on gender. It's hard to imagine how she will be able to have a conversation with a baby if she doesn't know the gender. Maybe she will ask. Gender identity is one of the components of the social environment and is discussed later in the chapter when we revisit this scene.

NAEYC Program Standards 2 and 3
Curriculum and Teaching

The social environment is harder to talk about than the physical environment because it is far less visible. You can stand and look around the physical environment to evaluate it. But you have to catch behaviors as they happen in order to see the social environment.

A good deal of Part 1 and some of Part 2 focus on the social environment without calling it that. The environmental chart in Appendix B outlines the social environment. This chapter discusses aspects of the social environment that haven't been discussed elsewhere.

Identity Formation

Because in the past most infants and toddlers were at home or in kinship care, not much thought was given to their identity formation. It was a process that just happened naturally. Times have changed; great numbers of infants and toddlers are now in out-of-home care, and their identity development has begun to be a concern.

Infants and toddlers are in the process of forming a sense of self. They aren't quite sure yet who they are, what they like, and where they belong. Their identity formation comes as they absorb the images of themselves they see reflected in their caregivers' eyes. They learn by identifying with their caregivers and imitating them. They can pick up their caregivers' personal traits and attitudes. Infants and toddlers learn from caregivers' perceptions of how people act in different situations and how people act toward them. They observe how emotions are expressed. From all these observations, infants and toddlers figure out how they appear to others. They begin to develop attitudes about how they and others should be treated. They also learn what to feel under what circumstances. From countless daily little interactions with their caregivers, infants take in numerous impressions and incorporate them into their identity. For the first time in history, great numbers of those caregivers are not family members.

The Principles in Action

Principle 1 Involve infants and toddlers in things that concern them. Don't work around them or distract them to get the job done faster.

Kaleb is the only dark-skinned child in the toddler center. The director is most worried about his identity formation, and staff members have had several antibias trainings. She is pleased to see how staff members are working with their various biases and how equitably they treat all the children. Today, however, there is a substitute who has had no training, and while the director is watching her, she picks up what she assumes are some unconscious behaviors. First, she notices that when children need a tissue, the substitute gets one and wipes their noses—that is, until Kaleb needs one. She takes the box to Kaleb, offers a tissue, and suggests he wipe his nose. Then she holds out the wastebasket for him to throw the used tissue in. After seeing the tissue episode, the director decides to stay in the room and pay closer attention to the substitute. Diapering presents another scene that disturbs the director. The substitute diapers the children she is supposed to, all but Kaleb. When it's his turn, she says she needs to take her break. The director asks her to diaper Kaleb first. When she does, she hands him a toy to play with and diapers mechanically, ignoring the child and focusing only on the task. She doesn't say a word to him and takes half the time that she took with the other children. The director asks another caregiver to take primary responsibility for Kaleb the rest of the day.

1. What messages do you think Kaleb might have been picking up from the substitute?
2. How might the substitute's behaviors have influenced Kaleb's ideas about himself, and his body and its products?
3. Should the director have done more than she did?
4. If she had confronted the substitute with her observations, how do you think the substitute might have responded?
5. Do you have some feelings about this scene?

According to J. Ronald Lally, the following are lessons that infants and toddlers learn from their caregivers that may become part of the sense of self.[1]

- What to fear
- Which behaviors are appropriate
- How messages are received and acted upon
- How successful they are at getting their needs met by others
- What emotions and intensity level of emotions they can safely display
- How interesting they are

The responsibility for caregivers, administrators, and policy makers is enormous. No one can afford to ignore the effect of caregivers on infants' and toddlers' sense of self. Society may see those who care for the youngest children as just babysitters, but the reality is that they are, as Virginia Satir, author and therapist, used to say, "people-makers." If caregivers are untrained, underpaid, and working in substandard programs, there's no telling what the results of their people-making might be.

Identity is made up of many facets, one of which is **self-concept**. An important reason for studying the emotional environment is to bring clarity to the way a child's identity is formed by the people with whom the child interacts. We start with a look at the environmental influences on self-concept. Self-concept, which relates to attachment, is made up of the child's perceptions of and feelings about himself or herself. Self-concept comes from body image as well as cultural and gender identification. The social environment, the way a child is treated by adults and children, affects self-concept and influences the degree of self-esteem.

Attachment

NAEYC Program Standard 1

Relationships

The prerequisite for high self-esteem in infants and toddlers is attachment. From attachment comes the feeling "I matter to somebody; who I am and what I do is important because somebody cares." All the self-esteem activities in the world won't make a difference if the child's basic attitude is "Nobody cares about me."

"Caring" in the sense of attachment has to happen at home, but it is important in child care too. It seems as though "caring" is what infant-toddler programs are all about because of all the caregiving focus. But "caring" the feeling is different from "caring" the action (taking care of). You can care for a child, wash his bottom and feed his face, without really caring for him. And you can't *make* yourself care for him (in the feeling sense). You can make yourself respect the child, and that may help the caring feeling come. Respecting the child will help you deal with all of him, not treating him as a bottom or a face, and in turn he may feel better about himself and reveal more of himself to you. That may help the caring feeling come.

What If You Don't Feel Attached?   But what can you do if you are respectful and you still find a child doesn't "matter" to you? Here are a couple of ideas.

Observe the child. Step back and really pay attention to her every move. Try to understand her. See if you can view the world from her perspective. Do a "child study" in which you make a series of short observations over a period of time, and then put them together and examine them for evidence of growth. Carry a notebook around in your pocket, and every chance you get, make notes about what you see this child doing. Be very detailed and specific. Note body posture, quality of movement, facial expressions, and tone of vocalizations. Try hard to be very objective—don't judge; just observe. If you get good at stepping into and out of an **observation mode**, you can do it quickly and effectively many times during the course of a day. In addition, at the end of the day, write some anecdotal records— notes about what you remember about the child that day and what you remember about your interactions with her. These reflection records as well as on-the-spot observations will provide you with material for your child study in the course of a few months. Observations alone may help your feeling for this child grow.

Observation can have powerful effects. One student who was required to do an extensive child study chose a child she didn't like very much. She reported that it was the best choice she could have made because after she really got to know this child and began to understand him better, her feeling for him changed.

Children are influenced by the images adults carry of them. You might guess that the teacher feels good about this child and that he feels good about himself as well.

Be aware that we all carry around in our heads unconscious images that influence our expectations of others as well as our own behavior toward them. These images can be very powerful, and it is important to become aware of them in order to change them.

Self-Image

Children are influenced not only by the images of them that adults carry around but also by the image they have of themselves. Part of self-concept is **self-image**—that is, one's own perception of oneself that relates to body image and awareness. **Body awareness** is a major task of infants and toddlers and grows as their motor skills develop. As they learn what capabilities their bodies have, they develop an image of themselves. You can watch a nine-month-old backing down off a couch he has crawled up on and get an idea of his body awareness. The child with good body awareness knows where he is in space and how far to back up before putting his feet over the edge of the couch. He can guess how far it is to the floor, so he is able to slide off and remain in control. The infants and toddlers at the Pikler Institute had excellent body awareness.

When working with children who have physical disabilities, it is important to take their body awareness and self-image into account. If you focus only on their

NAEYC Program Standard 2
Curriculum

lack of skills, they'll have some difficulties with self-concept. Pay special attention to whatever abilities they have, emphasizing what they *can* do rather than concentrating on what they can't do. Take a strength-based approach.

As children develop competence, their self-concept expands. They take pride in accomplishments. Thus the thrust for independence and the development of self-help skills relate to body image and the growth of self-concept.

Cultural Identity

Cultural identity is also a part of self-concept. The culture or cultures we come from influence every detail of every action of our lives, including how close we stand to people, where and when we touch them, gestures we make, what we eat, how we talk and think, how we regard time and space—how we look at the world. You bring your culture to your work with infants and toddlers. You also absorb the culture of the program itself, or if you don't absorb it, you are influenced by it. You are teaching infants and toddlers culture every day in everything you do. In a program where the children and caregivers are of the same culture, and it is compatible with the culture of the program, there is real consistency. Those children don't think about culture—it's so much a part of them.

In fact, few of us think about culture until we encounter someone who comes from a different one. This can happen to infants and toddlers quite early when they go into child care. The question is, How does exposure to different cultures affect infants and toddlers? What do they do with a second or third set of cultural messages? This is no new phenomenon: Throughout history, members of one culture have been involved in raising the children of another.

One theory is that children who are raised biculturally or multiculturally have a greater understanding and acceptance of differences in people. They may also be more willing to see beyond cultural differences and relate to people as individuals, regardless of their cultural differences. This is the theory behind the push at present for multicultural education. The goal in multicultural education is to help children appreciate their own culture and cultural differences. The advocates of multicultural education see it as a way to fight bias of all kinds and racism in particular.

A Multicultural, Multilingual Infant-Toddler Curriculum But what is a **multicultural, multilingual curriculum** in an infant-toddler center? It is easier to talk about what it is *not* than about what it is. It is not just pictures stuck on walls, rotating ethnic foods, music from many cultures, or celebration of holidays. Infants and toddlers do not gain much understanding of culture or learn other languages from those devices, though you may choose to include some of those components in your program for various reasons, including your own enjoyment and satisfaction or that of the parents.

The point of a multicultural, multilingual curriculum is to keep children connected to their families and their culture. Language plays a big part in helping children continue to feel that they belong to their families and also feel at home in the center or family child care setting. Many infant-toddler programs, for a number of reasons, have an English-only focus. School readiness is one reason. Pressure to have children fluent in English before kindergarten creates a lot of pressure on staff and administrators. Lack of bilingual staff is another reason programs take an English-only approach.

Programs that ignore a child's home language and regard a child who doesn't speak English as deficient can cause problems and have an impact on cultural identity and self-esteem. Head Start and other programs for low-income children are looking carefully now at addressing the linguistic needs of what are called **dual language learners**. The term not only includes children whose home language is not English, but also monolingual English-speaking children who can learn another language in child care programs. Addressing the needs of dual language learners goes a long way toward promoting cultural identity and expanding positive views of diversity.

Supporting home language, no matter what it is, represents an important part of this trend. For too long educators have focused on the deficiencies of what have been called limited English proficient (LEP) children without regard to the development they already have in their home language. Labels can be harmful! Careful attention to home language promotes healthy development. Those children in English-only programs who do not speak and understand English can be stunted in their language and cognitive development. Furthermore, an English-only focus can create gaps between children and their families and cause issues with identity formation. It was thought in the past that bilingualism causes language delays. Research seemed to prove this when assessments of English language learners were done only in English without regard to how proficient they might be in their home language. Assessments such as counting vocabulary words in English may show that bilingual English language learners have fewer words than monolingual English speakers. In reality bilingual children who have support in continuing to develop their home language while learning English score higher than monolinguals when assessed in both their languages. Bilingualism is a benefit—not only to children whose home language is not English, but to English-speaking children as well. Ultimately, the whole society gains when the numbers of bilingual citizens and residents increases. In many countries in the world most of the population is bilingual, and in some countries being trilingual is the norm.[2]

Ideally, a multicultural, multilingual approach includes supporting home language and helping children continue to develop in their first language, while also helping them to develop in English. The same goes for culture. Ideally, the children are supported in their home culture while learning about another culture or cultures. How does the staff learn about the home cultures of the children? Such information comes from the families themselves. Some of this you may be able to just observe. It helps to ask. By asking, you may open up a dialogue about cultural differences. All of this may turn out to be very interesting and valuable to you.

However, none of this makes a real difference to the infants and toddlers in your care. What does matter when you care for children from a culture different from your own is that you listen to what their parents want for them in their day-to-day care. This means discussion of caregiving practices. It also means potential conflict when your beliefs and values clash with those of the parents. For example, take a parent who does not understand your goals for each child to become independent. She may insist on spoon-feeding her child way beyond an age you feel is appropriate. Or take a parent who stresses independence beyond your own goals. She may ask you to allow a toddler to sleep or eat whenever or wherever he or she wants without regard to any kind of schedule. Or a parent may want to keep siblings together even though the age difference makes your environment inappropriate for one or the other. Or a parent may ask you to help her with toileting her child even though the child is far younger than you think appropriate. Or a parent may ask you to dress or not to dress his or her child in a certain way, or in certain kinds of clothes you don't approve of. All of these can be cultural issues.

A true multicultural infant-toddler approach in such cases would be to invite parent input and then figure out what to do with it. Some requests are easy to respond to immediately; others take more talking, clarifying, understanding, and perhaps negotiating. Still others go against your very deeply held values and beliefs, standards, or regulations, and no amount of talking or negotiating will convince you to comply with the parent's wishes. Sometimes when a serious conflict like this occurs, the parent has other choices for child care, in which case he or she may find someone who is more able to comply. But often the parent has no other choice, so difficulties arise.

One way some caregivers get around these difficulties is to stop discussing the issue, pretend to go along with the parent just to keep peace, and then keep doing what they believe in when the parent leaves. That approach can leave the child in the position of coping with a culturally assaultive environment while in child care. Imagine yourself in a culturally assaultive environment. How would that feel?

It is much better to work continually toward resolving the conflict. It's good practice for all of us to open up and expand our cultural awareness by being persistent in resolving difficult dilemmas that arise when parent beliefs and practices conflict with caregiver beliefs and practices. It may be that you and the parent will come to an agreement that it won't hurt the child if out-of-home child care is one way and home is another way. Or it may be that together you'll find some middle ground. It may even be that you'll change your practices once you understand the parent's point of view, or she will change hers when she understands your point of view.

Culture is one aspect of identity formation; race is another. The two may go together, but they don't always. Although race is a social construct, not a biological fact, racism makes it imperative that caregivers not be color-blind when it comes to identity formation. Children in infant-toddler programs need attention

Reflect

Imagine yourself in a culturally assaultive environment. If you can't imagine such an environment, pick an environment you feel most comfortable in and imagine its opposite. How would it feel to spend a good part of your waking hours in such an environment? What relationship do your own imaginings and experience have to caring for culturally diverse children?

to their perception of racial identity, and caregivers need to look closely at the message children receive and may incorporate into their sense of self. Some children can develop a negative racial identity without specific kinds of support and interventions. Other children grow up with an inherent sense of racial superiority unless adults around them pay careful attention to the environment and the messages those children are receiving. In other words, without awareness on the part of the adults in children's lives, the experiences involved in identity formation can be very different for white children than for children of color. Parents may be aware of the importance of incorporating a positive sense of a racial self and working at home toward that. Caregivers can join in that effort by being constantly vigilant about what children learn in the program about themselves based on the color of their skin, the messages they receive, the treatment of their family, and the images from the media.

Even as toddlers, children begin to perceive power relationships, and the group they perceive to be in power in the program can influence their identity formation. When white children observe that the group in power looks like them, they assume they are members of that group and have the same rights. Those observations can grow into a feeling of entitlement and a sense of self-worth, which can be magnified by seeing discrimination in action and taking in negative stereotypes of people with whom they don't identify. When children of color observe that the group in power is not like them, especially if they observe and/or experience prejudice, discrimination, and exposure to stereotypes, they are less likely to grow into a feeling of entitlement and sense of self-worth.

Both groups need specific kinds of interventions if they are to move from feelings of superiority and inferiority to perceptions of equity. Because they are so young, talking is less effective than showing. Infants and toddlers learn through direct experience. That means we need to be sure that all children's experiences are positive ones and do *not* include:

- Exposure to stereotypes, prejudices, and negative images that influence their attitudes or with which they might identify.
- Observations of interactions among adults that give them the impression one group of people is better than the other.
- Personal interactions that show lack of respect.

See Figure 13.1 for a checklist for equity in identify formation in infant-toddler programs.

Gender Identity

Part of self-concept is **gender identity**. Most children are aware quite early whether they are a boy or a girl, and their feelings about their gender influence how they perceive themselves. You can see one way they learn about gender if you recall the behavior of the new caregiver in the scene at the beginning of the chapter. Adults influence children's ideas of how they are supposed to be

Figure 13.1 Checklist for Equity in Identity Formation in Infant-Toddler Programs

1. Children see themselves and their families represented in the staff, pictures, photos, and books. They hear their home language spoken.

2. Diversity is welcomed, and the program is considered an inclusive one.

3. Children see and hear adults interacting with each other in respectful and equitable ways across lines of color (also across lines of culture, ethnicity, gender, age, ability, religion, sexual orientation, and family makeup).

4. Staff is well trained in developmentally appropriate practices and in how to include culturally appropriate and individually appropriate practices as well.

5. There is an initial and ongoing process for finding out what each family wants for their child (or children) in terms of actual caregiving behaviors.

6. There is an openness to creating consistency of care for each child by adapting the policies and practices of the program to meet each family's deeply held values and related practices.

7. If families in the program all appear to be of similar background, effort is made to uncover existing invisible diversity.

8. If the families are of similar background, effort is made to counteract media stereotypes and expose children periodically to people who are different from those they know.

according to their gender, and this influence starts early. Remember that Brian was mainly noticed for his size, strength, and bravery, while Brianna was only acknowledged for her sweetness and appearance. Even without the words, the differential way each was touched and handled gives a strong message.

Throughout this book we have mentioned sex role stereotyping. The information has come mostly in the form of questions designed to heighten your awareness of sex role stereotyping.

Children can grow up with a severely limited view of their capabilities and potentials by being taught narrow sex roles. These teachings start early, as shown in the chapter opening scene. The expectations even at birth can be very different for a boy baby than for a girl baby. Those expectations influence a child's self-concept. If you expect boys to grow to be strong, brave, unemotional, and capable, you act differently toward them than you do toward girls. If you expect girls to be sweet, kind, attractive, emotional, and not too smart, they might just try to live up to your expectations.

You can see for yourself how people treat boys differently from the way they treat girls with a simple observation. Just keep track of what adults, especially strangers, say to very young children. They are much more likely to comment to girls on appearance and clothes. Boys are noticed for their deeds and less often for appearance.

Children learn about what is expected of their gender by such simple, innocent remarks. They also learn from the clothes they are given to wear. (It's hard

Reflect

Observe yourself interacting with infants and toddlers. Do you treat boys differently from girls? If yes, why? If no, why not?

Figure 13.2 Strategies for Expanding Children's Ideas about Gender Roles

1. Be careful not to treat boys and girls differently. Observe yourself closely!

2. Model expanded gender roles yourself.

3. Avoid exposing children to media messages that show stereotyped gender roles.

4. Watch your language so you don't link occupations to gender.

to crawl and climb in a dress.) Toys give messages too. When boys are encouraged to play with tools, construction sets, and doctors' kits, they get one message. When girls are given dolls, play dishes, and makeup kits, they get another message. Children learn about expected gender roles from television, books, and, above all, role models. If the family child care provider waits until her husband gets home to fix the screen door and makes it clear that she never touches tools, she is giving a message. When centers leave their tricycles unrepaired until a man comes on the scene, they, too, are giving a message.

If current trends continue, the children in infant and toddler programs today will grow up into a world of a variety of job opportunities for both sexes. The days when men and women were restricted from certain jobs are mostly in the past. Yet if children grow up with a limited view of their capabilities because of the narrow sex roles taught to them, their freedom to qualify for these jobs will be limited.

Figure 13.2 offers four ideas about how to offer both the boys and the girls you work with a broad view of their gender roles. First, be aware of treating boys and girls differently. Do you offer more support and sympathy to girls when they get hurt and expect boys to "tough it out"? Do you help girls when they need it and wait for boys to figure things out on their own? Do you offer girls dolls and boys blocks, or do you encourage and support both sexes to play with all the toys? Do you touch girls more than boys (or vice versa)? Do you talk to girls more than boys (or vice versa)?

Second, model expanded gender roles. If you're a woman, how often have you tried to fix something, or do you just put it aside, convinced you don't know how? Can you check your own oil? (Learn—it's easy.) If you're a man and you're reading this book, you've already expanded your gender role. Can you think of ways to expand it further?

Third, avoid exposing children to media messages that teach narrow gender roles. We hope the infants and toddlers in your program aren't watching any television, so you don't need to worry about that medium. Find books and pictures that show strong, capable women as well as nurturing men in a variety of occupational roles.

Finally, avoid linking occupations to gender—say "police officer" rather than "policeman," "firefighter" rather than "fireman." These are simple changes, but they make a difference.

Self-Concept and Discipline

Reflect

What do you remember about the way you were disciplined as a young child? Can you remember a situation that hurt your self-esteem?

The way you guide and control behavior can influence children's ideas of and feelings about themselves. The discussion here will center around ways to discipline that don't tear down self-esteem.

Much of what is appropriate discipline for infants and toddlers comes about naturally through meeting individual needs in a timely fashion and through setting up an environment that is appropriate to their age level. If they can't get to hot stoves, they won't touch them. If they can't reach TV remotes, they won't click them. If they have no access to steep stairs, you don't have to find ways to prevent them from climbing them. To a great extent, the environment sets the limits.

However, you do have to protect the children from hurting each other, and sometimes you do have to prevent them from ruining toys and furniture by banging, chewing, and throwing. You can do this by using a strategy called **redirection**. You redirect the child from what he shouldn't be doing to something similar that is OK to do. For example, if a child is throwing a toy car, give her a ball to throw. The closer the action is to what she is already doing, the easier it is to redirect. Redirection is close to distraction but not quite the same. Distraction is often used to keep a child from feeling emotion, whereas redirection is more about using the energy in an acceptable rather than an unacceptable way. Distraction is manipulative in a way that redirection is not. Sometimes redirection doesn't work and you must firmly but gently physically restrain the child (if a word won't do it) and remove the object or the child if he or she threatens to continue this behavior. If you remain calm and gently persistent, you won't be as apt to trigger rebellion as you would if you issue sharp warnings or commands. You do need persistence because older infants and young toddlers continually test limits. That's how they find out about you and the world they live in. Once they're satisfied you really mean it, the test is over—until the next situation, anyway. The way to preserve their good feelings about themselves as well as their sense of power while you enforce the limits is to avoid shaming, belittling, blaming, or criticizing them.

Don't Punish or Scold   Punishment, scolding, and anger have no place in the discipline of infants and toddlers. You may, of course, feel and express anger at times when you are not able to manage the behavior of the children you care for. That's normal and doesn't hurt anything. However, recognize that the anger is personal. Don't blame the children for it, and don't use anger to control their behavior. Find other ways to get the effect you want from them. When you use anger to get your way, the children will quickly pick up this behavior, and you'll find them trying it on you.

Punishment damages self-esteem. There are other ways to change undesirable behavior that not only leave self-esteem intact but that also actually enhance self-concept as children learn to control their own behavior and feel good about getting attention for staying within the limits and exhibiting prosocial behavior.

VIDEO OBSERVATION 13

Child in Sandbox (Redirection)

See Video Observation 13: Child in Sandbox (Redirection) for an illustration of a situation where guidance is needed. You'll see a girl sitting in the sand who keeps trying to put a sand-filled spoon in her mouth. Watch how the adult handles this situation. This is an example of redirection.

Questions

- How did you feel about the kind of redirection the adult was using? Would you have done it differently?
- What other kinds of approaches could have been used in this situation?
- What effect do you think this kind of redirection might have on the child's self-concept? How about the other approaches you came up with—might they have had a different effect on the child's self-concept?

To view this clip, go to **www.mhhe.com/itc10e**. Click on Student Edition, select Chapter 13, and click on Video Observations.

Define Unacceptable Behavior   Before you consider ways of changing behavior, you must first define what is undesirable behavior. The child's age will influence your definition. For example, the screams of a young infant are not undesirable behavior; they are communication and must be attended to. Touching and mouthing objects are not undesirable behaviors in older infants; they have a need to touch and mouth. Experimentation and exploration are not undesirable behaviors in toddlers; that's how they learn about the world.

No One "Right" Way   When considering alternatives to punishment, you have to realize that no one approach works for all the children all the time. What works depends on the child, the situation, and the origins of the behavior. For example, if a certain toddler behavior has in the past been rewarded by adult attention, it has been learned. Therefore, the approach is to "unlearn" it by removing the reward. At the same time, you must be sure to replace the attention the child has been receiving when you remove it from its connection with a particular behavior. Sometimes adults forget that there must be two parts to this approach of removing the reward from undesirable behavior. The children *need* the attention you're denying them. Find other ways to give it to them. Also be sure before you try this approach that you determine whether this behavior is communicating some other unfulfilled need. If that is the case, don't ignore the behavior; regard it as communication and fulfill the need.

Some behaviors are expressions of feelings. Accept the feelings. Help the child learn to express them in socially acceptable ways. What is considered an acceptable expression of feelings varies with the culture. Some people see screaming in anger as healthy; others find screaming unacceptable.

Changing Behavior in Toddlers   Here is a summary of six approaches to changing undesirable behavior in toddlers:

1. *Teach socially acceptable behavior.* Modeling is one of your most effective teaching methods. Children naturally pick up your behavior, so make sure it is the behavior you want to teach.
2. *Ignore the behavior you want the child to change.* Often it is being done for your benefit. (But of course don't ignore behavior that threatens safety or communicates a need—a hungry, crying baby needs to be fed, not ignored.)
3. *Pay attention to behavior that is socially acceptable.* Call attention to children for being gentle with one another, for taking care of toys and equipment. Make a fuss over desirable behavior (not undesirable behavior).
4. *Restructure the situation.* Perhaps there are too many choices of things to do, or not enough. Either situation can cause infants and toddlers to act in less than desirable ways. Maybe two children need to be separated for a while.
5. *Prevent harmful behavior from happening.* Stop the hitting before it occurs. Catch the biting before the teeth sink in. The strong reaction children get from the children they hurt can be very rewarding. That reward is cut off when the action is not allowed to happen. Such behaviors will decrease if you stay on your toes instead of letting them happen and then dealing with them afterward.
6. *Redirect the energy when appropriate.* When you must restrict a child, give several other choices of things he or she can do. ("I won't let you throw the block, but you can throw the pillow or the soft ball." "I won't let you bite Maria, but you can bite this washcloth or this plastic ring.")

"Time-Out"?   A word about **time-out**. Time-out—that is, removing the child who is misbehaving—is sometimes used as a blanket approach by caregivers who don't know any other methods of guiding behavior. Early childhood educator Marian Marion sees time-out as punishing and inappropriate.[3] It is controversial because it is misunderstood and often overused. Removing a child from a situation he can't handle is different from time-out. Sometimes toddlers are out of control because they are being overstimulated. Removing an out-of-control toddler to a quieter place for a short time helps him or her regain composure and control. Confining children, even by making them sit in a chair, as a punishment for an infraction of a rule is not the same as helping them gain control when they need to.

Once you perceive that a particular child has this need occasionally, you can help her learn to judge the situation and make the decision to leave on her own. The ultimate goal of discipline, after all, is to turn it over to the individual. Your approaches to discipline should lead eventually to self-discipline—the establishment of inner controls.

Cultural Notes   Feelings for or against the use of time-out can relate to cultural differences. When privacy is a cultural value, a child may be taken away from the group (whether it is called time-out or not) so the child can have time and space alone to gather himself or herself back together and regain control. This approach is used by those who stress independence and individuality. Not all cultures see the benefits of stressing those two characteristics. For some, belonging to the group is more important than the notion of individuality. From a collectivist orientation, time-out is like shunning and is an extreme punishment. No matter how kindly it is done, and with what intentions, cutting the child off from the group is punishment. It's important to be sensitive to differences in perspective.

Another difference in perspective relates to notions of authority, which Lisa Delpit has been writing about for a long time in both her older book, *Other People's Children*, and her newer one, *Multiplication Is for White People*. She writes about such subjects as the differences between the way some European Americans speak to children as compared with how some African Americans speak to them.[4] The soft-spoken request for a certain behavior is not recognized by some children as a command. They are more used to hearing the command form of the verb (tempered or not): "Sit down, please." "Stop banging your cup." These children may not pay attention to other forms of guiding behavior. A pleasant voice saying "It's not safe to stand up" or "I don't like it when you bang your cup" is ignored. Children who ignore adults whose tone or words don't convey authority can end up being labeled as problems. That isn't fair! Caregivers should be sensitive to children's differing backgrounds and learn to speak their language, even if it's just another form of English. That doesn't mean that those adults can't continue to behave in authentic ways that feel comfortable to them. It does mean that they have to *teach* children in their care that they mean it when they make a soft-spoken statement that sounds indirect. They teach by following up with action when the words alone don't work, which is a good approach to use with anybody's children!

One last point about self-concept and discipline: Not all cultures see the goal of discipline as establishing **inner controls**. From some perspectives, discipline always comes from an outside authority, whether it's a person or group pressure. Discipline is not something that is inside but is external to the individual.[5] Children who expect to be monitored may feel justified in misbehaving if no one is paying attention. Again, this difference in views of controlling behavior (internal control or external control) may result in a situation where children from diverse backgrounds end up labeled as problems unless caregivers are aware of the difference.

Modeling Self-Esteem by Taking Care of Yourself

NAEYC Program Standard 6
Teachers

It may seem strange to find a section on taking care of yourself in a book that focuses on caring for infants and toddlers. But some caregivers are poor models for the children they work with. The job demands sacrifice, it is true, and you need to put your own needs last quite often. But the job also demands high self-esteem. Children need to be around adults who see themselves as worthy, who respect and care for themselves. The opposite of the worthy adult is the adult whom everyone tramples on—the children, the parents, and the coworkers.

No one can tell you how to increase your worth in your own eyes, but Figure 13.3 presents some advice on how to take care of yourself. First, take care of your needs. You have the same range of needs that the children have (that is, physical, intellectual, emotional, and social needs). Don't neglect yourself. Eat right, exercise, pamper your body regularly with a swim, a hot bath, a walk, whatever you enjoy most. Stimulate your mind with a good book, a class, a game of chess. Feel your feelings; don't ignore them. Learn to express them in ways that are healthy for you and the children. Find ways to use anger to help yourself solve problems or gather needed energy for making changes. Nurture your social life. Build relationships. Build a broad base of support. The more choices you

Reflect

How do you feel about yourself? On a scale of 1 to 10, what is the level of your self-esteem? What do you do to increase your self-worth in your own eyes?

Figure 13.3 Some Hints about Nurturing Your Own Self-Esteem

1. Take care of your needs; don't neglect yourself. Take care of your physical, intellectual, emotional, and social needs.

2. Learn to be assertive. Don't let anybody take advantage of you.

3. Learn conflict management.

4. Learn time management.

5. Feel proud of what you do. You have an important job. Let people know that.

6. Play. Play renews energy and brings out your creative spirit.

have, the less chance you'll be let down. And don't hide your relationships from the children. It's good for the children to be with an adult who relates to other adults.

Second, learn to be assertive. Say no when appropriate. Family child care providers are especially famous for saying yes, yes, yes, until everyone in their lives is taking advantage of them. Don't let that happen to you.

Third, learn conflict management. Negotiation and mediation skills are important, not only in working with children but also with adults.

Fourth, learn time management. This set of skills helps you immeasurably by teaching you to use the time you have in ways that benefit you most.

Fifth, find ways to explain the importance of your job so that you can be proud of it. Don't apologize for what you do. The first years are the most important ones. The people who rear children (that is, you and the parents) are the people responsible for the future of their country.

And finally, play. Adults need to play just as children need to play. Play renews energy and brings out a creative spirit.

This chapter has covered a lot of territory—from *caring about* each child that you *care for* (and how to work toward that goal if it doesn't happen naturally) to *taking care of* yourself, with stops along the way to look at self-concept from the view of culture, gender, and discipline. The social environment is made up of all these factors and more! The next chapter examines another programmatic issue: adult relationships. Although it is in a chapter by itself, this topic is part of the social environment.

Appropriate Practice

Overview of Development

According to the National Association for the Education of Young Children, attachment is a foundational building block for identity formation. In young babies attachment brings a sense of belonging, which gives them security to use their senses and physical abilities to explore. Seeing himself or herself as an explorer and investigator becomes part of the child's early identity. Mobile infants come to see themselves as expert explorers if they are supported and encouraged. All this exploration relates to the identity issues of toddlers as they deal with the dual issues of independence and control.

Developmentally Appropriate Practice

Following are samples of developmentally appropriate practices that relate to the social environment:

- Adults respect infants' individual abilities and respond positively as each baby develops new abilities. Experiencing caregivers' pleasure in their achievements, infants feel competent and enjoy mastering new skills.
- Adults know that infants are curious about each other. At the same time, caregivers help ensure that children treat each other gently.

(continued)

Appropriate Practice *(continued)*

- Pictures of infants and their family members are hung on walls at heights where infants can see them.

Source: Sue Bredekamp and Carol Copple, eds., *Developmentally Appropriate Practice in Early Childhood Programs*, 3rd ed. (Washington, DC: National Association for the Education of Young Children, 2009).

Individually Appropriate Practice

Following are samples of individually appropriate practices that relate to the physical environment:

- Adults ensure that every child receives nurturing responsive care. In order to be individually appropriate and give nurturing responsive care to promote positive identity formation in all children, caregivers must know how to meet the specific needs of each child rather than take a general age and stage approach. They must give positive messages to the children (both verbal and nonverbal) that what they need is OK.
- Adults create an "inclusive" classroom, making sure that spatial organization, materials, and activities enable all children to participate actively. Adaptations need to be made in a way that indicates to children that who they are is just fine and they will be welcomed here.

Source: Sue Bredekamp and Carol Copple, eds., *Developmentally Appropriate Practice in Early Childhood Programs*, rev. ed. (Washington, DC: National Association for the Education of Young Children, 1997).

Culturally Appropriate Practice

Following are samples of culturally appropriate practices:

- Caregivers work in partnership with parents, communicating daily to build mutual understanding and trust and to ensure the welfare and optimal development of the infant. Caregivers listen carefully to what parents say about their children, seek to understand parents' goals and preferences, and are respectful of cultural and family differences.
- Some cultures find photographs uncomfortable or distasteful. As one mother said, "I was shocked when the teacher pulled out pictures of her family. In my country we only have pictures of people who have died, and we don't carry them around with us." In such a case, Bredekamp and Copple suggest that caregivers and parents confer in making decisions about how best to support children's development or how to handle problems or differences of opinion as they arise.

Source: Sue Bredekamp and Carol Copple, eds., *Developmentally Appropriate Practice in Early Childhood Programs*, rev. ed. (Washington, DC: National Association for the Education of Young Children, 1997).

Appropriate Practice in Action

Looking back at the Principles in Action on pages 290–291, consider the care the caregiver is giving Kaleb. Then look at the first item under the "Individually Appropriate Practice" section of the Appropriate Practice box and answer the following questions:

1. Is Kaleb receiving nurturing, responsive care?
2. Is the caregiver following principle 1?
3. From what you read in the Principles in Action, can you tell anything for sure about Kaleb's culture?
4. Do you think the caregiver's treatment of Kaleb relates to his culture?
5. How would you write an additional item under the "Individually Appropriate Practice" section that would address the risk to Kaleb's self-identify formation?

Summary

Although less visible, the social environment is as important as the physical environment and contributes to emotional well-being and socialization by supporting infants' and toddlers' identity formation and attachment.

Identity formation

- Identity formation is of special concern in infant-toddler programs because children under age three are in the beginning stages of learning who they are, what they can do, and where they belong.

Attachment

- Attachment affects identity formation and should be a priority in infant-toddler programs.
- Caregivers who don't feel attached can become more attached by
  o Closely observing the child
  o Trying to see themselves interacting in a caring mode with the child
  o Examining the image they hold of the child

Self-image

- Self-image is how children see themselves and includes the following characteristics:
  o Body awareness, which increases as movement develops
  o Cultural identity, which grows when the program regards families as partners and pays attention to cultural differences in ideas about what infants and toddlers need from adults. Language is a part of cultural identity and where there is language diversity, supporting home language is important.
  o Racial identity, which is different from cultural identity, though they may go together. Caregivers must pay attention to what message children are receiving about their race, even though the real issue is not race, but rather racism. Race is not a biological fact; it's a social construct.

Gender identity

- Gender identity relates to children's feelings about their gender as well as the following factors:
  o How their gender influences how they perceive themselves
  o How adults interact with them based on their gender
  o How adults model gender roles

Self-concept and discipline

- Self-concept can be deeply affected by the adult's approach to discipline and guidance.

- It is important that adults do the following to positively influence children's self-concepts:
  o Use positive ways to guide behavior, such as redirection
  o Define what is acceptable behavior in terms of developmental ages and stages
  o Be aware of cultural differences in ideas about discipline

Modeling self-esteem by taking care of yourself

- If children are to grow up knowing how to take care of themselves, they need role models who meet their own physical, mental, emotional and social needs.

Key Terms

body awareness 293
cultural identity 294
dual language learner 295
gender identity 297
inner controls 304
multicultural, multilingual
    curriculum 294

observation mode 292
redirection 300
self-concept 291
self-image 293
time-out 302

Thought/Activity Questions

1. What is the difference between self-concept, self-image, and body awareness?
2. Explain some of the issues around using time-out as a guidance strategy.
3. Try to see a child differently. Pick a child whose behavior bothers you and try to see the child without the troublesome behavior.
4. Imagine yourself working in a toddler program using the principles of this book and the ideas about discipline outlined in this chapter. You are confronted with a hard-to-handle child whose parent thinks she acts that way because you aren't behaving the way her daughter expects an authority to behave. Create a dialogue between yourself and this parent.

For Further Reading

Deborah Chen, "Inclusion of Children with Special Needs in Diverse Early Care Settings," in *Infant/Toddler Caregiving: A Guide to Culturally Sensitive Care*, 2nd ed., ed. Elita Amini Virmani and Peter L. Mangione (Sausalito, CA: WestEd and Sacramento, CA: California Department of Education, 2013), pp. 25–40.
Carol Brunson Day, "Culture and Identity Development: Getting Infants and Toddlers Off to a Great Start," in *Infant/Toddler Caregiving: A Guide to Culturally Sensitive Care*,

2nd ed., ed. Elita Amini Virmani and Peter L. Mangione (Sausalito, CA: WestEd and Sacramento, CA: California Department of Education, 2013), pp. 2–12.

Louise Derman-Sparks and Julie Olsen Edwards, *Anti-Bias Education for Young Children and Ourselves* (Washington, DC: National Association for the Education of Young Children, 2010).

Janet Gonzalez-Mena, *Diversity in Early Care and Education: Honoring Differences* (New York: McGraw-Hill and Washington, DC: National Association for the Education of Young Children, 2008).

Christine Gross-Loh, *Parenting without Borders* (New York: Penguin Group, 2013).

J. Ronald Lally, *For Our Babies* (New York: Teachers College Press, 2013).

Karen N. Nemeth and Valeria Erdosi, "Enhancing Practices with Infants and Toddlers from Diverse Language and Cultural Backgrounds," *Young Children* 67(4), September 2012, pp. 49–57.

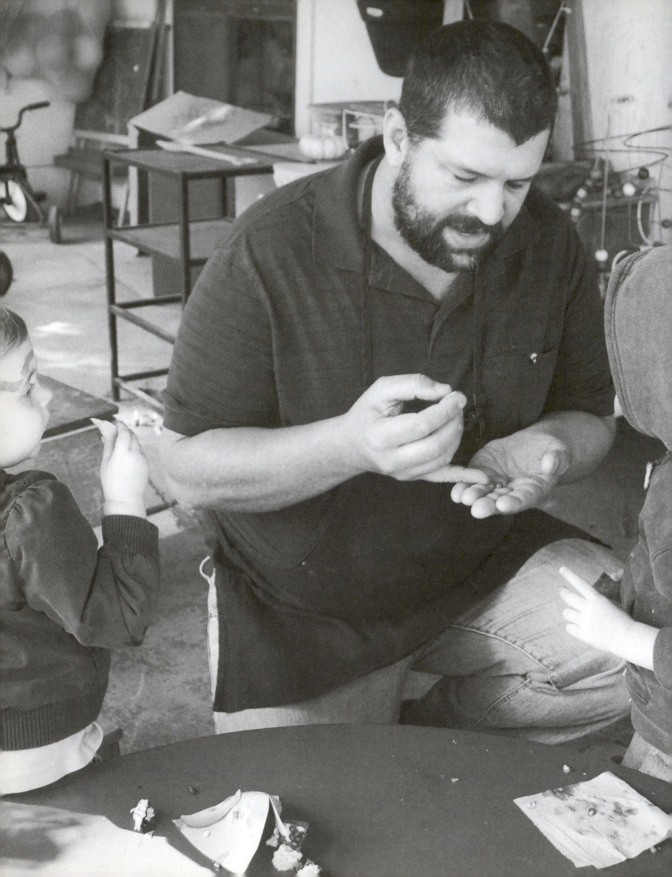

chapter 14

Adult Relations in Infant-Toddler Care and Education Programs

Focus Questions

After reading this chapter you should be able to answer the following questions:

1 What are the stages of caregiver development in relating to parents and other family members? Which is the stage to aim for and why?

2 If you have a service plan that focuses on the child, why do you also need one that focuses on the family?

3 What blocks communication with parents and what are some ways to open up communication?

4 What is parent education and involvement and how is it different if parents are partners instead of merely consumers of a service?

5 How are caregiver relations different for center staff than for family child care providers?

What Do You See?

A mother arrives to pick up her daughter. She is obviously in a hurry. Her daughter runs toward her, arms outstretched. The mother starts to smile, then takes a look at the knees of her little pink pants, which are bright green with grass stains. A big frown takes over the smile. She picks her daughter up a little brusquely. Muttering to herself, she strides over to the nearest caregiver. "How did this happen?" Her voice sounds strained.

How will the caregiver react in the face of this upset mother? You will find out later in the chapter. Her response is important. What she conveys to the mother has implications for whether it's a relationship-building response or one that breaks down the relationship. Although relationships don't usually hinge on just one response or one set of interactions, the goal of each interaction should be to help these two important people in this child's life have a positive relationship with each other.

Parent-Caregiver Relations

We discuss the relationship between caregiver and parent throughout this book. In this chapter we examine that relationship more closely. The subject of parent-caregiver relations is very important. Every professional who provides a service to others must develop a relationship with his or her clients. In the field of infant-toddler care, this relationship with the client—that is, the parent(s)—is vital because it affects the relationship of the children to the caregiver.

Although the term *parent* occurs throughout the chapter, it is important to recognize that in many cases it is the *family* to whom the staff or provider must relate. It is worthwhile to understand lines of authority and responsibility within each family.[1]

Caregiver Stages of Relating to Parents

Caregivers commonly go through three stages when they start working with children. It is important to recognize these in yourself and know that you can move to the next stage when you realize that your attitudes, feelings, and behaviors relate to being new in the field. (Of course, some people get stuck in a stage and don't move forward.)

Stage 1: Caregiver as Savior   Sometimes caregivers forget that their client is the parent(s), not just the child. They make their own decisions about what to do for the child without consulting parents as to their goals and desires. They may even have feelings of competition with the parent. If these competitive feelings are strong enough, they result in a **savior complex**, when caregivers see their role as rescuing children from their parents. The savior complex is a stage many caregivers go through when they first find themselves in charge of someone else's children.

The caregiver as savior is an interesting phenomenon. Not only is she out to save each child in her care from his parents (with a few exceptions, of course), but she plans to save the whole world through what she is doing with children! Stage 1 caregivers ride around on their high horses looking down on parents.

Stage 2: Caregiver as Superior to Parent   Most people move out of that stage when they realize that their charge is only part-time and temporary. They may influence children for part of the day while the child is in child care, but the parents are the predominant and permanent force in the child's life. It is the parents who give the child a sense of connection with the past and a view of the future. At about the same time that caregivers come to see the importance of parents in children's lives, they also begin to see individual parents' points of view. Caregivers in this second stage have more understanding about what influences the parents' child-raising practices.

During the second stage, caregivers come to see parents as the client. While still in the glow of the savior complex, caregivers work to change parents—to educate them. The difference between a stage 1 and a stage 2 caregiver is the perception of who the client is. The savior effect is still in operation as caregivers see themselves as superior substitutes for parents.

Stage 3: Caregiver as Partner to Parent and/or Family   The final stage comes when caregivers see themselves as partners—as supplements and supports to parents rather than as substitutes for the parent. The parent and caregiver *share* in the care of the child. This stage brings on a mutual relationship in which the caregiver and parent communicate openly, even when conflicts arise. In this stage, the caregiver is clear about how important it is to do nothing that weakens children's sense of belonging to their own family.

Being a support, a surrogate, a supplement doesn't make you any less professional. Look at architects. Their job is not to impose ideas on the client but rather to take the client's ideas and needs and, using professional expertise, come up with something that works as well as pleases. Communication is an important part of the process.

Reflect

If you are a caregiver, which caregiver stage of development are you in currently?

The Principles in Action

Principle 3 Learn each child's unique ways of communicating (cries, words, movements, gestures, facial expressions, body positions) and teach yours. Don't underestimate children's ability to communicate even though their verbal language skills may be nonexistent or minimal.

Emily has cerebral palsy. It is her first day in the family child care home, and her provider is trying to get to know her. She realized in the first five minutes that it would be a challenge to learn to read Emily's facial expressions and body language. Happily, her mother realized the difficulty the provider would have, so she offered to stay with her daughter the first few times so she could teach her the unique ways Emily has of communicating. The provider paid close attention to Emily and listened to her mother's interpretations of what she was seeing and hearing. Otherwise, the provider never would have known what pleased Emily and what didn't. Her facial expressions weren't what the provider was used to. Several times she guessed, but she was wrong. "She's hungry," her mother decided, based on when Emily had last eaten and her present agitation. "Let me show you how to feed her," she offered. Feeding didn't look so hard, but reading the hunger signs did. Now Emily has eaten, but she has started whimpering. The provider turns to the mother to understand what Emily is trying to convey.

1. Would this scene be different in any way if it were in a center rather than in a family child care home?

2. Some providers and caregivers ask parents not to stay very long because they want the child to get used to them. What do you think of that approach? Would that have worked in this case?
3. What about a child who doesn't have diagnosed special needs—should a parent stay the first few times to help the provider or caregiver get to know the child?
4. How would you feel about taking care of a child with Emily's condition?

The architect's responsibility is considerably less than that of a caregiver. The architect's goal is merely a structure; the caregiver is dealing with human lives.

Of course, the caregiver who is going through these three stages may be working in a family-centered program where the philosophy is to partner with parents. In that case, the new caregiver who is still in the savior stages may feel out of step with the program policy and practice. It may help that caregiver to understand that these are stages of development and that's why at first he or she feels uncomfortable. The chances are that stage 1 and stage 2 caregivers hired to work in a family-centered program will get the kind of training that will help them move through the stages faster than those who work in a purely child-centered program.

Communication with Parents and/or Family Members

Communication should be a major concern from day one. It's not just a matter of helping the parent understand the policies and practices of the center and finding out more about the child and family. It's even more important to use communication to start building a relationship with the family. So even though there may be a set procedure for the intake interview, including forms to fill out, if you keep your eye on the goal of creating a relationship, you'll have more success both at the beginning and down the line. One early job is to find out the needs of the child and family and then decide on a service plan.

Service Plan: Focus on the Child

What kinds of information should be discussed in the development of a **needs and services plan**? A needs and services plan is a form that guides the program in some of the specifics in working with each child. This form contains information from parents about their children's habits, special needs, ways of communicating, and daily routines. Such information should include when and how much the child sleeps; how the child goes to sleep; and the child's eating habits, needs, likes and dislikes, bowel function, liquid intake and output, cuddling needs, and **comfort devices**—for example, a blanket or a stuffed animal that children can use to soothe themselves. These items should be discussed when the child enters the program and on a daily basis thereafter. It may be hard to find "talking time," and shift changes may mean the child's caregiver is not present when the parent arrives, but simple written records give the information that may be of great importance to the parent and to the caregiver. (Did he just have a snack, or is he crying because he is hungry?)

Although it is difficult to find time to do it, writing down anecdotes is also useful because some parents appreciate hearing about what went on that day. But be careful about leaving a parent feeling guilty about the child's behavior. It's up to you to guide behavior while you are with the child. If you had a hard time that day, don't blame the parent for it. Also, when you're relating positive anecdotes, be careful that you don't make parents feel left out because of all the cute things the child did that they missed. If the child took a first step that day, you want to weigh your own excitement with the parents' possible disappointment of not having been there to see it. Of course, not all reports are happy ones. If a child has a significant fall, scrape, or bite, the parent needs to be called and the details need to be reported on an accident or incident form by someone who observed it. A copy of the report goes in the files and another one should be sent home. Minor bumps and scratches call for a simpler "ouch" report.

Be sure that while you're conveying information you are also listening. You need information too—about what happens in the other part of the child's life. Is she particularly fussy this week because something is going on at home? Is he tired today because he didn't sleep much last night, or might he be coming down with something? Are her bowels loose because of something she ate that didn't agree with her, or might she have picked up an infection? Listening is half of communicating.

Service Plan: Focus on the Family

The Parent Services Project (PSP) started by Ethel Seiderman is now nation-wide and addresses the development of the child and family together. Each participating program has a plan that includes services to the parents, not just a service plan for the child. The idea is to ensure the well-being of the parents as a way of caring for their children. One way to promote well-being is to bring parents together in ways that foster community building as parents make connections and develop social networks.

NAEYC Program Standard 7
Families

Staff in the national headquarters of the PSP organization train child care professionals to focus on positive attitudes about working with parents and practical activities to serve the family. The program builds on family strengths and resources and regards cultural sensitivity and inclusion as an important part of the work. What kinds of activities are written into the service plan? The activities differ from program to program depending on what the families in the particular program need and want. Each PSP program is tailor-made, so no two are exactly alike. A typical sampling might include a menu of adult activities such as support groups, classes, workshops, or leadership opportunities; family fun activities such as Friday night pizza parties with a rented video for entertainment; field trips on weekends to the beach, an amusement park, or the zoo; specialized child care such as respite care and sick child care; programs for men, for grandparents, for foster parents; multicultural experiences; or mental health activities.

Figure 14.1 A Summary of the Principles Under Which Parent Services Project Programs Operate

1. The way to ensure the health and well-being of children is to ensure the health and well-being of their parents.

2. Parents are the child's primary teachers, and they know the child best.

3. The relationship between parents and staff is one of equality and respect.

4. Parents make their own choices about the services they want.

5. Programs and services are voluntary.

6. Programs build on parents' strengths and are ethnically relevant and community based. Each community sets its own reality based on what is good for it.

7. Social support networks are a crucial element in the happiness, health, and productivity of people.

See Figure 14.1 for a summary of the principles under which the PSP programs operate. They should be guiding principles for *all* child care programs.

Communication Blocks

Sometimes it's hard to listen when you are angry with a parent. The source of your anger can be something as simple as a personality conflict or as deep as a basic attitude toward parents who leave their children to go off to work, especially when it seems there is no financial reason to do so. Ironically, some caregivers feel ambivalent about child care and whether it is good for children. Some family child care providers decide it is better for them to stay home with their children than go out to work, so they go into the business of caring for the children of other mothers who leave home to work. If a woman who made this choice sees it as a sacrifice, she may resent a mother who arrives in the morning well dressed, happy, and about to embark on what the caregiver perceives to be a more socially or intellectually stimulating day. This is an unfortunate situation and can cause hard feelings between caregivers and parents. A first step to solving this problem comes when the caregiver faces such feelings squarely, recognizing that anger or annoyance over child or parent behavior really springs from this particular source. What to do about it will become clearer once the feelings are acknowledged.

Sometimes it's hard to listen because a parent is angry. Parental anger is often misplaced, centering on some minor issue instead of the real source. Parents may cover their insecurities, their conflicting feelings, their feelings of guilt and stress with anger. Parents may sense uncomfortable competition—real or not—between themselves and the caregiver. Parents often feel threatened by competent caregivers. They worry that they are losing their children as they see them express affection for the caregiver. Parents who feel insecure about parenting

Reflect

Suppose you are a caregiver, and a parent is very angry about something you did with her child. How would you handle this situation? Would it make a difference if it was a father who was angry with you?

skills may hide that insecurity by acting extra wise or knowledgeable—even pushy. If you listen carefully enough, you may be able to detect the real message behind the words. Just as when children feel insecure you try to bolster their confidence in themselves, point out their strengths and competencies, and steer them toward successes, so you can take the same approach with an insecure parent.

Some parents actually need parenting themselves. They look to you as wise and capable and lean on you for support. You have to decide how much of this need you can fulfill. You can't be everything to everyone, and this parent's needs may be one burden too many for you. Then you have to decide whether you can put the energy into supporting the parent while you help him or her become self-sufficient, whether you have to redirect the parent to someone else, or whether you have to just set a limit and say no. Sometimes you can get parents together with each other, and they will form a mutual support system.

Sometimes it's hard to listen when you feel you're being attacked. You end up defending yourself instead of allowing the other person to really express what is on his or her mind. For example, a parent may say that all her child does is play in your program, and she wishes he were learning something. If you get defensive, show anger, and close down communication, you may never have a chance to create the kind of **dialogue**, or conversation using nondefensive language, in which you can listen to each other's points of view. But if you are able to listen, eventually you'll have a chance to point out all the child is learning through the caregiving and free play.

Opening Up Communication

You can open the communication by letting the parents know you heard them. This can be done by simply restating the parent's own words, which allows them to correct you or explain further. This approach is called active listening and also includes stating what the other person seems to be feeling. The idea is to really listen and let the other person know that you are listening. Adults who use this strategy all the time with children sometimes have a harder time remembering that it works with adults as well. As you establish a dialogue, you'll be able to get a better picture of what parents want as well as explain your approach and what you believe in.

Conferences Besides day-to-day informal encounters, **conferences** are important for communication. Setting aside time when parents and caregivers can sit down to talk to each other helps to develop relationships. When parents and caregivers have a warm and trusting relationship, infants and toddlers benefit. The first conference, called an **intake interview**, can set the pattern for communication, especially when the caregiver makes the family feel comfortable and at home. It's called an interview, but it should be thought of as a two-way conversation. Although it can be informal and warm, it is important that some matters be made clear from the beginning. One issue is that child care personnel are mandated to report any suspected child abuse. If such a situation should arise,

Reflect

What are your experiences with conferences? Do you remember parent-teacher conferences as a child? Are you a parent? Do you have experiences in the parent chair of parent-teacher conferences? Do any feelings come to you as you think about conferences?

parents who know about this requirement ahead of time won't feel betrayed or deceived when the caregiver files a report. Of course, this is a touchy subject and not one anyone wants to talk about. But from a legal point of view and for the protection of the child, the cards must be put on the table. Some programs have parents read a short statement concerning the mandate to report child abuse; they are asked to sign it to show they have read it. It's even possible that this policy acts as a prevention device.

In addition to the initial intake interview, periodic informal conferences help parents and caregivers develop their partnership, gain insights, and set long-range goals. It is important to help parents feel secure about such a conference. They may perceive themselves as being in the "hot seat." Some parents arrive at conferences with all the old feelings left from report card sessions in their elementary or high school days. In such situations, you need to do all you can to help them relax and feel comfortable so you have real communication.

Helping Parents Feel at Home   Start by looking at the environment in which you will conduct the conference. If you sit behind a desk with a file folder in front of you and a wall of reference books behind you, that gives the proceedings the tone that you are an expert, removed from the amateurs—the parents. Any insecurities they arrive with will be magnified in this setting.

Because you are in your own territory, it is especially important that you make the parents feel welcome and at home. If you know educational, psychological, or developmental jargon, try not to use it. That gets harder as you begin to see yourself as a professional. After all, professionals have their own way of talking that sets them apart. But just think how you appreciate the doctor who can explain your symptoms without sending you off to a medical encyclopedia. At the same time, don't talk down to parents. It's hard to communicate openly when one party is being patronizing.

If you have a specific goal for the conference, state it at the beginning. If it is to be just an informal give-and-take session, state that. Don't leave parents wondering why they have been asked to this conference. Use conferences to examine issues between you, explore problems and questions concerning the child, decide on ways to approach behavior that needs changing, exchange information, and develop goals. If the child is present at the conference, don't talk around him or her. Include the child in the conversation (even babies).

Issues of Parents of Children with Special Needs

Children with special needs and their parents have been integrated throughout this book and reflect the variety of issues that parents and families of children with special needs experience. In most ways parents of children with special needs are like other parents, but some may arrive in a conference with you with some emotional issues you may have to understand and work with. They may be in denial about their child's condition. Denial is a normal stage in coming to grips with something as serious as giving birth to a baby with special needs. Be gentle and understanding with parents in denial and be patient about helping them beyond this stage. It may take some time.

Some parents of children with special needs carry a heavy burden of guilt. They may not show this guilt to you, but it may affect your relations with them, especially if they have a sense that you blame them.

Anger may also be present in these parents. Though it may come out at you, it may well have nothing to do with you personally. Approach the parents' anger the way you do children's anger. Allow them to express their feelings without getting defensive or angry back.

Realize that these parents may have had a number of dealings with "experts" before they met you, and they may bring the issues from these experiences to their conference with you. Of course, not all parents of infants and toddlers with special needs will bring anger, guilt, or unresolved issues to their conferences with you. Some will have had positive experiences in working together with "experts" and will be ready to establish a partnership with you, their child's caregiver. But others will come with a lot of baggage, and if you recognize this fact, you can deal with it.

When Just Listening Is Not Enough   Sometimes parents and caregivers have disparate needs or differences of opinion that put them in conflict with one another. Just listening isn't enough; what is needed is a problem-solving or conflict-resolution approach. When this happens, it is important both to listen and to express your own feelings and position. When together you have defined the problem, then brainstorm potential solutions. It may be that there is a cultural difference that troubles both you and the parent. You don't see eye to eye on something such as toilet training, for example. If in the parent's culture the time to start toilet training is much earlier than you believe it should be started or than is the policy of your program, this is an issue about which you need to communicate. It may be hard to keep from arguing with the parent, but you'll get further if you try to understand each other. That's where dialoguing comes in. Instead of trying to convince the parent that one way is right and the other wrong, you need to sort out the differences. It may even come down to some basic conceptual differences. For example, at the Pikler Institute they never use the word *toilet training*. Instead they call it sphincter control, because it is only a matter of children gaining the muscle strength to manage their own elimination process. Because diapering, dressing, bathing, and feeding have been cooperative processes, sphincter control is all children need to take the next step, which is to use the toilet. That is very different from the kind of conditioning process that is involved in toilet-training babies.

Communicating with parents whose culture is different from yours may be very difficult, yet it is important that you accept the parents' ways of doing things as much as possible and try to carry out their wishes. That is easy to do when the ways and the wishes don't tread on your theories of what is good for children. It's much harder when what the parents want is in conflict with what you think is right. The problem is that theories are culturally bound.

Reflect

What are your experiences with cross-cultural encounters? Do you have feelings or ideas about those experiences?

There is no one right answer—no one truth. It is easy to forget that and get carried away telling people what is good for babies. You have to remember to listen to their ideas rather than just sell yours. For that reason, when you are deciding what is good for babies and toddlers, you have to take culture into consideration.

And while you are looking at culture, you also have to look at the difference in generational perspectives. The generation gap is real. If you are a grandmother and the parents of the children in your care are much younger, they may well have a different way of looking at what's good for children, even if they are of your same culture. The experience differential doesn't explain all the differences; you have to consider the times in which the person grew up. If you are 20 and many of the parents are twice your age, you have to recognize that they may have a different view. One isn't right and the other wrong; they are just different.

A gender difference may create a communication gap. The way a father perceives his child may be different from the way a mother does. Male caregivers' responses, reactions, and understandings of children may be different from those of female caregivers.

Let's revisit the scene at the beginning of this chapter and see how the caregiver handled the situation. Remember the mother who arrived to find her child had grass stains on the knees of her pink pants? The mother was in a hurry and was upset as she walked over to the nearest caregiver and demanded an explanation. We can't tell whether this is a cross-cultural, cross-generational, or cross-gender situation or not. It could be. But even if it is not, the goal is the same—to create a dialogue with the parent rather than getting defensive. Let's look at the rest of that scene. Try to keep out of a blaming mode and to stay in a problem-solving mode.

"How did this happen?" The mother's voice sounds strained. The caregiver looks concerned.

"We were outside this morning—it must have happened then. I'm sorry. I can see that you're pretty upset about it."

"You bet I am!" the mother says angrily.

"It's going to be hard to get out," the caregiver says understandingly.

"Yes, it is." There is a pause in the conversation. The caregiver waits, still attentive to the mother—maybe to see if the mother wants to say more. Then the caregiver adds, "You must be pretty mad at us."

At that the mother explodes. The words rush out on top of one another, first about her anger and then about how she is going to meet her fiancé's mother, and it's important that her daughter look her very best. She talks about how insecure she feels around the new family that she's about to become a part of. When she's finished, she looks a lot better. The frown is gone, replaced by a slightly nervous look.

"Do you have time to sit down for a minute?" the caregiver asks kindly.

"Not really," replies the mother, sitting down anyway. She's holding her daughter with tenderness now, and the child plays with her hair.

"I'm just wondering how we could keep this from happening next time," says the caregiver tentatively.

"You could keep her inside," says the mother immediately.

"I hate to do that," says the caregiver. "She loves to be outside."

"Yes, I know," admits the mother.

"Besides," continues the caregiver, "there are times when we are all outside, and there's no one inside to watch her."

"Well," says the mother hesitantly, "I suppose I could send her in jeans—but she looks so cute in her little outfits. . . . When I'm going someplace after work, like today, I want her to look nice." She thinks for a minute. "I guess it makes more sense to dress her up when I pick her up than to expect her to keep an outfit nice all day."

"It would sure make us feel better to have her in jeans instead of trying to keep her from getting her clothes dirty."

"Yes, I guess I can understand that. Well," she says, standing up, "I really do have to go. Thanks for listening to me."

This problem was resolved quickly and easily by the caregiver listening and not getting defensive and angry herself. This particular problem of clothes is not always solved so easily. Some parents do not want their children to be away from home in anything but good clothes. They won't be persuaded so easily that it's better for everybody if the child arrives in play clothes. Sometimes this reflects a cultural attitude about school and has to do with the family wishing to retain a certain image.

Whether communication comes easily or not because of age, gender, or cultural differences or just individual differences, there are some ways that you can facilitate it. Here are some tips for opening and maintaining lines of communication with parents:

- Regard communication as a two-way process. If you're having problems with a child's behavior, the parent probably is too. Make it easy to exchange information.
- Develop your listening skills. Learn to listen for the feelings behind the words and discover ways to encourage parents to express those feelings without offending you.
- Develop a problem-solving attitude, and learn techniques of communication, mediation, and negotiation to use during conflict management and resolution.
- Keep records so you can report specifics.
- Make time available when it is clear that a parent needs to talk. It helps to have a comfortable place to sit.
- Try to talk to each parent every day at arrival and pick-up, even if you're busy.
- Try to make parents feel welcome whenever they are around, even if they pop in and disturb your program. In some teen parent programs on high school campuses, mothers come by between classes. It is hard on some of the children for a while because they have to learn to handle the more frequent hellos and good-byes. But it is important for the staff to be understanding about these parents' needs even though it makes their job harder.

Parent Education

**NAEYC Program
Standard 7**
Families

Your job is not only infant and toddler education but **parent education** as well. Education involves not just knowledge, but knowledge along with attitudes and skills. If you build a relationship, parents will be influenced by you in all these areas. But if you set yourself up as an expert and try to teach them directly, you may run into trouble. Knowledge alone doesn't change attitudes. They change over time with exposure to different people's values, ideas, methods, and attitudes. Most parents leave a program knowing more and feeling different from when they first enrolled, even if they never attend any kind of formal lecture on parenting or child development. If you can involve parents, over time they will pick up knowledge of child development by watching other children and seeing what is common behavior, by reading what you suggest, and by asking questions and having discussions with you. Parent involvement works best when parents feel welcome to take part in the program and help out on the side. Mandatory involvement moves parents away from a partnership role, unless the program is set up especially for parent participation and parents choose it. In that case, the main purpose of the program is parent education, and it comes about through actively working with the children and through discussion groups, parent meetings, and guest speakers. This model is the ideal way to augment the knowledge building that happens naturally when parents spend time around a center, even just for short drop-off and pick-up sessions.

Parents of Children with Special Needs

Parents of children with special needs may need to learn different things than do other parents. If these parents have not been exposed to other children before they come to your program, at first they may learn more than they want to know about typical development. It can come as a great shock to some parents to compare their children for the first time with children who don't have special needs. Be extra sensitive to their feelings.

Most parents are eager to learn more if they don't feel threatened or pushed. An invitation to observe or participate either occasionally or regularly is welcomed by many parents and is a further means to parent education. In a family child care home, a father regularly stayed an extra half hour in the afternoon when he had time. He would sit and play the piano and interact with the children who approached him. He not only contributed to the program but also gained knowledge just by being there.

Skill building comes gradually too. Parents come to you with varying degrees of parenting skills. Most will gain more by being exposed to professional caregivers. However, a danger lurks when caregivers present themselves as models for parents.

VIDEO OBSERVATION 14

Girl Crawling through Low Window (Parent Ed Program)

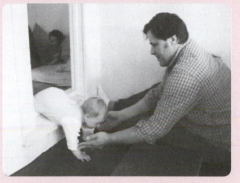

See Video Observation 14: Girl Crawling through Low Window (Parent Ed Program) for an example of a parent participation program. This particular one happens to have been started by Magda Gerber. Although you don't see the educarer (as Magda called caregivers), only the father, you can hear her voice encouraging and supporting his actions with his daughter. This is a good example of an infant solving a problem.

Questions

- This father is obviously nervous about leaving his daughter alone to solve the problem she had set up for herself. Do you think the caregiver was wrong in encouraging him not to help his daughter?
- What might be a cultural issue in this scene? Is it a specific cultural idea to allow, and even encourage, babies to solve problems by themselves?
- What would you have done if you had been the caregiver in this scene watching the father and his daughter?

To view this clip, go to **www.mhhe.com/itc10e**. Click on Student Edition, select Chapter 14, and click on Video Observations.

Early Care and Education Professionals

The parent role is different from your role as a professional caregiver, though it may look very similar at times. You don't have the shared history, nor will you be part of the child's future. You don't have the intensity of interest that brings about passionate exchanges. If the child "behaves just fine" with you and becomes a tyrant when the parent arrives, don't brag or feel superior. The explanation for the contrast is more likely to relate to the normal parent-child relationship and strong attachment than to your seemingly superior competence.

Children need competent caregivers, but they also need totally human, emotional, and connected parents. What you see as poor handling of a situation is more likely a parental handling rather than a professional handling. The two are different, though each should have many elements of the other. Parents operate (and should operate) more spontaneously from the gut level, reacting emotionally rather than responding reasonably. Of course, parents should also use their heads, should be objective now and then, and should build some of the competencies you have (which will happen to some extent through observing you). They should also gather information about child development and caregiving so they can *think* about what they are doing. But they should still parent mostly from gut reactions rather than from thought-out approaches. Parents should be far more human than competent. Caregivers also should be human and step out of their usual role now and then and interact intensely and passionately with children; but they should mostly be fairly objective and thoughtful in goals and reactions.

If you are both a parent and a caregiver, you can probably understand when you think about those times you handled things differently as a parent of your own child than you would have as the caregiver of someone else's. Perhaps at the time you felt guilty. But if you look at role differences, you can be glad that you are a normal parent. Your children deserve a real parent, not a professional caregiver. And other people's children deserve professional caregivers, not more parents.

That doesn't mean a professional caregiver should be cold and detached. If you've read this far in this book, you know that the message throughout has been to be real, to get connected, to feel your feelings. The point is balance. The balance swings more to feelings and spontaneity in the parenting role and more to thoughtfulness, objectivity, and planning in the caregiver role.

Relating to the Parents of a Child Who Isn't Doing Well

Sometimes, in spite of all your efforts in the parent relations and parent education department, you may have a child in your care who isn't doing well. He or she may be disrupting your whole program, taking a large portion of your time so that you have to worry about neglecting the other children. If you're in a center, the first step is to talk to other staff members (and the director). If you're in a family child care home, you may not have such a clearly defined problem-solving support group with which to discuss issues like this, but it is important that you find somebody—another child care provider perhaps.

You'll also want to talk to the parent(s)—not to place blame, but to get additional perspectives on the problem and further ideas for strategies to find ways to meet this child's needs. Teamwork and cooperation at home and in the program may work.

Or nothing may work. After trying and assessing various strategies, you may find that the child's behavior is still causing considerable turmoil. You'll probably also come to the conclusion that the situation isn't good for you, the other children, *or* the child. It is hard to realize that you can't meet every child's needs to the fullest extent. You may resist the idea that you can't be everything this particular family needs.

The next step is a **referral**. Perhaps some outside source can be of assistance to this family. Often that works. With specialized help the situation becomes tolerable, and you find you can meet the child's needs. But sometimes you have to realize that you've done all you can for a particular child, and it's time to ask the family to find care elsewhere. This is an extremely painful process for all concerned, but sometimes a necessary one.

Caregiver Relations

Staff relations are of extreme importance in a job as demanding as child care. In a family child care home, the issue is family relations, which is somewhat different. We'll deal with this subject briefly before discussing center staffs.

The Family Child Care Provider

Getting support is valuable if you are a family child care provider. But if the rest of your family is resentful, it may be hard to get their support. One family child care provider sat down and wrote out a contract with her family—husband and two preteen children—before she went into business. She felt it was important to be clear about the use of the house, which belonged to all four, and about what was or was not expected of each family member regarding the children in care. This contract was not something she forced them into; it was an agreement that they built together, considering everyone's ideas and feelings. In this family, the children were old enough to understand the contract, their rights, and their obligations. The contract saved the family a good deal of conflict.

In many family child care homes, conflict is the name of the game. If the children are younger, it's hard for them to understand why they have to share room, toys, even Mommy. Usually the agreements are less clear than a written and negotiated contract. As a result, a good deal of resentment, tension, and friction can arise. Some friction is, of course, normal but may be unexpected when a provider first goes into business. But in most families the advantages outweigh the disadvantages, and the friction falls into place with the other ordinary family conflicts.

Family child care providers also should look for support outside their own families. It is hard because you're tied to your home a good deal of the time, but if you look, you can find other family child care providers to talk to. The provider who worked out the contract with her family found another family child care provider in her own neighborhood through attending local support meetings. The two meet regularly at the park with their children (it's a short walk), so they have adult company as well as an outing for the children. No one can listen with more understanding to a family child care provider than another family child care provider. Find someone to talk to if you haven't already.

Center Staff

In a child care center setting, staff relations are different because you work together and are not related to one another. It's a strange situation to be around adults all day but seldom focus on them. That can create problems because you have little time to sit down and talk things out. Most child care staffs have staggered schedules, so the only time all the staff are there together is during the busiest time of the day, when the adults have little time to relate to each other. Some staffs working with older toddlers and preschool children are able to get together during naptime, but that won't work for most infant center staffs. In many centers, even breaks are staggered so that no two staff members are off the floor at the same time.

If child care were like other fields, there would be built-in time for staff meetings, for staff training, even provisions for staff renewal. But for many programs on a tight budget, those are unaffordable luxuries.

Obviously, staff members can seldom get off and talk to each other without the children around. And they need to talk to establish relationships, to settle conflicts, to share information on children and families, to set goals, to evaluate, and to share resources. Most of all they need adult contact to alleviate the isolation that adults who spend many hours a day with children commonly feel.

If you are new to the field and in a training program where you learn to focus almost exclusively on the children, you may be surprised to come into a center and see adults sitting around talking to each other while the children play. You may be quite critical if your training has made it sacrilege to focus on anything but the children when you are working (except on break). But over time, you may come to realize that those talks are important to staff members who work all day every day with very young children. And they are important to the children. How else are children to see adults relating to adults if their daily contact consists only of adults who focus on them and ignore the other adults present? Children need to see adults exhibit a wider range of behavior than what they see when the adults relate only to them.

In a three-hour program, it is still preferable to see adults concentrate mostly on the children, but that expectation is neither realistic nor desirable in all-day care. Of course, it isn't good policy to focus on adult relationships to the exclusion of the children and to the point of neglecting their needs. But if each child gets plenty of wants-nothing quality time when the caregiver is available to him or her during free play, as well as wants-something quality time during caregiving activities when the focus is on the individual child, the adult can relate to other adults while the children are present without neglecting the children.

Respect as the Key to Adult Relationships

Although the term *respect* has not been used so far in this chapter, that quality should underlie all the interactions adults have with each other—whether parent, family member, fellow staff member, or administrator—as well as with the children. Magda Gerber's influence of mutual respect and trust should be felt throughout the program, not just in the interactions between adults and babies.[2]

When Magda started talking about respectful care back in the 1970s, her ideas were new to those focused on infants and toddlers. She was proud of being some-what of a rebel. Nobody was using the word *respect* when talking or writing about infants and toddlers. Respect back then was something that young children had to learn to give elders. Gerber turned that around so that giving respect became a two-way process. By the end of the 1990s Magda was lamenting that she had lost her rebel status. Her ideas were everywhere and were no longer thought of as strange or new. The word *respect* is commonly used in the field of infant-toddler care. But from observations of how some caregivers treat parents and fellow caregivers, perhaps more attention should be paid to using the 10 principles when working with adults. Just consider these points:

1. *Principle 1 is about teamwork* and applies to adults as well as infants and toddlers. Do adults cooperate with each other, or do they work around each other to get the job done?
2. *Principle 2 is about quality time.* How often do adults spend quality time with one another? This question isn't about blaming anybody. The child care field makes it very hard to find time to really relate to each other in ways that build relationships. We need to advocate for our field to pro-vide for adult relationships. We also need to take advantage of the oppor-tunities that do arise.
3. *Principle 3 is about communication.* How hard do adults work to learn each other's unique ways of communicating? This is a big question if more than one language is spoken in the program. It's a smaller question if it means being sensitive to body language and getting to know each person well enough to be able to "read" him or her.
4. *Principle 4 is about investing time and energy to appreciate the whole person.* Do adults value some people more than others for particular qualities they have or do they appreciate each one for who he or she is?
5. *Principle 5 warns not to objectify people.* How often does one adult treat another as an object? It may be harder to see how principle 5 applies to adults because they are the same size, but when you consider status differences, prejudice, and bias, that may make principle 5 more meaningful.
6. *Principle 6 is about authentic feelings.* How honest are the adults in the pro-gram about their feelings? Do they hide them even from themselves, or do they bring their authentic selves to the relationships with the people they serve and work with?
7. *Principle 7 is about modeling.* Notice how many adults criticize others for particular behaviors that they themselves exhibit, although often they are not aware of that fact. Are you aware that we are more like our worst enemy than our best friend? Being consciously aware of behaviors and working on them is a worthwhile pursuit for all adults.

8. *Principle 8 is about recognizing problems as learning opportunities* and applies to adults just as it does to children. Infant-toddler programs are full of problems; working to solve them is part of the job and is good for the brain!

9. *Principle 9 is about trust.* Trust is an issue between caregivers and the families they serve, but it is also an issue among caregivers. Being trustworthy is a valuable trait and one to aim for.

10. *Principle 10 is about quality of development* and maybe brings us back to respect—self-respect. Caregivers need to develop an appreciation for adult development and learn ways to facilitate it rather than pushing it or criticizing other caregivers' or parents' shortcomings.

Appropriate Practice

Overview of Development

Each baby is different. No matter how well trained caregivers are, they need to learn about the babies in their care from the babies' families. Certainly, well-honed observation skills help caregivers get acquainted with each baby's needs, interests, and preferences, but no firsthand experience or training replaces what the family knows. Building a solid relationship from the time a child enters the program helps caregivers learn from the experiences and knowledge of the family. They also need to learn about the culture of the family, their goals, and their child-rearing beliefs. When caregivers value the family, the relationship becomes one of mutual support and learning. They are able to create an alliance. They maintain that alliance through regular and ongoing two-way communication between family and caregiver. The alliance is important when the infant is young and becomes a further source of strength and support when babies begin to move around. At that time babies enter a new stage of development mixed with feelings about separation and attachment. Working together, family and caregiver can support each other in discovering how to keep the infant feeling secure as they discuss safety issues and the need for changes in the environment both at home and

possibly in the program as well. Babies grow into toddlers whose feelings become more complex as they feel a conflict between independence and dependence, pride and shame, anger and tenderness—to name a few of the emotions toddlers experience. All these feelings challenge parents and caregivers. The adults can offer each other support through what can be a difficult time. Finally, toddlers are in the midst of their identity formation, which is rooted in the family and community. Only when caregivers know and understand can they support healthy identity formation.

Carol Copple and Sue Brededamp, eds., *Developmentally Appropriate Practice in Early Childhood Programs*, 3rd ed. (Washington, DC: National Association for the Education of Young Children, 2009).

Developmentally Appropriate Practice

Following are samples of developmentally appropriate practices that relate to the adult relations, particularly the family-caregiver alliance:

- Caregivers work in partnership with parents, communicating daily to build mutual understanding and trust.

- Caregivers help parents feel good about their children and their own parenting by sharing with them some of the positive and interesting things that happened with their children during the day.
- Caregivers and parents confer in making decisions about how best to support children's development or to handle problems or differences of opinion as they arise.

Source: Carol Copple and Sue Bredekamp, eds., Developmentally Appropriate Practice in Early Childhood Programs, 3rd ed. (Washington, DC: National Association for the Education of Young Children, 2009).

Individually Appropriate Practice

Following are samples of individually appropriate practices that relate to the adult relations:

- Caregivers and parents confer in making decisions about how best to support children's development or how to handle problems or differences of opinion as they arise.
- The key to meeting all children's needs is to individualize. Parents are the ones who know their children best. If children have special needs, it is even more important to talk to the parents and find out what they know and with what specialists they may be connected.

Source: Carol Copple and Sue Bredekamp, eds., Developmentally Appropriate Practice in Early Childhood Programs, 3rd ed. (Washington, D.C.: National Association for the Education of Young Children, 2009).

Culturally Appropriate Practice

Following are samples of culturally appropriate practice:

- Caregivers work in partnership with parents, communicating daily to build mutual

understanding and trust and to ensure the welfare and optimal development of the infant. Caregivers listen carefully to what parents say about their children, seek to understand parents' goals and preferences, and are respectful of cultural and family differences.

- Cultural and family differences can create goals and priorities that conflict with those of the center or family child care program. Toilet training in some families' traditions occurs in the first year of life instead of the second or third, for example. When caregivers set themselves up as experts on child development and judge families without understanding cultural issues, they put up barriers to working in partnership with families.

Source: Carol Copple and Sue Bredekamp, eds., Developmentally Appropriate Practice in Early Childhood Programs, 3rd ed. (Washington, DC: National Association for the Education of Young Children, 2009).

Appropriate Practice in Action

Look back at the Principles in Action on pages 313–314. Then return to this page and read the first item in the "Developmentally Appropriate Practice" section of the Appropriate Practice box and both items under the "Individually Appropriate Practice" section.

1. Do you think Emily's provider is showing evidence of a partnership with her parent's attitude?
2. What if the provider had felt insecure around the mother and, to keep her status as a professional provider, had pretended she was an expert in children with cerebral palsy? How might this scene have turned out very differently?
3. Is it more important to learn to read the signals of children who have special needs than it is to learn to read the signals of all children in your care?

This chapter has been about adult relations and their importance to the children in child care. Children need to see their caregivers as full human beings, and they can't if they don't see them in relation to other adults—their parents as well as other staff members.

Summary

Adult relations change and communication is enhanced when a program takes a family-oriented approach and regards parents as partners.

Parent-caregiver relations

- An important aspect of adult relationships in infant-toddler programs is realizing that caregivers tend to go through stages of relating to parents.
- Communication with parents is important and involves understanding what blocks communication and what opens it up. This understanding is especially important when working with parents of children who have special needs.

Parent education

- Parent education can occur informally as parents and other family members see what is going on in the program. Parent involvement can help family members feel welcome and encourage them to spend more time in the program, but it should be voluntary.
- The goal of parent education should not be to make the parent into a professional caregiver. Caregivers and parents have different roles, and that is as it should be.

Caregiver relations

- Caregiver relations take on different meanings depending on whether the caregiver is a family child care provider or a member of a center-based staff.
- Respect is a key component of all relationships—both those that adults have with children and those that adults have with each other.

Key Terms

comfort device 314
conference 317
dialogue 317
intake interview 317

needs and services plan 314
parent education 322
referral 325
savior complex 312

Thought/Activity Questions

1. Caregivers are mandated reporters. What does that term mean?
2. What are some ways to make parents feel comfortable during a conference with their child's caregiver?
3. Interview caregivers to see if you can tell in which stage of development they are. Is there anything to indicate that they are saving children from their parents, educating the parents to be as good as they are, or seeing parents as partners?
4. When thinking about communicating with and supporting parents, what additional issues may be present with a parent whose child has a disability or special need?
5. Suppose you work with someone from a culture different from your own who has very different ideas about child rearing and caregiving. What steps would you take to open up communication between the two of you?

For Further Reading

Linda Gillespie and Sandra Petersen, "Rituals and Routines: Supporting Infants and Toddlers and Their Families," in *Developmentally Appropriate Practice: Focus on Infants and Toddlers*, ed. Carol Copple, Sue Bredekamp, Derry Koralek, and Kathy Charner (Washington, DC: National Association for the Education of Young Children, 2013), pp. 102–104.

Janet Gonzalez-Mena, "Cultural Sensitivity in Caregiving Routines: The Essential Activities of Daily Living," in *Infant/Toddler Caregiving: A Guide to Culturally Sensitive Care*, 2nd ed., ed. Elita Amini Virmani and Peter L. Mangione (Sausalito, CA: WestEd and Sacramento, CA: California Department of Education, 2013), pp. 56–65.

Janet Gonzalez-Mena, *50 Strategies for Communicating and Working with Diverse Families*, 3rd ed. (Upper Saddle River, NJ: Pearson, 2014).

Karen N. Nemeth and Valeria Erdosi, "Enhancing Practices with Infants and Toddlers from Diverse Language and Cultural Backgrounds," *Young Children* 67(4), September 2012, pp. 49–57.

Mariana Souto-Manning, "Family Involvement: Challenges to Consider, Strengths to Build on," *Young Children* 65(2), March 2010, pp. 82–89.

Quality in Infant-Toddler Programs: A Checklist

1. Look for evidence of a *safe* environment:
   - ☐ No obvious safety hazards, such as electric cords, open sockets, broken equipment, toys with small parts, cleaning supplies within children's reach, unsecured doorways
   - ☐ No hidden safety hazards, such as toxic paint or toys containing toxic materials
   - ☐ Fire and disaster plan that includes how adults will get babies outside
   - ☐ Emergency numbers posted by telephone
   - ☐ Parents' emergency cards on file indicating what to do when the parents can't be reached in an emergency
   - ☐ Safe ratios maintained at all times (California law reads no more than four infants [children under two] to one adult)
   - ☐ Children allowed optimum risk-taking opportunities ("optimum" means failure involves learning but not injury)
   - ☐ Interaction allowed, but children protected from hurting materials or one another

2. Look for evidence of a *healthy* environment:
   - ☐ Sanitary diaper-changing process
   - ☐ Consistent hand washing after diapering and before eating
   - ☐ Proper food preparation and storage
   - ☐ Staff recognizes symptoms of common illnesses
   - ☐ Health policies that indicate when children are to be excluded from the program because of illness
   - ☐ Health records, maintained on all children, showing evidence that their immunizations are up to date
   - ☐ Regular washing of sheets and toys
   - ☐ Staff knowledge of infant and toddler nutritional needs
   - ☐ Food allergies posted prominently

3. Look for evidence of a *learning* environment:
   - ☐ Optimum amount of age-appropriate toys, materials, and equipment
   - ☐ Caregivers consider caregiving times as "learning times"
   - ☐ Free play valued above exercises, directed play activities, group times

☐ Environment includes plenty of softness, some seclusion, provisions for high mobility

☐ Environment developmentally appropriate for all children present any given day

4. Look for evidence that the staff's goal is to advance physical and intellectual competence:

☐ Staff's ability to explain how the environment, the free play, the caregiving activities, and the staff's relationship with the children make up the curriculum

☐ Staff's ability to explain how the curriculum promotes development of fine and gross motor skills and cognitive skills, including problem-solving and communication skills

5. Look for evidence that the program supports social and emotional development and that staff members provide positive guidance and discipline:

☐ Staff members encourage children to develop a sense of themselves through body awareness, by using their name, and through promoting cultural identification

☐ Staff members recognize and accept children's feelings and encourage appropriate expression

☐ Staff members guide behavior without using either physical or verbal punishment

☐ Staff members encourage creative social problem solving when children experience conflict with another child

☐ Staff members teach respect by showing respect

6. Look for evidence that the program strives to establish positive and productive relationships with families:

☐ Regular and ongoing communication with parents at pick-up and drop-off times emphasizing an *exchange* of information

☐ Friendly atmosphere

☐ Conferences and parent meetings

☐ Mutual problem-solving approach to conflicts

7. Look for evidence that the program is well run and purposeful and responds to participants' needs:

☐ Good record keeping

☐ Attention to infants' individual needs

☐ Attention to parents' needs

☐ Responsible program management

8. Look for evidence that the staff is professional:

☐ Is well trained

☐ Respects confidentiality

Environmental Chart

This chart shows how to set up both the physical and the social environment to promote development. Remember that rates of development vary a great deal among children. These age guides may not fit individual children, but the chart as a whole does reflect the *sequence of development*.

Level I: Development After Birth

Area of Development	Physical Environment	Social Environment
Physical *Large Muscles* Infants' primary task is head control • Can lift head briefly • Can turn head to clear nose for breathing • Most arm and leg movements are reflexive and are not under infants' conscious control *Small Muscles* • Cannot control hands—often keeps them clenched • Grasp whatever is put into hands because of reflexive action • Stare at objects, especially faces; begin to coordinate eyes	**Appropriate Toys and Equipment** • Crib or bassinet, a place to feel secure while sleeping • Mat, rug, or blanket in a safe space to lie unencumbered with room to move around • Few toys needed yet because environment is stimulating enough • Faces are interesting, and so is a bright-colored scarf • Don't put rattles or toys into hands because they can't let go of them	**Adult Role** • Use sensitive observation to determine infants' needs • Provide a feeling of security when necessary (wrap infants in a blanket and place in a small enclosed space) • Let infants experience wide open space, like the floor, at times • Provide peace and quiet and a minimal amount of stimulation—people infants associate with (caregiver and other children) provide enough stimulation • Put infants in a safe spot where they can be part of the center but not overstimulated • Call infants by name • Encourage infants to focus on caregiving tasks
Emotional/Social *Feelings and Self-Awareness* • Infants show only satisfaction or dissatisfaction • Does not differentiate self from the rest of the world	• Infants need to be where safe and secure and needs can be easily met • Large playpen provides safety from more mobile toddlers (should be large enough to hold both adults and children)	• Respond to infants' messages and try to determine real needs (remember that dissatisfaction is not always due to hunger)

Emotional/Social

Social

- May smile
- Make eye contact
- Are soothed by faces
- Respond to being held

Intellectual

- Can coordinate eyes and follow objects or faces as they move
- Respond to faces or objects they see
- Suck and gum objects that come near the mouth
- Display reflexes that are the beginnings of the sensory skills, which in turn provide the basis for the development of intellectual skills

Language

- Listen
- Cry
- Respond to voices

Appropriate Toys and Equipment

- Very young infants need a quiet, safe environment that is not overstimulating. After babies discover their hands, make available a limited variety of soft, washable, colorful toys to be looked at or sucked on (be sure there are no small parts to come off and be swallowed)
- Allow infants to move freely (though they can't yet go anywhere)
- Don't prop in infant seat or other restrictive device

- At this level, people are more important for language development than is physical environment
- Set up environment so that infants' needs are easily met and they don't have to wait for long periods of time

Adult Role

- Provide for attachment needs by having a consistent caregiver
- Hold during feeding
- Provide for infant-to-infant contact
- Minimum adult interference—infants should be free to develop at their own rates
- Give them faces to look at (especially that of the primary caregiver) and opportunities to see, touch, and gum objects
- Don't force anything on them
- Place them on their backs so they can have a broader view, both ears can hear, and they can use their hands

- Listen to infants
- Try to interpret their cries
- Talk to infants, especially during caregiving times; tell them what will happen; give time for a response; tell them what is happening as it happens

Level II: Month 3

Area of Development	Physical Environment	Social Environment
Physical *Large Muscles* • Beginning to lose reflexes and have voluntary control of arms and legs • Gaining some head control	**Appropriate Toys and Equipment** • Large playpen, big enough for caregivers and several infants • Variety of washable objects within reach of infants for them to look at and stretch for • Rug or mat for infants to lie on • Avoid restrictive devices	**Adult Role** • Sit with children periodically and watch attentively • Respond when called for • Don't continually distract with unnecessary noise or talk; entertainment isn't necessary • Allow infants freedom to explore through looking, sucking, stretching, and reaching
Small Muscles • Grasp reflex no longer takes over hands all the time • Reach for objects with both arms but with hands fisted • Swipe and miss	• Same as above	• Same as above
Emotional/Social *Feelings and Self-Awareness* • Show wider variety of feelings and use voice to express them • Begin to see hands and feet belong to them and begin to explore them, as well as face, eyes, and mouth, with hands • Begin to recognize primary caregiver • Respond differently to different people • Coo and babble when talked to	• People are more important than objects	• Provide for attachment needs because infants need to develop a primary relationship • Recognize and respect infants' feelings: talk about what infants seem to be expressing, especially during caregiving
Intellectual • Respond to what they see • Attend longer than at first • Look from one object to another • Can hold object on their own and manipulate to some extent • Give signs of remembering • When they hear a noise, they look for the source • Look and suck at the same time but have to stop sucking to listen	• Some interesting toys and objects for infants at this level of development include bright cotton scarves, soft balls, rattles, squeeze toys, plastic keys	• Encourage exploration and curiosity by providing a variety of objects of different textures, shapes, and sizes • Allow children freedom and peace to explore by putting them on their back in a safe area large enough for them to move freely • Provide for interaction with other infants
Language • Listen attentively • Coo, whimper, gurgle, and make a variety of other sounds • Cry less often • "Talk" to themselves as well as to others, particularly primary caregiver	• People are still more important than equipment or objects for language development • Avoid toys that make noise from some hidden device so the baby doesn't see where the noise is coming from. That includes many toys for babies including rattles and squeaky toys	• Talk to infants, especially during caregiving routines; prepare them ahead of time for what is going to happen. Allow time for them to respond after you say and indicate what you will do next • Respond to babbling and cooing— play sound games with infants

Level III: Month 6

Area of Development	Physical Environment	Social Environment
Physical *Large Muscles* • Have control of head • Turn from back to stomach and stomach to back • May move from place to place by rolling • May creep or inch forward or backward • May almost get to sitting while rolling over *Small Muscles* • Reach with one arm and can grasp at will • Hold objects and manipulate them • Can grasp with thumb and forefinger but not well yet • Change objects from one hand to the other	**Appropriate Toys and Equipment** • Need more open space and freedom than before • Need a variety of textures under their body—hard floor, rugs, grass, wooden deck, etc. • Need a variety of interesting objects to move and reach toward	**Adult Role** • Place objects far enough from them so that infants must work to get them • Provide plenty of room and motivation for moving around as well as manipulating and grasping objects • Provide for interaction with other infants • Keep infants in positions they can get in by themselves
Emotional/Social *Feelings and Self-Awareness* • Display a wider variety of feelings • Becoming aware of body parts • See difference between self and rest of the world • Respond to name • Have taste preferences • May want to start self-feeding *Social* • May respond with fear to strangers • Call to primary caregiver for help • Enjoy games with people (peekaboo)	• Space large enough for exploration and social interactions will promote relationships	• Talk to infants, especially during caregiving; place special emphasis on naming body parts • Call children by name • Encourage children to take over self-help skills as they are able
Intellectual • Visually alert a good part of waking hours • Recognize familiar objects • Can see and reach for objects they want • Can pick up and manipulate objects • Look for dropped objects • Can use several senses at once • Memory is developing **Language** • Respond to different voice tones and inflections • More control over sounds produced • Use a variety of sounds to express feelings • Imitate tones and inflections	• Infants continue to enjoy all the toys and objects listed in Level II under Intellectual Development • Can now appreciate a wider variety of objects at once • Place objects around a safe area so that infants have reason to move around and reach for them • Cloth or cardboard books	• Provide for attachment needs and let children use primary caregiver to provide security in presence of stranger • Respond to babies playing games like peekaboo • Allow children freedom to explore • Change or rearrange objects in the environment periodically • Provide for interaction with other infants • Respond to children's communication • Talk to children, especially during caregiving routines • During playtimes, comment on what children are doing if appropriate (be careful not to interrupt so the words get in the way of the experience)

Level IV: Month 9

Area of Development	Physical Environment	Social Environment
Physical *Large Muscles* • Crawl • May crawl stiff-legged • May crawl while holding object in hand • Pull to stand on furniture • May stand alone • May or may not be able to get back down from standing • Get into sitting position • May move along holding on to furniture *Small Muscles* • Can pick up small objects easily with thumb and forefinger • Explore and manipulate with forefinger • Growing in eye-hand coordination	**Appropriate Toys and Equipment** • Infants need more room to explore and a greater variety of objects, textures, experiences, toys • Plastic or wooden cars and trucks, play or real telephones, blocks, dolls, balls of different sizes, nesting toys • Pillows and low platforms (or steps) can be added to the environment to provide a variety of levels for children to explore • Rails or low furniture needed for standing or cruising	**Adult Role** • Watch for children who stand up but can't sit back down; help when they indicate they are stuck • Be sensible about helping children who get stuck; don't rescue them but promote problem solving • Provide open spaces and safe climbing opportunities • Allow children to explore with little adult interference • Encourage infants to use manipulative skills, such as pulling off socks, opening doors, taking apart nesting toys
Emotional/Social *Feelings and Self-Awareness* • Clearly attached to primary caregiver and may fear separation • Reject things they don't want *Social* • Feed selves biscuit • Drink from cup holding handle • Becoming sensitive to and interested in the moods and activities of others • Tease • Anticipate events	• Need the tools for self-help, such as cup and spoon	• Provide enough of a schedule for infants to come to anticipate the sequence of events • Allow opportunities for uninterrupted concentration • Encourage problem solving • Don't help until they're really stuck • Allow them to discover the consequences of their behavior whenever it is safe to do so
Intellectual • Remember games and toys from previous days • Anticipate people's return • Can concentrate and not get interrupted • Pull cover off toy they have seen hidden • Enjoy taking things out of container and putting them back • Solve simple manipulative problems • Interested in discovering the consequences of their behavior	• The objects and toys listed under Physical Development are also appropriate for promoting intellectual development • Also provide interesting and safe objects from the adult world—pots, pans, wooden spoons, and junk such as discarded boxes, both big and little (infants appreciate real objects as much as toys)	• Provide the opportunity for infants to become assertive • Help children interpret the effect of their actions on others • Give plenty of opportunities for children to develop self-help skills • Help children express separation fears, accept them, and help them deal with them • Provide for attachment to primary caregiver • Provide good models for children (adults who express honest feelings, neither minimized nor exaggerated)

Language
- Pay attention to conversations
- May respond to words other than own name
- May carry out simple commands
- Use words such as *mama* and *dada*
- Have intonation
- May repeat a sequence of sounds
- Yell

Appropriate Toys and Equipment
- Appreciate a greater variety of picture books

Adult Role
- Include infants in conversations
- Don't talk about them if they're present unless you include them (especially important at this stage)
- Promote interactions with other infants
- Respond to infants' sounds
- Encourage use of words
- Ask questions infants can respond to

Level V: Month 12

Area of Development	Physical Environment	Social Environment
Physical *Large Muscles* • Can stand without holding on • May walk but probably prefer to crawl • Climb up and down stairs • May climb out of crib *Small Muscles* • May use both hands at the same time for different things • Use thumbs well • May show preference for one hand • May undress self or untie shoes	**Appropriate Toys and Equipment** • Need lots of space both indoors and outdoors to enjoy crawling and practice walking • Need lots of objects to manipulate, explore, experiment with, and carry around	**Adult Role** • Provide for safety and plenty of movement • Don't push children to walk—allow them to decide when they are finished with crawling
Emotional/Social *Feelings and Self-Awareness* • Show wide variety of emotions and respond to those of others • Fear strangers and new places • Show affection • Show moods and preferences • May know difference between their possessions and those of others	• Provide an environment that encourages and facilitates self-help skills	• Provide for self-help skills • Acknowledge infants' possessions and help protect them • Give approval • Set reasonable limits • Accept uncooperative behavior as a sign of self-assertion • Give choices • Give and return affection • Accept and help infants deal with fears and frustrations
Social • Feed self • Help dress self • Obey commands • Seek approval but are not always cooperative	• Provide needed tools and equipment for self-help skills	• Encourage self-help skills
Intellectual • Good at finding hidden objects • Increased memory • Solve problems • Use trial-and-error method effectively • Explore new approaches to problems • Think about actions before doing them (sometimes) • Imitate people who are not present	• Children at this level enjoy most of the toys and household objects already mentioned but use them in more sophisticated ways • Also enjoy large beads to string, large LEGO blocks, small building blocks, stacking cones, wooden snap trains, etc.	• Promote active problem solving • Provide for interaction with other children • Set up environment so children see new and more complex ways to use toys and equipment
Language • Know words stand for objects • Begin to sound like they speak the language of their parents (use same sounds and intonations) • Use gestures to express self • May say two to eight words	• Toy telephones, dolls, and books promote language development at this level • Any toy can become a reason to talk as children play • Music promotes language development	• Promote interaction among children; children learn to talk from adults, but they practice as they play with other children • Give simple instructions • Play games with children • Sing songs and do finger plays • Encourage expression of feelings • Fill in missing words and expand utterance for children when responding

Level VI: Month 18

Area of Development	Physical Environment	Social Environment
Physical *Large Muscles* • Walk fast and well • Seldom fall • Run, but awkwardly • Walk up stairs holding a hand *Small Muscles* • Can use crayon to scribble as well as imitate marks • Better control at self-feeding	**Appropriate Toys and Equipment** • Need room to walk and run • Enjoy taking walks if adult isn't too goal oriented • Enjoy plenty of sensory experiences such as water play and sand	**Adult Role** • Keep the environment full and interesting but not chaotic; may need to change arrangement periodically and introduce new toys • Promote interactions among children • Allow for enough physical exercise
Emotional/Social • Imitate adults in dramatic play • Interested in helping with chores • Interested in dressing process; can undress to some extent • May be beginning to get some bladder and bowel control	• Provide the tools for dramatic play, such as dress-up clothes, dolls, housekeeping equipment, dishes	• Allow children to help as they are able • Set limits and gently but firmly enforce them • Encourage self-help skills • Help children with their interaction and talk them through aggressive situations
Intellectual • Can begin to solve problems in their head • Rapid increase of language development • Beginning of ability to fantasize and role-play	• Provide a variety of toys available on low shelves for children to choose from—small people, animals, doll houses, containers filled with small objects, measuring cups, spoons, etc.	• Provide a number of choices • Help children work on a problem uninterrupted • Encourage use of language
Language • May use words to gain attention • Can use words to indicate wants • May know 10 words • Enjoy picture books	• Books with clear, simple pictures	• Provide a variety of experiences and help children put language to them • Ask questions and encourage children to ask them too • Read aloud

Level VII: Month 24

Area of Development	Physical Environment	Social Environment
Physical *Large Muscles* • Run headlong, have trouble stopping and turning • Walk up and down stairs (may hold on) • Throw a ball • Kick a ball forward *Small Muscles* • Put on some easy clothing • Hold spoon, fork, cup but may still spill • Can use a paintbrush but don't control drips • Can turn the pages of a book	**Appropriate Toys and Equipment** • Low climbers and slides • Large balls, both lightweight and heavier • Low three- and four-wheeled, steerable, well-balanced vehicles, both with pedals and without • Swings children can get into and out of themselves • Hills, ramps, low stairs • Space to run • Large, lightweight blocks • Wooden puzzles with two to four large pieces • Pegboards • Stacking toys • Big beads to string • Construction sets (easy to put together) • Play dough • Rhythm instruments • Texture matching games • Feely boxes • Sand and water and toys to play with in them • Dolls to dress and mostly *undress* • Books • Felt pens, crayons, finger paint	**Adult Role** • Encourage freedom to move in any way they like (within limits, of course) • Allow for plenty of physical and sensory experiences • Encourage children to find new ways to combine and use familiar toys and equipment • Offer choices • Allow loving chases or loving wrestles • Play circle games and sing songs with movements (but not with the whole group as a circle time compulsory activity) • Encourage small-muscle use by offering a wide variety of choices • Offer a number of sensory activities • Allow children to use toys and materials in creative ways (within limits, of course) • Allow children to combine materials and toys in unique ways (within limits, of course) • Facilitate problem solving when children get stuck
Emotional/Social • May understand personal property concepts ("That's mine," "That's Daddy's") • May tend to hoard possessions; may resist sharing • Assert independence ("Me do it!") • Take pride in accomplishments • May say no even to things they want	• Provide space for personal possessions (cubbies or boxes) • Provide duplicates of favorite toys so sharing isn't such an issue • Provide plenty of things to do so sharing isn't such an issue • Hand puppets sometimes allow children to express their feelings • Art, music, and dramatic play experiences (listed under Small Muscles) allow children to express their feelings • Large-muscle experiences also allow children to express their feelings	• Respect children's need to hold on to their possessions • Model sharing rather than require it • Allow children to try things by themselves, even when you know you can do them better or faster • Help them have accomplishments they can take pride in

Intellectual
- Can identify parts of a doll—hair, ears, etc.
- Can fit forms into a form board
- Can solve many problems on their own
- Can work simple puzzles

Language
- Use personal pronouns (I, me, you) but not always correctly
- Refer to themselves by name
- Use two- and three-word sentences
- May know as many as 50 to 200 words
- Talk about what they are doing

Appropriate Toys and Equipment
- Provide books, puzzles, records, in addition to toys listed above, that allow choices and provide opportunities for concept development and problem solving

- Provide a good variety of books (children can use them carefully now)
- Pictures at child's eye level around the room, changed often, give children something to talk about
- Allow and set up "happenings"—experiences that give children something to talk about
- Provide for music experiences

Adult Role
- Provide a variety of choices of materials to use and ways to spend time
- Give freedom to use materials in creative ways
- Encourage problem solving
- Allow exploration

- Encourage conversation between children and between child and adult
- Help children speculate ("I wonder what would happen if . . .")
- Go places and talk about what you do and see
- Encourage verbalization of feelings and wants
- Help children begin to talk out differences instead of relying on hitting, kicking, and other negative physical behaviors

Level VIII: Month 36

Area of Development	Physical Environment	Social Environment

Physical

Large Muscles
- Walk, run with control, climb well, throw a ball with aim
- Jump in place
- Balance on one foot for a second or two
- May pedal tricycle

Small Muscles
- Put on shoes but don't tie laces
- Put on clothing except for buttoning
- Feed self alone and well
- Scribble with more control
- Draw or copy a circle
- Use paintbrush and control drips
- Use construction toys imaginatively
- May exercise bowel and bladder control

Appropriate Toys and Equipment
Need all the toys and equipment listed for the 24-month-old, but larger versions that provide more challenges. The 36-month-old can begin to use the equipment designed for preschoolers and is probably ready to move on from the toddler program.
- May enjoy some large wooden blocks, balance boards, planks, boxes, ladders for building
- Unit blocks and accessories to go with them
- Construction sets with more and smaller pieces
- Small-wheeled vehicles to go with blocks
- Sensory table
- Puzzles
- Objects to sort
- Flannel board and figures
- Small beads to string
- Wide range of art materials, including paint, collage, scissors, glue, crayons, felt pens, chalk
- Dolls and accessories
- Doll house
- Extensive dramatic play equipment
- Puppets

Adult Role
- Offer choices
- Can move gross motor equipment outside for this age group and expect them to be slightly more restrained inside
- Be careful about encouraging gross motor experiences in boys more than in girls (they should get equal encouragement; indeed, girls should get extra encouragement if they are reluctant)
- Allow plenty of choices
- Encourage children to use toys and materials in creative ways
- Find ways that older children can become involved in small-muscle manipulative activities without being interrupted by younger children who want to dump rather than build
- Keep small parts from younger children, who might put them in their mouths
- Encourage fine motor activities in both boys and girls (if boys are less interested, find materials that entice them)

Emotional/Social
- May show regard for people or possessions
- Play with sustained interest
- Play and interact with another child
- Willing to use toilet
- Can conform to group for short periods

- Provide space for personal possessions
- Provide plenty of materials to allow children to share feelings and to role-play, such as dramatic play equipment, dress-up clothes, puppets, dolls, small figures, musical instruments and experiences, art materials
- Books that children can identify with also help them express their feelings
- Have toilet readily available

- Begin to encourage sharing and cooperative play
- Help children get involved and stay involved in play activities by preventing interruptions by other children
- Can expect children to participate in short active group times, such as circle time
- Encourage interaction among children

Intellectual

- May count to two or three
- May draw face or very simple figure
- Can work simple puzzles
- More sophisticated problem solving
- Call self "I" and other people "you"
- Know he is a boy or she is a girl
- Know most of the parts of the body
- Compare sizes

Language

- Use plurals
- Converse in short sentences, answer questions, give information, use language to convey simple ideas
- Name pictures and label actions
- May have 900-word vocabulary
- Articulate fairly clearly

Appropriate Toys and Equipment

- The variety of construction materials, manipulative toys, dramatic play, and art materials listed above all contribute to intellectual development
- Objects to sort
- Plenty of puzzles
- Parquetry blocks
- Simple games such as Lotto
- Simple, hands-on science displays and experiments

- Setting up the environment for gross motor, fine motor, social, emotional, and intellectual experiences should provide plenty for the children to talk about
- Add to variety and complexity of books and pictures provided for two-year-olds
- Music experience
- Simple hands-on science displays and experiments

Adult Role

- Provide plenty of choices
- Encourage peer interaction during problem solving
- Encourage absorption, involvement with materials, activities, and people
- Encourage an inquiring attitude
- Encourage creative thinking
- Encourage children to think about past experiences as well as future ones
- Encourage development of number concepts in a natural context

- Encourage comparisons of size, weight, etc., of objects in a natural context
- Read books, tell stories, sing songs
- Embed language in all experiences
- Encourage questioning
- Encourage conversations
- Encourage speculation
- Encourage verbal conflict resolution
- Encourage verbalization of feelings
- Help children listen to one another
- Play language games such as Lotto

Notes

Chapter 1

1. We use the word *caregivers*, but others prefer *infant care teacher* or *infant-toddler teacher*, or *teacher*, or in the case of family child care, *provider*. Magda Gerber's Resources for Infant Educarers (RIE) used the term *educarer*. At the Pikler Institute the term is *nurse*, though the caregivers there have not studied medicine.
2. Linda Acredolo and Susan Goodwyn, *How to Talk with Your Babies Before They Can Talk* (Lincolnwood, IL: Contemporary Books, 1996).
3. See further explanation in Janet Gonzalez-Mena, *Diversity in Early Care and Education: Honoring Differences* (New York: McGraw-Hill, 2008).
4. Although expression of anger has been used as an example of relating in a respectful way to infants and toddlers, it is important to note that this particular example is culture bound. Not all cultures believe in the individual's right to express feelings unless that expression somehow serves the group.
5. The DVD *On Their Own with Our Help* is available through the RIE Store, at www.rie.org.
6. This hands-off approach is a cultural issue. In some cultures, children are taught that graciously receiving help is a skill to be learned and is more important than standing on their own two feet. See further explanation in Janet Gonzalez-Mena, *Diversity in Early Care and Education: Honoring Differences* (New York: McGraw-Hill, 2008).

Chapter 2

1. Anna Tardos, ed., *Bringing Up and Providing Care for Infants and Toddlers in an Institution* (Budapest: Association Pikler-Loczy for Young Children, 2007). Miriam David and Geneviève Appell, *Lóczy: An Unusual Approach to Mothering*, trans. by Judit Falk (Budapest: Association Pikler-Lóczy for Young Children, 2001).
2. Magda Gerber and Allison Johnson, *Your Self-Confident Baby* (New York: Wiley, 1998); Magda Gerber, *Dear Parent: Caring for Infants with Respect* (Los Angeles: Resources for Infant Educarers, 1998); Ruth Anne Hammond, *Respecting Babies: A New Look at Magda Gerber's RIE Approach* (Washington, DC: Zero to Three, 2009).
3. Nel Nodding, *Educating Moral People: A Caring Alternative to Character Education* (New York: Teachers College Press, 2002); ibid., *Starting at Home: Care and Social Policy* (Berkeley and Los Angeles: University of California Press, 2002); ibid., *The Challenge to Care in Schools* (New York: Teachers College Press 1992).
4. J. Ronald Lally, "Brain Research, Infant Learning, and Child Care Curriculum," *Child Care Information Exchange*, May/June 1998, pp. 46–48.
5. Patti Wade, letter to author, October 1978.
6. Abraham H. Maslow, *Toward a Psychology of Being*, 2nd ed. (New York: Van Nostrand, 1968), p. 51.
7. Albert Bandura's social learning theory is based on the idea that modeling is a powerful teaching tool. Bandura's research showed that people are influenced by each other's behaviors. Later researchers

became fascinated with how infants, starting at a very young age, imitate others. Albert Bandura, *Social Learning Theory* (Englewood Cliffs, NJ: Prentice Hall, 1977).

8. Paula J. Bloom, P. Eisenberg, and E. Eisenberg, "Reshaping Early Childhood Programs to Be More Family Responsive," *America's Family Support Magazine* 21(1–2), Spring/Summer 2003, pp. 36–38; Damien Fitzgerald, *Parent Partnership in the Early Years* (London: Continuum, 2004); Janis Keyser, *From Parents to Partners: Building a Family-Centered Early Childhood Program* (St. Paul, MN: Redleaf Press; Washington, DC: National Association for the Education of Young Children, 2006); Lisa Lee, *Stronger Together: Family Support and Early Childhood Education* (San Rafael, CA: Parent Services Project, 2006); Cherry A. McGee-Banks, "Families and Teachers Working Together for School Improvement," in *Multicultural Education: Issues and Perspectives*, 6th ed., ed. James A. Banks and Cherry A. McGee-Banks, (New York: Wiley, 2007), pp. 402–410; Ethel Seiderman, "Putting All the Players on the Same Page: Accessing Resources for the Child and Family," in *The Art of Leadership: Managing Early Childhood Organizations*, ed. Bonnie and Roger Neugebauer. (Redmond, WA: Exchange Press, 2003), pp. 58–60.

9. Urie Bronfenbrenner, *The Ecology of Human Development: Experiments by Nature and Design* (Cambridge, MA: Harvard University Press, 1979); ibid., "Ecological Models of Human Development," in *International Encyclopedia of Education*, 2nd ed., vol. 3, ed. Torsten Husén and T. Neville Postlethwaite (Oxford, UK: Pergamon, 1994), pp. 1643–1647; Urie Bronfenbrenner and Pamela A. Morris, "The Ecology of Developmental Processes," in *Handbook of Child Psychology*, vol. 1, *Theoretical Models of Human Development*, 5th ed., ed. William Damon (series ed.) and Richard M. Lerner (vol. ed.) (New York: Wiley, 1998), pp. 993–1028.

10. Barbara Rogoff, *The Cultural Nature of Human Development* (Oxford and New York: Oxford University Press, 2003).

11. Ibid.

12. David L. Kirp, *The Sandbox Investment* (Cambridge, MA: Harvard University Press, 2007).

13. Bruce Fuller and his colleagues looked long and hard at the idea of school readiness policies aimed at giving all children an equal start before they got to school. His conclusion was that though there was some evidence of benefit to children of low-income families if what was offered was comprehensive, not just academic skill-building, there is no evidence that middle-income children benefit from such policies. Fuller also pointed out that scientific evidence is only one factor in addressing early education, not the whole story because child rearing is more related to ideals than to science and school readiness. Bruce Fuller, *Standardized Childhood: The Political and Cultural Struggle over Early Education* (Stanford, CA: Stanford University Press, 2007).

14. Paul Tough, *Whatever It Takes: Geoffrey Canada's Quest to Change Harlem and America* (Boston: Mariner Books, 2009).

15. Ibid., p. 279.

16. For more information on HCZ and Baby College, see www.hcz.org.

17. See more about Early Head Start and the National Resource Center at http://www.ehsnrc.org.

Chapter 3

1. See www.pikler.org and www.RIE.org.

2. J. Ronald Lally, "The Impact of Child Care Policies and Practices on Infant/Toddler Identity Formation," *Young Children* 51(1), November 1995, pp. 58–67. In this article, Lally makes a compelling case for the importance of such practices as primary-caregiving systems.

3. Anna Tardos, ed., *Bringing Up and Providing Care for Infants and Toddlers in an Institution* (Budapest: Association Pikler-Loczy for Young Children, 2007); Miriam David and Geneviève Appell, *Lóczy: An Unusual Approach to Mothering*, trans. by Judit Falk (Budapest: Association Pikler-Lóczy for Young Children, 2001).

4. Janet Gonzalez-Mena, *Diversity in Early Care and Education: Honoring Differences* (New York: McGraw-Hill, 2008); Mubina Hassanali Kirmani, "Empowering Culturally and Linguistically Diverse Children and Families," *Young Children* 62(6), November 2007, pp. 94–98.

5. University of Texas Medical Branch at Galveston, "Mother's Milk: A Gift That Keeps on Giving," *Science Daily*, September 15, 2007.

6. American Academy of Pediatrics, "Breastfeeding Promotion in Physicians' Office Practices:

Phase II," *Breastfeeding: Best for Baby and Mother*, Spring 2004; www.aap.org/breastfeeding/newsletter3104.pdf.

7. American Academy of Pediatrics, "Merging Motherhood with the Military," Spring 2004; www.aap.org/breastfeeding/newsletter3104.pdf.

8. Anne Morrow Lindbergh, *Gift from the Sea* (New York: Pantheon, 1955), p. 104.

9. Mubina Hassanali Kirmani, "Empowering Culturally and Linguistically Diverse Children and Families," *Young Children* 62(6), November 2007, pp. 94–98.

10. For the complete study results, look for the "Feeding Infants and Toddlers Study" in the *Journal of the American Dietetic Association*, January 2004.

11. What you saw in that scene was based on an observation at the Pikler Institute in November 2003. The description is adapted from an article by Janet Gonzalez-Mena, "What Can an Orphanage Teach Us? Lessons from Budapest," *Young Children*, 58(5), September 2004, pp. 27–30. At the Pikler Institute, the idea of caregiving as curriculum is taken very seriously. Adults are trained in specific ways to carry out each caregiving routine, and the result is that the infants and toddlers in this residential nursery are trusting and secure in the relationships they have with their caregivers. Fulfilled with the kind of individual attention they get during those times of the day, they then are able to explore freely the rest of the time, playing alone and with each other with little or no adult interruptions. Granted, this is a very specific curriculum coupled with a good deal of training, and nothing is done casually. The approach has been developed, studied, and refined since 1946. We aren't suggesting that you adopt the model, but we are suggesting that the fact the Pikler Institute created their own unique curriculum through observation and research can inspire others to do the same.

12. A search of "diaper free" and "elimination communication" at the Amazon.com website in April 2014 showed eight books written in the last few years about how to potty train babies before a year old. Also, Kahwaty's book gives information about how to potty train not one infant, but two at the same time! Donna Hoke Kahwaty, "Toilet-Training Newborns: Parents Grab Hold of Trend to Potty-Train Infant Twins," *Twins*, March/April 2006, pp. 20–23.

13. A summary of findings on SIDS is by Neil K. Kaneshiro, MD, MHA, Clinical Assistant Professor of Pediatrics, University of Washington School of Medicine. Also reviewed by David Zieve, MD, MHA, Medical Director, A.D.A.M., Inc.; ADAM Health Illustrated Encyclopedia, 08/02/2009. S. M. Beal and C. F. Finch, "An Overview of Retrospective Case Control Slides Investigating the Relationship Between Prone Sleep Positions and SIDS," *Journal of Paediatrics and Child Health* 27(6), 1991, pp. 334–339; National Institute of Child Health and Human Development, NIH Pub. No. 02-7040, Back to Sleep Campaign pamphlet, September 2002; B. C. Galland, B. J. Taylor, and D. P. G. Bolton, "Prone versus Supine Sleep Position: A Review of the Physiological Studies in SIDS Research," *Journal of Paediatrics and Child Health* 38(4), 2002, pp. 332–338. The majority of findings suggest a reduction in physiological control related to respiratory, cardiovascular, and autonomic control mechanisms, including arousal during sleep in the prone position. Because the majority of these findings are from studies of healthy infants, continued reinforcement of the supine sleep recommendations for all infants is emphasized.

14. The suggestions in this chapter fit the overall philosophy of the book, which is based on the values of independence and individuality. It's important to note that not all cultures have these values. Therefore, these approaches to caregiving should be discussed with the families, and some agreement should be reached. See Janet Gonzalez-Mena, *Diversity in Early Care and Education* (New York: McGraw-Hill, 2008), for more information on how to communicate with parents regarding cultural issues. Also see Elita Amini Virmani and Peter L. Mangione, eds., *A Guide to Culturally Sensitive Care*, 2nd ed. (Sacramento, CA: California Department of Education and WestEd, 2013).

15. See note 13.

Chapter 4

1. For example, Deborah Carlisle Solomon, *Baby Knows Best* (New York: Little, Brown, 2013); Eva Kallo and Gyorgyi Balog, *The Origins of Free Play* (Budapest: Association Pikler-Loczy for Young Children, 2005); Alison Gopnik, "Let the Children Play. It's Good for Them!"

Smithsonian Magazine, July-August, 2012; David Brooks, "The Psych Approach," *New York Times*, September 27, 2012; Elena Bedrova and Deborah J. Leong, *Tools of the Mind: The Vygotskian Approach to Early Childhood Education*, 2nd ed. (Upper Saddle River, NJ: Pearson/Merrill Prentice Hall, 2007); David Elkind, *The Power of Play* (Cambridge, MA: DeCapa, 2007); Elizabeth Jones and Renatta M. Cooper, *Playing to Get Smart* (New York: Teachers College Press, 2006); Sharon Lynn Kagan, Catherine Scott-Little, and Victoria Stebbins Frelow, "Linking Play to Early Learning and Development Guidelines," *Zero to Three*, 30(1), September 2009; Dorothy Singer, Roberta Golinkoff, and Kathy Hirsh-Pasek, eds., *Play = Learning: How Play Motivates and Enhances Children's Cognitive and Social-Emotional Growth* (New York: Oxford University Press, 2006).

2. S. Rosenkoetter and L. Barton, "Bridges to Literacy: Early Routines That Promote Later School Success," *Zero to Three* 22(4), February/March 2002, pp. 33–38.

3. Papert's story has two major points. One is that when children play with concrete objects the way Papert did with gears, they build models that transfer what they learn through their senses to their minds, which then allows them to mentally manipulate ideas for further understanding. The other point is that Papert "fell in love with gears." Obviously someone supported and encouraged him and provided materials, but Papert was the one who made the choice to use them. Early play provided an important foundation for later learning and understanding. Seymour Papert, *Mindstorm: Children, Computers, and Powerful Ideas* (New York: Basic Books, 1980), p. vi.

4. Carla Hannaford, *Smart Moves: Why Learning Is Not All in Your Head* (Salt Lake City: Green River, 2005); Rae Pica, "Babies on the Move," *Young Children* 6(4), July 2010, pp. 48–49.

5. Elena Bodrova and Deborah Leong, *Tools of the Mind: The Vygotskian Approach to Early Childhood Education*, 2nd ed. (Upper Saddle River, NJ: Pearson/Merrill Prentice Hall, 2007).

6. The Significance of Grit: A Conversation with Angela Lee Duckworth, http://www.ascd.org/publications/educational-leadership/sept13/vol71/num01/The-Significance-of-Grit@-A-Conversation-with-Angela-Lee-Duckworth.aspx; Carol Dweck, *Mindset* (New York: Ballantine, 2007); Carol Garhart Mooney, *Theories of Attachment* (St. Paul, MN: Redleaf, 2010); Janet Gonzalez-Mena, "What Can an Orphanage Teach Us? Lessons from Budapest," *Young Children*, 59(5), September, 2004, pp. 26–30.

7. Magda Gerber, "From a Speech by Magda Gerber," *Educaring* 16(3), Summer 1995, p. 7.

8. J. McVicker Hunt, *Intelligence and Experience* (New York: Ronald Press, 1961), p. 267.

9. Judith Van Horn, Patricia Monighan Nourot, Barbara Scales, and Keith Rodriquez Alward, *Play at the Center of the Curriculum* (Columbus, OH: Merrill, 2007).

10. Abraham H. Maslow, *Toward a Psychology of Being*, 2nd ed. (New York: Van Nostrand, 1968), pp. 55–56.

11. "Once upon a Screen" Stephen Koepp, ed. *The Science of You* (New York: Time Books, 2013), pp. 106–109.

Chapter 5

1. R. Shore, *Rethinking the Brain: New Insights in Early Development*, rev. ed. (New York: Families and Work Institute, 2003), pp. 16–24.

2. K. Gallagher, "Brain Research and Early Child Development: A Primer for Developmentally Appropriate Practice," *Young Children* 60(4), July 2005, pp. 12–20.

3. M. Klaus and J. Kennell, *Parent-Infant Bonding* (St. Louis: Mosby, 1982), p. 2.

4. R. Restak, *The Naked Brain* (New York: Three Rivers Press/Random House, 2006), pp. 58–70.

5. Ibid., pp. 91–99.

6. R. Isabella and J. Belsky, "Interactional Synchrony and the Origins of Infant-Mother Attachment," *Child Development* 6, 1991, pp. 373–384.

7. M. Ainsworth, M. Blehman, E. Waters, and S. Wall, *Patterns of Attachment: A Psychological Study of the Strange Situation* (Hillsdale, NJ: Erlbaum, 1978), pp. 333–341.

8. O. Mayseless, "Attachment Patterns and Their Outcomes," *Human Development* 39, 1996, pp. 206–223.

9. H. Harlow, "The Nature of Love," *American Psychology* 13, 1958, p. 386.

10. J. Bowlby, *Attachment*, vol. 1 of *Attachment and Loss* (New York: Basic, 2000), p. 343.

11. J. R. Lally, "Brain Research, Infant Learning, and Child Care Curriculum," *Child Care Information Exchange* 121, May/June 1998, pp. 46–48.

12. C. P. Edwards and H. Raikes, "Relationship-Based Approaches to Infant/Toddler Care and Education," *Young Children* 57(4), July 2002, pp. 10–17.

13. A report from the National Joint Committee on Learning Disabilities, "Learning Disabilities and Young Children: Identification and Intervention," *Learning Disability Quarterly* 3, Winter 2007, pp. 63–72.

Chapter 6

1. J. M. Mandler and L. Douglas, "Concept Formation in Infancy," *Cognitive Development* 8, 1993, pp. 291–318.

2. M. H. Johnson, *Developmental Cognitive Neuroscience*, 2nd ed. (Malden, MA: Blackwell, 2005), pp. 186–204.

3. R. Samples, *The Metaphoric Mind* (Menlo Park, CA: Addison-Wesley, 1976), p. 95.

4. T. G. R. Bower, *Development in Infancy*, 2nd ed. (San Francisco: W. H. Freeman, 1982), pp. 87–99.

5. P. W. Jusczyk and R. N. Aslin, "Infants' Detection of the Sound Patterns of Words in Fluent Speech," *Cognitive Psychology* 29, 1997, pp. 1–23.

6. D. R. Mandel, P. W. Jusczyk, and D. B. Pisoni, "Infants' Recognition of the Sound Patterns of Their Own Names," *Psychological Science* 6, 1995, pp. 314–317.

7. T. Nakake and S. Trehub, "Infants' Responsiveness to Maternal Speech and Singing," *Infant Behavior and Development* 27, 2004, pp. 455–464.

8. J. E. Steiner, "Human Facial Expressions in Response to Taste and Smell Stimulation," *Advances in Child Development and Behavior* 13, 1979, pp. 257–295.

9. S. W. Porges and L. P. Lipsitt, "Neonatal Responsivity to Gustatory Stimulation," *Infant Behavior and Development* 16, 1993, pp. 487–494.

10. K. Simons, ed., *Early Visual Development: Normal and Abnormal* (New York: Oxford University Press 1993), pp. 439–449.

11. *A Parent's Guide: Finding Help for Young Children with Disabilities (Birth to 5)*, a publication of the National Dissemination Center for Children with Disabilities, downloaded from www.nichcy.org/ InformationalResources/Documents/nichcy%20 pubs/pa2.pdf.

Chapter 7

1. S. J. Fomon and S. E. Nelson, "Body Composition of the Male and Female in Reference to Infants," *Annual Review of Nutrition* 22, 2002, pp. 1–17.

2. P. M. Thompson and J. N. Giedd, "Growth Patterns in the Developing Brain," *Nature* 404, 2000, pp. 190–192.

3. P. Casaer, "Old and New Facts About Perinatal Brain Development," *Journal of Child Psychology and Psychiatry* 34, 1993, pp. 101–109.

4. M. A. Bell and N. A. Fox, "Brain Development over the First Year of Life," in *Human Behavior and the Development of the Brain*, ed. G. Dawson and K. W. Fischer (New York: Guilford Press, 1998), pp. 314–345.

5. K. Gallagher, "Brain Research and Early Child Development: A Primer for Developmentally Appropriate Practice," *Young Children* 60(4), July 2005, pp. 12–20.

6. E. Pikler, "Some Contributions to the Study of the Gross Motor Development of Children," *Journal of Genetic Psychology* 113, 1968, pp. 27–39.

7. E. Thelen and L. B. Smith, "Dynamic Systems Theories," in *Handbook of Child Psychology*, vol. 1, ed. W. Damon (New York: Wiley, 1998), pp. 563–633.

8. The *Bayley Scales of Infant Development (BSID)*, first published in 1969, was originally intended to measure three major developmental domains— cognitive, motor, and behavioral. The third, current edition, *The Bayley Scales of Infant and Toddler Development (Bayley-III)* adds two more domains— social-emotional and adaptive. See Nancy Bayley, *The Bayley Scales of Infant and Toddler Development*, 3rd ed. (San Antonio, TX: Pearson Education, 2005). Table 7.2 is based on the 1993 second edition; the milestones for motor development, however, have remained essentially the same since the 1993 revision.

9. J. Faulk, "Development Schedules Stimulating Adult Educational Attitudes," in *The RIE Manual for Parents and Professionals*, ed. M. Gerber, 2nd ed. (Los Angeles: Resources for Infant Educarers), 2013, pp. 101–107.

10. É. Kálló and G. Balog, *The Origins of Free Play* (Budapest: Association Pikler-Lóczy for Young Children, 2005), p. 16.

11. Emmi Pikler, "Data on Gross Motor Development of the Infant," *Early Development and Care* 1, 1972, pp. 297–310; S. Petrie and S. Owen, *Authentic Relationships in Group Care for Infants and Toddlers: Resources for Infant Educarers (RIE) Principles into Practice* (London and Philadelphia: Jessica Kingsley Publishers, 2005).

Chapter 8

1. J. H. Flavell, "On Cognitive Development," *Child Development* 53, 1982, pp. 1–10.
2. L. Berk and A. Winsler, *Scaffolding Children's Learning: Vygotsky and Early Childhood Education* (Washington, DC: National Association for the Education of Young Children, 1995), p. 22.
3. J. R. Lally, "Brain Research, Infant Learning, and Child Care Curriculum," *Child Care Information Exchange* 121, May/June 1998, pp. 46–48.
4. M. Diamond, *Magic Trees of the Mind* (New York: Plume, 1998), pp. 112–120.
5. S. Rushton, "Applying Brain Research to Create Developmentally Appropriate Learning Environments," *Young Children* 56(5), September 2001, pp. 76–82.
6. "Early Childhood Inclusion," A Joint Statement of the Division for Early Childhood (DEC) and the National Association for the Education of Young Children (NAEYC), 2009, http://community.fpg.unc.edu/resources/articles/early_childhood_inclusion.
7. Fact Sheet: "Including All Kids: Am I? Should I? Can I?" http://ecdc.syr.edu/includingallkids.pdf.

Chapter 9

1. L. Vygotsky, "Play and Its Role in the Mental Development of the Child," in *Play: Its Role in Development and Evolution*, ed. J. Bruner, A. Jolly, and K. Sylvia (New York: Basic Books, 1976).
2. A. L. Woodward and E. M. Markman, "Early Word Learning," in *Handbook of Child Psychology:* vol. 2. *Cognition, Perception and Language*, 5th ed., ed. W. Damon (series ed.), D. Kuhn and R. S. Sieger (vol. eds.) (New York: Wiley, 1998), pp. 371–420.
3. S. Begley, "How to Build a Baby's Brain," *Newsweek*, Spring/Summer 1997, pp. 28–32.
4. See Dr. Kuhl lecture at www.google.com, "Patricia Kuhl," "video on TED.com."

5. R. Restak, *The Naked Brain* (New York: Three Rivers Press/Random House, 2006), pp. 58–72.
6. D. L. Mills, S. A. Coffey-Cornia, and H. J. Neville, "Variability in Cerebral Organization During Primary Language Acquisition," in *Human Behavior and the Developing Brain*, ed. G. Davidson and K. W. Fischer (New York: Guilford Press, 1994), pp. 427–455.
7. A. Wetherby, "First Words Project: An Update, Florida State University," in *Proceedings of the NAEYC* (Portland, OR: National Institute for Early Childhood Professional Development, 2003).
8. R. Parlakian, "Early Literacy and Very Young Children," *Zero to Three*, September 2004, pp. 37–44.
9. L. Makin, "Literacy 8–12 Months: What Are Babies Learning?" *Early Years: Journal of International Research and Development* 26(3), October 2006, pp. 267–277.
10. B. Otto, *Literacy Development in Early Childhood: Reflective Teaching for Birth to Age Eight* (Columbus, OH: Pearson/Merrill, 2008), pp. 63–79.
11. Ibid., p. 80.
12. S. B. Heath, *Ways with Words: Language, Life, and Work in Communities and Classrooms* (New York: Cambridge University Press, 1983).
13. These core principles were developed by the Training and Technical Assistance Collaboration (TTAC), an interagency partnership in California dedicated to serving children with disabilities birth to age five. For more information, e-mail ttac@wested.org.

Chapter 10

1. F. Leboyer, *Birth without Violence* (New York: Random House, 1978).
2. R. Thompson and R. Goodvin, "The Individual Child: Temperament, Emotion, Self, and Personality," in *Developmental Science: An Advanced Textbook*, 5th ed., ed. M. Borstein and M. Lamb (Hillsdale, NJ: Erlbaum, 2005), pp. 391–428.
3. S. Chess and A. Thomas, *Temperament: Theory and Practice* (New York: Brunner/Mazel, 1996).
4. The Goodness of Fit model is discussed in A. Thomas and S. Chess, *Temperament and Development* (New York: Brunner/Mazel, 1977).
5. M. K. Rothbart, B. A. Ahadi, and D. E. Evans, "Temperament and Personality: Origins and Outcomes," *Journal of Personality and Social Psychology* 78, 2000, pp. 122–135.

6. S. C. Luthar, D. Cicchetti, and B. Becker, "The Construct of Resilience: A Critical Evaluation and Guidelines for the Future," *Child Development* 74, 2000, pp. 543–562.

7. A. H. Maslow, *Toward a Psychology of Being* (New York: Van Nostrand, 1968), p. 157.

8. Ibid., pp. 163–164.

9. L. Gilkerson, "Brain Care: Supporting Healthy Emotional Development," *Child Care Information Exchange* 121, May 1998, pp. 66–68.

10. K. C. Gallagher, "Brain Research and Early Childhood Development: A Primer for Developmentally Appropriate Practice," *Young Children* 60(4), July 2005, pp. 12–20.

11. The effect of labeling emotions is taken from G. Tabibnia, M. Craske, and M. Lieberman, "Linguistic Processing Helps Attenuate Psychological Reactivity to Aversive Photographs after Repeated Exposure," paper presented at the 35th Annual Meeting of the Society for Neuroscience, Washington, DC, November 12–26, 2005.

12. R. Shore, *Rethinking the Brain* (New York: Families and Work Institute, 1997), pp. 28–30.

13. Ibid., pp. 41–43.

14. Mark L. Batshaw, *Children with Disabilities* (Baltimore, MD: Paul H. Brookes, 2007), pp. 511–521.

15. Mary Beth Bruder, "Early Childhood Intervention: A Promise to Children and Families for Their Future," *Exceptional Children* 76(3), Spring 2010, pp. 339–345.

16. Ibid., pp. 350.

Chapter 11

1. T. G. R. Bower, *Development in Infancy*, 2nd ed. (San Francisco: W. H. Freeman, 1982), p. 256.

2. Jaipaul L. Roopnarine and Alice S. Honig, "The Unpopular Child," *Young Children* 49(6), September 1985, p. 61.

3. Doyleen McMurtry, early childhood instructor, Solano College, Suisun, CA.

4. J. R. Lally, "The Art and Science of Child Care," *Program for Infant/Toddler Caregivers*, WestEd, 180 Harbor Drive, Suite 112, Sausalito, CA.

Chapter 12

1. Janet Gonzalez-Mena, "What Works: Assessing Infant and Toddler Play Environments," *Young Children*, 68(4), pp. 22–25, 2013; Elizabeth Prescott, "The Physical Environment: Powerful Regulator of Experience," *Child Care Information Exchange*, Reprint #4, C-44, Redmond, WA 98052. This article was first published in 1968 and then republished in the November/December 1994 issue of *Child Care Information Exchange*. The entire article is now available to read online at www.ChildCareExchange.com, in the "Resources for You FREE" section.

2. Susan Aronson and Patricia M. Spahr, *Healthy Young Children: A Manual for Programs* (Washington, DC: National Association for the Education of Young Children, 2002).

3. Louis Torelli, "The Developmentally Designed Group Care Setting: A Supportive Environment for Infants, Toddlers and Caregivers," *Zero to Three*, December 1989, pp. 7–10.

4. See note 1, Prescott, "The Physical Environment."

5. Roger G. Barker, *Ecological Psychology: Concepts and Methods for Studying the Environment of Human Behavior* (Stanford, CA: Stanford University Press, 1968).

6. Éva Kálló and Györgyi Balog, *The Origins of Free Play*, trans. Maureen Holm (Budapest: Association Pikler-Lóczy for Young Children, 2005); Miriam David and Geneviève Appell, *Lóczy: An Unusual Approach to Mothering*, trans. Judit Falk (Budapest: Association Pikler-Lóczy for Young Children, 2001).

7. These ideas come from Molly Sullivan, who used them in her family day care home in Berkeley, California.

8. Elizabeth Jones and Elizabeth Prescott, *Dimensions of Teaching-Learning Environments II: Focus on Day Care* (Pasadena, CA: Pacific Oaks, 1978).

9. Louis Torelli, "The Developmentally Designed Group Care Setting: A Supportive Environment for Infants, Toddlers, and Caregivers," *Zero to Three* 10(2), pp. 7–10, 1989.

10. Ruth Money, "The RIE Early Years 'Curriculum,'" in *Authentic Relationships in Group Care for Infants and Toddlers: Resources for Infant Educarers (RIE) Principles into Practice*, ed. Stephanie Petrie and Sue Owen (London and Philadelphia: Jessica Kingsley Publishers, 2005), pp. 51–68.

11. Jim Greenman, "Designing Infant/Toddler Environments," in *Caring for Infants and Toddlers: What Works, What Doesn't*, vol. 2, ed. Robert Lurie

and Roger Neugebauer (Redmond, WA: Child Care Information Exchange, 1982).

12. Sherry Turkle, "Once Upon a Screen," *The Science of You*, ed. Stephen Koepp (New York: Time Books, 2013) pp. 106–109.

Chapter 13

1. J. Ronald Lally, "The Impact of Child Care Policies and Practices on Infant/Toddler Identity Formation," *Young Children* 51(1), November 1995, pp. 58–67.

2. The following have a good deal of information about the research showing advantages in bilingual education for even the youngest children. Karen Nemeth, *Many Languages, One Classroom: Teaching Dual and English Language Learners* (Beltsville, MD: Gryphon House, 2009); Jim Cummins, *Bilingual Children's Mother Tongue: Why Is It Important for Education*, http://iteachilearn.org/cummins/, 2008; Linda Espinosa, *Challenging Common Myths about Young English Language Learners* (New York: Foundation for Child Development, 2007); Patton O. Tabors, *One Child, Two Languages* (Baltimore, MD: Paul. H. Brookes, 2008).

3. Marian Marion, *Guidance of Young Children*, 6th ed. (Upper Saddle River, NJ: Merrill/Prentice Hall, 2003).

4. Lisa Delpit, *Other People's Children* (New York: New Press, 1995); *Multiplication is for White People.* (New York: The New Press, 2011).

5. In *Black Children: Their Roots, Culture, and Learning Styles*, Janice Hale-Benson discusses how discipline works in the black community. Every adult in the community is expected to firmly correct undesirable behavior even when someone else's child is the one misbehaving. Any misbehavior is not only immediately corrected but is reported to the parent as well. In other words, in the black community, there is a social control network that takes responsibility for all the children in that community. Children aren't on their own; they're always being watched by somebody. Hale-Benson says that this approach is different from that in schools, where the teachers don't watch so closely because they expect the children to develop inner controls. Therefore, children who are used to being diligently observed and controlled find themselves more on their own than they're used to. Parents who expect to be notified immediately of any misbehavior may find school a lax place where there seem to be fewer external pressures to keep children behaving properly. See Janice E. Hale-Benson, *Black Children: Their Roots, Culture, and Learning Styles* (Baltimore: Johns Hopkins University Press, 1986), p. 85.

Chapter 14

1. A teenage parent may rely on her mother or may at least need to consult with her mother. A wife may need her husband's approval to make decisions. Sometimes the grandmother, rather than the parents, makes decisions concerning her grandchildren. Some families have joint decision making. It's of no use to discuss a problem with a mother if she has no authority to make any decision. The family structures in some cultures leave someone other than the mother, or even the father, as the ultimate decision maker.

2. Polly Elam writes about the mutual respect and trust she experienced with Magda Gerber as her mentor in "Creating Quality Infant Group Care Programs," in *Authentic Relationships in Group Care for Infants and Toddlers: Resources for Infant Educarers (RIE) Principles into Practice*, ed. Stephanie Petrie and Sue Owen (London and Philadelphia: Jessica Kingsley Publishers, 2005), pp. 83–92.

References

References for the text are provided online at www.mhhe.com/itc10e.

Glossary

ability to predict The skill to expect or know what will happen.

accommodation From Piaget's theory, the process of taking new information into the mind/body in such a way as to readjust, refine, or expand previous mental categories.

activity Something that somebody does. A learning experience. Specifically, for purposes of distinguishing infant-toddler education from preschool education the word activity in this book relates to the processes of daily living (such as diapering, dressing, feeding) carried out by the adult with the cooperation of the child.

adaptive behavior Normal or useful. Adaptive behavior includes the ability to adjust to new situations and apply familiar or new skills or organize behavior to better fit a situation.

aesthetics Visually appealing. When adults value aesthetics, they demonstrate that value in the way they design environments for infants and toddlers.

anecdotal records A documentation method that briefly describes an activity, a snatch of conversation, a chant, and so on. Anecdotal records can be based on reflection or written on the spot.

assimilation From Piaget's theory, the process of taking new information into the mind/body by incorporating it into previously developed mental categories.

assisted learning Social interaction, according to Lev Vygotsky, supports early language development as well as problem solving. The belief is that children's learning is assisted by their interactions with more knowledgeable people; co-constructed.

attachment An enduring affectionate bond between a child and a person who cares for the child, giving the child a feeling of safety or security. Building a trusting secure attachment through consistency, responsiveness, and predictability shows children they can trust the caregiver to meet their needs (physical, mental, emotional). Attachment allows children to feel safe in their environment and therefore comfortable to explore and venture out.

autonomy Being independent and responsible for one's actions. Includes feelings of power and a sense of competence in making choices. The second stage of Erik Erikson's psychosocial development.

axon A filament extending from a nerve cell from which neural impulses are transmitted.

bilingualism Having the ability to speak and understand two languages.

body awareness Knowing where one's body is in space and learning its capabilities. Seen to emerge in infants and toddlers as their motor skills develop.

body wisdom Children's ability to be in their body, know what it needs, and have confidence in how it works and moves.

brain plasticity Capacity for regions of the brain and individual neurons within these regions to adapt and take on different functions as a result of experience.

caregiver presence Two ways of relating to infants that are a part of the two kinds of quality time. In wants-something quality time, the caregiver's presence is active. The caregiver has a task to perform, and though he or she may be gentle and responsive, the caregiver is giving direction to the interaction. The other type of caregiver presence is receptive; that is, the infant is the directive one who initiates the action and the caregiver responds to that action.

cephalocaudal An organized pattern of physical growth and motor control that proceeds from head to foot.

cerebral cortex The largest, most complex structure of the human brain; responsible for higher-level thinking and intelligence; surrounds the rest of the brain (much like a half-shelled walnut).

cognitive experience Gathering information, organizing it, and finally using it to further one's understanding and know one's world.

comfort device An object or action that may be of comfort to the child, also known as a transitional object. May be used during the departure of a parent or before naptime to help the child make the transition into a new routine.

conditioning A relearning of one's behavioral response to react in a certain way when presented with specific stimuli.

conference A meeting with parents arranged with a goal in mind, such as sharing information, thoughts, questions, and concerns, with the purpose of gaining insights and planning long-range goals collaboratively.

constructing new knowledge A view based on Jean Piaget's work that suggests that children don't passively receive knowledge through being taught but rather actively construct it themselves.

continuity of care A method used in child care to keep infants and toddlers with the same caregiver(s) over a period of time. Desirable for building trust and security through attachment. The time can vary, but two years is a goal, and three years is even better.

cultural identity Part of self-concept, cultural identity relates to everything we do; how we look and talk, what we eat, where we live, and how we look at the world.

curriculum A plan for learning that is all-inclusive and centers on connections and relationships with an infant or toddler in a caregiving center or family child care. Focus is on education and care that responds to and respects the child's needs in warm, respectful, and sensitive ways that promote attachment. Respectful and responsive curriculum is based on relationships that occur within planned and unplanned activities, experiences, and happenings.

dendrites Fibers extending from neurons that receive input from neighboring neurons.

dialogue Communication in which different points of view are listened to and nondefensive language is used to promote open communication and problem solving.

documentation A variety of records that represent children's learning, skill building, social-emotional development or thought processes. Documentation captures the processes and products of children's daily experiences and can be in the form of written records, but also can include photographs, tape recordings, and videos.

dual language learners children who speak a language other than English who are learning English. The term also applies to children whose home language is English, when they are in bilingual programs where they are learning another language. In some programs all the children are learning two languages.

emergent literacy The holistic, ongoing experience of becoming literate; it is the process of learning to read and write. This philosophy allows literacy to unfold naturally for very young children in a developmentally appropriate, responsive environment.

emotion Affective response to an event that is personally relevant. Emotions come from within the individual but may be triggered by an external event. Emotional states include happiness, surprise, anger, envy, and sadness.

environmental limit A physical barrier that keeps a child or a material out of or inside of a given space. Environmental limits may also be accompanied by a verbal limit, such as "the water stays in the pan."

exploration Act of discovering and examining one's environment, people, objects, and properties of objects through touching, mouthing, smelling, seeing, and hearing. Providing a safe, developmentally appropriate environment that accommodates the various abilities allows for exploration, which can result in a variety of discoveries.

expressive language The *result* of the process of refining sounds and messages received during the first 12 months; it culminates in the clear expression of the first word(s), usually at or by one year.

fast mapping The speedy (and sometimes not very precise) process of acquiring vocabulary by connecting a new word with an underlying concept after only a brief encounter.

feeling A physical sense or awareness of an emotional state. An emotional response to an event or interaction.

five senses Touch, hearing, smell, sight, and taste are all ways stimuli from the environment are taken into the central nervous system for processing.

floor time The opposite of time-out, when instead of having attention removed, a toddler who is exhibiting difficult behavior has an adult who pays full attention to the child (down on the floor) and is responsive rather than directive.

free play The name given undirected but monitored play when children have choices to pursue their special interests without continual adult control or expected outcome.

gender identity Part of self-concept, how a child perceives of himself or herself as a boy or girl. Influenced by the messages received from others and the media regarding expectations and relative value of boys and girls.

gross motor Physical movement that requires the use of larger muscles such as rolling over, pulling up, climbing, walking, running, jumping.

gross motor activity An activity using the large muscles of the arms, legs, and trunk, such as climbing, rolling, sliding, running, and so on.

happenings The preferred word in this book for learning activities occurring during infant-toddler play and exploration. A broad term intended to encompass the simplest event as well as more prolonged and complicated experiences. These are not happenstance events; they involve intentionality. Adult intention is one part, related to the planning, preparation, and facilitating that go into them. The intention of the child is equally important as adults observe, learn, and understand what the child is trying to do so they can facilitate if necessary. The word *activity* is avoided because it tends to put people in a preschool mode.

individualized family service plan (IFSP) A written plan for early intervention consisting of the child's level of development, the family's strengths and needs, goals for the infant and family, and the specific early intervention services needed to meet the goals. Developed by a team including parents and a variety of infant specialists.

infant stimulation An approach to infant education based on the idea that stimulating the senses helps infants develop. What is missing from this approach is the idea that infants left on their own in a rich sensory environment can make choices about what to take in. Having sensory experiences by choice is different from being stimulated by someone. Further, when the stimulation comes from the outside, infants can be overwhelmed and feel powerless.

initiative Sense of purposefulness and effectiveness. Energy related to creating, inventing, and exploring. Third stage of Erik Erikson's psychosocial development, occurring at the onset of preschool age.

inner controls Another word for self-control. The goal is to help children learn to control their own behavior instead of depending on someone or something outside themselves.

intake interview Interview conducted when a child is admitted to a program or center. A service plan for both the child and parent is assessed at this time to help meet their needs through the scope of the curriculum or outside resources.

intentionality Engaging in an action deliberately in a way that is congruent with one's purpose or goal.

interactional synchrony Mutually reciprocal behaviors that mesh, seen in caregiver-child interactions.

interactions Mutual and reciprocal actions that relate one to another. Through chains of respectful and responsive interactions caregivers build relationships with infants and toddlers in their care.

language The ability to produce symbols and sounds that represent meaning, influenced by emotional and social development. Development of language is context-dependent. The words (symbols), their pronunciation, and the methods of combining them used and understood by a large group (generalized meaning).

learning tool Anything that is safe and interesting can be a source of learning for an infant or a toddler. Some examples are books, scarves, flannel boards, cardboard boxes, and blocks.

limits Boundaries placed on a child's behavior. They can be physical boundaries from the environment, such as gates or locked doors, or verbal boundaries, such as reminding children to sit while they have food in their mouth. Children will test invisible boundaries in order to discover them.

literacy The ability to listen and speak, and eventually to read and write.

locomotion The ability to move independently; related in this text to large or gross motor skill development.

manipulation The ability to move skillfully with the hands and fingers; related in this text to small or fine motor skill development.

memory The ability to retain and recall past experience, including images or thoughts.

mirror neuron A special kind of nerve cell that reacts the same when an animal acts and when that animal observes another animal acting, leading researchers to theorize that this finding has an important relationship to infants' ability to imitate. The implications point to current research on early attachment, movement, language, and social cognition.

mixed-age groups Groups of children of varying ages, more common in family child care.

model To set an example by performing behaviors, actions, and interactive styles that others observe and imitate. Infants and toddlers learn from modeled behavior, so modeling can be a conscious teaching strategy and also a means of guidance.

mouthable A characteristic of a toy or material that makes it appropriate for infants and toddlers, who learn about the nature of objects and their properties by putting them in their mouths.

multicultural, multilingual curriculum Gaining an understanding of the families' caregiving practices, listening to how they would like you to be with their child, and incorporating this information into your caregiving with their child. Being respectful and reflective of the various cultures and languages in your community by addressing the linguistic needs of all children including the dual language learners.

myelinization The building or increasing of the myelin sheath that acts as an insulator around the axon with neural fibers allowing for efficient transmission of messages by the brain. Deterioration of the myelin sheath is caused in part by teratogen ingestion and could lead to delayed processing of information by the brain.

needs and services plan Information regarding the child and family's routine, habits, special needs, and ways of communicating. Also, any needs, concerns, or requests for social support or intervention. Opening communication between the family and community resources is one important goal of a needs and services plan.

neural pathways Information highways of the brain. Repeated stimulation strengthens some, and the ones that are neglected weaken and disintegrate.

neurons Nerve cells that send and receive messages and make up the communication system of the brain.

neuroplasticity Flexibility and responsivity. In the first few months, a child's brain is very flexible and responsive to all sounds. With time, neural connections are strengthened through repetitious, responsive interactions, therefore making more permanent connections and less plasticity.

neurotransmitters Electrical impulses that transmit messages to the brain via synapses.

object permanence The understanding that objects continue to exist even when out of direct perception or sight.

observation mode A particular state or way of being in which the focus is on paying close attention.

optimum stress The right amount of stress—that is, enough to energize and motivate the child toward activity, including problem solving, but not so much to hamper or inhibit the child's ability to act or solve a problem.

overstimulation Too much sensory input. An infant may show signs of being overstimulated by crying, turning away, or falling asleep.

parent education An approach to working with parents designed to meet parents' needs, such as the need for support and help or the need for information about techniques and practices that may be useful in guiding a child's development.

perception The processing and organizing of information that has been taken in through the senses.

philosophy of education A set of theories or concepts related to development, the acquisition of knowledge, and learning of skills.

play spaces Areas set up for play, which should contain a variety of stage-appropriate toys and equipment for whole-body play as well as fine motor manipulative play. Also, space should provide for a range in mood from energetic to mellow, as well as social and solitary.

positive reinforcement Response to an action or a behavior that strengthens the likelihood of that action or behavior being repeated. Also known as a reward.

preoperational stage The second stage in Piaget's theory of cognitive development. Marked by symbolic thought, where language and ability to pretend begin to appear, starting at around two years of age and lasting until about seven years of age.

pretend play Using one object, thing, or person to represent or stand for another. First appears around two years of age, when children can represent things through symbols and have the ability to think of their world when not directly experiencing it.

primary-caregiver system A system in which a caregiver takes primary responsibility for several infants or a small group of toddlers. In center settings where there is more than one caregiver per group, the effect is to have a caregiving team. That way children feel a strong bond with one person but also have another one or two adults with whom they are comfortable and familiar.

prosocial behavior Actions that benefit another person without rewards for oneself.

proximodistal An organized pattern of physical growth and motor control that proceeds from the center of the body outward.

receptive language The language a child understands. Before children say their first word, they understand much of what is said to them because they have made connections between sounds and sound patterns they have heard.

redirection A guidance strategy for changing children's unacceptable or disruptive behavior. The idea is to help children move their energy in a different direction and involve them in some positive activity. Redirection may look like distraction, but it is different.

referral An outside service that has been identified as a source of assistance to meet a particular family's needs.

reflexes Automatic or involuntary response system to touch, light, sound, and other forms of stimulation.

relationship The state of being related, an important requirement for infant-toddler education. A relationship between infant or toddler and caregiver develops as a result of respectful, responsive, and reciprocal interactions.

release time The time when caregivers in a team situation are released from responsibility for the rest of the group and can focus full attention on one child.

resiliency The ability to overcome adversity within one's development and continue to develop in a functionally adaptive manner.

resilient The quality of being able to cope with adversity and adapt in a positive way.

running records A method of documenting that gives a blow-by-blow, objective, written description of what is happening while it is happening. A running record can include adult interpretations about the meaning of the observed behaviors, but it must separate objective data from subjective comments.

savior complex A pattern that occurs when caregivers disapprove of parents and feel that they want to rescue the child from the family.

scaffolding A temporary structure of support provided by adults at an appropriate level to help children increase their competence at a given task or interaction. This structure of support can be seen in the use of words describing actions, questions to expand actions, temporary physical assistance, reflecting emotion, or providing for a challenging opportunity. Sometimes the mere presence of the adult or older peer is all that is needed to help a child to solve a problem, accomplish something, or fulfill a need.

selective intervention Interrupting children who need help to stay safe or interact positively. Selective intervention can also take advantage of teachable moments. Learning when to intervene appropriately is an important skill for caregivers in facilitating infant-toddler play.

self-actualization Sense of self-direction that brings about an extension and maturing of the personality. According to Abraham Maslow, this happens when one's physical, emotional, and intellectual needs are met. A point where one's needs relate to achievement and self-expression to realize one's potential.

self-calming devices Techniques, such as thumb sucking, that infants may use to calm themselves, to settle their emotional state, which may be inborn. The ability to calm oneself without relying solely on others.

self-concept Children's perceptions of the attributes and abilities they possess that they see as defining who they are. Self-concept is influenced by social context, gender identity, and culture.

self-esteem Personal assessment of positive worth. The aspect of self-concept that involves judgment of one's own worth.

self-help skills The skills children need to act independently, such as feeding themselves or putting on their shoes.

self-image The picture a person has of himself or herself. Part of self-concept, one's perception of oneself, relates to body image and awareness.

self-regulation The ability of a young child to organize his or her own behavior, often using self-help skills—especially language—to act in socially competent ways to get personal needs met.

sensitivity The degree of responsiveness of an individual to external conditions or stimulation. Some children with extreme sensitivity experience discomfort.

sensorimotor stage The coordination of sensory perception and muscle movement marked as the beginning of thinking. The first stage in Jean Piaget's theory of cognitive development.

sensory input That which comes in and is received through the eyes, ears, nose, mouth, and skin. This information is used to understand one's environment and interactions. Sometimes called "sensory stimulation."

sensory integration The process of combining and integrating information across the senses; it is critical to the development of perception.

social interaction A critical component of language development. Through imitation of the caregiver and the caregiver's response, children reinforce their understanding of how to interact with people in a social context.

social referencing The process of using another person's emotional reaction to a situation as a basis for deciding one's own reaction. An infant observes her caregiver's facial expression and/or body language before responding positively or negatively to a new situation.

strange situation From the research of Mary Ainsworth (1978), involves a series of departures and reunions between mother and infant to measure attachment. Today it is considered somewhat dated because of varying family lifestyles and child care arrangements.

stranger anxiety Distress an infant exhibits when faced with unfamiliar adults.

structure A plan or setup of a physical environment that gives a clear message or expectation that influences one's behavior in such a space. It is most important for an environment for young children to be structured in a developmentally appropriate manner.

synapses Gaps between neurons across which chemical messages are sent via neurotransmitters.

tactile perception The processing of information that comes through touch.

temperament An overall personality style based in genetic origin that develops within a social context.

three-R interactions An interaction that is respectful, responsive, and reciprocal. This interaction is a key part of effective caregiving. Interactions are linked together, creating a chain of interactions that build a partnership with the infant and are vital to relationships and therefore to growth, development, and learning.

time-out A guidance approach that involves removing a child from a situation in which he or she is behaving unacceptably.

toilet learning A method by which children learn to use the toilet independently, usually sometime during the third or fourth year of life. Children are old enough to learn to use the toilet when they show that they are physically, mentally, and emotionally ready.

toilet training A method by which children are helped before the third year to use the toilet through a kind of conditioning method that depends more on cultural traditions than it does on readiness.

trust To feel confident and secure within a relationship. The first stage of Erik Erikson's psychosocial development, which is the focus of the first year of life.

wants-nothing quality time Quality time in which the adult is available and responsive to the child but is not directing the interaction, activity, or play.

wants-something quality time Quality time in which the adult and child are involved in a task the caregiver has set up (diapering, feeding, bathing). The caregiver pays attention and includes the child in the process or task.

zone of proximal development According to Lev Vygotsky, the gap between a child's current performance and his or her potential performance if helped by a more competent child or adult.

Credits

Text and Illustrations

Chapter 5 Page 94, from Rima Shore, *Rethinking the Brain: New Insights into Early Development.* © 1997. Revised 2003. Families and Work Institute, 267 Fifth Avenue, New York, New York 10016. 212-465-2044. Website: www.familiesandwork.org; **Chapter 7** Page 139, from Bayley, 1993; Adapted from D.R. Shaffer and K. Kipp (2007). *Developmental Psychology: Childhood and Adolescent*, 7th Ed., Belmont, CA: Thomson & Wadsworth; Page 145, *Bayley Scales of Infant Development*, 2nd Ed. (BSID-II). © 1993 by NCS Pearson, Inc. Reproduced with permission. All rights reserved. Bayley Scales of Infant Development is a trademark, in the US and/or other countries, of Pearson Education, Inc. or its affiliates(s); **Chapter 9** Page 186, Table 9.1 adapted from *How Does Your Child Hear and Talk?* American Speech-Language-Hearing Association. © 2002 American Speech-Language-Hearing Association. www.ASHA.org. Used with permission; **Chapter 10** Page 224, from *Motivation and Personality*, 3rd Ed., by Abraham H. Maslow, p. 72. © 1970 Harper & Row. Adapted by permission of Pearson education, Inc., Upper Saddle River, NJ. Pyramid illustration used by permission of Ann Kaplan.

Photos

Chapter 1 Page 2, © Jude Keith Rose; **Chapter 2** Page 22, © Frank Gonzalez-Mena; **Chapter 3** Page 46, © Frank Gonzalez-Mena; Page 52, © Frank Gonzalez-Mena; Page 62, © Lynne Doherty Lyle; Page 64, © Frank Gonzalez-Mena; **Chapter 4** Page 70, © Lynne Doherty Lyle; Page 75, © Frank Gonzalez-Mena; Page 84, © Lynne Doherty Lyle; **Chapter 5** Page 92, © Frank Gonzalez-Mena; Page 96, © Frank Gonzalez-Mena; **Chapter 6** Page 112, © Lynne Doherty Lyle; **Chapter 7** Page 130, © Frank Gonzalez-Mena; Page 144, © Frank Gonzalez-Mena; Page 146, © Frank Gonzalez-Mena; **Chapter 8** Page 156, © Lynne Doherty Lyle; **Chapter 9** Page 182, © Frank Gonzalez-Mena; Page 192, © Lynne Doherty Lyle; Page 197, © Frank Gonzalez-Mena; **Chapter 10** Page 208, © Frank Gonzalez-Mena; Page 211, © Frank Gonzalez-Mena; Page 214, © Lynne Doherty Lyle; **Chapter 11** Page 234, © Lynne Doherty Lyle; Page 246, © Jude Keith Rose; **Chapter 12** Page 256, © Lynne Doherty Lyle; Page 265, © Lynne Doherty Lyle; Page 279, © Lynne Doherty Lyle; Page 281, © Lynne Doherty Lyle; **Chapter 13** Page 288, © Lynne Doherty Lyle; Page 293, © Lynne Doherty Lyle; **Chapter 14** Page 310, © Lynne Doherty Lyle.

Index